Daytrips
SAN FRANCISCO
& NORTHERN
CALIFORNIA

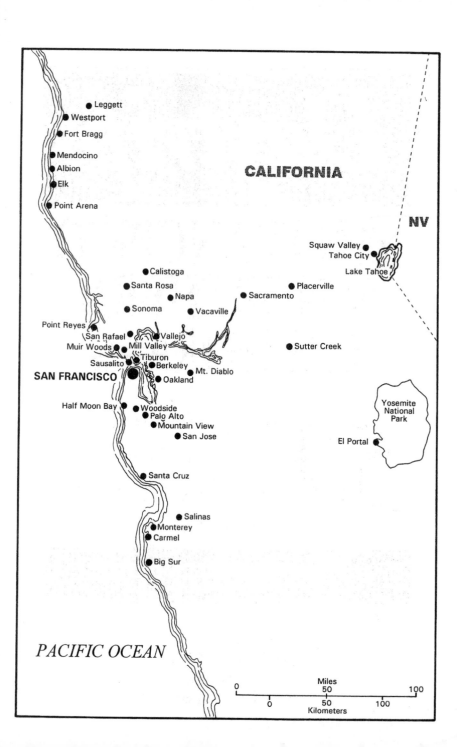

Daytrips

SAN FRANCISCO & NORTHERN CALIFORNIA

50 *one day adventures in the city, the Bay Area, and overnighting farther afield*

DAVID CHEEVER

HASTINGS HOUSE
Book Publishers
Norwalk, Connecticut

While every effort has been made to insure accuracy, neither the author nor the publisher assume legal responsibility for any consequences arising from the use of this book or the information it contains.

Distributed to the trade by National Book Network.

Edited by Earl Steinbicker, creator of the DAYTRIPS series.

ISBN: 0-8038-9441-4

Printed in the United States

10 9 8 7 6 5 4 3 2 1

Contents

6   CONTENTS

Introduction

It's hard to imagine anyone who would not want to go on a trip to San Francisco, whether for vacation or business or both. Besides the physical beauty, there's something about the air as well. Perhaps it's the constant fresh breezes off the ocean that sweep away the usual urban haze, and when the sun shines (which it does a lot in San Francisco), the place can be positively uplifting. When you stand on one of the sunny hills and look out over the blue, beautiful bay with white sailboats darting here and there, the feeling of exhilaration doesn't get much better.

Some people say the city is a tight place in terms of its geography, and that's quite true when you consider that it's almost an island. Well yes, it's a peninsula, but a relatively small one at that. That means daytrips are an ideal way to see San Francisco. There are many longtime residents who constantly pursue daytripping, getting to know their city because there is so much there. Just identifying the reputed 40 hills within the city would take some doing. The big urban parks and even the smaller ones can occupy plenty of your time.

Only about 400,000 people live in San Francisco proper. Many of the neighborhoods where these lucky people reside are showcases of lovely homes, quaint shops and renowned restaurants. Discovering these hidden spots is great fun and we've devoted several daytrips to this endeavor.

Of course the downtown area has its fabled attractions. In a geography test, not many people would miss the city where the pyramid office building resides. Union Square is usually seen as the heart of downtown and it has been transformed into an even more inviting plaza for shoppers, sun worshipers and those taking a pause from their hectic schedules. San Francisco never rests on its laurels, however, in terms of new attractions. A recently opened Children's Discovery Center and unique shopping area developed by Sony in SOMA (a burgeoning area South of Market) draw thousands every day. There are fascinating museums, antique churches, stores and restaurants flourishing in SOMA too.

One cannot forget the standbys; they also seem to get better every year. Fisherman's Wharf has a new light rail line that runs along the waterfront making access smoother now that the ugly Emarcadero Freeway has been demolished. Chinatown is Chinatown, but now you can take a walking tour of the area that teaches you how to buy fresh foods from the street vendors and make them into tantalizing Chinese dishes.

You want to shop? Of the 16 daytrips right in the city, about 14 have suggestions for shopping, and one whole daytrip is devoted just to shopping. After all, this is one of the favorite pastimes of residents and visitors in San Francisco.

Food. Well, it doesn't get much better than the range of restaurants available in Baghdad by the Bay. There has been a great rush to bring even more world-class chefs to San Francisco, with a lot of grumbling from restaurateurs in other parts of the world. Many are unhappy about this draft movement (some call it stealing) which has only heightened the city's reputation as a haven for foodies.

Across the famous bridge to the north is one of nature's—and man's—wonders. Exploring Marin County in all its fun, foibles and fascination occupies several daytrips. We'll also go beyond Marin to wine country. And this wouldn't be a worthy guidebook without a peek around the Mendocino Coast stretching north all the way to giant redwood groves. These daytrips are centered in Mendocino.

And across the bridge to the east are many more delicious destinations. We'll go to interesting islands in the bay that are seldom visited, to the region's tallest mountain and to tiny historic towns—one where Joe Dimaggio was born and another where playwright Eugene O'Neill wrote some of his most famous plays. Farther east are more treasures to behold. Gorgeous Gold Country. Year-round Yosemite. Sparkling Tahoe. Each of these names call forth history, scenic drama and fun. These daytrips are centered in the particular region to be visited.

Traveling south of San Francisco holds engaging daytrips as well. First there's the inviting coast with beaches and fascinating sea creatures to be enjoyed. Then the mountains beckon too, with hiking in deep redwood forests. Going south leads directly to all that high tech stuff to be inspected, touched and experimented with. And would you believe a 160-room mansion in San Jose built by a gun heiress who many years ago developed some intriguing high tech mechanisms, perhaps foretelling the region's current fame?

Also south of the city, but arranged into separate daytrips centered on the peninsula are the wondrous towns of Monterey and Carmel.

Weather is one of San Francisco's strong points. Admittedly, in the deep of winter, it can be chilly and rainy. During December to February, it's a good idea to take a raincoat. But it never snows, and most of the time the weather can be a joy. During summer, the fog might sweep in through the Golden Gate, and what a phenomena that is to watch. Usually the sun is shining brightly at the same time. Coastal areas will always be cooler than inland cities and towns.

Believe us when we say that the more your explore in San Francisco and Northern California, the more you won't want to leave.

A word about times and admission rates: we'd like to be totally accurate, but these things have a way of changing—and the costs usually don't go down. That's why we include phone numbers for almost every attraction and restaurant—(the latter have a way of disappearing altogether). If you have your heart set on visiting a particular museum or other attractions, by all means call ahead.

Happy Daytripping!

COMMENTS? IDEAS?

We'd love to hear from you. Ideas from our readers have resulted in many improvements in the past, and will continue to do so. And, if your suggestions are used, we'll gladly send you a complimentary copy of any book in the series. Please send your thoughts to Hastings House, Book Publishers, 50 Washington St., Norwalk, CT 06854, or fax us at (203) 838-4084, or e-mail to info@upub.com.

Section I

DAYTRIP
STRATEGIES

The word "Daytrip" may not have made it into dictionaries yet, but for experienced independent travelers it represents the easiest, most natural and often the least expensive approach to exploring many of the world's most interesting areas. This strategy, in which you base yourself in a central place and probe the surrounding region on a series of one-day excursions, is especially effective in the case of San Francisco and Northern California.

Time is a precious commodity today. You may not want to spend the whole day touring around a specified agenda. That's why these daytrips are of mixed length: some only take the morning, leaving the afternoon for relaxing by just gazing at the beautiful bay with a good book in hand; or you may want to be really ambitious and fill up your day in order not to miss much.

These one-day adventures are arranged in such a way that you can head in a direction and then cut short one trip to jump to another in close proximity if you see something that intrigues you. Or they can be hooked together to really get a feel of the place.

ADVANTAGES:

1. Freedom from a fixed itinerary. You can go wherever you feel like going whenever the mood strikes you.
2. Freedom from the burden of luggage. Your bags remain in your hotel while you run around with only a guidebook and a camera.
3. Freedom from the worry of reservation foul-ups. You don't have the anxiety each day about whether that night's lodging is okay.
4. The flexibility of making last-minute changes to allow for unexpected weather, serendipitous discoveries, changing interests, newfound passions, and so on.

5. The flexibility to take breaks from sightseeing and doing things whenever you feel tired or bored, without upsetting a planned itinerary. Why not sleep late in your base for a change?

6. The opportunity to sample different travel experiences without committing more than a day to them.

7. The opportunity to become a "temporary resident" of your base city. By staying there for a while you can get to know it in depth, becoming familiar with the local restaurants, shops, theaters, night life and other attractions—enjoying them as a resident would.

8. The convenience of not having to pack and unpack your bags each day. Your clothes can hang in a closet where they belong, or even be sent out for cleaning.

9. The convenience (and security) of having a fixed address in your base city or town where friends, relatives and business associates can reach you for fun or in an emergency.

10. The economy of staying at one hotel, perhaps on a discounted longer-term basis as a result of some kind of package plan. You can make advance reservations for your base without sacrificing any flexibility at all.

And, of course, for those who actually live in the Bay Area, daytrips can be the key to discovering some of the city's fascinating places that they either didn't know about or passed over before—one day at a time.

CHOOSING A BASE CITY

SAN FRANCISCO:
Years ago, San Francisco was known as Yerba Buena, and it almost missed being the principal city of the region. Ships could easily reach the tiny burg, but when the railroad emerged, trains from the East couldn't as easily take or bring goods and people across the water to a city hugging a peninsula. Thus Yerba Buena almost got eclipsed by towns in the East Bay that were more central in terms of transportation.

Let's say wiser heads (certainly those who appreciate beauty) prevailed and today San Francisco is the dominant hub in the region. Water access has served the city well over the years; today's train commuters can get to the city from the east through a tube under the bay.

GETTING TO SAN FRANCISCO:
By air: Most of the world's major airlines serve **San Francisco International Airport** (SFO), as do some of the smaller regional carriers. There is excellent access to the city via Airporter services, taxis and limos. Not nearly

as heavily used is the East Bay's **Oakland Airport** (OAK), which for some people is more convenient.

By train: No matter which direction you come from, all **Amtrak** train service arrives at Emeryville, east of San Francisco. From there you can take a motorcoach or rent a car to get into the city, about a 25-minute ride. ☎ 1-800-USA RAIL.

By bus: Service is available from anywhere in the country on **Greyhound.** The buses go right into the downtown bus terminal in the heart of the hotel district, making this a convenient way to arrive in town. ☎ 1-800-231-2222.

By car: Venerable Highway 1 runs up and down the California Coast and if you're averse to freeways and busy roadways, this can be lots of fun. It's quite slow in many places, but oh, so scenic. Coming from the north, a more direct route is Highway US-101, which shoots right over the Golden Gate Bridge (as does Highway 1). In many places, Highways 1 and 101 converge. Highway 101 is part two-lane road, part freeway and part multi-lane with local access (meaning periodic red lights). It then goes south.

The major freeway from the east is I-80, which takes you straight across the Bay Bridge and into the city. The north-south freeway is I-5. Coming from the north on that freeway, you will need to get on 505 and then take 80 into the city. Coming from the south on I-5, take 580 and then 80 across the bridge and into San Francisco.

ACCOMMODATIONS IN SAN FRANCISCO:

Even the bed and breakfast places in San Francisco surpass just about any other city. They range from simple clapboard houses to the Gothic **Archbishop's Mansion**. The latter is just what it says it was. The archbishop knew how to live well and you, too, can enjoy Victorian plush furnishings and fireplaces in each room. An excellent group of B&B's in the city and surrounding areas are those run by the **Four Sisters Inns**.

They offer lots of goodies: country breakfasts, morning newspapers, complimentary beverages, afternoon tea, knowledgeable concierges, evening turndownservice and home-baked cookies. The rooms are delightfully furnished, many with fireplaces. They have two properties downtown on Bush in San Francisco: the Petite Auberge and the White Swan Inn. There are three inns on the Monterey Peninsula: Green Gables Inn and Gosby House in Pacific Grove, and the Cobblestone Inn in Carmel. In Napa Valley, you can enjoy the Maison Fleurie in Yountville. ☎ (800) 234-1425 for reservations.

Hotels likewise range from intimate and quaint to world-class super hostelries. The **Hyatt** at the Embarcadero was one of the first to sport a huge open atrium lobby with dramatic sloping walls. It's worth a visit. In the grand and elegant category is the **Sheraton Palace** on Market Street (see Daytrip 13). Of course San Francisco is surrounded on three sides by water, creating a bit of isolation; thus most people stay in the city for convenience—and that's where the action is. Hoteliers know this, and so you can expect higher-than-normal room rates.

There are a smattering of motels on Lombard Street with more modest rates. Those few motels/hotels at Fisherman's Wharf are in the pricey column simply because of the location.

OTHER BASES:

There are clusters of daytrips far enough out of San Francisco so that overnighting in another city or town makes for a more enjoyable experience. Yes, you can drive to Monterey and back in a day—or Mendocino or Yosemite—but it would only leave you and hour or two for the fun of these places and that doesn't make much sense. You need time to take in the churning seacoasts, the dramatic mountains or the serenity of Lake Tahoe—so by all means try to work some of these overnighters into your schedule. This will lead you to some of the most interesting parts of Northern California.

For the mountainous area east of San Francisco—Gold Country, Yosemite and Lake Tahoe—a circuit is recommended. Certainly you can decide to alight in any of these fabulous spots and stay; we've just stitched them together so you can do it all.

CHOOSING DESTINATIONS

With fifty trips to choose from, and several attractions for each trip, deciding which are the most enjoyable for you and yours might be challenging. You could, of course, read through the whole book and mark the most appealing spots, but there's an easier way to at least start. Just turn to the Index and scan it, looking out for the special interest categories set in **BOLD FACE** type. These will immediately lead you to choices under such heading as Museums, Historic Sites, Water Sports, Adventure Activities, Beaches and the like.

The elements of one trip can often be combined with another to create a custom itinerary, using the book maps as a rough guide and a good road map for the final routing.

Some of the trips, listed in the Index as **SCENIC DRIVES** are just that. They are primarily designed for the pure pleasure of driving, with just enough attractions along the way to keep things lively. These are especially enjoyable if you're blessed with a car that's fun to drive.

GETTING AROUND

The driving directions assume that in the sections—other than those for overnighters—you're leaving from Union Square. Directions in the outlying areas are pretty clearly explained.

The route **maps** scattered throughout the book show you approximately where the sites are, and which main roads lead to them. In many cases, however, you'll still need a good up-to-date road map. These can be had from the San Francisco Convention and Visitors Bureau, or AAA has excellent maps.

Most of daytrips in this book are designed to be made by **car**, which provides freedom and flexibility. Public transportation in San Francisco is very good and can be lots of fun in the case of the **cable cars**. The city **buses**, called The Muni, are sometimes given as an alternative to driving on several daytrips. And going east or south, where it is practicable, we give you the CalTrain or BART **trains** as another alternative.

Once again, San Francisco is surrounded by water and so some daytrips can only be taken by **ferry**. Besides those ferry-only trips, these jaunty watercraft can give you an excellent look at the city from different perspectives. There are lunch and dinner cruises as well.

Tour companies abound with **vans** and **buses** of varying sizes. They offer structured tours so you can spend more time looking. **Tower Tours** offers tours of highlights in the city as well as to outlying areas.

FOOD AND DRINK

Several choice restaurants that make sense for daytrippers are listed for each destination in this book. Most of these long-time favorites of experienced travelers are open for lunch, are on or near the suggested tour route, and provide some atmosphere. Many feature foods typical of California's innovative cuisine. Their approximate price range is shown as:

$ —Inexpensive.
$$ —Reasonable.
$$$ —Luxurious and expensive.
X —Days closed.

As you might expect, San Francisco offers a cornucopia of foods. For example, if you like ethnic foods there's plenty of Chinese, Thai, Indian, Mexican, British, Spanish and Italian. Seafood that tantalizes should not be missed at dozens and dozens of spots from the shrimpy little places to grand palaces.

San Francisco's restaurants have been scanned by the *Zagat Survey*, which you may want to consult if you're especially serious about food.

With so many great parks and beaches, how about a picnic? There are delis galore and in many places we suggest picking up the fixings for an al fresco meal by the bay, at the beach or in a park.

PRACTICALITIES

WEATHER:

One of the great things about San Francisco's weather is that there are seldom big swings either from day to day or season to season. But there are some conditions to keep in mind: It is almost always cool right along the coastline, whereas inland is almost always warm; fluffy fog streams in through the Golden Gate (and sometimes anywhere in the city), usually during the summer months; rain can happen during the period December to February, but that's what makes the hills so green during this season.

There you have it.

OPENING TIMES, FEES, AND FACILITIES:

When planning a daytrip, be sure to note carefully the **opening times** of the various sites—these can sometimes be rather quirky. Anything unusual that you should know before starting is summarized in the "Practicalities" section of each trip.

Entrance fees listed in the text are, naturally, subject to change—and they rarely go down. For the most part, admissions are quite reasonable considering the cost of maintaining the sites. Places with free entry, especially those not maintained by governments, are usually staffed with unpaid volunteers and have a donation box to help keep the wolves from the door. Please put something in it.

Special **facilities** that a site might offer are listed in the *italicized* information for that site, along with the address and phone number. These often include restaurants or cafeterias, cafés, information counters, gift shops, tours, shows, picnic facilities, and so on. **Telephone numbers** are indicated with a ☎. **Area codes** for the entire state Bay Area are changing, so be sure to verify them.

SAFETY:

WATER. Have fun on the many beaches in Northern California, but please heed our warnings and posted signs in places where swimming is not advised or forbidden.

AUTOMOBILES. San Francisco is a safe place, but we advise you not to leave anything in your car. Don't make it a tempting target.

SUNTANS. Nearly everyone who comes to San Francisco is exposed to lots of sun. Prevent burns that are detrimental to your health by always wearing strong sunscreen, especially near the water.

CONSERVATION:

MARINE LIFE CONSERVATION DISTRICTS: Frequently you will see these government-protected areas. Do not disturb sea animals or other protected objects.

COASTAL SITES. The coastal areas of California, especially the many cliff sites, have a tendency to be crumbly. Many times signs warn visitors not to climb along the tops or walk too close along the bottoms. Heed those warnings.

HANDICAPPED TRAVELERS:

Access varies with each individual's needs and abilities, so no firm statement can be made about any site. Those that are generally accessible without much difficulty are indicated with the symbol &, but when in doubt it is always best to phone ahead.

GROUP TRAVEL:

If you're planning a group outing, *always* call ahead. Most sites require advance reservations and offer special discounts for groups, often at a substantial savings over the regular admission fee. Some sites will open specially or remain open beyond their scheduled hours to accommodate groups; some have tours, demonstrations, lectures, and so on available only to groups; and some have facilities for rental to groups.

TAXES:

All prices quoted are subject to change and without tax. There is a minimum 7.25 percent sales tax charged on most transactions (and it can go higher depending on where you are visiting). In addition, there is a hotel room tax of 10 percent. On rental cars, the sales tax is charged plus a $1.93 per day vehicle road tax.

SUGGESTED TOURS

Two different methods of organizing daytrips are used in this book, depending on local circumstances. Some are based on **structured itineraries** such as walking tours and scenic drives that follow a suggested route, while others just describe the **local attractions** that you can choose from. In either case, an **area map** always shows where things are, so you're not likely to get lost. Numbers (in parentheses) in the text refer to the circled numbers on the appropriate map.

Major attractions are described in one or more paragraphs each, beginning with practical information for a visit. **Additional sites** are worked into the text, along with some practical information in italics. All are arranged in a logical geographic sequence, although you may want to make changes to suit your preferences.

Walking tours, where used, follow routes shown by heavy broken lines on the accompanying map. You can estimate the amount of time that any segment of a walking tour will take by looking at the scaled map and figuring that the average person covers about 100 yards per minute or three miles per hour.

Trying to see everything at any given destination could easily lead to an exhausting marathon. You will certainly enjoy yourself more by being selective and passing up anything that doesn't catch your fancy, and perhaps planning a repeat visit at some other time.

Practical information, such as opening times and admission fees is as accurate as was possible at the time of writing, but will certainly change. You should always check with the sites themselves if seeing a particular one is crucially important to you.

*OUTSTANDING ATTRACTIONS:

An *asterisk before any attraction, be it an entire daytrip or just one exhibit in a museum, denotes a special treat that in the author's view should not be missed.

VISITOR INFORMATION

The addresses and phone numbers of major sights are given in the text wherever appropriate. These are usually your best source for specific information and current brochures. On a wider scale, valuable information and maps can be supplied by the **San Francisco Convention and Visitors Bureau,** 201 Third St., Suite 900, San Francisco, CA 94103-3185, ☎ (415) 974-6900, Internet: www.sfvisitor.org.

Section II

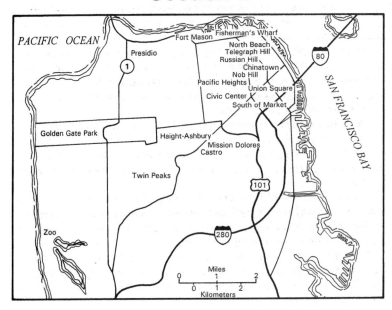

PACIFIC OCEAN

Fort Mason
Fisherman's Wharf
North Beach
Presidio
Telegraph Hill
Russian Hill
Chinatown
Nob Hill
Pacific Heights
Union Square
Civic Center
South of Market

SAN FRANCISCO BAY

80

1

Golden Gate Park

Haight-Ashbury

Mission Dolores
Castro

Twin Peaks

101

Zoo

280

Miles
0   1   2
0   1   2
Kilometers

DAYTRIPS WITHIN
SAN FRANCISCO

The majority of visitors to San Francisco, whether first-timers or frequent travelers, stay pretty much west of Van Ness Avenue. Within that area are the "biggies" like elegant shopping at Union Square, eating crab at Fisherman's Wharf or haggling to buy cloisonné enamel in Chinatown. Those are really wonderful activities, but there are nooks and crannies worthy of exploration by the most experienced of ESEFF (short for SF or San Francisco) travelers. We'll lead you to some of them.

There are two major urban parks and several smaller ones that are treats to behold. Gigantic Golden Gate and Presidio Parks are very entertaining, but when you climb your way to the top of much smaller Buena Vista Park above the Haight-Ashbury neighborhood, the views are staggering.

Museums, sports teams, concerts, harbor cruises and great food are certainly a magnet to keep most people in the confines of ESEFF.

GETTING AROUND
SAN FRANCISCO

While the many hills of San Francisco are part of the city's charm, walking them might cause some people to back off. You care not to use your feet, but you may miss some things too. This book contains many walking trips that you can shorten if you wish, and there are ways to cover the hills in a variety of vehicles.

MUNI BUSES:

San Franciscans are oftentimes not kind to their bus service. Unlike many other cities, the Muni doesn't have a set schedule. You wait at a bus stop until your route number comes along. It's not as bad as it sounds. We give you the bus numbers where the Muni is suggested. The fare is $1 and transfers are good for three hours. For information ☎ (415) 923-6317.

CABLE CARS:

They're crowded, slow and there are only three lines, but all that gets ignored as these little hillclimbers remain a big part of the city's charm. Perhaps that's because you won't find them anywhere else. The cost to ride a cable car one way is $2. For unlimited use, you can buy an all-day pass for $6. There's a three-day pass for $10 and seven-day pass for $15. The two main routes run from Union Square to Fisherman's Wharf and from the beginning of California at Market Street out to Van Ness Avenue.

FERRIES:

In the case of Alcatraz, you can only get there by ferry. But there are many other fun trips by ferries that crisscross the bay and tour you around the bay. You can even take the ferry to a baseball or football game. Several daytrips suggest the ferries. The two major ferry companies are **Blue and Gold**, ☎ (415) 705-5555 or 773-1188, and **Golden Gate Ferry**, ☎ (415) 923-2000.

BART:

The Bay Area Rapid Transit system serves the East Bay and the peninsula with a mostly underground web of routes. Except at commute time, these are quick ways to reach your destination. For daytrips where using BART is a good alternative, we show routes and fares.

CALTRAIN:

This train service only runs down to the peninsula. For visiting Palo Alto, home of Stanford University, we give you directions to the train station in San Francisco and the fare.

CAR:

For certain daytrips—like the 49 Mile Drive—only a car will do. For most others, we have tried to give you alternatives simply because parking can be such a hassle.

Trip 1
San Francisco

The 49 Mile Drive

An excellent way to see the highlights of San Francisco is to take the venerable 49 Mile Drive. After that, you can select those attractions where you might want to delve deeper.

The drive was originally mapped out in 1939 for the Golden Gate Exposition, with the idea of leading visitors on a winding route through the city's highlights and ending at the fairgrounds on Treasure Island. Interestingly, the route was modified over the years so that it no longer includes Treasure Island. Franklin D. Roosevelt was one of the first motorists to make his way over the original route and purportedly was duly impressed.

GETTING THERE:

By car, you can start anywhere on the route, but we suggest a lift-off from Union Square.

PRACTICALITIES:

If you start from the area around Union Square, it is a good idea to get started around nine o'clock, which is after heavy commuter traffic in the city core.

The entire route is marked by numerous blue-and-white seagull signs, although in places you will have to play detective—particularly around the Twin Peaks area. You may also run across construction somewhere along the line.

The weather should not cause problems any time during the year, although you may experience fog in the summertime along the coast and through the Sunset District.

FOOD AND DRINK:

Scott's Seafood Grill (2400 Lombard St., Marina District) It's hard to beat the seafood selection and preparation here. Nice starched linens and crisp atmosphere. Lunch and dinner daily. ☎ (415) 563-8988. $$

California Pizza Kitchen (438 Geary St.) A bustling place with innovative pizzas, pasta and salads. The service in this fun family place is usually pretty quick, with lunch and dinner daily. ☎ (415) 563-8911. $–$$

Cha Cha Cha (1801 Haight St., near GG park) If you like Caribbean atmosphere and food, this is the place. Not too spicy, so the whole family will enjoy. Lunch and dinner daily. ☎ (415) 386-5758. $–$$

Sanppo (1702 Post, Japantown) Full range of Japanese food served in a simple atmosphere. Try the teppan yaki. Lunch and dinner daily. ☎ (415) 346-3486. $

Speckman's (1550 Church St., Mission District) Old-World feeling place with hearty German food. Prepare to eat lots of food, or the owner will scold. Lunch and dinner. ☎ (415) 282-6850. $

LOCAL ATTRACTIONS:

Numbers in parentheses correspond to numbers on the map.

The beauty of this drive is that it introduces the first-time visitor to the cornucopia of places to see in San Francisco. You can't possibly see it all in one 49 Mile Drive, but it will whet your appetite for more. For those familiar with the city, it may just take you to places you've meant to go (like maybe the Haight or Twin Peaks), but have missed over the years.

The concept of a relatively long car trip for visitors to reach the city's highlights has held up pretty well when you consider it was introduced about 60 years ago. As we make our way around the drive, we'll only give you the top 16 attractions, but don't hesitate to stop anywhere along the way and explore.

Union Square (1) with its underground parking garage is considered the heart of the downtown shopping and hotel district. Go down Geary and turn left on Grant. From there, follow the route signs up over **Nob Hill** (2) and then back into **Chinatown** (3) *(see page 41)*. This is probably the best known of the many Chinese communities in America.

You will then go through **North Beach** (4) *(see page 44)* with its strong Italian accents in buildings, food and churches. Telegraph Hill is on the right above Columbus Avenue. Next is probably San Francisco's best-known attraction, **Fisherman's Wharf** (5) *(see page 50)*, the bustling heart of bayfront seafood restaurants, shops, attractions, fishing boats, museums and more.

Past Fisherman's Wharf is the first of two wonderful facilities turned over by the military some years ago. **Fort Mason's** (6) *(see page 64)* long Navy warehouses and piers now hold an eclectic mix of artist's studios, restaurants, exhibits, meeting halls and offices. Past the Marina Green is a treasure that stood sentinel over the bay for over one hundred years. The entire city gave a huge sigh of relief when the Army turned over the **Presidio** (7) *(see page 68)* for recreational use. Meadows, large stands of cypress and eucalyptus and minimal structures mean 1,500 acres of parklike hills and ocean vistas.

Next, the drive will take you along cliffs with some of San Francisco's western beaches far below, and then through an exclusive housing area known as Seacliff. A short distance later and you enter Lincoln Park. On a hilltop in the park is the stupendous *Palace of the Legion of Honor (8)*(see page 38)*, a museum patterned after its Paris namesake. The San Francisco version is overflowing with masterpieces of European art from medieval times into this century. This is a must.

The drive takes you out to the ocean again with the remarkable Cliff House clinging to the shore. There is a long stretch of beach along the Great Highway. This is not for swimming, but the ocean is particularly beautiful all along this four-mile stretch. Look for sea lions frolicking on the small rocks off the coast.

Nearly at the end of the Great Highway is the **San Francisco Zoo** (9)*(see page 31)*. This facility features the Primate Discovery Center, Gorilla World and Koala Crossing. After that, you make your way around Lake Merced, a large freshwater basin practically next to the ocean.

You will eventually take Sunset Boulevard through what is know as the Sunset District directly into **Golden Gate Park** (10)*(see page 26)*. It's hard to believe that this was once over 1,000 acres of sand dunes. Now it contains world-class museums, sweeping lawns and playing fields, bridle paths, lakes and huge displays of flowers—truly a wonder of urban planning.

At the eastern end of the park, you will skirt the infamous **Haight Ashbury** (11)*(see page 33)*, and then go past the University of California Medical Center on your way to **Twin Peaks** (12)*(see page 34)*. The scenic drive curls upwards to over 900 feet, affording a spectacular view of the city splayed out below.

As you twist and turn your way through neighborhoods at the foot of Twin Peaks, you soon come to the **Castro** (13)*(see page 36)*, known worldwide for its large gay population. This area is filled with terrific restaurants, antique shops, galleries and pocket parks. Next to the Castro is the Mission District with the well-known **Mission Dolores** (14)*(see page 36)*. This early Spanish mission was built in 1776, and the historic church in 1791.

The drive then spans some industrial areas and a portion of the Bayshore Freeway as it points you back into the city proper. It goes by the imposing and dignified **Ferry Building** (15), which was an important transport hub before the various bridges were built. As you turn left on Washington, the series of slender high rise buildings on your left is the **Embarcadero Center** (16). There are eight buildings connected on the second level for some of the city's best shopping. Offices occupy the upper floors.

When you turn left on Battery and make your way toward Market Street, you are in the heart of San Francisco's boisterous financial district. The landmark buildings in this neighborhood are the Transamerica Pyramid and the rose-colored Bank of America building. From there you can return to Union Square where this drive started.

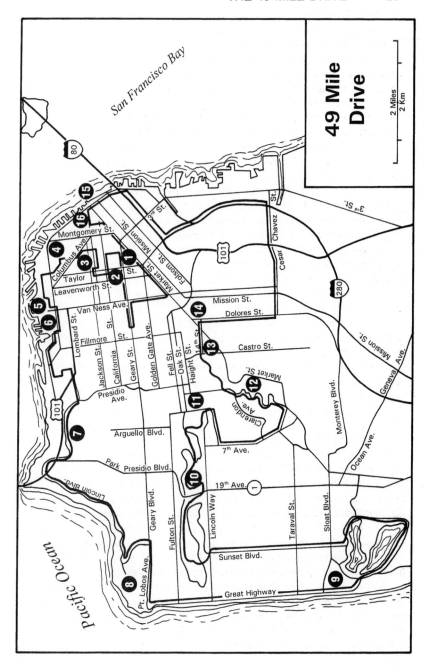

49 Mile Drive

2 Miles
2 Km

*Golden Gate Park/ Seacoast/Zoo

Be prepared for lots of stimulation and fun on this daytrip. The four world-class museums (not one should be missed) in Golden Gate Park provide plenty of intellectual stimulus for many visitors while the park's 1,000 acres of grounds feature many other offerings—walking, biking, golf, archery, boating, horseback riding and contemplation—to take care of just about anybody's needs.

The park got its start in 1871 when William Hammond Hall was appointed the first superintendent. These were called the Outside Lands and were mostly sand dunes with a few scrub plants. But Hall, as a civil engineer and surveyor, had had some success with reclaiming other parts of the distant city and he set about designing a park with meandering roads that would provide a place of respite for city dwellers. Did he ever succeed!

His successor, John McLaren, was as determined and talented. He took over in 1890 and planted thousands of trees and plants such that different blooms appear each month. It is a real tribute to these two visionaries that the park offers something for just about everyone.

Following the park visit, we will head out to the city's western border and follow that along the ocean to the evolving San Francisco Zoo.

GETTING THERE:

By car from Union Square, go west on Geary Street. Cross Van Ness and go several blocks, turning left on Webster Street. Approximately nine blocks later, turn right on Fell Street. After about 1.5 miles you will cross Stanyan which will take you to the park entrance a short distance later.

By Bus, from Union Square, board the #38 Geary and transfer to the southbound #44 O'Shaughnessy at 6th Avenue, which stops right in front of the museums.

PRACTICALITIES:

This daytrip cries out for comfortable shoes. Start fairly early so you can take advantage of the cornucopia of things to see and do. It may be chilly in the summertime, so take a light sweater. The two fine-arts museums are closed Monday and Tuesdays, so plan accordingly. On Sundays, John F. Kennedy Drive is closed to cars, allowing 7.5 miles of bicycling.

Keep in mind that three of the major museums in the park are free the first Wednesday of each month—if that fits into your schedule.

FOOD AND DRINK:

House (1269 9th Ave.) Very stylish interior that has nothing to do with a house. California Cuisine that will delight you. Try the Ahi Tartare or the Crab Cake appetizers. Lunch and dinner daily. ☎ (415) 682-3898. $$

Beach Chalet (1000 Great Highway) Great views across the Great Highway of the ocean rolling in make this a special spot. A variety of brews (how about Beach Blanket Blonde?) accompany a fun menu. Lunch Mon.–Sat., Sunday Brunch. Dinner daily. Reservations ☎ (415) 386-8439. $–$$

Shangri-La (2026 Irving St. in the Sunset District) This Chinese restaurant serves only vegetarian fare using all-natural earth-grown ingredients. No MSG either. Try the Mu-Shu with Chinese pancakes. Lunch and dinner daily. ☎ (415) 731-2548. $

Pluto's (627 Irving St. in the Sunset District) One of the most innovative buffet lines in San Francisco. Choose from three stations: Greens & Things; Meats & Poultry; and Veggies & Spuds. The Smashed Spuds of the Day are terrific. Lunch and dinner daily. ☎ (415) 753-8867. $

LOCAL ATTRACTIONS:

Numbers in parentheses correspond to numbers on the map.

We suggest jumping right into the museums. An excellent bargain is the Explorer's Pass which gives you a 25 percent discount to all four major attractions. It can be purchased at any one of the museums except the Japanese Tea Garden.

Golden Gate (GG) Park is by no means just museums: There are at least two dozen sporting opportunities in the park including golf, tennis, boating, horse back riding, archery, bicycling and much more—to say nothing of the numerous trails, walks and bike paths throughout. We'll get to some of those later.

*ASIAN ART MUSEUM (1), Tea Garden Drive, GG Park 94117, ☎ (415) 379-8800. *Open Wed.–Sun. 9:30–5. Adults $7, seniors $5, kids 12–17 $4; under 12 free. First Wed. of the month free to all.* ♿.

As you step into the galleries of this fascinating facility (opened in 1966), you are transformed into a world of paintings and statuary from China, Japan, India and southeast Asia. Not just art, but the collection of 10,000 pieces also includes textiles, architectural elements and other applied arts. Naturally, only portions of the collection can be shown at any one time, so exhibits are rotated constantly. Perhaps the highlight for many visitors is the expansive and famous Avery Brundage jade collection. (It should be noted that the Asian Art Museum will move into the Old Library at the Civic Center by the year 2000).

*M.H. DE YOUNG MEMORIAL MUSEUM (2), Tea Garden Drive, GG Park 94117, ☎ (415) 750-3600. *Open Wed.–Sun. 9:30–5. Adults $7, seniors $5, kids 12–17 $3; under 12 free. First Wed. of the month free to all. Gift shop and café.* ♿.

This museum got its start in 1894 during the Midwinter International Exposition held in the park. Its namesake was a newspaper publisher who really got things going by pushing for expansion of the facilities and collections.

Interestingly, the collection has mostly concentrations of American and British art, but also has a sizable collection of African art. The American collection spans the period from Colonial times to the present; the British collection from 16th through the 19th centuries. It is estimated that only 10 percent of the total collection is on exhibit at any one time, so look for different showings all the time. One of the exhibits you won't want to miss is about 100 paintings from Mr. and Mrs. John D. Rockefeller.

*CALIFORNIA ACADEMY OF SCIENCES (3), Music Concourse, GG Park 94117, ☎ (415) 750-7145. *Open daily 10–5, Memorial Day weekend through Labor Day. 9–6 rest of year. Adults $8.50, seniors and kids 12–17 $5.50, first Wed. of each month free to all.* ♿.

This is a must for families. The Academy offers something for everyone with its three main exhibits called **Earth, Ocean and Space**. The natural history section of the museum includes **Wild California** with dioramas of California landscapes and animals. The **Gem and Mineral Hall** includes stunning samples of California gold along with other examples of the state's minerals, while the **African Safari** is a vaulted hall with examples of big game. One of the most interesting earth exhibits is a tiny area where visitors stand on a platform that replicates earthquakes of various magnitudes. Be prepared for some real shakin'!

The **Steinhart Aquarium** is renowned for its display of over 12,000 specimens. The many galleries contain salt and fresh water fish, mollusks, eels and much more. Feeding time for the dolphin and seals is very popular. For children, there is a replica of a California tidepool where, with the help of a trained guide, kids can touch the various sea creatures.

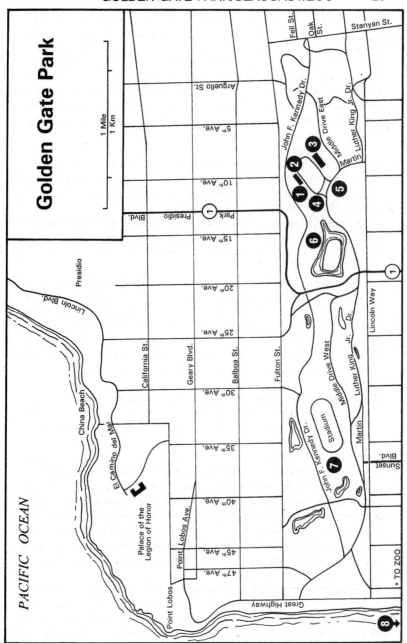

Golden Gate Park

The **Morrison Planetarium** changes shows constantly, so call for the latest program. Whatever is planned, you will see fascinating night shows under a 65-foot-high dome. The **Laserium** is a dazzling display of multi-colored patterns drawn on the planetarium roof.

*JAPANESE TEA GARDEN (4), Tea Garden Drive, GG Park 94117, ☎ (415) 668-0909 *Open daily 9–6. Adults $2.50, seniors and kids 12 and under $1. Gift shop and tea garden.* ⅙.

This is a place of great beauty and restfulness. The landscaping reflects many of the lovely aspects of gardens in Japan with displays of azaleas, bonsai trees and bamboo. Ponds and unusual bridges are found throughout the garden. Of special interest is the Moon Bridge, which can be climbed even though it is very steep. The reason it arches so steeply is that its reflection in the water below forms a circle like the moon.

As a suggestion, take time for a cup of green tea in the tea house looking out over neat gardens and a reflecting pond. It will slow down your pace. Guided walks, after admission is paid, are available Sundays and Wednesdays year-round; May to October Monday, Wednesday, Saturday and Sunday. All narrated walks start at 2 p.m. and take about 45 minutes.

Just across Martin Luther King Jr. Drive is the **Strybing Arboretum and Botanical Gardens** (5) with thousands of trees, plants and shrubs. Spacious meadows are intertwined with gardens featuring species from Mexico, Africa, South America and Australia. The largest, naturally, is a garden replete with plants native to California. *Free.*

Stow Lake (6) circles around Strawberry Hill. Stylish electric motor boats can be rented for about $13 per hour depending on the number of passengers. If you're willing to work, row boats are $9.50 an hour and pedal boats are $10.50. Pedal surreys are also available. *Hours are 9–4 daily, summer hours are 9–5.* ☎ *(415) 668-6699.*

The area west of Crossover Drive includes dozens of activities including several meadows for picnics. **Golden Gate Park Stables** (7) is a full equestrian facility located at the intersection of John F. Kennedy Drive and 36th Avenue. The stables offer lessons as well as guided trail rides. One of the most popular is a one-hour Beach Ride outside the park along the Pacific Ocean for $25. ☎ *(415) 668-7360. Open daily 8–6.*

Miles of bike trails wind through the park. Bikes and rollerblades can be rented from **Golden Gate Park Skate and Bike**, 3038 Fulton St. and 6th Ave. ☎ *(415) 668-1117. Bike rates are $5 an hour or $25 for 24 hours; rollerblades are $6 per hour or $26 for 24 hours Open 10–6 daily. Safety gear provided.*

Golfers can swing their way through a nine hole par 3 course located off JFK Drive. ☎ *(415) 751-8987 for reservations. Rates are $10 on week-*

days and $13 on weekends. Clubs can be rented for $6 and pull carts for $3.50.

For those who like to walk, there are numerous guided tours. One of the more interesting is a 90-minute stroll around **Strawberry Hill**. Learn the history of Stow Lake, the Pioneer Log Cabin, Sweeney's Observatory and blooming Rose Garden. Meet at the entrance to the Japanese Tea Garden at 11 a.m. from May–October. Also during the summer months there's a two-mile loop walk that takes in 11 points of interest in the eastern section of the park. A three-mile walk extends the length of the park and adds another 15 of the park's features.

Get on either Martin Luther King Jr. Drive or John F. Kennedy Drive and head downhill for the ocean. Turn left, which puts you on the Great Highway running along the beach. After 2.5 miles, turn left at Sloat Boulevard. This will take you to the **San Francisco Zoo** (8). Highlights of this evolving facility include the Primate Discovery Center, Insect Zoo and the Children's Zoo. We say "evolving" because the SF Zoo has begun a multi-million-dollar makeover that will propel it into the world-class category of the top two or three zoos on Earth. That's not to say it isn't lots of fun now.

You can make your way on foot through flamingos, bears, sea lions, lions and tigers and many more wondrous animals, or take a tram. *The tram is $2.50 for adults and $1.50 for kids. Open every day of the year. Adult admission is $9, kids 12–16 $6. There are two snack bars as well as a sit-down restaurant called the Terrace. Gift shop.* ☎ *(415) 753-7080. Partially* ♿.

Neighborhoods around Twin Peaks

The Twin Peaks, right smack in the middle of San Francisco, have no residential or commercial buildings on them, but they are surrounded by some of San Francisco's most interesting neighborhoods. Who hasn't heard of Haight Ashbury? Probably not quite as well known, but nonetheless making a name for itself is the Castro District. On the way there, as we come down off Twin Peaks, we'll pass through Noe Valley, which has become one of the classier addresses in San Francisco these last few years. It wasn't always that way. The Mission District has quite a history too.

We'll take you to—and through—these neighborhoods for a fun tour of the communities that sit in the shadow of Twin Peaks. And we must not forget the trip up Twin Peaks themselves, which affords a breathtaking view of the city and its famous bay—it's a 360-degree view of the entire city.

GETTING THERE:

By car from Union Square, go west on Geary Street. Cross Van Ness and go up over Cathedral Hill. After several blocks, go left on Webster for nine blocks and turn right on Fell. After about 1.5 miles, turn left on Masonic to Haight Street.

PRACTICALITIES:

You will be in and out of you car a lot, so it's a good idea to take only stuff that you can carry with you. There will be some spectacular views, so bring along your camera.

In Haight-Ashbury, most stores open at noon during winter and 10 in the summer.

FOOD AND DRINK:

The Sausage Factory (517 Castro St.) Small but comfortable spot that serves a good range of Italian food. Their raviolis are reputed to be some of the best. Try the Sole Dore if you're there on Friday. Open for lunch and dinner daily. ☎ (415) 626-1250. $–$$

Squat & Gobble (1428 Haight St.) The kinda funky place you would expect in Haight Ashbury. Great crepes. Try the Hawaiian or Special Salsa. Open for breakfast, lunch and dinner daily. ☎ (415) 864-8484. $

People's Café (1419 Haight St.) This restaurant lives up to its name serving simple, but wholesome food. Their specialities are egg dishes like Benedict and Florentine. Breakfast, lunch and dinner daily. ☎ (415) 553-8842. $

Fire Wood Café (4248 18th St. in the Castro District) Lovely building holds a terrific place for salads, pizza and pasta. Their salads come with 3 fixings you choose, like caramelized onions, roasted red peppers, etc. Open for lunch and dinner daily. ☎ (415) 252-0999. $

Fuzio (469 Castro) Nicely decorated with a good selection of Mediterranean foods. Try some of the Universal Pastas like Firecracker Pork Fusilli or Rigatoni Alfuzio. Lunch and dinner daily. ☎ (415) 863-1400. $

SUGGESTED TOUR:

Numbers in parentheses correspond to numbers on the map.

Ambling around the **Haight-Ashbury District** (1) at times seems like stepping back to the 1960s when the hippies took over the whole place. There's still some of that, which we'll explore, but the district has also become respectable with Baby Boomers buying up lots of the real estate.

Right at the corner of Haight and Masonic you can get your quick fix of 60's retro at the **Positively Haight Ashbury** store at 1400 Haight Street. The front lets you know what's going on pretty quickly. It looks 60's, smells 60's (incense and all that kind of stuff) and sells 60's. It's really a tie-die department store with all manner of jewelry, blouses, skirts, scarfs and the like with the distinctive tie-died look.

The Haight has plenty of funky shops and restaurants in about a ten-block area. Down the street to the left are a series of interesting shops starting with **Pipe Dreams** at 1376 Haight. As you might imagine, they sell all manner of smoking equipment including water pipes and even Zippo lighters. You'll also find intriguing jewelry and clothing. Also worth a visit—selling about the same things as Pipe Dreams—is **Golden Triangle** at 1340 Haight. Check out **Gargoyle** at 1310. They sell candles, oils and clothing. In a slightly more conventional vein is **3D Interiors** at 1312 Haight, offering very stylish yet unusual take-apart furniture. This you won't find at home.

On the other side of the street is **Bound Together** at 1369, which calls itself an Anarchist Collective Bookstore. Lots of interesting volumes, so go figure what they mean by their slogan. Almost next door is **Recycled Records** at 1377 Haight. This is a small, self-contained marketplace where they buy, sell and trade unusual and hard to find tapes, CDs and records.

If you've had enough of the remnants of the hippie era, then head east on Haight Street and turn right on Buena Vista West. This steep street runs alongside **Buena Vista Park** (2). At its summit, the 36-acre park rises some 569 feet, which means spectacular views of the city and the bay. This is an old park built in 1870, laced with strenuous trails and featuring an ancient redwood grove and a children's playground. As you go up this road, there appear some pretty substantial homes including one of the two **Spreckels Mansions**. The one at 737 Buena Vista West (the other one is even bigger on Washington Street in Pacific Heights—see Daytrip 12) was a B&B for a while, but is now a private residence.

Turn right on Frederick Street and then left on Clayton. A short distance up at the top of a rise at a second stop light is a confusing intersection. You want to bear right and get on Twin Peaks Avenue. After a block or so, Twin Peaks Avenue turns left. As the name implies, this will take you to the summit. And what a spectacle is in store for you when you reach the top! Market Street seems to spill out directly from **Twin Peaks** (3), leading the eye straight to the Ferry Building and the downtown highrises. The view back toward the ocean may at times be obscured by fog, but it moves pretty fast so you will probably also be able to see the coastline. The gangly tower on the third hill in this area is **Sutro Tower** (built originally to broadcast television signals), which remains an embarrassment to San Franciscans. They seem resigned to having this blight on their lovely hills.

Go down Twin Peaks the opposite way from the way you came up. At the bottom of the hill, turn right on Portola Drive and immediately move left to turn on O'Shaughnessy Boulevard. The road winds down pretty steeply along **Glen Canyon Park** (4). This narrow park has huge stands of eucalyptus and redwood along both sides of the steep glen. At the stop sign, turn left on Elk. A short distance later on the left is the entrance to the park, which includes a wide path up the middle of the steep canyon for walking, jogging and biking. As you go up Elk it becomes Diamond Heights Road. Look for the second Diamond Street (after Addison) and turn right.

As you proceed along Diamond Street, you will pass through **Noe Valley** (5), which has become a very good address in San Francisco. That wasn't always true, but it is said that real estate prices on the other side of Market Street pushed Baby Boomers to find new areas, and many have settled in Noe. Turn right on 24th Street, leading you to Noe's "Little Village," which boasts a variety of shops, public houses, outdoor cafés and restaurants.

Retrace your route and go back to Diamond. Turn right. Just before you get to 18th Street, there is an innovative private school called **Live Oak** in a pink building on the right. What makes it unique is that it combines generations. The basement is a community center for senior citizens and on the upper floors are kids in grades K–8. The seniors periodically help out with

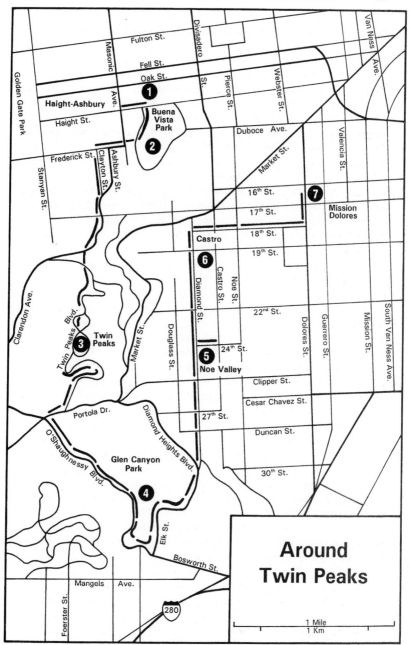

Around
Twin Peaks

1 Mile
1 Km

the kids, which has been very rewarding for both. It's called Intergenerational Learning; as the population ages we are expected to see more and more of this.

Turn right on 18th Street, leading you straight in the **Castro District** (6). For whatever negatives you might have heard about the Castro, be assured that it is an area of energy and creativity with many interesting places to shop and eat. The **Browser's Nook** at 530 Castro sells antiques and has dozens of new stained glass Tiffany-type lamp shades. If you've never been in a gay bookstore before, go ahead and visit **A Different Light** at 489 Castro. You may not want to buy such volumes as "International Gay Expressions," but it may open your eyes as to what interests people who lead a different lifestyle. Worth a visit is the **Castro Theater** at 429 Castro. This landmark is one of the last of the many ornate San Francisco neighborhood film palaces. The exterior alone is pretty gaudy with colorful tiles at ground level and soaring rococo columns reaching to the roofline. The lush interior is big—seating 1,600. None of the cramped little shopping mall cineplexes for the Castro. The showings are mostly revival classics. ☎ *(415) 621-6120.*

Since 1989, Ms. Trevor Hailey has been conducting walking tours of the Castro called "Cruisin' the Castro." She will definitely entertain you as she helps you learn "how and why San Francisco got to be literally the Gay Mecca of the world." Cost is $35 per person, including brunch. ☎ *(415) 550-8110 for reservations.*

Next head down 18th for several blocks, which becomes the **Mission District.** At Dolores Street turn left and go up two blocks. On the left is **Mission Dolores** (7), reputed to be the oldest building in San Francisco. Of the 21 California Missions, this is the third most northerly and the sixth to be established under the direction of Father Junipero Serra. What makes the story most interesting is that the first mass was celebrated under a makeshift shelter on June 29, 1776, and thus the City of Saint Francis had its official beginning five days before the signing of the Declaration of Independence. The actual building was completed in 1791, making it the oldest intact mission in California.

There is a tour of the old Mission church, the bigger basilica next door, a small museum (it's really a small room) and cemetery. *Cost is $2. The Mission is open 9–4:30 May–Oct. and 10–4 Nov.–April.*

The corner of Dolores and 16th might be considered "Church Crossroads." The Mission is Catholic; across Dolores is a major Lutheran Church; and across 16th is a new Jewish Synagogue.

*Art in the Park and a Seacoast Walk

Lincoln Park is one of three major parks in San Francisco. This one sits up high on a headland where the Pacific Ocean sweeps into San Francisco Bay. As a result it affords magnificent views all the way from the Golden Gate Bridge down the Great Highway. The park started out as a cemetery for the city's various ethnic groups, but the graves were moved in the late 1800s. The renowned John McLaren *(see Daytrip 2),* who almost single-handedly built Golden Gate Park, also landscaped this one.

Sitting at the very highest point in the park is a splendid gift from one individual to San Francisco. The wife of one of the city's wealthiest citizens, a sugar baron, gave the California Palace of the Legion of Honor in 1924 to honor the Californians who died during World War I. We'll explore this treasure.

A sizable chunk of the park is devoted to an 18-hole golf course that is only one of two in the city of San Francisco. It is very hilly, but quite popular. Just below the museum is an old railroad right-of-way that can be walked, run or biked called the Coastal Trail. It is well worth exploring as well.

On the south side of the park is Clement Street, which has been called a "feast for food lovers" because of the multiplicity of ethnic eateries strung along about ten blocks.

GETTING THERE:

By car from Union Square, go west on Geary Street. Cross Van Ness and go one block, turning right on Franklin Street. Approximately seven blocks later, turn left on California Street. After about two miles, turn right on 25th, which will take you to El Camino Del Mar. Turn left and this will take you to Lincoln Park.

By bus, take bus #38 to 33rd and Geary. From there, it's an uphill walk to the museum.

PRACTICALITIES:

There's an optional walk along the seacoast, so wear comfortable shoes. Remember to leave nothing in your car. In summer, it can be foggy in this part of the city, so take along a sweater or light jacket.

FOOD AND DRINK:

India Clay Oven Restaurant (2435 Clement St.) They use a tandoori clay oven that quickly chars meats, poultry and seafood. Special lunch buffet (all you can eat) for $5.95. Indian breads freshly oven baked. Lunch and dinner daily. ☎ (415) 751-0505. $-$$

Cliff House (1090 Point Lobos Ave.) Go there just because of where it is and its history. Over a 100-year period, this is the third edition. Clinging to the cliff at the start of the Great Highway, the views are awesome. Good seafood and salads. Lunch and dinner daily. ☎ (415) 386-3330. $-$$

Greco Romana (2448 Clement St.) First-place winner at the SF Fair Premier Pizza Contest. The dough and sauces are made fresh daily. Also daily Greek specialties like moussaka, spanakopita, pasticio and more. Lunch and dinner daily. ☎ (415) 387-0626. $

Loui's (902 Point Lobos) Just a little farther up the coast is this intimate and very friendly spot. Great views as well, but not as formal as the Cliff House. Standard fare served well. Breakfast, lunch and dinner. ☎ (415) 387-6330. $

SUGGESTED TOUR:

Numbers in parentheses correspond to numbers on the map.

Proceed along 25th until you get to Lake Street, then turn left. This will deliver you into an exclusive neighborhood called **Seacliff** (1). Of special interest at 129 24th Avenue is the home where Ansel Adams grew up, when this part of the city was out in the country. The house is not open to the public, so please respect the owner's privacy.

Continue along Lake Street, turning right at the end. This will run into El Camino del Mar. Turn left and it will lead you right into the park. A short distance later is a treasure not to be missed:

*CALIFORNIA PALACE OF THE LEGION OF HONOR (2), 34th and Clement, San Francisco, CA 94121, ☎ 863-3330. *Adult admission $7, kids 12–17 $4, seniors 65+ $5. Open Tues.–Sun 9:30–5. Admission is free the second Wed. of each month. Gift shop. Restaurant.* &.

If it looks like a classical French palace, that is because it was patterned after the Palais de la Legion d'Honneur in Paris, where Napoleon first established his new civil and military order. It is a three-quarters reproduction.

The Legion of Honor was given to the people of San Francisco by Mr. Spreckels in 1924 at the urging of his wife Alma deBretteville Spreckels. Mrs.

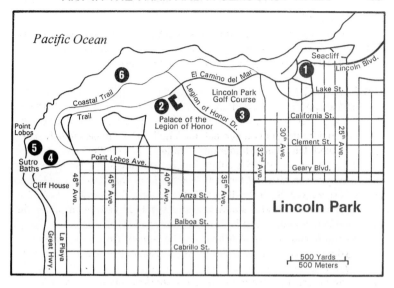

Spreckels was fascinated with the work of the sculpture August Rodin, and so she gave not only the building, but also her collection of almost 60 Rodin pieces, some of which she bought directly from the sculptor. A casting of *The Thinker* resides imposingly in the entry courtyard.

The museum has over 20 galleries surveying about 4,000 years of art. The permanent collection features many outstanding European pieces and paintings from Renoir, Seurat, Cézanne, Degas, Monet, Manet and more. The collection is basically broken down into seven periods. Within **Ancient Art** are such treasures as an Assyrian wall relief, ca 885 BC from northern Iraq. The **Medieval** collection is represented by a monumental religious sculpture and jeweled objects presented against a backdrop of early tapestries. To represent the **16th Century**, there are works from the Netherlands and stunning early Italian paintings. The High Renaissance is represented with paintings by Titian and Tintoretto and two masterpieces by El Greco, including a painting of St. Francis, the patron saint of San Francisco.

Highlights of the **17th–18th Century** collection are Italian and French art including works from Steen, Hals and Rubens and Rembrandt. The British collection includes works from Gainsborough, Reynolds, Raeburn and Constable. The **19th–20th Century** shows a variety of nationalities. There are popular works by Manet, Monet, Renoir, Degas, Seurat and Cézanne, ending with two important works by Picasso.

A careful survey of the building in the 1980s showed that, in spite of very sturdy original construction, the landmark building needed to be made seismically secure. For two years ending November 1995—the museum's 75th anniversary—the Legion of Honor got quite a makeover that included seismic strengthening, restoration of historic features and the addition of 35,000 square feet of space for exhibits, storage and a new restaurant. To many frequent museum visitors, all the classic beauty remains, but now the building is even more pleasurable.

There are changing exhibitions all the time, so call to find out what is currently showing.

If all that art stimulation has you needing to stretch your other muscles a bit, the 18-hole **Lincoln Park Golf Course** (3) is cheek-by-jowl with the museum. They say of the course that you may walk it once, but never after that. It is very hilly, but the views are outstanding. *Rates are $23 weekdays and $27 weekends. Carts are $11.* ☎ *750-GOLF for tee times.*

If golf is not your thing, we recommend getting in your car for a trip out of the park on Legion of Honor Drive to **Lands End** (4). Go straight across to Geary, which becomes Point Lobos Drive. Turn right. Look for a parking lot marked Merrie on the right just as the road starts to dip down to the Great Highway.

Just below you are the ruins of the grand **Sutro Baths** (5). There's no record of why Adolph Sutro wanted to build this enormous, elegant monument in 1881, but build it he did—over three acres and at a then-astronomical cost of $250,000. After you entered through the classic Greek portal, inside were one fresh water tank, five salt water tanks at various temperatures and one salt water tank at ocean temperature (which meant very chilly). To show the magnitude of the operation, there were 20,000 swim suits and 40,000 towels for rent. There were lots of amenities: three restaurants; natural history exhibits; galleries of sculptures, paintings, tapestries and artifacts from Aztec, Mexican, Egyptian, Syrian, Chinese and Japanese cultures; and finally a 3,700-seat amphitheater. It all cost 10 cents to enter. Today you can explore the remains of the Baths, but use caution as you climb over the concrete ruins.

At the far end of the parking lot is a little uphill path to the **Coastal Trail** (6). This magnificent walking path will lead you around the complete headland. There are constant views of the Golden Gate Bridge and the Marin Headlands. Because you are on a cliff above the ocean crashing on the rocks below, make sure you stay on the trail. If you are ambitious, the trail covers about five miles all the way to the Golden Gate Bridge and Lands End. Over the course of the trail, you will pass from thick vegetation and matted Cypress trees and then come out into the neighborhood of Seacliff where the trail passes down regular streets. There are terrific opportunities to discover Baker Beach and China Basin.

Chinatown/North Beach/Telegraph

This daytrip is mostly about discovering two of San Francisco's most influential ethnic neighborhoods. Who can say what kind of a city it would be without the Chinese and Italians? What is wonderful is that both populations still thrive and have maintained much of their culture, albeit the Chinese more strongly. It is interesting to note that their neighborhoods abut each other.

We will take some time to carefully explore Chinatown and North Beach. Some people ask where the beach is in North Beach. In fact there was a beach here years ago, before the engineers filled many of the small bays and inlets around San Francisco. Even if you've been to both before, there's so much to see that you're bound to find something new.

This daytrip will end with an interesting, but steep climb to Telegraph Hill where the famous Coit Tower shines down on the surrounding area.

GETTING THERE:

On foot from Union Square, go east (down) on Post or Geary to Grant Avenue. Turn left and at Bush and Grant you will find the Chinatown Gateway.

By bus from Union Square, take a #30 (and get a transfer) that will go up Columbus Avenue. Get off at Washington Square and take a #36 up to the tower.

PRACTICALITIES:

Since the distance from Chinatown Gateway to Coit Tower is slightly less than 1.5 miles, it makes sense to walk this daytrip. That's especially pertinent when you consider that the wait for a parking stall at Coit Tower can be an hour during heavy summer visitor periods. Wear comfortable walking shoes.

FOOD AND DRINK:

Enrico's (504 Broadway) This sidewalk café has embraced the likes of Janis Joplin, Hunter Thompson and Bill Cosby along with writers, actors, artists, socialites and neighborhood residents. Pizzas and hearty pastas lead into entrees like honey-cured pork chops. Lunch & dinner daily. ☎ (415) 982-6223. $$

Kan's (708 Grant in Chinatown) This white-tablecloth Chinese spot has fed Streisand, Bogart, Travolta, Sandra Bullock, Elvis, Marilyn Monroe and many other celebs. Try it yourself. You may become a celebrity. Mostly Cantonese lunch & dinner daily. Dim sum. Reservations ☎ (415) 362-5267. $–$$

The Stinking Rose (325 Columbus in North Beach) Their slogan is "We season our garlic with food." Many excellent Italian dishes, all served with garlic. All kinds of garlic accouterments for sale too, like cookbooks, clothing, fresh, bottled and canned cloves. Lunch and dinner daily. ☎ (415) PU-1-ROSE. $–$$

Washington Square Bar & Grill (1207 Powell in North Beach) Typical San Francisco seafood and pasta place. Dark wood, waiters in starched aprons, and yes, great food. Lots of sports memorabilia on the walls. Lunch and dinner daily. ☎ (415) 982-8123. $–$$

San Francisco Brewing Company (155 Columbus Ave. in North Beach) Enjoy a meal while they brew beer right in the same room. Very aromatic. House beers are Albatross and Emperor Norton lagers plus Gripman's Porter. Burgers, sandwiches, salads. Lunch and dinner daily. ☎ (415) 434-3344. $

SUGGESTED TOUR:

Numbers in parentheses correspond to numbers on the map.

As soon as you pass through the Chinatown Gateway (known as the "Dragon's Gate"), the tempo changes. Chinatown has a certain bustle to it that's not found many other places—except perhaps Hong Kong or other Chinatowns in America. Just passing along Grant Avenue shows a whirlwind of goods. The jewelry may look familiar, but some of the foods, herbs, incense and decorative goods are obviously foreign.

Turn right on Polk Street and shortly you will see **St. Mary's Square** (1) with members of the Chinese community engaged in the slow movement Tai Chi and other forms of exercise. At the other end of the square across California Street is the red-brick **St. Mary's Church**. This was built in 1854 and withstood the 1906 earthquake and fire. While the church was gutted, the walls survived. It seems only appropriate that the foundation granite was quarried in China, but the red bricks came from New England. There are interesting historical photos inside. *Open daily. Free.*

As you go along Grant Avenue again, keep in mind that this is the oldest street in San Francisco. It originally was Yerba Buena and was named af-

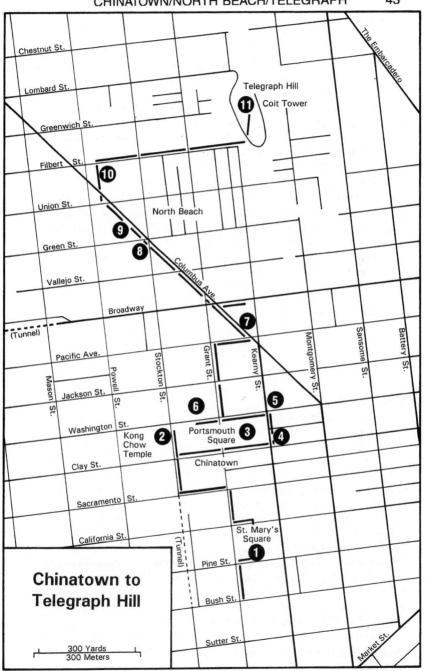

Chestnut St.

Lombard St.

Telegraph Hill

11 Coit Tower

Greenwich St.

Filbert St.

10

Union St.

North Beach

9

Green St.

8

Vallejo St.

Columbus Ave.

Broadway

7

(Tunnel)

Pacific Ave.

Jackson St.

6

5

Washington St.

Kong Chow Temple

2 Portsmouth Square **3** **4**

Clay St.

Chinatown

Sacramento St.

California St.

St. Mary's Square

1

Chestnut St.

Mason St.

Powell St.

Stockton St.

Grant St.

Kearny St.

Montgomery St.

Sansome St.

Battery St.

The Embarcadero

(Tunnel)

Pine St.

Chinatown to Telegraph Hill

Bush St.

Sutter St.

Market St.

300 Yards
300 Meters

ter Ulysses S. Grant in 1885. Turn left on Sacramento and right on Stockton. On the uphill side of the street is the **Kong Chow Temple** (2) on the fourth floor at 855 Stockton. This is a small temple—with intricate carvings and strong odor of burning incense—where Chinese residents light incense sticks and leave fruits and other foods to show their loyalty to overseas Chinese. Praying at the temple for humility and honesty is also part of the ritual. Harry Truman came to this very temple in 1948 asking for a prediction of the election outcome. Of course they were right and neither Harry or Bess ever forgot that.

Next walk down Clay to Kearny where you will find **Portsmouth Square** (3), generally considered to be the center of life in Chinatown. The square is where the first pubic school in California was built. Here you will see all manner of activity, especially school groups. Walk across the footbridge over Kearny to the **Chinese Cultural Center** (4), which rotates exhibits of Chinese arts and crafts. The Center offers two walking tours of Chinatown. The Chinese Heritage Walk emphasizes the achievements, social progress and history of the Chinese in America. *Cost is $15 and it is conducted Sat. and Sun. at 2. Weekday tours are possible at 10:30 by advance reservation.* The Chinese Culinary Walk/luncheon explores and explains the different styles of Chinese cooking and how to shop for ingredients. This walk culminates with a dim sum luncheon. Cost is $35 conducted daily at 10:30. ☎ *(415) 986-1822 for reservations.*

Next go up Washington, where you will pass a small branch of the **Bank of Canton** (5) at 743. What is unusual about this spot is that for many years it housed the telephone exchange for Chinatown, where the operators not only had to speak several Chinese dialects, but also had to memorize all the numbers in the area since most customers refused to use the phone book. Keep going and turn right into Ross Alley. At 56 Ross is the tiny **Fortune Cookie Factory** (6). See how they make those little delicacies. Buy them fresh. Find out where they get the fortunes.

As you stroll along Grant, look for Pacific Avenue and turn right. One block later is Columbus Avenue. Turn left. Now you have effectively left Chinatown and entered North Beach. This is the beginning of the large Italian neighborhood that flourished for many years. Here you will find cabarets, jazz clubs, galleries, every type of Italian restaurant, and of course, plentiful adult entertainment.

On the left, look for the **City Lights Bookstore** (7), founded in 1953 as the nation's first all-paperback bookstore. It was started by poets, and to this day has an upper floor devoted to poetry. What also makes this store unusual is its publication of avant-garde material. *Open daily 10–midnight.*

Turn right on Broadway and within steps you will see why this has been called the Barbary Coast. Live sex shows, adult movies, and other such offerings proliferate. At the corner of Broadway and Columbus is the **Condor** nightclub, which is reputed to have staged the first topless show in the mid-1960s. Today, the Condor continues to prosper—as a sports bar.

Walk up Columbus Avenue and enjoy the strong smell of garlic and other spices from the numerous Italian restaurants lining the boulevard named for Christopher Columbus. At 1435 Stockton, just off Columbus, look for the **North Beach Museum** (8) above the Eureka Bank. Besides documenting in photos the various ethnic groups that make up the area, there are exhibits of the people who helped sculpt the whole neighborhood during the Beat Generation. *Open 9–4 Mon.–Thurs., and 9–6 on Fri. Admission is free.* ☎ *(415) 626-7070.*

At Green Street, renamed "Beach Blanket Babylon Boulevard," look for **Club Fugazi** (9) where they stage the zany live show Beach Blanket Babylon on Wednesdays through Sundays. *Tickets range from $20–50.* ☎ *(415) 421-4222.* The building itself is a nifty restoration of an old community center.

Next on the right is Washington Square with a statue of Benjamin Franklin. How do you figure that? On the other side of the square is the huge **Saints Peter and Paul Church** (10), called the "fisherman's church" because many of its parishioners once made their living from the sea. The imposing, twin-steepled church has a magnificent, intricately carved white marble altar worth a visit inside. Purportedly, Cecil B. deMille showed up as the church was being built in 1922 to film sequences for his blockbuster movie *The Ten Commandments. Open daily.*

Head up Filbert Street following the signs to the "Coit Tower Steps." You will climb past some attractive residences on your way to Telegraph Hill. In the early days the hill was a key in directing ship traffic in the bay. **Coit Tower** (11) is another of those wonderful San Francisco stories. Apparently Lillie Hitchcock Coit loved San Francisco, but she especially loved firefighters since they rescued her from a burning hotel when she was eight. Using a smidgen of her wealth, she had Coit Tower built in 1933 for $118,000 as a memorial to San Francisco's firemen. Lillie used the same architect who designed City Hall and the Opera House (see Daytrip 14). Inside are about two dozen stylized murals of California life during the period, painted as a commission for the depression-era WPA. The tower is only 210 feet high, but stands out strikingly because of its position atop 220-foot Telegraph Hill. You can take an elevator to the observation deck 21 stories up. *Gift shop. Adult admission is $3, seniors $2, kids under 12 $1. Open daily 10–7.*

There are hill paths (footpaths) around Coit Tower that offer stunning views. Coming up the way we did along Filbert from Washington Square is perhaps the easiest. Once on the top on the east side, look for the **Greenwich Steps** practically at the tower, or down a bit farther the **Filbert Steps**. The Filbert Gardens along the steps make this the most popular of the hillpaths. Each of these is pretty challenging. The steepness was caused by dynamite blasting in the 1800s when fill was needed to round out the shoreline. Some visitors go down the Greenwich Steps and up the Filbert Steps or vice versa.

Trip 6
San Francisco

Strolling the Waterfront

The idea behind this daytrip is to take a leisurely stroll along San Francisco's lovely eastern shoreline before diving into the fun and frenzy of Fisherman's Wharf. And speaking of the waterfront, it has truly been transformed since they tore down the ugly, elevated Embarcadero Freeway. It opened up vistas and improved access and now the city has planted trees along a wide swath of previously dark and forbidding roadway.

Like a lot of high traffic areas, the waterfront is becoming gentrified. The hulking pier fronts along this stretch were once the scene of heavy movement of goods from all over the world, but they now house restaurants, architect's offices, design studios, various water activities—and even parking. Containerized freight spelled the death-knell of the San Francisco waterfront as far as shipping was concerned. Most that has now moved to Oakland.

The route we will follow is actually called the Bay Trail that goes all the way to the Golden Gate Bridge and across to Sausalito. In fact, the Bay Trail loops entirely around the bay and is about 400 miles long. We'll only tackle about 1.5 miles of it during this daytrip.

GETTING THERE:
   On foot from Union Square, go east (down) on Post or Geary to Market and turn left. Walk straight down Market to the Ferry Building on the waterfront. You will go past Justin Herman Plaza with its unusual, angular fountain.
   By bus, go to Market and catch a J,K,L, M or N Muni to the Ferry Building.

PRACTICALITIES:
   From the Ferry Building to the Cannery in Fisherman's Wharf is a 1.5-mile walk. Comfortable shoes are a very good idea. It can be sunny along the waterfront, so sunglasses will serve you well.
   Winter (usually October–May) hours can be shorter, but most everything is open by 10 in the morning.

FOOD AND DRINK:

Scoma's (Pier 47 in Fisherman's Wharf) They have their own fishing dock, so you know it's fresh. This is where locals come for seafood. Try Lazy Man's Cioppino, spicy abalone and the crabcakes. Lunch and dinner daily. ☎ (415) 771-4383. $$–$$$

Alioto's (Pier 8 at Fisherman's Wharf) Established in 1928, this is the best-known restaurant on the wharf. The second-floor dining room affords unreal views. Wide range of seafood as expected. Lunch and dinner daily. Reservations ☎ (415) 673-0183. $$–$$$.

Fog City Diner (1300 Battery) Classy chrome and tile diner has been the site of dozens of TV commercials and movies. They serve a wide variety of fresh fish and shellfish dishes. Salads and sandwiches too. Lunch and dinner daily. ☎ (415) 982-2000. $–$$

Il Tornaio (1265 Battery in Levi Plaza) Lovely setting right on the Plaza. It started as a baking school in Milan and expanded to the US with several locations. Superb pastas and other Italian dishes—and breads too. Different region of Italy featured monthly. ☎ (415) 986-0100. $–$$

SUGGESTED TOUR:

Numbers in parentheses correspond to numbers on the map.

As you come to the end of Market Street and cross the Embarcadero, you will see **Justin Herman Plaza** (1) on the left. The fountain made of angular pilings, seemingly thrown in a heap, can be climbed on, around and through. Designed by Canadian Armand Vaillancourt, it was opened in 1971. This site is popular with the lunchtime crowd. In good weather, jazz groups, jugglers and other buskers can be seen performing.

The **Ferry Building** (2), while somewhat overshadowed by taller buildings that have shot up in the neighborhood, is nonetheless an inspiring structure. It's interesting to note that when it is lit up at night, you can see it from anywhere along Market Street. The classical revival-style building (modeled after the Moorish bell tower of the Seville cathedral) was designed by A. Page Brown in 1892 and dedicated in 1898. During its heyday, the Ferry Building was the pre-bridge transportation hub of the entire Bay Area, serving over 50 million ferry passengers a year. Today it is the site of the World Trade Center. You can take a sloping stairway up to the third floor and along the way see some stylized murals of the economies, people, dwellings, flora and fauna and transportation of the Pacific.

You can still take ferries from this location to Sausalito, Larkspur and the East Bay—and even 49ers and Giants games at 3Com Park. *For the games, the ferry leaves at 11:15 in the morning on game day. The fare is $15 roundtrip. There are six departures a day to Alameda (see Daytrip 33) and one to Vallejo and Marine World (see Daytrip 32). ☎ (415) 247-1604 for reservations.*

As you make your way along the Bay Trail, note that the imposing pier fronts have large numbers that from this direction from the Ferry Building are odd, and south of the Ferry Building are even. **Pier 3** holds an interesting old ferryboat called the **Santa Rosa** (3), built in 1927. It floats and is used as an office building today, but you can go up on deck for good look at the Bay Bridge and Treasure Island. *Open 9:30–4 Mon.–Sat. Free.* **Pier 7** was once one of San Francisco's heavy-lifting docks, but is now lined with antique lampposts, benches and fishermen.

Be sure to look for tall, black-and-white posts spaced about every 100 yards along this route. They give brief, but interesting bits of history about the bay and the city including one that lists the numerous shipwrecks around the Golden Gate.

For you sailors, **Pier 17** will hold a good deal of interest. Housed here is a retail shop and headquarters for True America, one of this nation's contestants for the America's Cup in 2000. *The store is open 10–6 Mon.–Fri. and 12–5 on Sun.* It carries all manner of nautical wear and gifts touting this particular boat.

At **Pier 23**, cross the Embarcadero to see one of the loveliest small urban parks in America. **Levi Plaza** was built and dedicated to the employees of Levi Strauss, which is headquartered in the area. The Plaza features dramatic fountains, cool lawns, small streams and plenty of benches for contemplating the beauty of the area. When you cross back over the Embarcadero, look for Pier 31 where you will find **Hornblower Cruises**. This is the largest dinner cruise line on the bay, offering dinner/dancing and sightseeing nightly. *All-inclusive cost (except bar) for a three-hour cruise is $61.50 Sun.–Thurs., $70 Fri. and $74.50 Sat.* ☎ *(415) 788-8866 for reservations.*

Soon you will come to a festival marketplace called **Pier 39** (4). This bazaar-like center has plenty of food, shopping and attractions to keep the whole family happy. Toward the back is an attractive merry-go-round. Upstairs is a fairly recent addition to the retail scene in the form of the **National Park Store.** This non-profit retail outlet offers nature, history, travel, art, photography and literature of the national parks of the west. Well worth a visit. Next door is another unusual shop called The Marine Mammal Center connected to the same facility in the Marin Headlands *(see Daytrip 17).* The store has exhibits on the sea lions next door as well as quality merchandise that supports the center.

At the entrance is the **Pier 39 Aquarium, Underwater World** (5). This aquarium you view from the inside out because you walk through more than 300 feet of crystal-clear tubing that's actually submerged. All around you are hundreds of sea creatures you can see up-close-and-personal. *Open daily in summer 9–9 and winter 10–8:30. Cost is $12.95 for adults, $9.95 for seniors 65+ and $6.50 for kids 3–11.*

Among the most fascinating sights at Pier 39 are the sea lions on the west

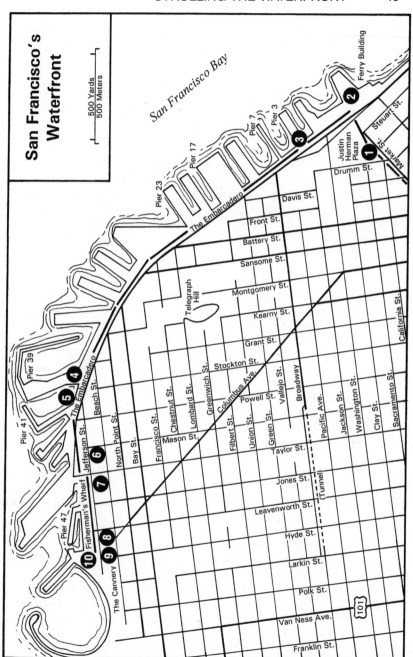

San Francisco's Waterfront

500 Yards
500 Meters

San Francisco Bay

side of the pier. On about two dozen floating pads are dozens of these sleek, furry mammals in all sorts of antics. Some pads are completely empty, while others are piled high with bulbous bodies to the point of being way over-crowded. Some are honking, others are arguing while the majority are just hanging out. The usually come here in January. It's a real show. *Pier 39 guides conduct a short course on sea lions Mon.–Fri. at 11 a.m.*

At Pier 41 are the **Blue and Gold Ferries**. They have an extensive offer-ing that includes bay cruises and trips to Tiburon, Sausalito (both $11 round-trip), Muir Woods ($32), Angel Island ($10) and—the most popular—Alcatraz ($11)*(see Trip 7)*. There are 10 Alcatraz departures a day, but it's a good idea to book as far in advance as possible. ☎ (415) 773-1188. A bar-gain way to see Alcatraz (by cruising by and not landing on it) and six of the city's other highlights—SF Zoo, M.H. deYoung Museum and California Academy of Sciences *(Daytrip 2)*, California Palace of the Legion of Honor *(Daytrip 4)*, Exploratorium *(Daytrip 9)*, and the SF Museum of Modern Art *(Daytrip 13)*—is to purchase a **City Pass** for $29.95 for adults, $19.95 for seniors 65+ and $17.95. Valid for one week, it gives you admission to all seven attractions at a considerable savings.

If walking's got you down and you'd like to hop on a bike for the rest of the Bay Trail, **Blazing Saddles Bike Rentals,** also at Pier 41, is the answer. You might want to go all the way to Sausalito over the bridge—a trip of nine miles. They include a computer to track your mileage, a route sheet, locks, helmet, packs and water bottle. *Rates start at $25 per day for a basic moun-tain bike. Kids' bikes and tandems too.* ☎ *(415) 202-8880 to reserve, espe-cially in summer.*

The next pier is 43½, which has long been abandoned. Note the rail tracks still in place, since this was where the trains from Marin County were ferried across to the city in the early days before the Golden Gate Bridge. Worth checking out next at 156 Jefferson Street is San Francisco's original sourdough bakery. French baker Isadore Boudin came to California for the Gold Rush and started baking a wonderful tart bread with a hard crust and soft inside that continues to this day. **Boudin French Bread Bakery** has good eats as well as lots of that tangy sourdough to consume there or ship home. They say San Francisco sourdough is the best because the salt air combines with the spores to make an unbeatable taste found nowhere else in the country.

The Wax Museum (6), 145 Jefferson at the corner of Mason, claims to be one of the world's largest museums of this type with over 200 figures. There's everything from King Tut's tomb to religious themes. The old-famous and the new-famous are represented with likenesses of such luminaries as William Shakespeare and Elvis. There are 14 presidential exhibits—luckily they're not next to the Chamber of Horrors with all kinds of unpleasant monsters. *Open 9–11 daily. Adults $11.95, seniors 65+ $8.95, kids 6–12 $5.95.*

In the same block is **Ripley's Believe It or Not** (7) at 175 Jefferson. It has two floors and 11 galleries. Ripley himself, an artist, reporter, explorer and collector, was said to be as unusual as the artifacts he gathered. There are many of Ripley's personal treasures on display as well as dozens of other oddities—like the two-headed calf, a portrait of Van Gogh made from toast, a double-eyed man from China with two sets of pupils in each eye—and more. If you know of an unbelievable fact or unusual item, submit it to the museum manager and you too can become part of the Ripley legend. *Open 10–10 daily. Adults $8.50, seniors 60+ $7.00, kids 5–12 $5.50.* ☎ *(415) 771-6188.*

If you turn right on Jones at **Pier 47**, you'll find the family-run **Old Wharf Smokehouse** (the official address is "Foot of Jones"). Not only does Trudy Svedise sell delicious smoked seafood, but her husband will take you deep-sea fishing if you so desire—and then smoke your fish for you after you come in. The rate is $85 per person which includes a license, use of equipment, and of course the wisdom of the skipper in catching sea bass, halibut or salmon depending on the season. They go out at 5:30 and fish until 3, depending on the weather. ☎ *(415) 775-6655.*

The Cannery (8), at the corner of Jefferson and Leavenworth, is a large, multi-story brick building that was a fruit cannery at one time. It now houses dozens of shops and restaurants. On the upper level is the **Official Museum of the City of San Francisco** (9). This modest facility shows the major phases in the city's life: its origins as a Spanish garrison, its renown as a Gold Rush boom town, and finally its place as "Earthquake City." Some of the early photos of the devastation of the 1906 earthquake are very interesting. Among other trivia, you'll learn that fortune cookies are of Japanese origin after all, and not Chinese. They were invented in 1909 at the teahouse in Golden Gate Park's Japanese Tea Garden. *Open Wed.–Sun. 10–4. The museum is free, but accepts donations.*

The final destination in this fascinating area of the city is one of the few floating museums in the world, the **Hyde Street Pier** (10). Through various shoreside displays you can learn how perilous a voyage around Cape Horn could really be, and how little space crew members existed in during coastal runs. See meticulously restored cabins. Look for riggers at work aloft using traditional shipwright's skills.

It is possible to tour the *Balclutha,* a square-rigger that sailed around Cape Horn; *C.A. Thayer,* the last commercial sailing vessel operating from the West Coast to ports primarily in Asia; *Eureka,* a sizable side-wheeler ferry used to take people across the bay; *Hercules,* an ocean-going tug used for hauling uncut logs from the Northwest to San Francisco; *Eppleton Hall,* an unusual tug with a paddle wheel and *Alma,* one of the last San Francisco flat bottom scows used to haul bulk cargo across the bay. *Winter hours are 9:30-5 daily and summer hours 10–6. Adults are $4, kids 12–17 are $2 and seniors 62+ are free.*

*Alcatraz by Ferry

It's hard to know exactly why over one million visitors a year are so attracted to a rocky, windswept island practically in the middle of San Francisco Bay. They go there to look at a string of jail cells in some somber old buildings. But just try to walk up to the ferry at Fisherman's Wharf without prior arrangements for a ride to Alcatraz. It's almost impossible to get there without an advance reservation—in summer, plan ahead several days.

The fascination is probably due to a bunch of movies about Alcatraz, and how they each added to the legends of The Rock. It is a fact that three prisoners took several years to scratch their way out with sharpened spoons. They were never seen or heard from again. Did they escape? We'll never know. Famous prisoners—like Al Capone—spent their final days there. Maybe it's the terrific view of San Francisco that is in part the reason thousands stream there every year.

Even the National Park Service, which runs Alcatraz, has discovered that it's difficult to separate fact from fiction in researching the history of *la Isla de los Alcatraces*, which means Isle of the Pelicans. Under the Federal Prisons Bureau from 1933–62, the folklore of Devil's Island or "Hellcatraz" supposedly was allowed to flourish to perpetuate The Rock's image as a dread, escape-proof citadel.

GETTING THERE:

There is only one way, and that is **by ferry** from Pier 41 at Fisherman's Wharf. The Blue & Gold Fleet offers ten departures a day to Alcatraz starting at 9:30 in the morning and ending at 2:15 p.m. There are 13 return trips.

The fares are: Adult (with cell house audio tour) $11.00 and (without audio tour) $7.75; seniors 62 + (w/tour) $9.25 and (w/o tour) $6.00; kids 5–1 (w/tour) $5.75 and (w/o tour) $4.50.

PRACTICALITIES:

By all means call ahead for reservations as soon as you know when you'd like to go. ☎ *(415) 705-5555 or 773-1188.*

The island can be blustery and chilly, so take along a sweater or light jacket. Sunglasses are a very good idea.

FOOD AND DRINK:

Swiss Loui's (Pier 39) Delicious Italian selections. See the sea lions below as they cavort like a circus act. The View Bar is well named. The California Wine Store is well worth a visit. Lunch and dinner daily. Reservations ☎ (415) 732-7917. $$

Lou's Pier 47 (Pier 47) Interesting mix of Cajun and San Francisco seafood. Terrific oyster stew, dungeness crab and cioppino. Sunny outdoor seating. Live bands Mon.–Fri., noon–4, Sat. & Sun. until 2 p.m. ☎ (415) 771-LOUS. $–$$

Pompei's Grotto (340 Jefferson St.) This is a family-operated trattoria that's the consummate wharf restaurant. Italian dishes with lots of seafood like prawns, cracked crab, calamari and more. Pleasant atmosphere. Lunch and dinner daily. ☎ (415) 776-9265. $–$$

Boudin Bakery (Pier 39) Old-time bakery from Gold Rush days. Try chowder or chili in a sourdough bread bowl. Plan to take home any of the many varieties of sourdough breads. Breakfast, lunch and dinner daily. ☎ (415) 421-2259. $

LOCAL ATTRACTIONS:

Numbers in parentheses correspond to numbers on the map.

*ALCATRAZ PRISON, in the middle of San Francisco Bay, ☎ (415) 546-2700. *Open every day. Free admission, but see information above for ferry fees. Visitor center with multi-media video, exhibits and shop. No food. Partially &.*

As you cover the one-and-a-quarter miles from the San Francisco pier to Alcatraz, the closer you get the more verdant it looks. It's a little surprising to see that trees, bushes and flowers—lavender lippia, orange nasturtium, pink ice plant—abound. Not bad for a twelve-acre island that is essentially waterless. It all has to be brought to the island from other sources or collected from rainwater. Not only is there no natural water, but almost no soil either. Tons of topsoil was brought originally from Angel Island (Daytrip 8) so this barren island could sustain—among other things—small garden plots for prison guards.

The dominant features of the island, however, are the silent buildings sitting on the rocky escarpment that rises 135 feet out of the bay. Someone once said it looks something like to a bombed-out European hill town from World War II. Part of that is due to the damage inflicted on Alcatraz by Native Americans who occupied the island from 1969–71. The Indians, who claimed Alcatraz as their birthright, gutted many of the prison's buildings. At one time, 400 Indians occupied Alcatraz—beating by a couple of hundred the highest number of prisoners on the island in its heyday.

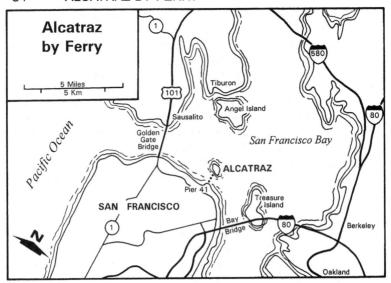

When the Rock's futu1re was in doubt, the GSA first tried to sell the island and then considered four possible uses for the inaccessible rock: as a gambling resort; a space museum; a monument to Native Americans; and as a university for Indians. In the process several buildings were razed by the General Services Administration leaving considerable rubble still visible around the old Parade Grounds.

Visitors land at the only dock on the island. It is the same one where hundreds of prisoners took their first steps into a world of terribly dark and dreary confinement. In anticipation of the island being used as a fort, the federal government built Sally Port in 1857 right above the jetty landing. This guardhouse, with its onetime moat and drawbridge, is another reminder that this is hardly a pleasant little spot for vacationing.

Just before Sally Port is the Visitor Center in one of the old barracks buildings. Here you will find fascinating exhibits and a multi-media show that gives a complete history of the island.

Since 1854 Alcatraz has been successively a major West Coast lighthouse, a fortification, a U.S. military prison, an Army disciplinary barracks, a federal penitentiary, an American Indian stronghold—and finally a visitor attraction. It was named Alcatraz (after the hundreds of pelicans that lived there) in 1775 by the explorer Juan Manuel de Ayala. The U.S. government bought the island in 1848 and built the first Pacific Coast lighthouse six years later. Fort Alcatraz was carefully built around the lighthouse ten years after that in 1858. The fort was fitted with about 100 cannon and housed 400 men to protect San Francisco and the bay from foreign intruders.

In 1909, the feds had prisoners build the first cell house for the Army, and that was the beginning of the island's use as a prison. It was 1934 when the Federal Bureau of Prisons made the decision to build Alcatraz into a hardened bastion to house its more incorrigible criminals. To show how bad they were, they were the ones who could not be confined at any other federal prison because of their horrific behavior.

There are park rangers available for a series of tours. Some examples are: Alcatraz as Indian Land; Time in The Rock; Escapes. You can also wander on your own through the areas open to the public. As you leave the dock, the road angles steeply up through a tunnel and past old fortifications and staff barracks. At the main prison cellblock with its heavy steel bars, you get to inspect the claustrophobic cells, mess hall, library and most appalling of all, the dark holes where prisoners were put in solitary confinement. An audio tour gives a good deal of detail.

Even the cells were pretty awful, measuring only nine feet long by five feet across. Prisoners spent almost the entire day alone in these cramped spaces with only a toilet and bunk. You get to see rows and rows of these prisoner pigeonholes along "Broadway," which the captives nicknamed the corridor between Cell Blocks C and B.

The Rock's administrative code was "Complete Control." Number 5 of the Alcatraz Prison Rules and Regulations said, "You are entitled to food, clothing, shelter and medical care. Anything else you get is a privilege."

At no time did the big house's 450 cells hold more than 250 captives. The staff ran as high as 100. This did not prevent three inmates—Frank Lee Morris, and John and Clarence Anglin—from tunneling out with sharpened spoons in 1962. The feat took years, and they were never found. Their seemingly successful escape was a factor in the Prison Board's decision to phase out the aging institution. Attorney General Robert Kennedy signed the closure order.

On March 21, 1963, the last of the Rock's inmates—27 pale men in wrist and leg shackles—were transferred to other federal penal institutions. Alcatraz is now a component of the Bay Area's 75,000-acre Golden Gate National Recreation Area created by Congress and signed into law by President Nixon in 1972.

Trip 8
San Francisco

Angel Island by Ferry

They say there are 14 islands in San Francisco Bay and that Angel Island is the largest at 700-plus acres. The dome-shaped island rises more than 700 feet above sea level at the summit of Mt. Livermore.

At one time, it was heavily wooded with native trees among which the Miwok Indians hunted and gathered food for six thousand years. Early sailors practically clear-cut the oak and madrone trees, and dubbed it Wood Island. The same man who discovered Alcatraz (see Daytrip 7) also landed here in 1775 and gave it the name *Isla de los Angeles* after the quiet cove where he anchored his ship. In the early 1800s the denuded island became a cattle ranch. When California achieved statehood in 1850, the Army took the island for a garrison.

Besides the physical beauty of the place, the scattered, empty (and in many cases boarded up) buildings make it seem like a ghost island. You can feel the spirits of an army camp, quarantine station, immigration center and prisoner-of-war camp. We'll learn about these permutations as we travel around the island.

The military took its leave of Angel Island in 1962, and the place languished and decayed for some time. Credit for saving the island and preserving it for our enjoyment go to two individuals. Caroline Livermore was a Marin County resident who pushed mightily for the island to become a state park. She succeeded and the mountain in the center of the island is named for her. A lot of credit goes to a retired physician by the name of Robert Noyes who several years ago formed the Angel Island Association that went about preserving historic buildings on the island. Also part of their work was making the facilities and some of the buildings accessible for the disabled.

GETTING THERE:

You can get there by private boat or either of three ferries. The **Blue and Gold Ferry** leaves Pier 41 at Fisherman's Wharf at 10:40 in the morning on Saturdays, Sundays and holidays (except Thanksgiving, Christmas and New

Year's Day), arriving about 50 minutes later; it departs the island at 4:50 in the afternoon. The round trip fee is $10 for adults, $9 for juniors 12–18 and $5 for kids 5–11. ☎ *(415) 773-1188.*

The **Angel Island State Ferry** leaves Tiburon four times a day on weekdays starting at 10; weekends every hour on the hour from 10–5; return trips are 20 minutes past the hour. The fee is $6 for adults, $4 for kids 5–11 and $1 for bikes. ☎ *(415) 435-2131.* To get to Tiburon, cross the Golden Gate Bridge and follow Highway 101 to the Tiburon Blvd. exit. Go into downtown, from which the ferry departs.

PRACTICALITIES:

Depending on how you want to tour the island—on foot, by bike or on the tram—wear appropriate clothing. In summer it can be foggy in the city, but warm and sunny on the island—you never know. Be prepared. Take sunglasses.

The Angel Island Company offers tram service and bike rentals. The **Tram Tours** run four times daily on weekends and holidays and three times daily on weekdays Apr.–Oct. ☎ *(415) 435-1915.* The cost is $10 for adults, $9 for seniors 62+ and $6 for kids 6–12. **Bike rentals** include helmet. Basic bikes are $10 an hour or $25 for the day; expert bikes are $14 an hour or $30 per day; tandems are $20 an hour or $45 per day and kids trailers can be rented for $5 an hour or $10 per day. You can take your own bike on the ferries, but it's usually a first-come-first-served situation.

Stable, two-person kayaks can be rented from **Sea Trek** weekends and holidays May-Oct. The rates are $100 per person which includes a picnic lunch, instruction, the tour and all equipment. ☎ *(415) 488-1000.*

FOOD AND DRINK:

Rooney's Café & Grill (38 Main St. in Tiburon) Located in one of the very old buildings in town, this small spot serves up wonderful sandwiches and pastas. Sunny outdoor seating in good weather. Lunch daily and dinner Wed.-Sun. ☎ (415) 435-1911. $–$$

Sweden House Bakery & Café (35 Main St. in Tiburon) Everything baked is made fresh on the premises. Delicious croissants and other goodies call residents to this gathering spot in big numbers. Outdoor seating has a view of the city. Breakfast, lunch and dinner daily. ☎ (415) 435-9767. $

SUGGESTED TOUR:

Numbers in parentheses correspond to numbers on the map.

You have choices on Angel Island. The Perimeter Road circling the island is about five miles and you can cover the place on foot, by bicycle or on a tram. Depending on how curious you are, you might add another mile

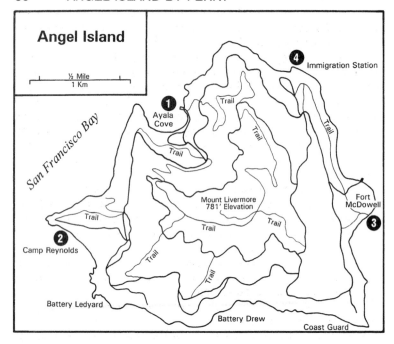

looking at some of the historic sites. Most people go around on foot since the scenery can be appreciated best at a walking pace.

The road is both paved and gravel in places and be assured it is not totally flat, providing some hilly challenges now and then. Mount Livermore, 781 feet tall, can only be ascended on foot.

One of the wonderful things about Angel Island is that there are no motorized vehicles, except a few utility vehicles used by the State Park Service—and the trams. That means if you bike or walk, it is one of the few places in America where you won't have to constantly fight cars, trucks and buses. Many visitors have commented on the sense of freedom from not having cars zipping around every turn.

The ferries all land at **Ayala Cove** (1), honoring Juan Manuel de Ayala who named the island. At one time it was called Hospital Cove because the U.S. Public Health Service quarantined ships and their cargoes here when they were suspected of harboring contagious diseases. That went on for about 50 years until the mid-1950s.

You will be greeted by good facilities that include restrooms, picnic tables, snack bar and an information booth. A few paces away is a **Visitor Center**, offering historical displays and a 20-minute video tour. At each of the significant stops around the island, there are docent-guided tours of the historic sites.

As you leave the Visitor Center for the Perimeter Road, you can go left or right. It is suggested you go right since the grade is better for biking and walking and the history unfolds more logically.

Boarded-up **Camp Reynolds'** (2) red brick hospital is the first building you will come to. Built in 1863, it was the Army's first installation on the island. Down a dirt road is the main part of the camp, which you might want to explore. Among the quaint wooden buildings that remain are some officer housing that was built on Yerba Buena Island and barged to this site, an officer's home and the adjoining bake shop. The latter two can be toured with docents. At the water's edge is the huge, red-brick quarter-master's storehouse, which is used by school groups for overnight field trips.

As the road winds around the shoreline, you will be treated to views of San Francisco and the surrounding area that are outstanding. Since the island is only a little over three miles from the city, it seems very close. Sausalito is obviously closer and therefore even more in your lap. And the westerly view of Golden Gate Bridge is quite unusual.

There are various military fortifications indicated by signs along the road, and if that sort of things interests you, by all means take the time to explore them. **Battery Ledyard** and **Battery Drew** are big concrete bunkers the Army built around the turn of the century to protect the bay from marauding invaders. They never fired a shot.

Next at the south east point of the island is the **Coast Guard Station** that isn't open to the public. But do stop for the views of the East Bay all along this stretch of road.

Another half-mile or so and you come to **Fort McDowell** (3), at one time the largest garrison on the island. You will pass **Quarry Point** which, before the days of environmentalism, was actually a sizable hill that got flattened to build buildings in San Francisco. This fort got its start in 1909 when construction started in earnest on what would become the biggest induction center for incoming soldiers—with overseas assignments—in the country. The many facilities at the fort served the military continuously through World War II.

The neat thing about exploring the fort is that you can make it right down to the beach, one of the few places on the island where you can go beach-combing. There's a Visitor Center at Fort McDowell that is a good place to get oriented. It will explain the massive buildings where 600 men lived in the largest barracks on the West Coast. The old, gray post hospital is pretty imposing as well.

Back on the Perimeter Road, after a short distance, you will come to the **Immigration Station** (4) on the northeast shoulder of the island.

Angel Island has been called the "Ellis Island of the West" because the Station was originally built to process an anticipated flood of European immigrants entering the U.S. through the newly-opened Panama Canal. It opened on January 21, 1910, in time for World War I and the closing of America's "open door" to immigrants from Europe.

The facility instead served as the detention center for the majority of approximately 175,000 Chinese immigrants who came to America between 1910 and 1940 seeking escape from the economic and political hardships of their homeland. At any one time, 600 men and women were detained on Angel island.

What these newcomers found when they reached America was discrimination and a series of restrictive anti-Asian laws, including the Chinese Exclusion Act of 1882. The law was passed after the economy soured in the 1870s and unions wanted to restrict the cheap Asian laborers brought to fish, build the railroads and farm. Although all Asians were affected, 97 percent of the immigrants processed through the Station were Chinese.

After the earthquake and fire of 1906 destroyed records that verified citizenship, many Chinese residents of California were able to claim citizenship for themselves and dozens of "paper children."

Citizenship papers were then sold to prospective immigrants; entire villages would often purchase papers from one representative in the hopes that he would return from "Gam San" or "Gold Mountain" and share his expected wealth. Immigration officials responded to the deception by detaining all working-class Chinese immigrants for interrogation.

Typical questions asked were: How many stairs lead up to your house? How many chickens do you own? Recite your family history. Those who did not match those of their "paper parents" were deported.

According to Immigration Station docents, almost 15 percent of the detainees were sent back. Rather than face the humiliation of being sent back to their villages, which had pooled meager resources to buy the citizenship papers, many deportees committed suicide.

The Chinese immigrants were held on the island for weeks, months, even years while awaiting hearings or appeals on their applications. In contrast, immigrants passing through Ellis Island were processed within hours or days and merely had to pass medical hurdles.

To vent their frustrations and their forced idleness and isolation (authorities separated family members to prevent exchange of information and routinely inspected letters and gift packages), detainees wrote poems expressing their anger, despair, homesickness and loneliness.

The poetry, written and intricately carved on the walls in the classical style of the Tang Dynasty, was recorded by two detainees in the early 1930s and rediscovered in 1970. Some of the writing on the walls is still legible today.

In the now sparse and barren rooms, one can only imagine the isolation and lack of privacy each detainee was forced to endure. Crowded into bunks three tiers high, the men and women imprisoned in the cramped dormitories lived in constant mistrust of each other. The women's bathroom, with its almost total lack of privacy, was the site of many suicides.

Although complaints about unsatisfactory conditions and mistreatment were filed frequently—the first filed only a few days after the Station opened—bureaucrats were slow to address the charges and did not abandon the detention center until a fire on August 12, 1940 destroyed the administration building.

Three months later, on November 5, a group of Chinese immigrants, 125 men and 19 women, were loaded onto ferries and transferred to temporary quarters in South San Francisco. On this seemingly ordinary day came the end of a sad and bitter era: The Ellis Island of the West had finally closed its doors.

But the use of Angel island for processing and holding foreigners wasn't over. The same barracks used for the Asian immigrants in the 1800s were again pressed into use service during WWII to hold Japanese, Italian and German prisoners of war. Today, these barracks hold a museum that bespeaks the tough conditions under which these foreigners were held. Be sure to visit the museum for a moving experience. *Open daily 11-3:30.*

With its stupendous views, the remaining distance to Ayala Cove will lift your spirits after the heavy experience of the Immigration Station.

Trip 9
San Francisco

*Northern Waterfront & Environs

Legend has it that some of the ground you will cover today (and in the previous Daytrip #6) is made of massive amounts of fill including rubbish, horse manure, and even dead cats! That's because San Francisco's original serrated shoreline of sandy coves and rocky promontories hindered construction of deep water piers. Leave it to the engineers who planned a great seawall that would neatly round out the city's northeast waterfront. Construction took 46 years, from 1878 to 1924.

All that work, money and time seems to have turned out a stunning waterfront. San Francisco is surrounded on three sides by water, giving it 29.5 miles of shoreline. For this daytrip, we'll only cover about two miles of it starting at Hyde Street and going north and west. During this trip, you'll experience an established maritime museum as well as several smaller ones in a former military installation. Beyond that is a magnificent wide swath of lawn with unbelievable views of the Golden Gate Bridge and the Marin Headlands.

Finally, we will end up at a unique entertainment center of which *Newsweek* said, "There are two models for great American amusement centers . . . Disneyland and the *Exploratorium*. This place feeds all the senses." Should be a fun day.

GETTING THERE:

By bus, go to Market and catch a #42 Muni, getting off at Hyde.

By cable car, catch the Powell/Hyde line that will take you to Aquatic Park.

By car, go west (up) on Geary or Sutter to Van Ness. Turn right and follow it until you come to North Point and turn right.

PRACTICALITIES:

This walk is about two miles along the waterfront, so wear comfortable shoes. Sunglasses are a wonderful idea if it's sunny.

FOOD AND DRINK:

The Mandarin (Ghirardelli Sq. Woolen Mill) Northern Chinese cuisine in a palace-like setting with huge pillars, jade green floor and stone and wood-hewn statues. Dignitaries frequent the place. Specialities are Pot Stickers, Glazed Walnut Prawns & Mu Shu vegetable. Lunch & dinner daily. ☎ (415) 673-8812. $$

Greens (Bldg. A, Fort Mason, Marina Blvd. and Buchanan St.) Art on the walls and a sweeping view of the bay combine to make this location for solid vegetarian fare appealing to all. Lunch Tues.–Sat. Café dinners Mon.–Fri. and prix fixe Sat. dinner. Takeout a specialty. ☎ (415) 771-7955. $$

McCormick & Kuletto's (900 North Point in Ghirardelli Sq.) Unreal view of the bridge, Marin and Sausalito. Mussels, crab, shark, salmon, snapper, trout and plenty of other seafood dishes to please. Huge wine list. Open for lunch and dinner daily. Reservations ☎ (415) 929-1730. $–$$

La Pasta (in Ghirardelli Sq.) Choose from over 20 fresh pasta dishes while you enjoy the great view of the Bay. The potato gnocchi (small potato dumplings in a buttery sage sauce) is excellent. Lunch and dinner daily. ☎ (415) 749-5288 for reservations. $–$$

Buena Vista (corner of Hyde and Beach Sts.) While the name suggests a great view, that's not really the case. But the "BV," as it's known by locals, is a favorite hang-out. Legendary Irish Coffee and other libations. Sandwiches, salads, etc. Breakfast, lunch and dinner daily. ☎ (415) 474-5044. $

SUGGESTED TOUR:

Numbers in parentheses correspond to numbers on the map.

We suggest you start this daytrip at the corner of Hyde and Beach Streets. Just below this is the **Cable Car Turnaround** where sometimes the gripman will call on nearby passengers to help out with the turn. To the right and below the Turnaround is a grassy area called **Aquatic Park** (1) where you can hang out and watch the swimmers (in almost any weather) stroking across the small bay created by the Hyde Street Pier on the right and the Municipal Pier on the left. The water may be calm because of the piers, but the temperature is hardly conducive to swimming—any time of year.

Ghirardelli Square (2), the famed chocolate factory, looms above this area. It has an interesting history as one of San Francisco's early, premiere businesses. Domingo Ghirardelli started out in Italy, then made his way to Peru. But the lure of the Gold Rush brought him to San Francisco in 1849.

He stayed in the gold country supplying chocolate to the miners until 1852, and then came to the city. Ghirardelli was an enterprising sort and his empire included chocolate, wool, and mustard; names that designate the various buildings in the square to this day. But chocolate gave way to merchandising in the early 1960s, so that today you can find over 50 shops, galleries and restaurants on three levels. Stop by the information both and pick up a map for a self-guided tour of the Square with historical markers to tell the full story.

As you go along Beach Street, at the foot of Polk Street you will come to the **Maritime Museum** (3) at 900 Beach. For a free museum, this one is stocked with fascinating seafaring exhibits. Huge mast sections, jutting spars and painted figureheads tell the story of the lives of the people who built ships and sailed on California's waterways. One-of-a-kind artifacts and historic photographs chronicle the excitement of the California Gold Rush. The story of the West Coast whaling industry is told in an exciting fashion. In the Steamship Room, displays and models trace the revolution of steam technology—from the tiny "mail packet" steamers to giant cargo vessels. Panoramic photos of early San Francisco, juxtaposed with recent views, challenge you to recognize the once-sleepy little village of 1848 in the busy skyline of today. *Hours are 10–5 daily. Free.*

Next, take the steps down from the Museum and make your way left on the Bay Trail as it circles Aquatic Park. The promontory with large cypress trees marks the beginning of **Fort Mason** (4). As in much of the rest of the country, base closures along San Francisco Bay have prompted conversion of military bases into civilian use. This fort on the San Francisco side of the Bay and Fort Baker on the north side, which both trained gun turrets on the entrance to the Bay, are now part of the huge **Golden Gate National Recreation Area**, one of the nation's newest national parks. Today the lower part of Fort Mason (the upper part was retained by the Army) is a thriving cultural center filled with theaters, museums and shops.

Besides such community resources as California Tomorrow, California Lawyers for the Arts, Friends of the River, the Ploughshares Fund and others like it, Fort Mason houses several small, but impressive museums. **The Mexican Museum** (5) collects, preserves, exhibits, interprets and promotes the artistic expression of the Mexicano and Latino people through visual arts and other multi-disciplinary forms. The museum store is called La Tienda, which has a broad selection of handcrafted gifts from Mexico and Latin America. *Located in Bldg. D, 1st floor. Open Wed.–Fri. noon–5 and Sat., Sun 11–5. Admission is $3.*

The **Museo ItaloAmericano** (6) is dedicated to researching, collecting and displaying the works of Italian and Italian-American artists. It also offers educational programs for the appreciation of Italian art and culture. Facilities include a gallery with changing exhibits, a library and gift shop. *Located in Bldg. C on the 1st floor. Open Wed.–Sun. noon–5. Admission is $2.* ☎

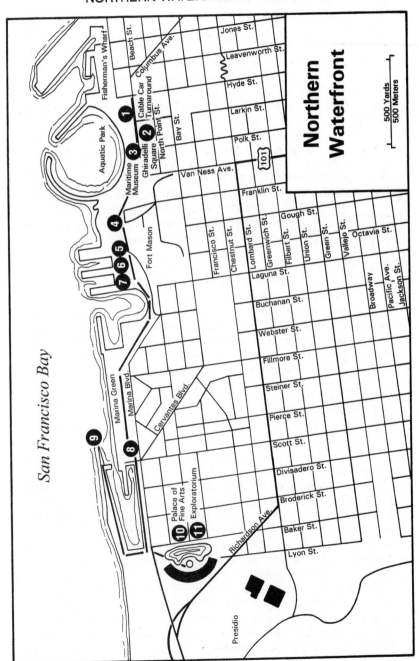

(415) 673-2200. **Magic Theater** (7) has won international recognition as an outstanding American playwright's theater. Substantial new plays by writers like Pulitzer Prize-winner Sam Shepard and poet/playwright Michael Mc-Clure have been presented at the Magic, as well as innovative works by emerging writers. *Bldg. D, 3rd floor. ☎ the box office at (415) 441-3687 for current showings.*

Head out of Fort Mason in the other direction from which you came. You will round a small yacht basin and then head toward the **Marina Green** (8). To the left, residences in the Marina District command even higher prices than most of the rest of San Francisco simply because of this giant lawn and their proximity to the bay. Hardly a moment goes by without some sort of activity taking place on the Marina Green. Kite flying is very popular. Joggers, walkers and bicyclists can cause heavy traffic on weekends. And of course, the many-splendored yachts tucked into the basin can be seen making their way in and out of the sheltered harbor.

Just past the yacht harbor is Lyon Street. Turn right and, just for fun, go to the end of the breakwater where you will see the **Wave Organ** (9). It's been called one of the world's most unusual musical instruments and is made up of a series of underwater pipes. These pipes are meant to pick up the tidal movement and play them back to listeners. Don't expect a symphony, but it's a kick nonetheless.

When you come back, cross at Lyon Street and this will take you to the **Palace of Fine Arts** (10). The neo-classical Palace—which is really not a palace, but an open-air series of structures—was built just for the 1915 Panama-Pacific Exposition and was expected to be torn down thereafter. The Palace was but a small section of the sprawling exposition in celebration of San Francisco's rebirth after the 1906 earthquake and the opening of the Panama Canal. San Franciscans liked the graceful colonnade of Corinthian columns that was left behind after the rest was demolished, and so it was spared. But because it was originally only built of wood and plaster as a temporary structure, it deteriorated badly and was a considerable eyesore for many years. Finally in 1962, it was rebuilt using stronger materials. It is a peaceful spot with a soaring dome in the middle, lagoon and plentiful weeping willow trees.

Now on to the:

*EXPLORATORIUM (11), 3601 Lyon St. San Francisco, CA 94123 (in a building that curves along the arch of the Palace), ☎ (415) 563-7337. *Open daily in summer (May–Oct.) 10–6 and Tues.–Sun. in winter 10–5. Wed. until 9:30 p.m. Adult admission $9, seniors $7, kids 6–17 $5 and 3-5 $2.50. Free first Wed. of the month. Museum shop and café. &.*

Its name is actually Exploratorium, the Museum of Science, Art and Human Perception. But that's kind of long-winded, so the museum says of itself that "it's a playground for you mind." Each of the 650 interactive displays is designed to teach you a little something about our world—while you play. That's what the Exploratorium is all about; having a lot of fun while learning.

Exhibits like the Distorted Room are carefully designed to challenge your senses and turn your world inside-out. There's the Anti-Gravity Mirror and exhibits where you can stick your hand in a tornado, fly by computer over the Bay, or just relax and blow monster bubbles. The Tactile Dome is an adventure in touch. In a pitch-black environment, you crawl, climb, slide and explore the most amazing and startling textures. It's a little like a maze, a little like a fun house, a little like a game of Pin the Tail on the Donkey. *Advance reservations for the Tactile Dome are suggested.* ☎ *(415) 561-0362.*

Kids love it, but adults can find plenty to keep themselves amused. If you read *Scientific American,* it's "The best science museum in the world." Further accolades have come from *Good Housekeeping* which lists the Exploratorium as one of the 10 best science museums in the nation.

Presidio and Across the Bridge

For two hundreds years, the Presidio served as a military garrison protecting the southern entry to San Francisco harbor. What's remarkable is that three nations saw the strategic significance of this key headland: It was in Spanish hands from 1776–1822; it was under Mexican control during the years 1822–48; and finally, the United States took over in 1848. In 1994, the military turned over this 1,400-acre treasure to the National Park Service, making it a permanent part of the massive Golden Gate Recreation Area.

The Presidio got started when a Spanish expeditionary force marched north in the late 1700s and discovered the great inland harbor of San Francisco. It was in September, 1776 that an adobe quadrangle and living quarters were built and the Presidio de San Francisco was dedicated. It looked considerably different then than now; in those days it was mostly hilly sand dunes and scrub bushes. Today, this lovely wooded area contains thick forests of eucalyptus and cypress, beaches, grassy hillsides, marshes and both sandy and rocky shorelines.

The community and the National Park Service are still working on the transformation of the Presidio from military post to huge urban park. The plans are working with and around 800 existing buildings, a research facility, a golf course and a national cemetery. Hiking and biking trails wind through the various built facilities and natural elements of the Presidio.

The Presidio is also the southern anchor for the much admired Golden Gate Bridge. During this daytrip, we'll explore the Presidio and then take a walk across the magnificent structure that stretches 1.7 miles across the mouth of the bay.

GETTING THERE:

By car, go up either Geary or Sutter to Van Ness. Turn right and go about one mile to Lombard and turn left. Go straight into the Presidio on Lombard.

PRACTICALITIES:
We plan some walking during this daytrip, so wear comfortable shoes or boots. Sunglasses are helpful if it's a sunny day.

FOOD AND DRINK:

Alegrias Food from Spain (2018 Lombard) Full range of popular foods from Spain. Tapas, paellas, zarzuelas and other Spanish dishes. Live flamenco guitar in typical Spanish decor. Lunch Wed.–Sat. Dinner nightly. ☎ (415) 929-8888. $

Samui Thai (2414 Lombard) Six times listed in the *SF Zagat Survey*, this Thai restaurant has a wide reputation for tasty foods and great service. Try the Ga Gee Gai, which is slices of chicken with yellow curry, sweet potato and coconut milk. Lunch Wed.–Sun. Dinner daily. Closed Tues. ☎ (415) 563-4405. $

Liverpool Lil's (2942 Lyon St. next to the Presidio) Great pub food in a pub-like setting. Typical English fare includes Steak & Kidney Pie. Also meatloaf plate and sandwiches. This spot is a favorite of locals. Lunch and dinner daily. ☎ (415) 921-6664. $

The Grove (2250 Chestnut in the Marina) Comfortable local coffee house where Marina residents like to hang out. Try the Pesto Tortellini or the Pad Thai. Gourmet salads and sandwiches too. Breakfast, lunch & dinner daily. ☎ (415) 474-4843. $

LOCAL ATTRACTIONS:
Numbers in parentheses correspond to numbers on the map.

The **Presidio** (1) has a high-minded purpose as a new kind of park. It is dedicated to not only preserving and protecting its own resources, "but also to finding solutions to environmental, cultural and social issues of global significance." That is in contrast to the days when it served warriors from the Civil War, through World Wars I and II—and then in the 1950s and through the Cold War as headquarters for Nike defenses located around the Golden Gate.

To honor its past, the **Presidio Museum** (2) was established in one of the wooden buildings that was once the post's hospital. With its strategic and colorful past, the museum has lots to work with—including exhibits of the growth of San Francisco from an isolated outpost to the modern city it is today. You can see what soldiers wore in those early days as well as the weapons they used. Well worth a visit. *The museum is on Lincoln Boulevard at the intersection with Funston. It is open noon–4 Wed.–Sun. Admission is free.* ☎ *(415) 556-0865 for exhibit information.*

You will pass **Letterman Hospital** (3), which is no longer in use primarily because the buildings were constructed before San Francisco passed its stringent earthquake building code—and these structures don't meet the newer code. The 100-year history of the Army's Letterman Hospital follows

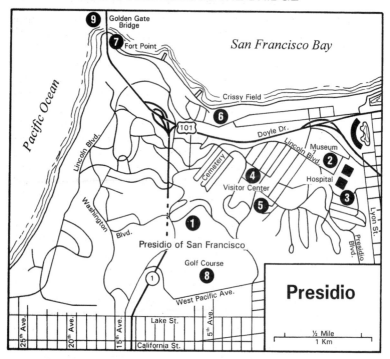

the story of how the United States became a world power. The hospital be-gan as a result of the Spanish-American War and closed as the Cold War ended. During the Second World War, Letterman became the nation's busiest hospital, treating the sick and wounded on their way back from the Pacific battlefields. This facility is significant because it was the Army's first permanent general hospital. Periodically, docents conduct sessions called "Civil War Medicine" where you can find out how soldier's wounds and ill-nesses were cared for using techniques that were modern 130 years ago.

Within The Presidio is one of the finest collections of military buildings and structures in the nation. And the Letterman complex is one of the many areas that contributes to the vast array of architectural styles, set in a park-like setting. To the right of the Parade Grounds is a row of early brick bar-racks. Be sure to go to Building 102, the **Presidio Visitor Center** (4), where you'll find all manner of information including current events. *Open daily 9–5, except Christmas and New Year's.* The **Presidio Officer's Club** (5) can be seen at the upper end of the Parade Grounds. Designed in the Spanish Mission style, it was built around the original adobe remains of the first gar-rison constructed by the Spanish in 1776. It is not open to the public.

At the water's edge within the Presidio is **Crissy Field** (6). Long ago, this area was a vast tidal marsh with lagoons that collected water from the three streams that run down through the Presidio. It changed considerably in 1915 when it became part of the Panama Pacific Exposition. A few years later, it was built as the only Army Air Service coast defense station in the western United States. Over the years, Crissy has been a part of several significant aviation events. In 1925, there is the story of the first flight to Hawaii originating from this very spot. What made this flight unbelievable is that the pilots ran out of gas about 400 miles from the Hawaiian Islands. They cut pieces of canvas from the lower portion of the wings to make sails and actually sailed the airplane to Honolulu! Was this the first flight—or the first flight/sail? Plans call for transforming the rather desolate Crissy back into marsh and lagoons with a grassed airfield. You can call for information and reservations for a "Crissy Field Aviation Walk," where you learn about the airfield's role in early aviation history. ☎ *(415) 561-4323.*

As you drive along the road at Crissy Field, keep on going and it will take you to **Fort Point** (7). Note that the Golden Gate Bridge, soaring overhead, was designed and built to avoid this old fortification. The fort was built between 1853–61 at a cost of about $2.8 million. The outer walls are 5–7 feet thick to shield 90 arched gun rooms known as casements. Its strength comes from more than 8 million bricks and granite from quarries in China as well as California. There are guided tours, audio tours and self-guided tours. *Open Wed.–Sun. 10–5. Admission is free.* From time to time Park Rangers conduct a thrilling "Candlelight Tour of Fort Point." Tour the old fort by the light of candle lanterns and stars. ☎ *(415) 561-4323 for reservations.*

Nearly at the top of the Presidio—near the Arguello Gate—are what are known as the Serpentine Grasslands. These few spots of open land contrast with the heavily wooded majority of the post. For 110 years, the Presidio sat on windswept grasslands and barren sand dunes. In 1883, W.A. Jones sought to "beautify the post, sharpen the contrast with the surrounding city and thereby accentuate the power of government." Between 1886–97, 100,000 trees of 200 types were planted. "The main idea is to crown the ridges, border the boundary fences, and cover the areas of sand and marsh waster with a forest that will generally seem continuous and thus appear immensely larger than it really is," according to Jones. He succeeded quite nicely.

Also near the Arguello Gate is the **Presidio Golf Course** (8) at 300 Finley Road. This is a beautiful public course that winds among the trees and valleys of the Presidio. *Mon.–Thu. rates are $35. After 4 p.m., there's a twilight rate weekdays of $25. Fri. rates are $45; twilight $30. Weekends and holidays are $55; twilight $35.* ☎ *(415) 561-4653 for reservations.*

There's a neat "Mountain Lake to Fort Point Hike" that retraces 3 miles of the trail used by the originator of the Presidio. You can explore the west side of the Presidio this way and learn both the cultural and natural history of the park's past, present and future. ☎ *(415) 561-4323 for reservations and information.*

Follow signs to **Golden Gate Bridge** (9). There's a small park right by the Toll Plaza. Here you'll find a gift shop, snack bar and restrooms. This is a good place to stop before your walk across the bridge. This great red-orange span opened to pedestrians on May 27, 1937 and to vehicular traffic the next day. It was some celebration. President Franklin D. Roosevelt pushed a telegraph key in the White House, every fire station in San Francisco and Marin County sounded, every church bell rang, every fog horn hooted. Ships bayed. Car horns honked. Four hundred planes flew overhead and two great ocean liners steamed underneath.

Lots of people are credited with creating the Golden Gate Bridge, but one individual must be given the lion's share for pushing and prodding for 13 years against tremendous business and political opposition. Joseph B. Strauss—a Chicago engineer who had built bridges all over the world—is considered the mastermind along with his associates Clifford Paine and Charles Ellis and consultants O.H. Ammann, Charles Derleth and Leon Moisseiff. It was remarkable that they got the job done in the depths of the Great Depression, because it was 1930 when voters of six Bay Area counties approved bonds for construction of the bridge. Construction started on January 5, 1933. Strauss said of his achievement, "It took two decades and 200 million words to convince people that the bridge was feasible; then only four years and $35 million to put the concrete and steel together." What an understatement.

Maybe some statistics will interest you. The length of the bridge is 1.7 miles. Its center span is 4,200 feet. The two soaring, hollow towers reach 746 feet (65 stories) into the sky. Its two great cables contain enough steel wire (80,000 miles) to encircle the equator three times. Every year, 40 million vehicles pass over this panoramic strand using six lanes. The car toll ($3) is collected coming into the city, but the pedestrian and bike ways are free.

The Golden Gate Bridge isn't really golden but instead has always been painted International Orange. Its designers rejected carbon black and steel gray, selecting the color because it blended well with the span's natural setting. Thank goodness. It's also said that this paint is not only the most resistant to showing wear from the elements of sun, wind, rain, salt spray and fog, but it's also the most visible in the fog. Author Susan Cheever said, "I don't know who decided to paint it (the Golden Gate Bridge) orange, but God bless them. When you drive up over Nineteenth Avenue and see the bridge rising before you, it's like seeing the towers of Chartres when you're driving out of Paris."

The bridge has been continuously open, with few exceptions, since it's completion. It's only been closed three times due to weather—in 1951, 1982 and 1983 due to gusting winds over 70 miles per hour. San Francisco's curve of soaring steel is recognized the world over as a symbol of the city by the bay.

Urban Hill Country/ Nob and Russian

You can find people who say there are really 40 hills in San Francisco, but two of the best known—of the famous four—are Nob Hill and Russian Hill. We'll explore both in this daytrip, plus make a couple of excursions along the way.

Nob Hill's name comes from its colorful history. Among the first to build their ornate palaces there were the railroad barons known as the Big Four—Charles Crocker, Leland Stanford, Mark Hopkins and Collis Huntington. Close behind came another two known as the Bonanza Kings of the Comstock Lode—James Flood and James Fair. In one way or another, they all left their legacy atop this famous hill. They were the "Nabobs" where some say Nob Hill got its name.

The 1906 earthquake shook this hill particularly hard and brought about probably one of the city's first urban renewal projects by knocking or burning down many of the grandiose wooden villas of the Nabobs. The result was the Crocker family gave the land under Grace Cathedral where their mansions once stood to the church. Stanford Court, the Mark Hopkins Hotel and the Fairmont sit on properties that were the original site of Nabob's homes. The imposing brownstone James Flood erected at 1000 California Street in 1886 survived—one of the few structures to do so on Nob Hill—and became the ultra-exclusive Pacific Union Club. Behind it is Huntington Park where that family's mansion sat originally.

GETTING THERE:

On foot from Union Square, go north up Powell to California and turn left. The summit of Nob Hill is two steep blocks up.

By cable car, take either the Powell/Mason or the Powell/Hyde lines to California Street. Walk up the two blocks to the summit.

PRACTICALITIES:

This is hill country that is best discovered and appreciated on foot, so wear comfortable shoes. When it rains, take an umbrella and remember that the sidewalks can be slippery.

FOOD AND DRINK:

Charles Nob Hill (1250 Jones) The famous Aqua seafood restaurant downtown is the sister to this French nouvelle supper club serving light French cuisine. Dinner Tues.–Sun. Reservations ☎ (415) 771-5400. $$$

The Big Four (1075 California in the Huntington Hotel) This spot got its name from the Big Four Railroad Barons mentioned above. Continental cuisine in a wonderful atmosphere of old San Francisco. Dinner daily. Reservations ☎ (415) 771-1140. $$$

Bella Voce (950 Mason in the Fairmont Hotel) Terrific Italian food in this magnificent hotel. Wide selection of pasta dishes with an emphasis on seafood. Lunch and dinner daily. ☎ (415) 772-5199. $–$$

The Bread & Honey Tea Room (334 Mason St.) Definitely British ambiance in the King George Hotel. Splendid Continental breakfast daily, but the real treat is English afternoon tea served Mon.–Sat. Sandwiches, fruits, crumpets. ☎ (415) 781-5050. $

SUGGESTED TOUR:

Numbers in parentheses correspond to numbers on the map.

At the corner of Powell and California is the **Stanford Court Hotel** (1). This is considered the downhill anchor of Nob Hill (although the posh, newish Four Seasons down on Sutter is crowding the old gang), built on the site of Leland Stanford's original mansion. Look carefully at the stone foundation along Powell and California streets. This is from the original Stanford home. When you reach the corner of Mason and California one block up, on your left is the stately **Mark Hopkins Hotel** (2), a Registered Historic Landmark. Part of the history of this site is that it was California's first cultural center in 1893. The Mark, which opened as a hotel in 1926, has a long history of debuts, dinner dancing, Junior League doings and high profile honeymoons. You may want to journey up to the hotel's **Top of the Mark Bar** for an awe-inspiring view all around the city and its beautiful bay.

Cross over California Street; on the corner is another of the Crown Jewels atop Nob Hill. **The Fairmont Hotel** (3) officially opened in April, 1907 on the site of mining baron James Fair's mansion. The building was to open just after the 1906 earthquake, but was delayed when the interior was destroyed by fire. This is a notably cinematic hostelry hosting such films as Hitchcock's "Vertigo," "Kiss Them for Me" starring Cary Grant and Jayne Mansfield, "Towering Inferno" starring Charleton Heston, "The Rock" with

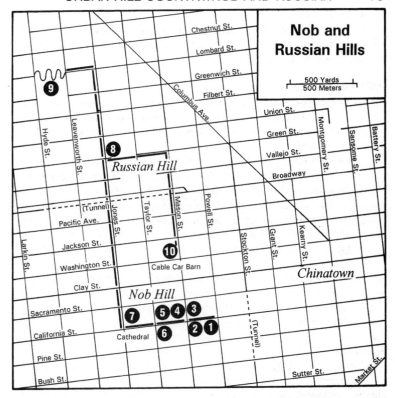

Sean Connery and Nicholas Cage and "Sudden Impact" starring Clint East-wood—to mention just a few. On our TV screens, the Fairmont was featured in the "Lifestyles of the Rich and Famous."

The richness of the lobby comes from not only the marble columns, soft velvet furniture and gold leaf, but the thickness of the carpet. If you walk to-ward the east end of the hotel, there is a glass elevator—added in 1961—that will whisk you to the Fairmont Crown, 24 stories above street level. It is claimed that a bride and groom, along with a six-person wedding party, can enter the glass trolley at the lobby level and by the time the elevator reaches its peak, the ceremony culminates leaving the newlyweds literally on top of the city.

Another neat feature of the Fairmont is the **Roof Garden**, open to the public. From the main lobby, veer right and turn left at the elevators. Walk past the gift shops to the end of the ramp and look for the sign; the garden is on the left. It seems like a putting green interrupted by flower beds. The entire yard sits under the shade of three 30-foot date palm trees. Very pleasant.

In the north hallway on the ground floor are several dozen excellent photos of the 1906 earthquake damage, including a panel showing the burned-out Fairmont. For $6,000 a night, you can rest your weary bones in the Fairmont's fabled Penthouse. Few people get to see it, even the help.

On the northeast corner of Mason and California is the **Pacific Union Club** (4), which was the original James Flood mansion. It too was one of the few survivors of the horror of the 1906 earthquake and fire. Only a handful of members may enter, and the club is irreverently called the P-U Club. It remains as aloof as ever behind its solid brass filigree fence that says: "Stay away. This is the exclusive domain of modern-day magnates."

In this same block is **Huntington Park** (5), a legacy of Collis Huntington of the Big Four mentioned earlier. Across the street is the legendary **Huntington Hotel** (6). The Huntington's 140 rooms and suites have secluded a succession of royals (Princess Margaret, Princess Grace and Prince Charles), and it's a favorite hideaway of celebs (Alistair Cooke, Luciano Pavarotti, Lauren Bacall and Leontyne Price to mention a few).

At Taylor and California streets is the great, gray eminence of **Grace Cathedral** (7), considered the largest Gothic structure in the west and third-largest Episcopal cathedral in the nation. The Crocker family donated the entire block to the Episcopal Diocese of California after the 1906 fire destroyed their two huge residences. It took a long time to complete the cathedral: the cornerstone was laid in 1910, construction started in earnest in 1927 and it was finally completed in 1964 with installation of the massive, round Rose Window (made in France) above the entry doors. These doors are replicas of those created by Lorenzo Ghiberti for the Baptistry in Florence, called the Doors of Paradise. The original 15th-century portals were deemed by Michelangelo to be the gates of heaven—and their 10 rectangular reliefs depict scenes from the Old Testament.

On Fridays from 7–8:30, walking prayer services are held in the cathedral's unique labyrinth. *Tours are conducted Mon.–Fri. at 1 and 3, Sat. at 11:30 and 1:30 and Sunday at 12:30 and 2. The cathedral is open Sun.–Fri. 7–6 and Sat. 8–6. Sunday services are 7:30, 8:30 and 11 in the morning and 3:30 in the afternoon for Evensong. You can pick up a brochure for a self-guided tour.*

Head north on Jones Street and walk approximately eight short blocks, which will put you at the apex of **Russian Hill** (8). It is a large area stretching some 35 blocks that got its name from Russian sailors buried in its soil. The hill encompasses four historical districts and once offered refuge to the literary likes of Jack London and Mark Twain. One of the city's best views awaits visitors at Jones and Vallejo streets, called the "Vallejo Crest." Gorgeous gardens, and in some instances large trees, surround brown-shingle country cottages that were built as an expression of rebellion against the city's gingerbread Victorian houses elsewhere.

There's one of San Francisco's many neat hillpaths on the east side of the crest. Take the steps down through lovely gardens. Cross Taylor and take more hillpath steps winding down through Coolbrith Park.

When you get to Mason, turn right, or if you're ambitious, another easy five blocks the other way will take you to Lombard and the **Crookedest Street in the World** (9), between Leavenworth and Hyde. Legend has it that the street was so steep that city engineers wanted to close it after some gruesome accidents. Suddenly, a junior engineer came up with the idea of curving the street to make it passable. Now its graceful curves of red brick hold wondrous displays of plants and flowers, and the houses lining the street are among the handsomest in the city.

If you walk back along Mason going toward Nob Hill, at the corner with Washington is the antique **Cable Car Barn** (10). While it says it's a museum, this is the real place where it all happens; the giant wheels that propel the cable cars can be seen along with the machine shop that keeps everything working. You can go downstairs for a look at what happens under the streets where the little hillclimbers take their passengers. There are also photos and memorabilia plus some very early cable cars. Gift shop. Well worth a visit. *Open in winter 10–5 and summer 10–6.* ☎ *(415) 474-1887 for more information. Free.*

At this point, your legs may have rebelled, and so you might consider taking a cable car right from this spot back to your hotel.

Go West to Pacific Heights

It seems that most visitors take the Powell/Mason or Powell/Hyde cable cars to such places as Fisherman's Wharf. The California Line sees far greater use from San Franciscans on their way to work and shop, so it seems very appropriate to grab the cable car mostly used by residents to head out to the poshest residential section of San Francisco.

Pacific Heights is usually considered that area from Franklin west to Baker, north to Pacific and south to California. What makes the neighborhood so desirable is that it generally runs along a ridge that's about 300 feet above the bay, affording spectacular views for many of the Victorian mansions built here.

They aren't all mansions. But the big ones are really big—and they're the ones where San Francisco's titans have settled. Big-name lawyers, bankers, financiers and even a well-known author inhabit this place. Sprinkled here and there in Pacific Heights are various consulates of foreign nations.

Within Pacific Heights is a pleasant urban park and just beyond that is one of the city's best neighborhood shopping areas.

GETTING THERE:

On foot and cable car from Union Square, walk north up Powell to California. Catch the California Line cable car all the way to Van Ness, which is the end of the line.

By cable car, take either the Powell/Mason or the Powell/Hyde lines to California Street and transfer to the California Line.

PRACTICALITIES:

After you get off the cable car, it will be about a three-mile walk round-trip depending on whether you make discoveries that take you off the track.

Wear comfortable walking shoes and be prepared for a few hills. That's what San Francisco is all about.

FOOD AND DRINK:

Ruth's Chris Steakhouse (1601 Van Ness) Steaks are the major fare, and they are excellent. All corn-fed U.S. prime beef. The seafood gets raves as well, serving Maine lobster and other tasty fish dishes. Dinner nightly. ☎ (415) 673-0557. $$

Vivande (2125 Fillmore) Stylish Italian restaurant serving some of the best and freshest Italian food in the city. They make their own pasta and sausage daily. Try the frittata. Gourmet deli, Italian pottery and wines on sale. Lunch and dinner daily. ☎ (415) 346-4430. $–$$

Pauli's Café (2500 Washington St.) This is a typical neighborhood café serving simple meals. What makes it fun is that it's a kind of meeting places for the neighborhood. Spinach and cheese raviolis are excellent. Breakfast, lunch and dinner daily. ☎ (415) 921-5159. $

Ten Ichi (2235 Fillmore) Very good Japanese restaurant serving a wide variety of sushi and other Oriental dishes. Chicken katsu is deep-fried chicken with plum dipping sauce. Yum. Lunch and dinner daily. ☎ (415) 346-3477. $

SUGGESTED TOUR:

Numbers in parentheses correspond to numbers on the map.

Be sure to enjoy the cable car ride up Nob Hill and straight out California to where this line ends at Van Ness Avenue. You may already know you're riding a National Historic Landmark. These are the only vehicles of their kind left in the world today, and they are over a 125 years old. All that wear and tear nearly brought the demise of this most San Francisco tradition.

The first attempt to do away with the little hillclimbers was in 1947 when the city announced they would be replaced with buses. But a determined lady by the name of Frieda Klussman rallied the citizens, who voted overwhelmingly to keep the cable cars.

In 1982, city officials took a good look and decided again to mothball the fleet due to deterioration over the years. It was deemed that $60 million would be needed to bring the system up to speed in terms of safety and convenience. Somehow the city prevailed on corporations and individuals (from around the country) and the federal government, so that eventually all the money was raised.

It took two years of what was likened to open-heart surgery to tear up four-and-a-half miles or 69 blocks of street. These streets were dug up section by section to make way for new cables, tracks, turntables and utility lines. The cable cars themselves needed extensive repair.

Finally in 1984, the ordeal was over. The celebration was typical San

Pacific
Heights

500 Yards
500 Meters

Francisco; huge crowds lined the tracks, bands played, helicopters hovered and TV cameras whirred. At noon, a thunderous cheer went up as bells clanged among the other commotion and the jaunty centenarians paraded into another century of service with the mayor (and who else?—Tony Bennett) leading the parade.

The sad plight of overworked horses is said to have inspired Andrew S. Hallidie, a London-born engineer and metal rope manufacturer, to invent the cable cars. "Hallidie's Folly" made its maiden run on August 2, 1873. The inventive Hallidie designed the system so that the gripman (sometimes called the "Celestial Navigator") pulls back on a lever, which closes a pincer-like grip on the endless cable kept constantly moving at 9.5 miles per hour in its slot 18 inches below the street. The usually colorful gripman also tends the hand and foot brakes (wood is used against the metal rails) and dings the brass bell. Many gripmen have become quite the showmen, known for their own particular tune played on the bells. There's even an annual Gripman's Bell Ringing Contest with pretty nifty prizes.

At one time there were eight lines operating along 112 miles of track. Today there are only three lines covering 8.8 miles: the Powell-Mason Line, the Powell-Hyde Line and the California Line. But, oh how those three lines are used. The recent annual count was 9.6 million riders. It cost $2 to ride the cable cars one way. For unlimited use, you can buy an all-day pass for $6; a three day pass for $10; or a seven day pass for $15. Well worth the money.

After you get off the cable car at the end of the line, cross Van Ness and go up to Franklin. At California and Franklin is the **First Church of Christ, Scientist** (1). This structure, built in 1911, is another excellent expression of the Italianate school of design. Detailed arches over doors and windows blend with lovely stained-glass windows.

Across the street are three very large mansions in a row stretching up California. On the corner is the **Edward Coleman House** (2), a registered Historic Landmark. Today, it is used as law offices and is closed to the public. Stretch your neck up to take a look at the next handsome Victorian mansion at **1818 California** (3), examining the detail in the trim over windows and doors. What is amazing about this property is that the gardens have been preserved on not one, but both sides of the mansion. It's pretty unusual to see open ground in this part of town—unless it's a park.

Next is **1834 California** (4), exuding the same stateliness of its cousins below. None of these mansions are open to the public and are only for viewing from the outside.

Go back to Franklin, turn left and walk three blocks to Washington. In the next block is the **Haas-Lilienthal House** (5) at 2007 Franklin. This one you can go into. *Open Wed. 12–4 and Sun 11–5. Admission is $5 for adults and $3 for seniors and kids.* This 1886 Queen Anne mansion is a great example of the way people lived in that era. The interior woodwork is dark and the ornamentation pretty detailed and fussy. The house was built by a wealthy San Franciscan by the name of William Haas. It got its hyphenated name because his daughter, Alice Lilienthal lived there until 1972. After her death, it was given to the Architectural Heritage Foundation, which maintains its offices at the mansion. ☎ *(415) 441-3004 for more information.*

The Foundation offers a two-hour walk to learn more about the Victorian mansions and row houses in the neighborhood, starting at 12:30 on Sundays. *Cost is $5 for adults and $3 for seniors and kids.* ☎ *(415) 441-3000 for more information.*

Jay Gifford conducts a terrific **Victorian Home Walk** where you learn about the architecture, lifestyle and history of this fascinating era. He takes small groups on a leisurely-paced walk that lasts about two and a half hours through areas of Pacific Heights and Cow Hollow. Among the 200 or so Victorians you will see is the one where *Mrs. Doubtfire* was filmed. *The tour starts daily at 11 from the St. Francis lobby at Powell and Geary. Cost is $20, including transportation.* ☎ *(415) 252-9485 for reservations.*

Next head up Washington Street. At the corner of Washington and

Gough is **Lafayette Park** (6). Steep steps and paths lead up to the summit where the views are pretty spectacular, looking out across the bay to Alcatraz, Angel Island and parts of Marin County. Neighbors run their dogs, and seniors sit enjoying the sun and the view. If you look north along the edge of the park, across Washington is the **Spreckels Mansion** (7) at 2080. The original owners were the same family that donated the Palace of the Legion of Honor in Lincoln Park (see Daytrip 4). They used the same architect for their home and the Palace. He created the similar grandeur that is apparent in both structures. Adolph Spreckels made his money in sugar both on the mainland and in Hawaii (on Maui there's a residential area called Spreckelsville named after him). The mansion, sometimes called the "Parthenon of the Pacific" for its columns and overall design, was built in 1912. It is not open to the public. Since 1990, best-selling author Danielle Steele has made this her home.

Walk along Washington where you will see a variety of homes—from the spectacular to the simple. Streets here, like many other parts of the city, get pretty steep. Hill dwellers have their own dicta:

—Don't charge downhill in brand new leather-soled shoes; they're to cement what skis are to snow;

—Don't open the door on the downhill side with a bag of groceries on the front seat since apples, cantaloupes, oranges, round roasts and toilet paper roll for blocks;

—Don't pretend you're Steve McQueen in the "Bullit" chase scene; you'll rupture your shocks or get a ticket or both.

This area has some of the steepest streets in San Francisco. According to the City Bureau of Engineering, Fillmore between Vallejo and Broadway is a 24-percent grade. But that one is the least steep of the 10 steepest streets in the city. The prize-winner for steepness is Filbert between Leavenworth and Hyde, which has a grade of 31.5 percent. The surest way to get a rise out of a visitor in an automobile is to zoom down Filbert's 31.5-percent grade and up intersecting Jones' 29-percent pitch. Sensing the car is about to somersault, some passengers have been known to scream. Even the most blasé blanch.

For those of you walking on this daytrip, keep in mind the old saying, "When you get tired of walking around San Francisco, you can always lean against it."

When you come to Fillmore Street, turn left for one of the most interesting shopping experiences in San Francisco. The **"Fillmore District"** (8) is fiercely proud of its unique neighborhood feel with dozens of one-of-a-kind flower shops, boutiques, cafés and restaurants. Yes, there's a Starbucks (which the residents fought against), but most are originals.

The anchor is clearly **Fillamento** at 2185 Fillmore. They offer stunning home furnishings with a touch of the Oriental. There's lots of bamboo, tasteful furniture, lots of unique gifts and even an extensive array of calligraphy materials. Someone said this store is what Gump's used to be. Next door at 2123 Fillmore is **Sweet Inspirations**, which offers up very fancy candies and baked goods.

Across the street is **Dorn-Foxroft, Ltd.** at 2123 Fillmore. They will sell you antique prints, decorative framing and accessories. **Cottage Industries** at 2326 Fillmore imports masks, statues, yard goods and gifts from 35 countries with a focus on Africa, Indonesia and India. Also at 2326 Fillmore is **Stroke of Genius,** a ceramic painting studio where you can create your own pottery. They say you can paint all day for $10. **Aumakua** has an array of hand made collectibles, jewelry and gifts. Find them at 2238 Fillmore.

The Fillmore District has about a dozen coffee houses where the citizens gather to talk, read and think. **Tea and Company** at 2207 Fillmore is a contrarian outfit offering more than 50 different teas—and no coffee. They say, "we cover our bountiful planet, through sub tropic regions, into tropical rain forests, across sun-ripened isles, over rugged mountain peaks, and back home, in order to bring you life's most incredible flavors and good health." All this in a splendidly modern and comfortable atmosphere.

*SOMA (South of Market)

The area south of Market Street represents about one third of the land area of the city. Much of it is landfill and for most of its existence the area was heavily industrial. Some sections of it were kind of seedy too, with flop house hotels and street people in great numbers. It hasn't all changed, but about fifteen years ago a rebirth started with construction of the spectacular new Moscone Center along Howard Street. That brought several classy new hotels into the area.

And then the city accentuated the renewal with the installation of one of the most enjoyable urban gardens anywhere. Soon museums were popping up, and even the venerable old Catholic Church along Market got into the act with a major retrofit (for earthquake protection) and renovation. A whole new multi-million dollar playground/recreation area built with children and their parents in mind was tagged onto the Moscone property. It is great fun.

For most cities that would be enough. But the Sony Corporation has installed a spanking new facility called Metreon which could be called an entertainment city. Movies, IMAX Theater, shops and the like make this facility a welcome addition to the area south of Market.

GETTING THERE:

On foot from Union Square, take Geary to Market and walk along until you come to New Montgomery. Turn right.

PRACTICALITIES:

Depending on how much of the territory you want to cover, this will be about a two-mile walk round-trip. Comfortable shoes are recommended. Lots of opportunities to take great photos exist, so bring along your camera.

FOOD AND DRINK:

Eppler's Bakery (90 New Montgomery) Good spot for a quick bite. Sizable bakery with lots of goodies for everyone. Limited soup/sandwich menu. Breakfast and lunch daily. ☎ (415) 546-4166. $

Clouds (atop Yerba Buena Gardens) Terrific view of the fountains and gardens from this small lunch spot. San Francisco Bay Chowder is a specialty. Also try Grilled Garlic Chicken. Open for lunch daily. ☎ (415) 278-0432. $

Fourth Street Bar & Deli (corner of Fourth & Mission) Colorful eatery geared to sports fans. Lots of sports memorabilia. The TKO is a burger topped with Cheddar Cheese and chili. Goods salads too. Open daily for lunch and dinner. ☎ (415) 442-6734. $

Willow Street Wood-fired Pizza (150 Fourth St.) Try the Hawaiian pizza with Canadian bacon, Maui pineapple and tomato sauce. Excellent pastas too. The Spicy Vegetable Fusilli is a hot item. Sandwiches as well. Lunch and dinner daily. ☎ (415) 538-8400. $

SUGGESTED TOUR:

Numbers in parentheses correspond to numbers on the map.

While the real story of the SOMA area is renewal, we'll begin this daytrip with an oldie, but truly goodie. Stop at the **Palace Hotel** (1) at 2 New Montgomery for a real treat. In 1875, the Palace debuted as the world's largest and most luxurious hotel. It was huge at seven stories towering over what was then a dusty frontier town. This hotel is the spectacular creation of William Chapman Ralston, who among his many achievements founded the United Bank of California (Daytrip 15). With his silver dollars he also built one of the first conglomerates that included—besides the hotel and bank—woolen mills, dry docks, carriage and watch factories and irrigation projects.

The hotel was gutted in the 1906 earthquake and fire, but was rebuilt true to the refinements of that era with vaulted ceilings, ornate gilding and Austrian leaded crystal chandeliers. Make sure to check out the famous Garden Court with columns that soar above marble floors toward a huge, luminous stained-glass ceiling. It is truly from another era. Besides other meals, they serve High Tea in the Garden Court from 2–4:30 daily. ☎ *(415) 512-1111 for further information.*

Turn left on Mission and at 678 you will find the **California Historical Society** (2). Its photographic collection contains over half a million images documenting the history of California in both the 19th and 20th centuries. It also has about 3,500 manuscripts in its collection that include diaries and letters of Gold Rush miners, early settlers and ranchers, as well as material from 19th-century businesses, political organizations and historical figures. Small, but interesting exhibits change about once a quarter in the Gallery. *Open 11–5 Tues.–Sat. Admission is $3 for adults.* ☎ *(415) 357-1850 for more information.*

Turn down Third Street to the:

*SAN FRANCISCO MUSEUM OF MODERN ART (3), 151 Third Street, San rancisco, CA 94103, ☎ (415) 357-4000. *Adult admission $8, seniors $5,*

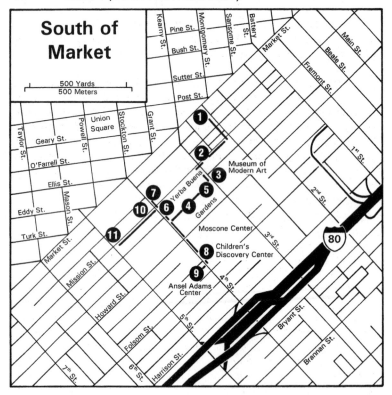

students $4. Half-priced on Thursday evenings from 6–9. Open daily 11–6 in winter and 10–6 in summer. Closed Wednesdays and major holidays. Gift shop open daily 10:30–6:30. Caffe museo open every day except Weds. ♿.

This superb structure, designed by Swiss architect Mario Botta and opened in 1995, is highlighted by a 125-foot cylindrical skylight that can be seen all the way to the Bayshore Freeway. Contemporary art affects people in different ways, and so may the collection and changing exhibits of the SFMOMA affect you. But stimulation seems to be the key word when describing the portions of the 15,000 works of art on display at the museum, including those pieces by Picasso, Matisse, Albers, de Kooning and Calder.

The exhibitions start on the second floor with pieces from the museum's permanent collection. Here you will find works from the modern masters, such as an exhibit titled "From Matisse to Diebenkorn," an extensive presentation of paintings and sculpture from 1900–80. There are also superb pieces from California artists that include paintings, sculpture and design work. The third floor changes pace with a large photography exhibit, including over 150 photos from the 19th century to the present. The fourth floor exhibits contemporary art from 1960-96 in an ever-changing selection of painting and sculpture. On the fifth floor is contemporary art covering four decades. Several gallery tours are conducted daily.

Across the street is **Yerba Buena Gardens** (4). Planted on top of the Moscone Center North, the gardens are divided into three parts: the Esplanade; Sister Cities; and the East Garden. The 5.5-acre Esplanade is ringed with 20 species of trees and an abundance of flowers. The "Butterfly Garden" is in the northeast corner. On the upper terrace of the Esplanade is the Sister Cities Garden, which is home to a diverse collection of flowering plants from San Francisco's 13 sister cities around the world. A curved, wooden bench the length of half a city block faces north, overlooking a 200-foot-wide reflection pool and the San Francisco skyline. The flowing pool cascades into a 22-foot high, 50-foot-wide waterfall over the granite-walled Martin Luther King, Jr. memorial below.

Separate from the main concourse is the East Garden, tucked between the theater and gallery in what is called the **Yerba Buena Center for the Arts** (5). Within the Center, the theater presents a diverse number of performances that include such favorites as the Family Matinee Series, Jazz Series and Artist-in-Residence. ☎ *(415) 978-ARTS ext. 2787 for current showings.* Just to the west is the two-story Gallery that presents works of artists in residence at the Center for the Arts. The exhibits can be very moving with such pieces as a table setting of dictators' favorite meals down through history. *The gallery is open Tues.–Sun. 11–6 and until 8 p.m. on the first Thursday of each month. Adult admission is $5 for adults, $3 for seniors and students. Free the first Thursday of each month. Gift shop.* ☎ *(415) 978-ARTS, ext. 2787 for more information.* ♿.

Right next to The Gardens is the spectacular multi-story **Metreon** (6) at Fourth and Mission, better known as the Sony Entertainment Center. This 350,000-square-foot four-story complex is filled with things for the whole family to do including: A 15-screen Sony Theatres first-run motion picture complex with 4,500 seats; a 3-D SONY-IMAX Theatre with a screen 80 feet tall and 100 feet wide; "Where the Wild Things Are" interactive playscape; "The Way Things Are Workshop" learning and entertainment attraction; "Open reality" interactive adventure zone; and numerous retail stores such as a "Discovery Channel Destination" flagship store and a Sony Style store offering the finest selection of hardware and software products from Sony. Microsoft opened its first-in-the-nation store right here. There's food aplenty, too, with such goodies as "The Night Kitchen" food services area and the "Taste of San Francisco," offering the latest culinary sensations from a select variety of Bay Area chefs.

Directly across the street is the historic **St.Patrick's Catholic Church** (7). As the name would suggest, this is the church for the Irish in San Francisco and, prior to the great earthquake and fire of 1906, it counted 30,000 parishioners. The church has led a perilous, but historic life for close to one and a half centuries, getting started in 1851 in a rented hall. The first church on this site was dedicated in 1872, but completely destroyed in the earthquake and fire, then rebuilt using the same bricks. The 1989 earthquake shook it pretty well, and so now it has undergone an earthquake retrofit and reconstruction. The marble inside is white, green and gold for its Irish heritage.

As you make your way down Fourth Street, you will come to the **Children's Discovery Center** (8) on the corner of Fourth and Folsum, built over the underground Moscone Center. Ten years in the making, this $56 million urban playground has something for everyone. Of special interest is the antique carousel that was refurbished and hauled up from Long Beach in Southern California. The 34,000-square-foot Studio for Technology will be entered through an upside down cone. Here kids may make their own TV shows, sculpt clay figures and animate them and learn stagecraft, special effects and lighting. If you want athletic action, there's a huge ice skating rink and a bowling alley. Two acres are devoted to a landscaped playground that includes slides, a sand pit, labyrinth, climbing nets and an artificial stream that kids can dam and change the water flow. Parents will be thrilled with the Child Care Building for up to 90 toddlers.

Just down the street on Fourth is the **Ansel Adams Photography Center** (9) at 250. While there are galleries devoted to photos from many well-known photographers, one entire gallery shows Adams' work. Very stimulating. *Open 11–5 Tues.–Sun. Adult admission is $5, $3 students and $2 for seniors.* ☎ *(415) 495-7000.* Walk back up Fourth to Mission and turn left for the **Cartoon Art Museum** (10) at 814. Located on the second floor, this smallish museum is a must for those who love comic books and funnies. The museum was founded in 1984 by a small group of aficionados. Its purpose is the preservation, collection and exhibition of cartoon art in all its forms. The museum's permanent collection numbers 10,000 pieces featuring art works from the late 1700s to the present. There is a Children's Museum, interactive CD ROM room and a main exhibition gallery packed into 6,000 square feet. *Open Wed.–Fri. 11–5, Sat. 10–5 and Sun. 1–5. Adults $5, seniors and students $3 and kids $2.* ☎ *(415) CAR-TOON for further information.*

In the next block at the corner of Fifth and Mission is the **Old U.S. Mint** (11). This Federal Classic Revival building was opened in 1874, but closed in 1994. Unfortunately there are no more tours. The building is a National Historic Landmark. While unused, it stands as a monument to the boom days of the California Gold Rush. According to early reports, the Mint was built to "stand up for centuries." The first critical test of the Mint came in 1906 during the great earthquake and fire. Amazingly, the Mint withstood the ravages of that tremendous shaking and fire. At that time, the subtreasury and the bank buildings lay in ruins. Until the banks could open, the Mint assumed the responsibilities of administering the relief funds and other monetary affairs of the crippled city.

Civic Center and Japantown

The Civic Center and Japantown are really two different worlds even though they're fairly close together, but that's what San Francisco is all about. Obviously, the Civic Center is home to solid, imposing government edifices serving the literary, cultural, financial and legal needs of San Francisco's citizens. We can enjoy it as visitors as well. And enjoy it we will because the whole area has been done with such style. The old has been refurbished into stunningly rehabilitated structures to serve well into the millennium. Besides the historic landmarks, there are also the fairly new and impressive places like Symphony Hall that add luster to the whole scene. And there's the quite new—like the recently opened public library—that also contribute to a fulfilling daytrip.

Japantown, on the other hand, is all about an important ethnic group and its place in the city's multi-ethnic mix. San Francisco's Japanese are far less numerous (about 1.5 percent) than it's Chinese population (almost 29 percent), but they have also influenced the city in many ways—which we will explore. A shopkeeper in Japantown, when asked the size of the Japanese population in San Francisco, said it has gotten smaller over the years, "because the rich ones have moved down to the Peninsula." That contrasts with the Chinese population, which has pretty well stayed in the city.

Don't expect Japantown to be like Chinatown. The heart of it is basically a city block devoted to serving the cultural, food, household, and floral needs of its surrounding citizens.

GETTING THERE:

By car from Union Square, go west on Geary to Van Ness and turn left. About eight blocks south is the Civic Center.

By bus, take the # 38 on Geary, or the # 2, 3 or 4 on Sutter and get off at Laguna, Buchanan or Webster Streets.

PRACTICALITIES:

There is street parking just off the Civic Center that usually is available after the morning rush hour, or the Civic Center Plaza garage between Polk and Larkin, Grove and McAllister. Enter on McAllister. If you park on the street, be sure to feed the meter since fines begin at $25. There is indoor parking in the Japantown Center. Entrances are on Geary between Laguna and Webster, Fillmore between Geary and Post, and Post between Webster and Laguna.

FOOD AND DRINK:

Millennium (246 McAllister St.) Combination Old-World San Francisco and modern decor where innovative and very tasty vegetarian dishes are served. This is not your image of a veggie restaurant. This is world-class. All are organic and dairy-free. Open for lunch Tues.–Fri. and dinner Tues.–Sun. ☎ (415) 487-9800. $$

Absinthe (398 Hayes St. at Gough) Beautifully, but simply decorated French brassiere in a lovely neighborhood. New cuisine menu for appetizers and entrees. Try the Lavender Creme Brulee with shortbread cookies for dessert. Lunch and dinner Tues.–Sun. Reservations ☎ (415) 551-1590. $$

Stars Café (500 Van Ness at McAllister) Very popular spot serving such entrees as Braised Short Ribs with roasted Brussel spouts and acorn squash. Also excellent wood oven fried pizza. Lunch Mon.–Fri. Dinner daily. Reservations ☎ (415) 861-4344. $$

Isobune Sushi Restaurant (1737 Post in Japan Center) The sushi comes floating by on little boats and all you do is snatch it off. Wide range of terrific sushi, plus sushi plates. Open lunch and dinner daily. ☎ (415) 563-1030. $–$$

Sapporo-ya (Kinokuniya Bldg. in Japan Center) Excellent menu of Japanese noodle dishes. They make their own noodles on the premises. You can watch them making them right in front. Lunch and dinner daily. ☎ (415) 563-7400. $

SUGGESTED TOUR:

Numbers in parentheses correspond to numbers on the map.

Close by the Civic Center, and a good place to get started on this daytrip, is the old **Masonic Temple** (1) at 25 Van Ness. Just looking at the structure from the outside tells you this is something important. For one thing, there's what looks like a huge marble saint standing precariously in a parapet at the corner of the building. Inside, take the elevator to the sixth floor, where you can see the original gold leaf dome—now surrounded by offices. In the basement is the **New Conservatory Theater**, a three-theater complex offering seldom-performed musicals and avant-garde plays. *For a current schedule ☎ (415) 861-8972, ext. 73.* Also in the basement is SF Street Artists

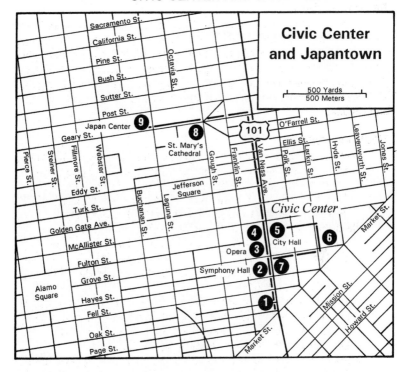

Civic Center
and Japantown

500 Yards
500 Meters

Program that since 1972 has encouraged talented Bay Area artists by licensing them to sell their works on the city's streets in five areas: Hallidie Plaza, Justin Herman Plaza, Union Square, Fisherman's Wharf and Point Lobos near the Cliff House.

In the next block is another interesting building that's not strictly part of the Civic Center, the **San Francisco Public Schools Administration Building** at 135 Van Ness. This looks like it should be a library or other impressive public building with its Art-Deco styling, but it's nothing but offices inside. Good looking nevertheless.

At the corner of Van Ness and Hayes is the **Louise M. Davies Symphony Hall** (2). Like a lot of buildings in San Francisco, this one hasn't been without controversy. Built in 1980 for $33 million, the acoustics were troublesome for many years, and so in 1992 they did a $10 million retrofit. All seems well now. It was designed by the well-known architectural group of Skidmore, Owings and Merrill (the same firm that designed the curving Edmund Brown State Office Building at Van Ness and McAllister as a bookend to the Davies) and is named after the lady who gave $5 million towards construction. *Tours of the hall are available on request on Wed. and Sat. Cost is $5.* ☎ *(415) 552-8338 for reservations. The Symphony season runs* *from September through May. Ticket prices range from $11 to $78. Call 864-6000 for ticket information. Gift shop.* &.

The next imposing structure, at 301 Van Ness, is the **War Memorial Opera House** (3). The first Opera House at Mission near Third was destroyed by the 1906 earthquake. While San Francisco has a long history of loving opera, it wasn't until 1918 that a group came together to consider a new performance area at the Civic Center. With the end of World War I, the decision was made to name this building and its neighbor after the war and its veterans. But after lots of machinations about money and power, the Opera House finally opened in September 1932 with a performance of *Tosca.* The ornate 3,000-seat Opera House is also home to the San Francisco Ballet, but its real claim to fame is as the birthplace of the United Nations. Most of the plenary sessions of the U.N. Conference took place here. *The ballet season runs from January through May with tickets ranging in price from $7–95.* ☎ *(415) 865-2000 for ticket information. Opera runs from Sept. to Jan. Tickets are $10 to 140.* ☎ *(415) 864-3330 for ticket information. Gift shop.* &.

Across a landscaped plaza is the Opera House's mirror image in the solidly imposing **Veterans' Building** (4), also completed in 1932 to honor the soldiers of WWI. Within this building is the modest Herbst Theater where President Truman and other heads of state and dignitaries signed the United Nations Charter on June 26, 1945. There are frequent performances and lectures of many different types in the Herbst. ☎ *(415) 392-4400 for information about showings and ticket prices.* Also in this building is the **San Francisco Art Commission Gallery,** which has a small showing of California artist's work along with exhibits on the third and fourth floors. *The ground floor gallery is open Wed.–Sat. 12–5:30. Free, but donations welcome.* ☎ *(415) 554-6080 to find out what's on exhibit.*

Across the street is the towering **City Hall** (5), built in 1915 as the anchor for the Civic Center. It is a monumental building with 500,000 square feet of office space, which is roughly three times the size of the state capitol in Sacramento. To be assured of its size, consider that it is a foot taller than the U.S. Capitol in Washington. This National Historic Landmark was badly damaged by the Loma Prieta earthquake in 1989, and so a massive rebuilding and retrofit was undertaken starting in 1996. Lost in much of the political brouhaha has been whether it cost $180 or $250 million to rehab the place. In any case, the huge dome, modeled after St. Peter's Basilica in Rome, the graceful stairways and the historic Light Courts on the main floor have been brought back to their original magnificence—to say nothing of the millions spent to stabilize the place. Well worth a visit.

As you walk out the west side of City Hall, there is a wide esplanade leading to two more imposing public buildings across Larkin. On the left is the **Old Main Library**, which is being readied for the galleries and collection of the Asian Art Museum (see Daytrip 2) when its moves from Golden Gate Park around 2000. It was originally designed by architect George Kelham and opened a year before the Opera House. Its next-door neighbor is the stunning **New Main Library** (6). You get the idea of the importance of art to the library when you first catch sight of the sculpture on the northwest corner, called *Double L Excentric Gyratory*. This magnificent building shows a Beaux Arts facade on the Larkin side in keeping with the rest of the Civic Center, but changes and goes to a contemporary exterior on the Grove and Hyde Street sides in keeping with the commercial activity on Market Street. It was designed by New York architect James Ingo Freed and San Francisco architect Cathy Simon. Inside is a unique configuration of open spaces and smaller intimate corners that contribute to a sense of grandeur and welcome.

Artwork inside includes a three-story interior wall with 50,000 annotated cards from the old card catalog—sort of nod to nostalgia since the computer long ago dispensed with the old cards. On the fifth floor are two works: a spiral staircase in the glass-enclosed Reading Room and a companion piece that is suspended from the high ceiling outside the room. The library is open every day from 10–5, except noon–5 on Sunday. Café and store. ☎ *(415) 557-4400.* ♿.

Right behind the new Library is the **United Nations Plaza** commemorating the birth of that august body at the Civic Center.

Before any other major meeting places were available in area, the city constructed what is now called the **Bill Graham Civic Auditorium** (7) in 1915. Designed by architect John Howard, it had its name changed in 1964 after the famous San Francisco rock promoter by the same name. Major concerts and plays are staged here. ☎ *(415) 991-8000.*

As you head up Van Ness, turn left on Geary. At the top of the rise is what's called **Cathedral Hill.** Here you will find grand monuments to the Lutherans, Unitarians, Baptists and Catholics. Crowning the hill is the ultramodern **St. Mary's Cathedral** (8), built in 1970. Covering two city blocks, the building is shaped like a drawn-up, sculpted cross that rises 19 stories from the ground. The interior spaces are dramatic with bronze friezes and soaring stained-glass windows. *The cathedral is open for self-guided tours daily. There are free organ concerts on Sundays at 3:30.* ☎ *(415) 567-2020 for more information.*

Just over the hill is the **Japan Center** (9). Today, more than 12,000 citizens of Japanese descent live in Japantown, or Soko, as it is often called. Historically in the 1920s and '30s, Soko was a 20-block area roughly surrounded by Fillmore, Sutter, Laguna and O'Farrell. The first Japanese arrived in the early 1860s, but it wasn't until the 1906 earthquake and fire that they were driven to this part of the city. As they settled here, they built churches and shrines and opened typically Japanese shops and restaurants. The neighborhood took on a very Japanese character and before long became a miniature Ginza known as *Nihonmachi* or Japantown.

In the Japan Center (which is the large shopping center in the middle of Japantown), take some time to visit **Katsura Gardens** whose slogan is "Think small—grow a bonsai." Here you will see some terrific examples of the art of bonsai. They tell you that any type of tree or shrub can be bonsai-ed, but some—like juniper, azalea, quince and willow—work better. If you're tempted to buy one to take back home, they regularly ship via UPS. *Open Mon.–Sat. 10–5:30.* In the Miyako Mall section of the Japan Center is a wonderful store called **Genji Antiques.** They have a large selection of traditional wooden Tansu chests as well as antique kimonos, table runners, Buddahs and the like. *Open 10–5 daily.* Be sure to visit the **Ikebono Ikebana Society of America** office next to the Kintetsu Restaurant Mall. Here you will see stunningly simple, but beautiful flower arrangements in the traditional Japanese style. *Open 9:30–5 Mon.–Sat.*

Wall Street of the West

There are only a small handful of what are called "Money Centers" in the United States. New York, of course, and following that Chicago and Dallas. The next tier are called "Regional Money Centers," which encompasses most of the other major cities in the U.S. San Francisco is clearly a Money Center. Here there's a Federal Reserve Bank, a longtime Mint and the head-quarters of three of the top ten banks in America. That's why San Francisco has been called "The Wall Street of the West."

That may be in large part due to the 1849 Gold Rush, which had such a dramatic affect in shaping so many parts and pieces of San Francisco. Great wealth was created during the Gold Rush, and not just among those who struck it rich in the hills. Lots of business people stayed behind in the city and prospered mightily by supplying food, materials, banking, information and the like to the mining operations. Much of that heritage is on display in the financial district of San Francisco. That's what we'll discover during this daytrip.

GETTING THERE:

On foot from Union Square, go down Post Street until you reach Montgomery. Turn left for this daytrip.

PRACTICALITIES:

The round trip from Union Square is about 1.5 miles, so wear comfortable shoes. A lot of the interesting spots on this daytrip are open only during the weekdays since this is the Financial District, so keep that in mind when you plan your day.

FOOD AND DRINK:

Carnelian Room (atop the Bank of America Bldg.) Breathtaking views every which way around the bay from more than 50 stories. You pay for the view, but the food is excellent as well. Reservations ☎ (415) 433-7500. $$–$$$

Vertigo (600 Montgomery in the Transamerica Pyramid) The setting next to the Redwood Park and the excellent food make this a memorable meal. Try the Lamb Three Styles and Champagne Poached Oysters. Lunch Mon.–Fri., dinner daily. Reservations ☎ (415) 433-7250. $$

Tadich Grill (240 California) This is the oldest restaurant in California, founded in 1849. It's been operated for three generations by the same family. A great spot for seafood and friendship. Busy at lunch where it's open Mon.–Sat. Same for dinner. Reservations ☎ (415) 391-1849. $$

Mac Arthur Park (607 Front St.) This longtime spot also sits across from an unusual urban park. They do excellent barbecue—ribs and chicken. Popcorn Shrimp and Garlic Mashed Potatoes are always popular. Reservations ☎ (415) 398-5700. $–$$

Enrico's (7 Spring St. between Calif. and Sacramento) Down a tiny alley is this authentic Spanish cuisine restaurant. The Cazuela de Rope is a Catalan style monkfish casserole with poor man's potatoes. Excellent. Open for lunch Mon.–Fri. and dinner Mon.–Sat. Reservations ☎ (415) 989-1976. $–$$

SUGGESTED TOUR:

Numbers in parentheses correspond to numbers on the map.

As you turn left on Montgomery, the tall buildings and rather narrow street give the effect of a dark and shadowy urban canyon. This is where many of the big deals in the west are done. Most of the big West Coast banks are headquartered in San Francisco, as are oil companies and brokerage houses. With them come the mega law firms and the many-tentacled accounting firms. You soon feel why this has been called "The Wall Street of the West."

At the corner of Montgomery and Bush is the stately **Russ Building** (1) at 235 Montgomery. Among the many skyscrapers in San Francisco, this one is probably the most prestigious because of its beauty and history. Constructed of glazed terra-cotta over structural steel, the lobby features vaulted Gothic Revival ceilings complemented by solid brass elevator doors. They say the history of the building is the history of San Francisco itself. Emanuel Charles Christian Russ, a Polish exile who was a silversmith, came to the city in 1847 before the Gold Rush and bought the entire block the building now sits on for $75. He and his nine children needed a place to stay, so they bought the wood from the ship they came around the Cape on and built the family home. He opened a little jewelry store. Then came the Gold Rush. Some of Russ' sons went off to mine gold, and did very well at it, but he stayed behind and housed more and more of the burgeoning population on his property at Montgomery, Bush, Kearny and Pine. He became the pre-

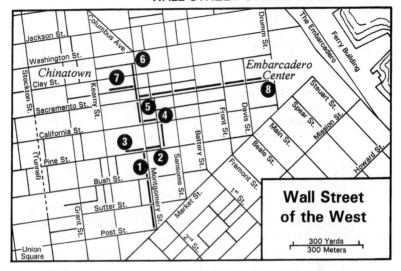

mier gold assayer, and his fortune grew. He bought more and more land. It's the All-American story.

Next, turn down Pine and have a look at the **Pacific Coast Stock Exchange** (2) at 301 Pine. This imposing building has been called the largest stock exchange outside of Wall Street. Note the two scowling granite dogs guarding the exchange, almost like temple dogs outside a Buddhist Temple. Visitors are not allowed inside the building. Go back to Montgomery and cross to the uphill side. Set back in mid-block is the entrance to the A.P. Giannini Plaza. Enter there and take the escalator up to the lobby of the **Bank of America World Headquarters** (3). See if you can feel the pulse of business flowing through the lobby. There's a certain energy to the place; all the men in expensive gray suits and ties and all the ladies in equally expensive pin-striped business suits are rushing here and there to make deals. As you walk outside toward California Street, there's a nondescript, dark piece of sculpture on the left. It has been called, derisively, "The Banker's Black Heart."

As you walk down the many steps to California Street, cross to the other side and go to 400 California, which is the **Union Bank of California** (4) headquarters. From the outside, you can't help but be impressed with the classic Greco-Roman style with its Corinthian colonnade. As you step inside, isn't this how a real bank lobby should feel? Four stories tall with filtered light coming through huge windows; the place exudes money. They call it the Main Banking Hall, otherwise known as the "Grand Old Lady of California Street." This was the first commercial structure to rise out of the ruins of the great 1906 earthquake. In 1905, the bank decided to build a new headquarters and so the site was cleared and the Sierra white granite for the building was quarried. Progress on the new building came to an abrupt halt, however, on April 18, 1906 when the earthquake and fire practically destroyed the city. Undaunted, the bank pushed ahead with the building's completion in 1908. That prompted the popular cry, "Don't talk earthquake, talk business!"

Downstairs in the main Banking Hall is the **Museum of Money of the American West**.This small site has an interesting collection of the most famous gold nuggets from the Gold Rush. Also on display are coins and paper money from western states that had their own private coinage. *Open 9– 4 Mon.–Fri. Free.*

Head back up California to Montgomery and turn right. In this block, at 420, is the **Wells Fargo History Museum** (5). Wells Fargo, one of the most famous names in American business, began banking and express operations in San Francisco in 1852. The company takes its name from its founders, Henry Wells and William Fargo. This was the era of the Gold Rush in California when thousands of people from around the world came to seek their fortunes. Wells Fargo provided a variety of banking and express services for this horde. In 1861, Wells Fargo operated the famous Pony Express between Sacramento and Salt Lake City. The company's stagecoach empire reached its zenith between 1866 and 1869 when it had 3,000 express offices around the world.

On display in the museum are artifacts and memorabilia important to the development of the American West. The most prominent display is the century-old Wells Fargo stagecoach. Mark Twain called it a "cradle on wheels." Long-ago passengers, who had their anatomy rearranged during a long ride, called it many other things—mostly unprintable. Upstairs is a reproduction of the stagecoach, which you can enter and hear a tape recording of what a bouncy journey in one of these critters was really like. Other exhibits include gold, money, treasure boxes, postal envelopes, art, tools, photography and more. *Open 9–5 Mon.–Fri.* ☎ *(415) 396-2619. Free.*

As you make your way along Montgomery, note the plaque at 550 Montgomery.It marks this building as a National Historic Landmark because it was the headquarters of the Bank of Italy from 1908-21. It was from this very place that A.P. Giannini launched the original system of bank branches that transformed the nature of banking in California and the nation. Bank of Italy became the gigantic Bank of America under his dynamic leadership, with over 1,000 branches in California and hundreds more around the world. A.P. would be shocked to learn that his beloved B. of A. was merged with NationsBank, which is the prevailing name.

In the next block is one of San Francisco's most famous (among many) landmarks. The **Transamerica Pyramid** (6) at 600 Montgomery was a source of great controversy when it was announced in 1969, but nowadays the slender, pyramidal configuration is embraced by all. Architect William L.

Pereira chose the design because it allows more light to reach the street than a conventional box-like building, to say nothing of the tremendous image the building has brought to Transamerica itself. At 48 floors, it is the tallest building in San Francisco with a height of 853 feet including the 212-foot spire. The 48th floor is the smallest with only 2,025 square feet. Two windowless wings rise vertically from the 29th floor. They contain elevators on the east side and a stairwell on the west. The main lobby usually has changing contemporary art shows, and to the north side is an unusual way to see the city. Since the tower is closed to public viewing, the company has installed four TV cameras at the very top. Visitors can control these cameras to see a broad panorama, or zoom in for a closer look. Good fun. Free. Be sure to visit the Redwood Park adjacent to the building.

Next turn up Commercial Street to visit the **Pacific Heritage Museum** (7) at 608, a building-within-a-building. Because San Francisco has always been the money headquarters on the West Coast, the United States Sub-Treasury was built here in 1875 on the site of the original mint. Some of the old building has been preserved and you can observe antique mint operations though a glass wall. The Bank of Canton wanted a new headquarters, so they commissioned Skidmore, Owings and Merrill to design their handsome 17-story building around the old building. Contemporary Asian artist's work is also on display. *Open Tues.–Sat. 10–4. Free.* ☎ *(415) 399-1124.*

If you walk along Montgomery to Sacramento and turn right, it will take you to the **Skydeck at Embarcadero Center** (8), located at the top of One Embarcadero on the 41st floor. It is San Francisco's only indoor-outdoor viewing observatory, offering 360-degree panoramic views of America's most photogenic skyline. What's fun are the interactive touch screen computer kiosks that provide historical and cultural information about life in the Bay Area. Tickets can be purchased at the Skydeck ticket booth on the street level of One Embarcadero. *Admission is $5 for adults, $3.50 for seniors 62+ and students, and $3 for kids 5–12. Open Wed.–Fri. 5–10 p.m., weekends and some holidays 10 a.m.–10 p.m. Closed major holidays.* ☎ *(415) 772-0566 for more information.*

Shop, Shop, Shop

It is pretty well known that shopping is one of the two favorite things for visitors to do in San Francisco—and shopping is almost always combined with the other favorite, sightseeing. The range of goods offered is immense. There are huge emporiums with multiple floors of goods next to tiny galleries featuring local ethnic artists and boutiques catering to the exotic. And we can't forget the street merchants who legally sell their wares in selected sites around the city (see Daytrip 14, which also talks about the Japanese Cultural Center shopping area).

While you may find interesting little shops as you make your way around the city, this daytrip will attempt to highlight some of the concentrated areas for excellent shopping—starting with the center of the city, Union Square. This is not to be confused with Union Street, in another part of the city offering terrific shopping—which we will cover in this daytrip. We'll also cover Crocker Galleria, San Francisco Shopping Centre and Embarcadero Center.

You will find shopping information in other sections of this book, too. Daytrip 3 touches on interesting shops in Haight-Ashbury and the Castro; Daytrip 5 covers Chinatown and North Beach; Daytrip 6 tells about Fisherman's Wharf's multitude of shops among its many other attractions and Daytrip 9 briefly explores Ghirardelli Square.

Can you spend money in San Francisco shopping? You bet. Try it and see how easy it is.

GETTING THERE:

On foot, start from Union Square and go down Post. Directions to specific shops in this area are highlighted in the Local Attractions section. To get to shopping areas outside the immediate Union Square area, directions are given in the same section.

PRACTICALITIES:

Most stores in San Francisco open at 10 in the morning and many stay open until about the same hour in the evening. You should have no problem using major credit cards; personal checks are another matter. There is a 8.5 percent sales tax on all purchases; however, if you are from outside California and have your goods shipped home, there is no tax.

FOOD AND DRINK:

The Iron Horse (19 Maiden lane) Recently remodeled, but retains its Old World charm. A large selection of elegant Italian dishes prepared with SF flair. Lunch & dinner Mon.–Sat. Dinner only Sun. ☎ (415) 362-8133. $$

Armani Café (1 Grant Ave., inside the Emporio Armani Boutique) Have a light Italian lunch with cappucino or wine. Open for lunch daily. ☎ (415) 677-9010. $$

Harbor Village (4 Embarcadero Center) Terrific Cantonese dishes include dim-sum, stir-fried and fresh seafood. Open daily for lunch and dinner. ☎ (415) 781-8833. $$

Café de Paris l'Entrecote (2032 Union St.) Typical French café. The name spells out its specialty. Plenty of fresh seafood. Lunch and dinner daily. Weekend entertainment. ☎ (415) 931-5006. $$

Grande Café (501 Geary St.) Probably the grandest café you've ever seen, with elaborate decorations. Terrific food too. Try the Poached Mussels. Breakfast, lunch and dinner daily. ☎ (415) 292-0101. $–$$

LOCAL ATTRACTIONS:

Numbers in parentheses correspond to numbers on the map.

It is said the hub of San Francisco's shopping district is the well-manicured 2.6-acre plot planted with palms, Irish yew, boxwood and bright flowers called **Union Square** (1). The reason the square has a slight rounding is because below it is a garage holding up to 1,000 cars. A California Registered State Landmark plaque at the park's Geary/Powell entrance records that Union Square was deeded to the public on January 3, 1850. Its name derives from a series of violent pro-Union demonstrations there on the eve of the Civil War.

Since the significance of many San Francisco landmarks is measured by whether they survived the 1906 earthquake and fire, be assured that the flying figure of Victory atop the 97-foot Corinthian column in the center of the square did just that.

Let's start this shopping fest at the upper end of the square with a visit to **Porsche Design** at 343 Powell. You won't find the cars here, but how about one of their $6,000 mountain bikes in shocking yellow? A bit more modest is a $98 kids' model of the sporty Boxster. There are leather goods, patio furniture, watches and more that all came from the Porsche Design Studios in Germany. ☎ *(415) 434-4629.*

Head up Powell to the **Powell Street Gallery** at 535. See the works of 28 mostly Bay Area artists on three floors of this historic landmark building. The Empire-style mansion was built by a Republican gambler for his mistress in 1910. He eventually married her, but when she found him with another, she shot him. This is one of the few owner-managed galleries in the city. ☎ *(415) 439-4444.*

At the corner of Post and Powell is the upscale **Saks Fifth Avenue** at 384 Post. Some may only dream of making purchases in this wondrous emporium, which gives shoppers a thorough course in what is current in fashion and accessories. *Café.* ☎ *(415) 986-4300.*

On Post in mid-block is the inestimable **Tiffany's**, displaying the closest thing to crown jewels America has to offer. No, you can't have Breakfast at Tiffany's. On display are items from the company's permanent collection, including many sterling silver trophies. Feast your eyes on the Vince Lombardi trophy and many others. *350 Post.* ☎ *(415) 781-7000.*

At the corner of Post and Stockton is one of the newest **Niketown** stores at 278 Post. The store, while selling all manner of Nike goods on four floors, is really a tribute to America's love of sports and its many sports heroes. Dynamic displays of athletes performing. ☎ *(415) 392-6453.*

Farther down on Post, be sure to stop at **The North Face** with its extensive selection of rugged yet comfortable outwear and sportswear. This store also offers tents, packs and sleeping bags and is known world-wide for its complete line of outdoors goods. *180 Post.* ☎ *(415) 433-3223.* Practically next door is a slick way to shop for kitchen devices, foods and accessories at San Francisco's own **Williams Sonoma** at 150 Post. ☎ *(415) 362-6904.*

No trip to San Francisco would be complete (at least no shopping trip) without a ritual visit to **Gump's** at 135 Post. ☎ *(415) 982-1616.* It started in the Gold Rush in 1849 and hasn't let up since. A bigger-than-life Buddha greets you as you enter. The statute is lighted by soaring cloth Japanese lanterns custom-made for Gump's. Asian antiques, art glass, unique jewelry and a garden shop are only the beginning. For your patio, there's a $1,800 outdoor candle with 20 wicks that resembles a big wheel of cheese.

At the corner of Post and Grant is stately **Shreve & Co.,** San Francisco's answer to all the other fine jewelers from around the world. It stands tall in its offering of silver jewelry, china, crystal and an extensive collection of gifts. ☎ *(415) 421-2600.*

Next turn right on Kearny and right again when you head up Maiden Lane. This narrow two-block mall is closed to vehicles from 11–4 daily. Now a quiet and sedate street, at one time it was one of the raunchiest red light districts in the city. Architecturally, its chief attraction is the distinctive yellow brick structure housing **Folk Art International** at 140. Designed by Frank Lloyd Wright in 1949, the building, with its spiral interior ramp, was the prototype for Wright's Guggenheim Museum in New York. It has a very comfortable feeling where tribal pieces and art from such places as Asia,

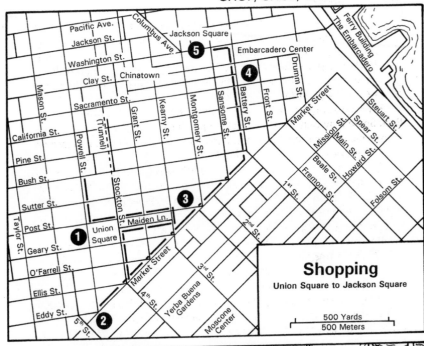

Shopping

Union Square to Jackson Square

500 Yards
500 Meters

Shopping

Around Union Street

1,000 Yards
1 Km

Tibet, Latin America and New Guinea are featured. They offer a good selection of books on Wright and his work. **Chanel** can be found here also along with many other interesting boutiques.

Turn left on Stockton, where you will find two towers of retailing; **Macy's** at 135 (☎ (415) 362-2100) and **Neiman Marcus** of publicity fame at 150 (☎ (415) 362-3900). Both are worth visits for their unique and fashionable offerings.

At the corner with O'Farrell is the venerable kid emporium **FAO Schwartz.** This is three floors of honking, clicking, blinking, singing and dancing fun where you can buy amusements for young people from $1 to $25,000. Ask any of the many personal shoppers to help you with a selection. Schwartz has even set it up so you can have private parties in the store after hours. Perish the thought of hosting a birthday party for your kids among all these temptations. ☎ (415) 394-8700.

If you turn left on Market, at the intersection with Grant Street is one of the most unusual retail store locations in the country. What is called the **Emporio Armani Boutique** at 1 Grant is actually quite a large store housed in an imposing granite structure that was formerly a Wells Fargo Bank branch. Guaranteed you'll deposit some money here. *Café.* ☎ (415) 677-9400.

If all that traipsing around hasn't worn you out, why not head back down to Market Street to enter the multi-story **San Francisco Shopping Centre** (2) at the corner of Fifth and Powell Streets? It's one of the few vertical malls in the country, with an unusual spiral escalator to sweep you up among the eight floors of upscale, trend-setting retailers. Actually, the top four floors are occupied by one of the country's largest **Nordstom** store, that famous Northwest retail emporium with its legendary customer service. They also offer a full treatment European spa. The other floors are home to 90 other leading retailers. Among the many, you might consider a visit to **Imposters**, which offers designer-like faux jewelry. ☎ (415) 541-4922. **Going to the Game** features heaps of college and pro logo wear with a pink 1957 Corvette plunked right in the middle of the store. **Afterthoughts** offers approximately 20,000 types and styles of pierced earrings. **d.b.a Socks** has jazzy underfootwear for kids and Moms and Dads. They have a popular item called Toe Socks that are like gloves for your feet with individual fingers (toes?) with hand-sewn designs. It's true. You wear them with sandals.

Next up is the **Crocker Galleria** (3), which can be reached on foot by walking back down Market to Montgomery. The Galleria is bounded by Post, Kearney, Sutter and Montgomery. Modeled after Milan's vast Galleria Vittorio Emmanuel, the three-level pavilion features 40 elegant boutiques, restaurants and services under a spectacular glass dome. Here you'll find the best of American and European designers, one-of-a-kind collectibles and treasures. **Gianni Versace** is probably the best-known shop here, carrying a complete collection of men's and women's clothing, accessories, watches and home furnishings. Rest or enjoy a picnic lunch in two rooftop gardens.

To get to **Embarcadero Center** (4), it's best to catch a Muni bus on Market Street to Battery, or you can walk these three long blocks. The Center is bounded by Sacramento, Clay, Battery and Justin Herman Plaza. Built by the Rockefeller family in the early 1970s, the center covers eight blocks. It encompasses three levels of open-air landscaped terraces that includes over 120 shop and restaurants. There are many well-known shops like **Liz Claiborne** and **See's Candies** along with dozens of San Francisco originals. **Waldeck's Office Supplies** is a 44-year-old institution whose name belies its extensive offering of San Francisco postcards, stationery and other visitor goods. This center has worked hard to offer entertainment, including a theater complex, the **SkyDeck** on the top of one of the office buildings that offers spectacular views from an indoor/outdoor observatory deck, ice skating in winter and walking tours of its renowned sculpture collection.

Close at hand is **Jackson Square** (5), which lies between Montgomery and Sansome, Jackson and Clay. Built during the Gold Rush days, these many red-brick buildings were once warehouses, hotels and saloons. Most have been lovingly restored and now house a variety of galleries and decorator and antique outlets. The **Jackson Square Art & Antique Dealers Association** is made up of 25 of the finest antique shops on the West Coast. Here you'll find American, Continental and English furniture, silver, tapestries and carpets, porcelain and ceramics and Oriental art plus scientific instruments. *463 Jackson St.* ☎ *(415) 397-6999.*

Next we go off to Cow Hollow and its well-known **Union Street Shopping Area** (6). By bus, take No. 41 westbound from the Financial District on Sacramento or along Columbus Avenue. Get off at the corner of Franklin, which is the beginning of the seven-block-long Union Street Shopping Area. In a change of pace for this portion of the shopping daytrip, we'll point out some of the interesting historical sites along the way and let you find your own favorites among the 200-plus shops and restaurants.

Cow Hollow is the old-time vernacular for the valley lying west of Van Ness Ave between Russian Hill and the Presidio. The first dairy was established in 1861 in what was then a green dale watered by the surrounding hills. The bucolic era ended with the late 1800s. Eventually, handsome Victorian houses replaced the tanneries, slaughterhouses and sausage factories that had sprung up in the area. Union Street's regeneration began in the late 1950s with a few stylish antique shops and home furnishing showrooms.

Especially noteworthy along the route are **The Octagon House** at the corner of Gough and Union, built in 1861. It is a perfectly-preserved heirloom, restored inside and out by the National Society of Colonial Dames. *It is open the second and fourth Thursdays and second Sunday of each month. Donations accepted.* Next is **1851 Union Street,** which was originally a stable facing Washerwoman's Lagoon. In a cul-de-sac off the south side of Union's 1900 block is **Charlton Court**, said to have been a milkwagon loading yard; a trio of 1873-96 Victorians at numbers 2,4 and 5 have been genteelly restored into the Bed and Breakfast Inn.

Home to several shops and restaurants at **1980 Union** is one of the district's most striking Victorian compounds, fashioned from three circa-1870 residences, including a pair of wedding houses (identical bungalows joined by a common center wall). At 1981 Union is the old **Laurel Vale Dairy**, said to be virtually all that remains of Cow Hollow's dairy industry. Today it houses Earthly Goods women's apparel. The three-story **Cudworth Mansion** at 2040 Union was built in 1870 by James Cudworth, one of the district's first dairymen. It now houses several boutiques. Finally at 2325 Union is **St. Mary The Virgin Episcopal Church**. This is one of the last vestiges of Cow Hollow, with its Eternal Fountain fed by a spring that once watered the district's herds.

Section III

DAYTRIPS AND OVERNIGHTING
NORTH OF
SAN FRANCISCO

Like the people who live north of San Francisco, those who visit this same area can become fiercely partisan. From the Marin Headlands and Sausalito hugging the shore immediately over the Golden Gate Bridge all the way several hundred miles north to the towering groves of the Redwood National Forest, you would be hard pressed to find more geographic beauty and diversity.

Within that span just described we must not forget the two terrific, but quite different wine valleys—Sonoma and Napa—or the 65,000-acre seashore/mountain playland called Point Reyes. Beyond that is old-fashioned Mendocino, crafted mostly by New Englanders. Just nine miles north of Mendo is the little choo-choo called the Skunk Train that takes you into and through dense redwood forests.

On the west side of this huge territory is the sparkling ocean, sometimes calmly making its way into secluded bays and other times crashing furiously onto sea stacks and other dark, rocky coastal outcroppings. If you pick spots we lead you to, you can play in the ocean in many different, fun ways.

GETTING AROUND—NORTH

Let's face it, this whole area—and most other parts of California outside of urban areas—have always been car country. Below are some alternatives.

FERRY:

You can reach some southern areas of Marin County by ferry. The Blue and Gold Fleet will take you to Sausalito or Tiburon for an $11 round-trip fare. They have five daily departures for each town that leave from Pier 41. The same company has trips to Vallejo where you can catch a limo to Napa. For Blue and White Fleet ☎ (415) 705-5555. For the ferry/limo package ☎ (800) 294-6386. Daytrip 24 has more information on the package and other transportation alternatives to Napa.

TOUR BUS:

Tower Tours leads folks on a three-and-a-half-hour motorcoach tour of Muir Woods that also includes Sausalito. The fare is $28 for adults and $13 for kids 5-11. ☎ (415) 434-8687.

BY CAR:

The choices are essentially the wonderfully scenic Highway 1 that mostly chugs along the dramatic coastline north of the city of San Francisco, or the more direct Highway US-101. In places they come together. You may want to map out your route to enjoy some of both.

ACCOMMODATIONS—NORTH

As we point out in Daytrips 26-29 from Mendocino north, your time will be much more enjoyable if you headquarter in that area and make daily forays from a central location—rather than trying to make these trips from the City of San Francisco. It could be done, but you wouldn't have a lot of fun.

Accommodations in the Mendocino/Fort Bragg areas are some of the most storied in the country. They range all the way from the bed and breakfast where Ala Alda and Ellen Burstyn filmed *Same Time Next Year* to the B&B where Jessica Fletcher hung out during the shooting of *Murder She Wrote*.

By far the best way to get a handle on the accommodations that will suit you best is to call (800) 262-7801. **Mendocino Coast Reservations** has a full range of motels, hotels and B&Bs to choose from, and they are very helpful.

VISITOR INFORMATION

San Rafael Chamber of Commerce
817 Mission Ave.
San Rafael, CA 94901
☎ (800) 454-4163
www.sanrafael.org

Napa Valley Visitors Bureau
1310 Napa Valley Town Center
Napa, CA 94599
☎ (707) 226-7459
www.napavalley.com/calistoga

Sonoma Valley Visitors Bureau
453 1st St. E
Sonoma, CA 94576
☎ (707) 996-1762

Superintendent
Point Reyes National Seashore
Point Reyes, CA 94956
☎ (415) 663-1092

Fort Bragg-Mendocino Chamber of Commerce
332 N. Main St., P.O. Box 1141
Fort Bragg, CA 954367
☎ (800) 726-2780 or (707) 961-6300
www.mendocinocoast.com

Sausalito and Marin Headlands

Sausalito and the Marin Headlands are the entry point to one of America's—let alone California's—most interesting pieces of real estate. A total study in contrasts, Marin County geographically holds huge open pastures for dairy cows, sophisticated cities like Sausalito, rough-hewn fishermen's shacks, homes for the rich and famous on Belvedere Island, a wild and untamed coastline, beaches, redwood forests and more. Rising like a huge sentinel looking down on the whole place is 2,560-foot Mount Tamalpais.

Marin attracts a unique blend of professional, well-educated entrepreneurial people, along with its share of aromatherapists, soothsayers, organic farmers and other whimsical types. The population of a quarter million has pretty much stabilized due to restrictive zoning, the Golden Gate Bridge as a barrier and the fact that Marin declined to become part of the underground transportation system of the Bay Area, called BART. Besides the bridge and a few ferries, the only other way to get to Marin is via helicopter or landing craft along the dangerous coastline.

Modern-day Sausalito has been compared with a typical Mediterranean village hugging a hill along the coastline; quaint, red-tiled roofs, magnificent yachts at anchor in the bay and open-air restaurants. It is all of that, but that image belies the town's past when it was a fishing village and then a haven for saloons and bordellos. During WWII, Sausalito took on a very industrial tone as a sizable shipbuilding center on the west coast.

The city itself is tiny at 2.14 square miles and only 7,500 citizens, most of whom live clinging to the rather steep hillside on which the city sits. It was first inhabited by Miwok Indians and later discovered by Spanish explorer Juan Manuel de Ayala who named his discovery "Saucelito" meaning Little Willow.

GETTING THERE:
By car from Union Square, go up either Geary or Sutter to Van Ness. Turn

right and go one mile to Lombard, then turn left. Approximately 11 blocks later, bear right onto Richardson, which will lead you directly to the Golden Gate Bridge. On the other side of the bridge, take the Sausalito off-ramp at Alexander Avenue. Turn left where it says 101 to San Francisco. Watch for the brown signs to Marin Headlands. You are on Conzelman Road.

PRACTICALITIES:

Sausalito and the Marin Headlands can be windy and chilly, especially in summertime, so take along a sweater or light jacket. Generally speaking, the attractions in and around Sausalito open around 10 in the morning, so plan accordingly.

FOOD AND DRINK:

Alta Mira Hotel (125 Bulkley Ave.) High on the hill above town, the views are staggering. Suitable menu with good seafood selections. Try the Sausalito Seafood Salad. Lunch and dinner daily. Reservations ☎ (415) 332-1350. $$–$$$

Scoma's (588 Bridgeway) Jutting out into the water on its own pier built in 1891, this restaurant brings you up close and personal with the bay. Very fresh seafood and authentic Italian dishes. Dinner daily and lunch Thurs.–Sun. Reservations ☎ (415) 332-9551. $$

Chart House (201 Bridgeway) This was Madame Sally Sanford's original eatery called Valhalla. Today it has a very nautical interior including outstanding ship models. Enjoy terrific steaks and seafood at the edge of the bay. Dinner daily starting at 5:30. Reservations ☎ (415) 332-0804. $$

Winship Restaurant (670 Bridgeway) Built in 1875 as a general store, this spot is located in the oldest brick building in town. They even turn sandwiches into a really full meal. Try the seafood chowder. ☎ (415) 332-1454. $–$$

"No Name" Bar (757 Bridgeway) Good old-time bar built around the turn of the century. Gained fame as a hangout of literary and counter-culture luminaries. Simple pub food. Lunch and dinner daily. Music in the p.m. except Monday. ☎ (415) 332-1392. $

SUGGESTED TOUR:

Numbers in parentheses correspond to numbers on the map.

As you climb quickly along the coast, you are entering the huge **Marin Headlands** (1). Astonishingly, the bridge seems practically in your lap. The first chance to take in the bridge, the sweep of the bay and the city is to stop at **Battery Spencer**. This is one of many abandoned gun emplacements all along this once heavily fortified coastline. Because you are high up—nearly at the level of the top of the bridge towers—the views are staggering.

Continue up Conzelman as it winds along the twisting coast. Far below

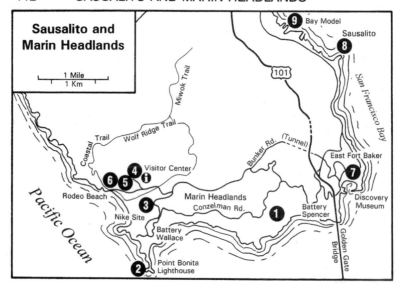

is the ocean crashing up against the steep shoreline. The road continues to climb and at one point you can turn right on McCullough Road and head for the Visitor Center. We suggest keeping left and following the rim road, which soon becomes quite narrow and one way. Enjoy the ocean views as they open up before you.

This same road will take you to the entrance to **Point Bonita Lighthouse** (2), which still operates to protect shipping from the vagaries of the churning ocean and ofttimes poor visibility around the Golden Gate. The only access is by walking a stimulating trail out over a bridge to the lighthouse, but the views are breathtaking. *Open Sat. and Sun. 12:30–3:30.* Past the lighthouse is one of dozens of decidedly low-tech coastal defenses in the form of **Battery Wallace** that could fire guns a grand total of 17 miles out to sea. You can wander around in the battery. At the end of the road is **Bird Island Overlook.** This island, once part of the coast line, provides protection for a wide variety of sea birds, primarily cormorants in winter and brown pelicans in summer. About seven miles off the coast—on clear days—you may be able to see the **Farallon Islands**, which are among the largest seabird nesting sites in America. It is estimated that 300,000 birds nest on these tiny dots in the Pacific Ocean.

Head back the way you came. As you head down, on the left is the **Historic Nike Missile Site** (3). Many Bay Area residents may not be aware, but in the mid-1950s the military built a concentration of coastal defenses around the Golden Gate in the form of long-range, buried Nike missiles. This one was closed in 1974 and is preserved as the last of its type in the nation. If this sort of thing interests you, rangers and volunteers operate the elevators to bring the missiles out of the ground during demonstrations. *Open Mon.–Fri. and the first Sun. of each month 12:30–3:30.* ☎ *(415) 331-1453.*

Follow Bunker Road until you see signs for the **Marin Headlands Visitor Center** (4) in an old church. This is an important orientation point for the whole Headlands experience. There are modest exhibits of the natural history of the Headlands, and a neat Miwok Indian shelter that gives you an idea of how these first settlers lived. Be sure to pick up a map here. Rangers lead interpretive hikes and conduct other programs of interest to visitors. *Open 9:30–4:40 daily.* ☎ *(415) 556-7940 for more information.* &.

When you leave the Center, watch for signs to turn left to the beach. Soon on the right you will see signs for the **Marine Mammal Center** (5). This is a unique clinic and hospital founded in 1975 that provides rescue, rehabilitation and release of seals, sea lions, whales, dolphins and otters. Over 800 volunteers work closely with veterinarians and other medical staff to treat patients for a variety of health and environmental problems. This is a terrific experience for the whole family. *Open daily 10–4. Free, but donations are a must in the form of membership. Gift shop.* ☎ *(415) 289-7325 for more information.*

Just down the road is **Rodeo Lagoon and Beach** (6). The lagoon is actually a wildlife estuary that is a mix of fresh and salt water. Because of that it attracts ducks, egrets and brown pelicans at different times of the year. During winter, the lagoon may swell due to heavy rainfall and break through to the sea. For much of the year, however, the beach is a wonderful place for walking. Swimming is out due to potentially heavy seas and undertow. Listen for the rocks rumbling on the incoming waves.

The buildings on the right are part of **Fort Cronkite**, which today is mostly used for conferences and meetings. At the end of the road is the first of many, many superb trails through the Headlands. The **Coastal Trail** winds along the coast showing some very deep coves and crashing ocean below. It eventually meets up with a gently sloping wagon road (the old Julian Road) built by the Army in the late 1860s. This trail goes about 1.5 miles to the **Wolf Ridge Trail.** It is very important to stay on the trails and not take shortcuts across switchbacks. Of the hundreds of miles of trails throughout the headlands, several are for mixed use by hikers, bikers and equestrians. You can travel many of the trails on horses provided by **Miwok Stables** at 701 Tennessee Valley Road. They offer one-, one-and-a-half- and two-hour guided trail rides throughout the Headlands. There's also a Pelican Inn Lunch Ride that's lots of fun. *Open Tues.–Sun. 9–4:30.* ☎ *(415) 383-8048 for rates, reservations and information.*

As you leave the area on Bunker, stop for a moment to reflect on how we all came to be able to enjoy this magnificent piece of real estate. Rolling hills that were once mostly dairy farms and the rugged coastline were held for years by the military so that today we can all enjoy this marvelous part of the 72,000-acre Golden Gate Recreation Area. According to a publication of GGRA, the Headlands, "shaped and changed by generations of human activity, is no longer a wilderness. But the wild heart of these rolling hills, rocky ridges, sheer coastal cliffs and quiet coves still beats today. The expanse of open land provides a unique counterpoint to modern life in the cities around it."

Soon you will come to the one-way "Five Minute Tunnel," which got its name because the light is set for five minutes to let opposing traffic through the tunnel. When you come to Alexander Avenue turn left. About half a mile down the road, look for signs on the right for Fort Baker and the **Bay Area Discovery Museum** (7). This complex of buildings features hands-on exhibits and programs primarily for children (although adults will find it fascinating as well) that tell all about beaches, ponds, hillsides and woodlands of the Bay Area. There's a crawl-through Underwater Sea Tunnel and life-size Discovery Boat plus the Maze of Illusions. Make your own animated video. *Open Tues.–Sun. 10–5 in summer and Tues.–Thurs. 9–4 and Fri.– Sun. 10–5 in winter. Closed major holidays. Adult admission is $7, $6 for kids one and up. Café and gift shop.* ☎ *(415) 487-4398 for more information.* ♿.

If you go back the way you came, it will take you straight into **Sausalito** (8). Downtown has been declared a National Historic Landmark, and as you walk along Bridgeway, you will see why. There are dozens of historic buildings reflecting the various phases of the city's past—fishing village, wartime shipyard and home to wealthy commuters. If you stop by the Visitor Center, pick up a $2 map of the fascinating Sausalito History Walk. It will guide you to 26 neat points of interest including the foundation for William Randolph Hearst's original castle. He left Sausalito in a huff before it was built and went south to build the monstrous San Simeon after the city fathers scolded him for having a mistress.

Most visitors only make their way along the level Bridgeway, but much of Sausalito's charm can be found on the upper reaches. Expect quite a climb along tortuously curving roads, but the houses are fascinating. The views from up here are also worth the effort. If you feel ambitious, look for El Monte Lane just before Village Fair. This is one of the many famous Sausalito hill-paths. The many steep steps will tax your heart and legs, but tucked above the fray is the Old-World gracious **Alta Mira Hotel.**

Practically at the end of the main drag is one of the Bay Area's more fascinating attractions, **The San Francisco Bay-Delta Model** (9) at 2100 Bridgeway. The Bay Model is a three-dimensional representation of the San Francisco Bay and Delta capable of simulating tides, currents, river inflows and other variables affecting water quality and movement in the huge estuary. The model, operated by the Army Corps of Engineers, spreads out over 1.5 acres and is built out of 286 five-ton concrete slabs.

There's an introductory video on the bay and the model at the Visitor Center to get things started. You can take a self-guided tour following a map provided, or there is an audio tour available with headphones and cassettes. Many of the Model's exhibits are interactive, where you can learn the history and ecology of the bay and delta. You can also explore the docks where three Army Corps debris vessels are tied up and where the *Wapama*—a vintage 1915 lumber schooner—sits in dry dock. *Bookstore and art gallery. Admission is free. Hours are Tues.–Sat. 9–4 in winter; and Tues.–Fri. 9–4 and 10–6 weekends and holidays in the summer.* ☎ *(415) 332-3871.*

For a change of pace, you can experience the bay at water level in a sea kayak. In Sausalito, **Sea Trek Kayaking Service** offers sit-on-top kayaks for about $10 an hour or $45 for a full day. No previous kayaking experience is necessary. In summer, they offer half- and full-day instructional programs. ☎ *(415) 488-1000 for reservations.*

Sausalito Bike Rental will rent you a suspension mountain bike and head you to a terrific bike path that eventually goes right up Mt. Tamalpais. Many shorter routes are available. Adult bikes are $39 a day (or $10 an hour), kids are $25 a day ($7 an hour) and tandems are $59. Located at the Ferry Plaza. ☎ *(415) 331-4448.*

If the open ocean calls you, **Caruso's** will happily take you out from Sausalito and through the Golden Gate. Salmon season is March–October, but they go out almost every day for halibut and striper. A day trip leaves at 6 a.m. and costs $55; an afternoon trip leaves at 3:30 p.m. and costs $45. ☎ *(415) 332-1015.*

Tiburon and Paradise Drive

Of all the fascinating towns ringing the bay, Tiburon hasn't always been given its due. Sausalito has always been a star, but some say Tiburon has even more to offer. It's a bit farther up the highway and well worth the trip.

Tiburon and its sibling Belvedere stick out into the bay to create Richardson Bay. Along the shore, there are wetlands and a bird sanctuary that we will explore.

In the 1880s an entrepreneur by the name of Peter Donohue brought the railroad to Tiburon. To do that, he had to carve a tunnel in the major hill behind the city so the trains could go on to San Rafael, farther north. The tunnel is still there although the trains are long gone. His genius was that the train connected up with ferries that took the whole gang into San Francisco. This was before the Golden Gate Bridge was built in 1937. Tiburon is still a major ferry terminal for trips into the city.

At one time, Tiburon had a lagoon at its backside lined with "arks" or houseboats. When the lagoon was filled in 1940, another entrepreneur, Fred Zelinsky, purchased the arks and put them up on pilings. Today, "Ark Row" is a series of buildings that form a popular shopping and dining area of Tiburon.

The gentrified downtown of today wasn't always that way. In the late 1880s to the 1930s, Tiburon was a bustling, rowdy railroad town. The original buildings on Main Street served railroad workers, shopkeepers and their families, and residents of cattle and dairy ranches that dotted the peninsula.

GETTING THERE:

By car from Union Square, go up either Geary or Sutter to Van Ness. Turn right and go one mile to Lombard, then turn left. Approximately 11 blocks later, bear right onto Richardson, which leads directly to the Golden Gate Bridge. On the other side of the bridge, go about six miles on Highway 101 and take the Tiburon Boulevard Highway 131 Exit.

PRACTICALITIES:

Tiburon is a good walking city, so wear comfortable shoes. Depending on the time of year, the breeze off the bay can be chilly, so it's always a good idea to take along a sweater or windbreaker.

FOOD AND DRINK:

Sam's Anchor Café (27 Main St.) Longtime favorite of San Franciscans. Outdoor seating on the deck is very popular on sunny days. Try the Oysters Brian in garlic. All the seafood is excellent. Lunch and dinner daily. ☎ (415) 435-4527 for reservations. $$

Tutto Mare (9 Main St.) Bayside seafood restaurant that specializes in delicacies from the coastal regions of Italy. Great variety of pasta dishes for all tastes. Lunch and dinner daily. ☎ (415) 435-4747. $$

Guaymas (5 Main St.) If you like Mexican food, you'll find the authentic regional menu very much to your liking. You can make a meal on appetizers, or feast on the large portion entrees. Great views. Lunch and dinner daily. ☎ (415) 435-6300. $$

Marin Joe's (1585 Casa Buena Dr., Corte Madera) Wonderful family has run this spot for over 40 years. They specialize in mesquite-broiled steaks, fish and chops. Hearty meals for breakfast, lunch and dinner daily. ☎ (415) 924-2081. $–$$

SUGGESTED TOUR:

Numbers in parentheses correspond to numbers on the map.

After you turn off Highway 101, go for about a mile on Tiburon Boulevard. Turn right on Greenwood Cove Road and then left. Up ahead on the right is the **Richardson Bay Audubon Center and Sanctuary** (1). A variety of birds and other animals make their home at this 11-acre sanctuary on Richardson Bay. One of the only remaining unaltered bay wetlands, the refuge is an excellent place to observe migrating waterfowl and shore birds. The Center also offers educational programs and a self-guided nature trail. *Open 9–5 Wed.–Sun. Adult admission is $2, kids $1.* ☎ (415) *388-2524.* In 1957, the **Lyford House** was barged from its original location at Strawberry Point to the Audubon Center. This stunning Victorian residence was built in 1876 by Tiburon's first developer, Dr. Benjamin Lyford. *Open Nov.–April on Sundays 1–4. Admission is included with the bird sanctuary.*

When you come to Beach Road, turn left. You will wind a short distance up a hill to Esperanza. Turn left and this will take you to **Old St. Hilary's Church** (2). This simple white sanctuary sits on top of a hill overlooking the town of Tiburon. Built in 1886 of redwood from the surrounding area, it is one of the few surviving examples of Carpenter Gothic in its original form and location. *Open 1–4 Wed. and Sun., Apr.–Oct.*

Go back the way you came, but go across Beach Road for **Downtown Tiburon** (3). We will start our walking tour at the corner of Beach and Main

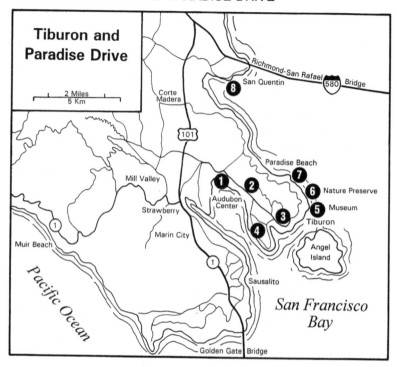

Tiburon and Paradise Drive

2 Miles
5 Km

Street, which at this point is sometimes dubbed **"Ark Row."** As you look to the left, at one time all of that area was a lagoon with arks (houseboats) tied up along a wharf. Before Main Street branches off, there was a drawbridge built in the 1880s to let out water craft of various sizes. Take the left branch of Main Street.

At 122 Main Street is the **Ranch Building** built in the 1870s and the oldest structure on Ark Row. At 112 Main is what's called the **Cottage**, built in the 1890s. It has a secret staircase that led to a stash of hidden, illicit booze during the rumrunning years. At the end of Ark Row, at 104 Main, is one of the original **Arks** built in 1895. As you continue on, at 72 Main is the old **Fleming Rooming House**, a relative newcomer built in 1918. Mrs. Fleming carefully screened the Pacific Northwest trainmen before renting rooms.

As Main Street bends to the left, the next series of historical structures were all built in the 1920s along the waterfront when Tiburon transformed from an agricultural to a railroad economy. A **Saloon** was built in 1925 at 35 Main with a trapdoor access to the bay for bringing in illegal liquor. Across the street at 34 Main was the **Beyries General Store and Hotel,** reportedly a bordello. At 27 Main is one of Tiburon's better known spots. **Sam's** (see info in Food and Drink above) is the oldest continuously oper-

ating restaurant in Tiburon. The saloon was fully operational during prohibition.

Retrace your steps and when you get in your car, turn left on Beach Road
for a driving tour of **Beautiful Belvedere** (4), one of the most exclusive residential areas in the nation. You'll see why as we make our way around the
island. Belvedere is Italian for "beautiful view."

But first, at 52 Beach Road, is the **Social Saloon of the S.S. China.** This
is actually the Victorian drawing room of a passenger and cargo sidewheeler
that plied between San Francisco, Japan and China. It was salvaged when
the ship was burned for scrap in 1886. While not large, it exhibits a
$600,000 restoration of the incredibly detailed interior with 22k gold leaf,
walnut woodwork, cut-glass floral window panes and oil burning chandeliers. *This museum is open Sundays and Wednesdays from 1–4 April–October.* ☎ *(415) 435-1853. Free.*

It's hard to believe—seeing the million-dollar mansions that line the
streets of Belvedere nowadays—that at one time this was just another place
to graze cattle. Israel Kaslow was the first resident, settling in around 1885.
But he was subsequently tossed off the island by John Reed, who went on
to develop Mill Valley (see Daytrip 19). In any case, what eventually developed is like few other neighborhoods, with its winding roads, tight lanes and
steep stairways—lots of stairways—all among heavy vegetation. The island
is a mile and a half long and less than a mile wide.

We suggest you navigate along Beach Road (which eventually becomes
Belvedere Avenue after Buena Vista) ever so carefully because of the narrow roadway. When you take into consideration the stupendous views, it
becomes clearer why this is such an exclusive enclave. If you go all the way
around the island, at a stop sign take Oak Avenue down, which rejoins
Beach Road.

At Tiburon Boulevard, turn right. As you leave downtown, the area opens
up to grassy areas, walkways and an incredible view of Angel Island along
what is now Paradise Drive. A short distance along this esplanade is the
Train and Ferry Terminal Museum (5). This was the original passenger and
freight depot of the San Francisco and North Pacific Railroad. In recent
years, it has been called the "Donohue Building" after the railroad's founder.
Built of redwood and board-and-batten, it is a classic Victorian railway
building of that era. *The Museum is open Wed.–Sun. 10–4. Admission is
$3.* ☎ *(415) 435-5490.*

A bit farther on Paradise Drive is the **Lyford Tower**, built in 1889. On the
National Register of Historic Places, this sandstone tower was built by Dr.
Benjamin Lyford as the southern gateway to "Lyford's Hygeia," a planned
community with a health spa. It was the first subdivision on the Tiburon
Peninsula.

Paradise Drive is one of California's most interesting shoreline drives.
The distance is about nine miles, and along the way you will have spectac-

ular views of the city, the East Bay and Angel Island. It's very curvy, so pull over often to safe lookouts.

At 2.3 miles, there's the trailhead for the **Tiburon Uplands Nature Preserve** (6). If you have time, be sure to take this short .7 mile trip through native forests of madronne and oak.

Around mile 3, you can reach the bay via the **Paradise Beach Park** (7). Here you'll find full facilities. There's a big lawn area and many spots for picnics. Try your hand at the horseshoe courts, or fishing from the pier. *The park is open 7 a.m.–8 p.m. daily. Admission is $7 per car on weekends and $5 on weekdays.* ☎ *(415) 435-9212 for more information.*

If you look north across the inlet you can see the yellowish hulk of San Quentin Prison jutting out on a promontory. If you want to visit the museum there, follow Paradise Drive and go north on Highway 101. Follow the exit and signs for The Richmond/San Rafael Bridge. Take the last Marin County exit before the bridge to the **San Quentin Museum** (8). You have to check with the guard at the gate to gain access to this smallish museum. There are several interesting displays: Great Escapes; Inmate Life; Prison Labor used to Build California's Roads; and History of the Death Penalty. On display are photographs, artifacts and a tiny replica of the prison's infamous gas chamber. *Open Tues., Fri. and Sun. 11–3. Sat. 11:45–3:15. Adult admission is $2, kids are $1.* ☎ *(415) 454-8808.*

*Muir Woods and Mill Valley

Redwoods are the highlight of this daytrip. In particular, coast redwoods that have survived and thrived for thousands of years in that narrow fog-shrouded band from the Oregon border south to Monterey. The fog plays an important part in helping these redwood giants grow to upwards of 300 feet since it collects on the branches and condenses and drips off, providing up to ten inches of precipitation a year beyond normal rainfall.

Another contributor to the redwoods dominance in this part of the world is its cinnamon-colored bark. The bark is unusually thick and resistant to such destroyers as fire and pests.

Redwoods were first logged in the Oakland hills during the 1820s, and farther south in Monterey a short time later. It was the Gold Rush, though, with its huge demand for lumber that propelled the logging industry in this part of California. The first sizable lumber mill got going in Eureka in 1850, and it soon had 300 competitors, mostly north of San Francisco in Mendocino and Humboldt counties.

Like a lot of other things during the Gold Rush, the logging of redwoods became excessive and haphazard. While environmentalists didn't exist then, nonetheless there was a movement to preserve some of the more scenic areas. In 1908, Teddy Roosevelt thankfully established Muir Woods and several other redwood enclaves in California.

GETTING THERE:

By car from Union Square, go up either Geary or Sutter to Van Ness. Turn right and go one mile to Lombard, then turn left. Approximately 11 blocks later, bear right onto Richardson, leading directly to the Golden Gate Bridge. On the other side of the bridge, go about 3.5 miles on Highway US-101 to the Mill Valley/Stinson Beach exit. Follow signs to Muir Woods.

PRACTICALITIES:

Muir Woods is very popular, especially with those taking a bus visit. They usually arrive fairly early in the morning and disgorge their passengers for short walk into the forest. Thus it's best to arrive around mid-morning. And if you take the self-guided tour deeper into the park, you will probably have it mostly to yourself.

The park is cool, shaded and moist all year. Daytime temperatures average between 40 and 70 degrees, so a sweater or jacket is advisable.

FOOD AND DRINK:

Panache Dance & Dinner Club (639 Blithedale Ave. in Mill Valley) Classy place with fine dining. The real treat is the live band and dancing after 9. Dinner daily. ☎ (415) 388-2493 for reservations. $$–$$$

Frantorio Ristorante (152 Shoreline Hwy. in Mill Valley) You'll find the extra-virgin olive oil on-premises production fascinating with its traditional stone crusher. This spot features Italian cuisine with a Mediterranean flair. Lunch and dinner daily. ☎ (415) 289-5777. $$

The Buckeye (15 Shoreline Hwy. in Mill Valley) Imposing roadhouse with a fine menu. BBQ mussels in grilled garlic bread, smoked Sonoma duck and bread smoked pork shank are a few of the specialities. Lunch and dinner daily. ☎ (415) 331-2600. $$

Piazzo D'Angelo (22 Miller Ave. in Mill Valley) Authentic Italian trattoria in downtown Mill Valley. Outdoor dining in good weather. Wood-burning pizza oven and rotisserie. They also bake fresh breads and pastries daily. ☎ (415) 388-2000. $–$$

SUGGESTED TOUR:

Numbers in parentheses correspond to numbers on the map.

*MUIR WOODS NATIONAL MONUMENT (1), Mill Valley, CA 94941, ☎ (415) 388-2595. *Open daily from 8 to 8. Entrance fee of $2 for adults and free for kids. Visitor Center and gift shop with snacks. Self-guided walks throughout the park. ♿ on paved trails.*

According to the National Park Service, the forest along Redwood Creek in today's Muir Woods was spared from logging because it was hard to get to. Noting that the area contained one of the Bay Area's last uncut stands of old-growth redwoods, Congressman William Kent bought 295 acres here for $45,000 in 1905 (the park has been expanded to 560 acres today). He then gave the land to the federal government. Teddy Roosevelt wanted to name it after Kent, but he pushed for it to honor the famed conservationist John Muir.

Philosopher, scientist and author Muir said, when told of the naming, "This is the best tree-lover's monument that could possibly be found in all

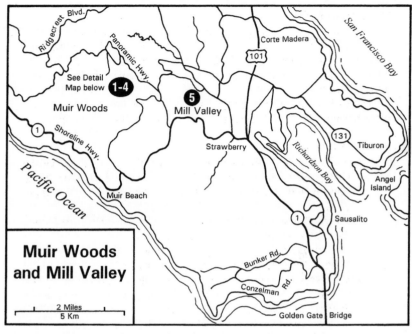

Muir Woods and Mill Valley

2 Miles
5 Km

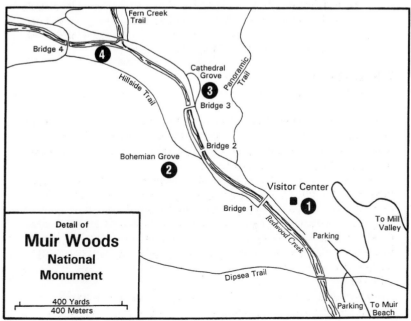

Detail of
Muir Woods
National
Monument

400 Yards
400 Meters

the forests of the world. You have done me a great honor, and I am proud of it."

One of the first impressions as you enter the park is the aroma; earthy and refreshing. Since animal life in a redwood forest is limited because the shaded conditions provide scarce food, you'll probably notice that it's quiet. And cool. The temperature averages about 65 degrees with little sunlight filtering through the layers of redwood branches that reach up to 250 feet.

All these conditions make for a wonderful walk through Muir Woods. As you start from the Visitors Center, you can decide whether to go the full six miles on the paved trail, or make two shorter loops. If you opt for the shortest, cross over Bridge 2 and make a loop back through the **Bohemian Grove** (2). To continue past Bridge 2 will take you to **Cathedral Grove** (3) where you can double back a bit and cross Bridge 3 to take you back to your car. Going farther takes you to Bridge 4. From there you can go back on the Hillside Trail that eventually rejoins the paved trail heading back to the parking lot.

For most of the walking, you will go along **Redwood Creek** (4), which originates high on the slopes of Mt. Tamalpais. This creek runs year-round, providing nearby trees and animals with water. It is host to diverse aquatic creatures including fish, crayfish and salamanders. In summer, the creek slows to a trickle, but watch out in the winter when it can become a torrent. In its rain-swollen winter condition, the creek breaks through the sand barrier at Muir Beach, and adult steelhead and silver salmon move up the creek to spawn.

If you are interested in more strenuous hiking, the **Panoramic Trail** leads off the paved trail just before Bridge 2. This trail eventually leads to several others that can be taken to the summit of Mt. Tamalpais. Farther up is the **Fern Creek Trail** that follows its namesake again up to Tamalpais. Probably the most well-known trail in this area is the **Dipsea Trail.** This one runs from Mill Valley, over Tamalpais and then on to Stinson Beach (see Daytrip 20). Every year since 1905, the Dipsea Race has been run over this tortuous course, a distance of 7.1 miles. It should be noted that a 91-year-old gentleman still runs the race and has since 1931. He's won it a couple of times in his heyday.

Experienced trail guide Tom Martell has been walking the Marin County trails (and those of 35 countries) for the last 20 years. He can turn a trip to Muir Woods into a real adventure by "showing out-of-towners what the locals do for outdoor fun." He offers a **Trail Walk Package** with lots of goodies including transportation, picnic lunch, snacks and lots of information delivered with a sense of humor. *Cost is $49.95.* ☎ *(415) 845-0856 for reservations.*

Muir Woods does not allow pets or smoking, nor the removal of any flora. Camping and picnicking are also forbidden. The Park Service is firm in its request that guests stay on the trails. People have been known to toss coins in the creek, which is unsightly and toxic to aquatic life. Resist.

Next we will explore **Mill Valley** (5). Turn left when you leave the parking lot and when you come to the stop sign, go straight across to Sequoia Valley Road. Follow this route (which changes names several times) right to the center of town. Sometimes called the "Switzerland of America," Mill Valley's streets wind up narrow, heavily forested hillsides and through deep canyons. Standing sentinel over most of Mill Valley is The Mountain—Mt. Tamalpais.

Originally a logging town, Mill Valley takes its name from the 1836 sawmill, built by John Thomas Reed. Reed was one of the principal suppliers of redwood to the Presidio in San Francisco. The railroad also played a part in the town's history. In 1889 a resort was opened in Mill Valley and so the Pacific Northwest Railroad built a spur to service that facility.

The town got another boost in 1896 when "the crookedest railroad in the world" began service winding up the slopes of 2,600-foot Mt. Tam. It was quite a wild ride as it swerved around 281 corners and chugged up steep slopes to the summit. The railroad ended in 1931, but this same roadbed is used today for biking and walking up to the summit—if you're so inclined.

Mill Valley has always been resistant to growth, even during its various boom times. In 1902, the women of the town founded the Bernard Maybeck-designed **Outdoor Art Club** to try to slow the cutting of redwoods and native plants. Today, the ambiance of the old train depot comfortably coexists with trendy eateries and upscale boutiques along Miller and Throckmorton Avenue.

A terrific walk in Mill Valley (if you haven't had enough in Muir Woods) is up Throckmorton to **Old Mill Park**, nestled in a large stand of redwood trees. In the park is the shell of Reed's original mill. Alongside it is the actual car #9 of the Gravity Train—squeeze handbrake and all. We suggest you continue this walk along Cascade Creek. This stream was pivotal in Mill Valley's growth. This rushing stream fueled John Reed's original sawmill from whence the town got its name. Start at Old Mill Park and follow Cascade Drive. This narrow, quiet road winds through tall redwood trees and by lovely homes nestled among these giants. Look for a sign that says "Three Wells," and take the path down to the creek. As you walk along the shore of the creek, you will come to round pools carved in the creek bed. The aim of this walk is to reach Cascade Falls. Look for the marker. If you take the lower fork, you can see the modest falls with a pool below. Some people have been known to take a dip in this chilly but refreshing water. If you take the upper fork, you go above the falls and there are two more wells carved out of the rock by the swirling water.

When you go back to town you may want to explore some of the interesting shops. **Dowd's Barn** at 157 Throckmorton has been around since

1892. Lots of pre-owned stuff in a fun atmosphere. There's an ersatz barn-yard out front where the original store burned down. **Start to Finish Bicycles** at 116 Throckmorton will rent you a mountain bike so you can explore the town and mountain further. *A front suspension bike is $35 per day and a full suspension is $50. They have trail maps for $6.* ☎ (415) 388-3500.

In the tradition of Mill Valley's avant garde, you can get completely relaxed at the **Center for Massage Therapy** at 125 Throckmorton. Get the kinks out from all that walking we've put you through with a 30-minute massage for $40 or an hour for $57. You can spend an hour in the hot tub and sauna for $12. ☎ *(415) 388-8770.* Don't miss **Capricorn** at 100 Throckmorton, where they have blended new gourmet kitchen stuff with a terrific collection of antiques. It works splendidly.

Beach, Lagoon and Mountain

The area to be covered today is essentially a big chunk of central Marin County that's not too far from San Francisco. The area includes a coastal drive that offers several beaches (including swimable Stinson Beach), a huge lagoon and 6,200-acre Mt. Tamalpais State Park with its three peaks that climb to over 2,500 feet.

After you cross the Golden Gate Bridge and turn off for Highway 1, you have entered a large portion of the huge Golden Gate National Recreation Area. It is about 70,000 acres that stretches from the Presidio in San Francisco all the way north to Olema near Point Reyes. We will only cover a small portion of that today.

GETTING THERE:

By car from Union Square, go up either Geary or Sutter to Van Ness. Turn right and go one mile to Lombard, then turn left. Approximately 11 blocks later, bear right onto Richardson, leading directly to the Golden Gate Bridge. On the other side of the bridge, go about 3.5 miles on Highway US-101 to the Mill Valley/Stinson Beach Exit on Highway 1. Follow signs to Stinson Beach.

PRACTICALITIES:

Even though it can be sunny when you start the day, along the coast in summertime the fog may roll in and cool things down considerably. So take along a sweater or light jacket. If you are inclined to go in the ocean, pack a swim suit and towel.

FOOD AND DRINK:

Mountain Home Inn (810 Panoramic Hwy.) High on the slopes of Mt. Tamalpais, you'll find sweeping bay views, good food and trailheads to redwoods, waterfalls and ocean vistas. Lunch & dinner daily. ☎ (415) 381-9000. $$

Pelican Inn (Hwy. 1 in Muir Beach) A well-done early English pub. Hearty English fare daily for breakfast, lunch and dinner. Ploughman's Lunch, Bangers & Mash and Cottage Pie. Rustic but comfortable rooms too from $170. ☎ (415) 383-6000 for reservations. $–$$

Stinson Beach Grill (3465 Shoreline Hwy.) They serve oysters grown just up the coast for the freshest anywhere. Grilled, Cajun, on the half shell. Other selections include Charcrusted Chutney Lamb. Lunch & dinner daily. ☎ (415) 868-2002. $–$$

Sand Dollar (3458 Shoreline Hwy.) Casual beach atmosphere with lots of good basic foods. Probably serves the best Boston Clam Chowder anywhere. Burgers, shakes and the like. Lunch and dinner daily. ☎ (415) 868-0434. $

SUGGESTED TOUR:

Numbers in parentheses correspond to numbers on the map.

When you turn off the freeway onto Highway 1, you will wiggle and wind you way through several miles of canyon leading to the ocean. Always in the distance is the sea, beckoning you to come closer.

You'll eventually get there after six miles. About five miles after leaving the freeway you will find the home to the **Zen Center** and **Green Gulch Organic Farm** on the left of the highway. They grow excellent organic veggies you can buy from the source. The buildings are very interesting. *The Center is open daily 9–4, but closed during the noon hour or when certain meditation programs are going on.*

Your next stop should be **Muir Beach** (1). This tidy little village is the first settlement along the coast north of San Francisco. It is a town of houses built on tiers that overlooks a rocky cove and the Pacific Ocean. Be sure to wander around the place. The beach itself isn't ideal for swimming, but great for walking. It sits at the mouth of Redwood Canyon where Redwood Creek from Muir Woods (see Daytrip 19) empties into the Pacific Ocean. Facilities include picnic tables and restrooms.

By all means stop by the **Pelican Inn** for a taste of Old England. They brought most of the building over from the Old Country. Great flower gardens.

At one time the area was a heavy producer of flowers, but water has become a problem. Now, heather is about the only crop left. Look carefully at the hills for this fragrant flowering plant.

As you travel along Highway 1, in another three miles is **Slide Ranch** (2) at 2025 Shoreline Highway. This a working ranch where kids can learn via hands-on experience such activities as milking a goat, spinning wool, gathering eggs and picking vegetables. The beautiful ocean setting offers kids the

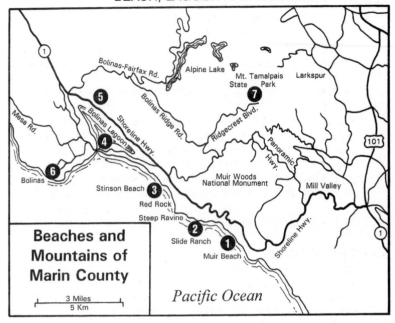

Beaches and Mountains of Marin County

3 Miles
5 Km

Pacific Ocean

opportunity to reach inside a tide pool or watch for whales in the winter months. Slide is a pioneer in the field of environmental education and teaches children teamwork, responsibility and respect for nature. Visitors can walk around and join in the programs. *Open weekends and holidays. Admission is by donation.* ☎ *(415) 381-6155 to pre-register or walk down to the office for further information.*

Highway 1 cruises along the coast above the ocean, and four miles beyond the ranch are signs to two other beaches—**Steep Ravine** and **Red Rock Beaches.** Neither are particularly suitable for swimming and aren't very large. Because of the steep cliffs on either side, Red Rocks is popular as a nude beach. They make you work because you have to park on the road and hike down a considerable distance.

If you can hold off until **Stinson Beach Park** (3), you will find a three-mile-long stretch of good sand. Stinson is the most popular swimming beach north of San Francisco primarily because it is pretty well protected from the fierce riptides along this coastline. There are lifeguards during the summer months. The beach park includes a terrific five-acre picnic area, restrooms and showers. *The park is open 9 a.m.–10 p.m. daily. No pets or fires on the beach.*

The village of Stinson Beach is weather-beaten homes and quaint shops and galleries. Be sure to visit **Stinson Beach Books**, one of the fun independent booksellers. It's crowded and in the corner is a wood-burning stove for those chilly winter days. Annie Rand has owned the store since 1976, and she'll search out good beach reads for you. ☎ *(415) 868-1922 for weather and surf information.*

If you want to make it into the waves, surfboard rentals are available at **Live Water Surf Shop** at 3450 Shoreline Highway. A surfboard is $25, boogie board $8 and a wetsuit $10—all per day. ☎ *(415) 868-0333.*

Periodically in the summertime, the fog can roll in along this stretch of the coast. Many visitors are curious as to why that happens during the warmer months since it would be more logical during the winter. Essentially, the water is quite cold below the surface just off the coast, but during the summer the warm California current comes along and forces the cold water upwards. That tends to turn the water cold and in the process relatively warm air passes over it causing condensation. That's when a fog bank occurs.

When you see the fog streaming in through the Golden Gate Bridge—or even along this coastline—in the summer that has a lot to do with warmer inland temperatures rising and pulling the fog inland. Don't despair, however, that the fog will ruin you daytrip because it usually burns off mid-morning.

When you leave the beach park, turn left. You can take a left on Seadrift Road, bringing you out onto the narrow peninsula that forms the lower portion of **Bolinas Lagoon** (4). If not, stay on the highway headed for the town of Bolinas. The lagoon is actually a large Nature Preserve managed by the county. Migratory waterfowl find this an ideal habitat. In the southern section of the lagoon is Pickleweed Island where you can watch the antics of the harbor seals that inhabit the place.

After 4.5 miles, you will come to **Audubon Canyon Ranch** (5). This 1,500-acre wildlife sanctuary is open on weekends and holidays 10–4 and serves as the trailhead for several interesting walks/hikes. There is a small Visitor Center with exhibits and a bookstore. A half-mile up on the Henderson Trail is a lookout with telescopes so you can observe the great blue heron and egrets nesting in the ravines. *Donations accepted.* ☎ *(415) 868-9244 for more information.*

Continue on the highway and turn left at Olema/Bolinas Road and left again on Horseshoe Hill Road. This will take you through a pastoral area to the village at the end of the point—isolated **Bolinas** (6). This is a low-key place where dogs sleep in the middle of the street. A left brings you to Duxbury Point. To the right is Agate Beach. The few citizens—many of whom are artists and writers—like it quiet and calm. Be sure to stop by **Smiley's Schooner Saloon and Hotel** at 41 Wharf Road. The oak backbar is a work of art. The simple rooms are furnished with beautiful black walnut armoires and headboards.

If you now retrace your route back along Highway 1, just past Stinson Beach is the **Panoramic Highway**. Take a left and be prepared for some dramatic scenery as you climb through a portion of the 6,200-acre **Mt. Tamal-pais State Park** (7). You climb quickly and the views are breathtaking back to the beach. Signs will direct you to the summit, but be aware that you turn left on Southside Road, which becomes the Pan Toll Road. In a recent *Wall Street Journal* story, they said, "only California's Mount Tamalpais can claim to be the best spot on Earth to shoot a car commercial." Name the auto brand and they've made a commercial or commercials for it here. The *Journal* story quotes Tom Saputo, a freelance creative director, "A religious experience . . . the perfect road . . .a driving fantasy." There you have it. If Hollywood and New York find this road nirvana, in all likelihood you will too.

There are actually three peaks: The West Peak is 2,560 feet, Middle Peak is 2,490, and the East Peak is the highest at 2,571 feet above sea level. We suggest going to the right to the East Peak. Near the summit is a Fee Area where there is a charge of $5 per car, seniors $4. Take a plank walk (made from old Gravity Train ties) up to the summit where the views are breathtaking of the city, East Bay and the mountains beyond.

It is believed that the mountain was named by the Miwok Indians who combined two of their words: "tamal" meaning coast and "pais" meaning mountain. Popular folklore speaks of the mountain's resemblance to a sleeping Indian maiden. Whatever the stories, it can be said with certainty that Mt. Tamalpais is Marin's most visible attraction.

If you can tear yourself away from the view, there are some wonderful hiking trails. About 200 miles of paths weave through the park and pass such sites as the **Old Railway Grade.** The sunny upper slopes of the mountain are covered with madrone, chaparral and oak trees. Without much effort, you can expect to see deer, bobcat, fox and raccoon. One of the thrills of Mt. Tam is watching the black hawks circle at eye level to prey on mice and field rodents. It is said these red-tailed hawks can see eight times better than humans, and thus they can spot a tiny mouse hidden in the weeds.

Camping is available at three sites in the park: Pan Toll near park headquarters, Frank Valley Horsecamp, and Steep Ravine Environmental Camp. ☎ *(415) 388-2070 for reservations and current rates.*

There is a Visitor Center staffed by volunteers with irregular hours. Snack shop too. The newest addition to Tamalpais is the rebuilt **Gravity Train Barn**. It is a faithful reproduction with interpretive displays and a working replica of the historical open-air cars that used gravity alone from the top of the mountain to the bottom. Along the way, the 30 train passengers wound past 281 curves at 12 miles per hour. The cost was $1.50.

To return to San Francisco, go back down and go left. Follow signs to Mill Valley.

*Point Reyes

The Point Reyes National Seashore was created in 1962 when President John F. Kennedy signed legislation to preserve the nation's dwindling undeveloped coastline for future generations. These 65,000 acres of spectacular wilderness include steep cliffs, a rocky coastline with thunderous surf and hidden beaches, calm moors, rich open meadows of wildflowers and windswept hillsides.

Point Reyes is actually a huge triangle that sticks out into the ocean. It is connected to the mainland by about 15 miles of land, but that attachment is tenuous since it runs right along the famed San Andreas Fault.

An interesting (and perhaps scary) fact is that during the 1906 earthquake in the area, the Point Reyes Peninsula heaved itself 20 feet north in one movement. You can see the evidence of Mother Nature's handiwork on a half-mile loop trail where fences got separated and buildings were flattened.

In fact, the peninsula is still moving north, albeit very slowly at about two inches a year. Scientists have traced its origin 300 miles south of where it is now.

The peninsula has been compared to the moors of Scotland. Quiet and misty, the awesome wildness is a symbol of California's undisturbed coastline. Often blanketed by fog while the inland valley remains warm, Point Reyes' advantageous location has enabled the natural occurrence of many distinct habitats. Over 45 percent of the North American bird species have been sighted here, and nearly 20 percent of California's flora is represented on the peninsula.

There is so much to do—beach walking, hiking, picnicking, horseback riding, camping and sightseeing—that you are guaranteed to have a very full daytrip.

GETTING THERE:

By car from Union Square, go up either Geary or Sutter to Van Ness. Turn right and go one mile to Lombard and turn left. Approximately 11 blocks later, bear right onto Richardson, leading directly to the Golden Gate Bridge.

Continue on Highway US-101 approximately 8.5 miles. Look for the Sir Frances Drake Boulevard turnoff. Go another 21 miles to Olema and follow signs for the Visitor Center.

PRACTICALITIES:

Because Point Reyes sticks out into the ocean, it can be breezy and cool, especially in the summertime. Take a sweater or light jacket. There are lots of good trails, so comfortable shoes are recommended. Consider taking along a lunch to enjoy at one of the many picnic spots, since there are not a lot of restaurants in the area.

FOOD AND DRINK:

Olema Farm House (10005 State Hwy. 1) This warm spot is in the first house built in Olema in 1845. Beer batter fish and chips and local seafoods are specialities. Try the homemade oyster stew. Lunch and dinner daily. ☎ (415) 663-1264. $–$$

Barnaby's (12938 Sir Francis Drake Blvd. in Inverness) Wonderful spot right on Tomales Bay. BBQ and garlic oysters from the farm down the road. Mussels in season. Specialty is the chicken apple sausage they make. Also great homemade desserts. ☎ (415) 669-1114. $–$$

Perry's Delicatessen (12301 Sir Francis Drake Blvd. in Inverness Park) Good deli with all the fixings for a fun picnic. BBQ chicken, burritos, calzones. Breakfast, lunch and dinner daily. ☎ (415) 663-1491. $

The Gray Whale (12781 Sir Francis Drake Blvd. in Inverness) Best vegetarian pizza in three counties. Also pastas, salads and sandwiches. Lunch and dinner daily. ☎ (415) 669-1244. $

SUGGESTED TOUR:

Numbers in parentheses correspond to numbers on the map.

*POINT REYES NATIONAL SEASHORE, Point Reyes, CA 94946, ☎ (415) 663-1092. *Main Visitor Center open weekdays 9–5, weekends and holidays 8–5. No admission fee. The water is potable, but always check with the NPS. Fire permits are needed all year. No firearms and no pets. Partly &.*

A good place to start is the handsome **Bear Valley Visitor Center** (1), located on Bear Valley Road off Highway 1 near Olema. Here you will find comprehensive exhibits on the plants, animals and people of the area. These displays give an excellent overview of the natural and cultural history of the Point Reyes National Seashore. There is also a seismograph so you can check on the earth's movement. Point Reyes is laced with 140 miles of trails for hiking and biking, and good maps are available. *Make reservations for* backpack camping, ☎ (415) 663-8054. The National Park Service stresses these are not drive-in campsites.

Just outside the Center is the fascinating **Earthquake Trail.** It is a half-mile loop that for a portion takes you along the San Andreas Fault. You can see where a farm fence got separated by 20 feet when the 1906 earthquake hit the area. The trail also offers interesting interpretive displays about these powerful earth movements. Another short path will lead you to **Kule Loklo,** a replica settlement of the Coast Miwok Indians. You may remember from other daytrips that the Miwoks were among Marin County's first inhabitants. Parts of Miwok life have been re-created in the village with tepee-like bark houses and an underground ceremonial house.

Located behind the Visitor Center is the **Morgan Horse Ranch.** This working ranch trains horses for the National Park Rangers. Self-guided exhibits, corrals and demonstrations are a part of the ranch's ongoing interpretive program. ☎ (415) 663-1763 for more information.

Farther along on Bear Valley Road you will see a lefthand turnoff for Limantour Road. This eight-mile drive will give you a real taste of Point Reyes. For a while you travel through dense forest of Douglas fir and then suddenly you are in the open. Part of the openness is evident from a recent forest fire that denuded hundreds of acres. That's why fires are not allowed, except on certain beaches and with a permit. Periodically you will see trailheads. The Coastal and Muddy Hollow Trails are for hiking and biking, while such trails as Laguna and Bayview are just for hiking.

At the end is the real treat. **Limatour Beach** (2) is a popular recreational area for strolling and picnicking. If you turn right and walk along the beach, it will take you to **Drakes Bay** (3) with the staggering white cliffs behind it, which have been compared to the White Cliffs of Dover. The beach has no lifeguard and swimming is not recommended. There are facilities.

When you come back up Limatour, at Bear Valley Road turn left, taking you back to Sir Francis Drake Boulevard. As you drive along this road, keep in mind you are atop the San Andreas Fault. Your next stop should be **Inverness** (4) on the western shore of **Tomales Bay** (5). Inverness was named after a city in Scotland because many believe it has the same feel as the moors and coastline of that country. In the late 1800s, Inverness was a heavily forested town with a flourishing summer resort. The quaint town has a market with fresh local fish, a small store called Bellwether, a Post Office and some remaining piers.

As the road bends left toward the end of the peninsula, you will see Mount Vision Road on the left. Driving up this winding road will take you to 1,300-foot **Mount Vision** (6) for some spectacular views of the peninsula. At the end is the trailhead for a multi-use Inverness Ridge Trail.

As you travel toward the lighthouse, you will pass thousands of acres of windswept open pasture. Dairy cows have been grazing on these rolling

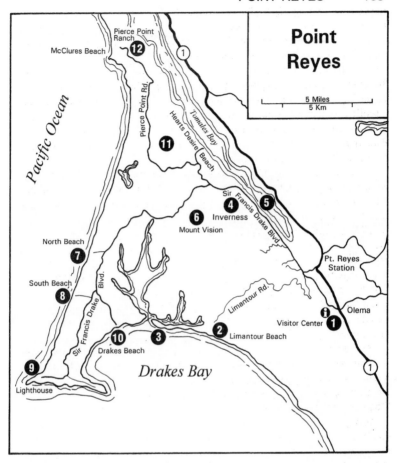

hills for 150 years. There are periodic signs indicating historic ranches, most of which date back to the mid- to late-1800s.

A few miles farther on you will see a turnoff on the right for **Point Reyes Beach North** (7), and a few miles beyond that **Point Reyes Beach South** (8). These beaches are part of an almost 30-mile-long, wide white strand that's perfect for walking or jogging. Facilities. Heed the warnings against going in the water which read: "DANGEROUS SURF. Surfing, wading and swimming not advised. Shark area, strong undertow, currents and sneaker waves. Enter at your own risk." Got it?

At the very western end of the peninsula is the **Point Reyes Lighthouse** (9), almost 300 feet above the rolling ocean below. Built in 1870, the lighthouse is a half-mile from the parking lot and down 300 steep steps. On a platform near the lighthouse is one of the best areas to view gray whales, who migrate along this coast going south from December through February and north March through May. These gentle giants travel singly or in pods of three. Two things make the whale viewing excellent at this spot: you are very high up; and these whales travel at almost a walking pace of 4–5 miles an hour—so there's lots of time to see them in action.

The tiny Lighthouse Visitors Center has exhibits on whale migration and lighthouse operation. It and the lighthouse are open Thursdays to Mondays 10–5. The stairs to the lighthouse have the same hours, but they are closed when the wind exceeds 40 miles per hour. Speaking of weather, be prepared for fog and wind. It is said this is the windiest place on the West Coast and one of the foggiest in the United States. ☎ *(415) 669-1534 for more information.*

As you head back north on Sir Francis Drake Boulevard, look for the turnoff on the right for **Drakes Beach** and the **Kenneth C. Patrick Visitor Center** (10). The beach is one of the best in Northern California. As a matter of fact, *Sunset Magazine* has rated Drakes among the top ten in California, calling it the "Most Historic Beach." The cliffs may intrigue you, but do not walk along the top or bottom since they crumble easily. Enjoy the sand and the water, although swimming can be dangerous.

Historians have long debated exactly where the English explorer Drake landed in 1579, but locals claim it was Drakes Bay, defined by the lighthouse point and Arch Rock about 15 miles across the water. Drake, as you may remember from your school days' history, was quite the explorer and privateer—which means he was a pirate. His lone ship ran into trouble near this area and luckily he was able to come into the bay to fix the bottom. He stayed several weeks and mingled with the Miwok Indians.

The Visitor Center provides exhibits detailing the 16th-century maritime exploration and the indigenous marine environment. A large salt-water aquarium contains plants and animal life from Drakes Bay. *Because it is staffed by volunteers, the Center is usually open Sat. to Wed. from 10–5. Free, but you can make donations. Snack bar open the same hours as the Center.* ☎ *(415) 669-1250 for more information.*

On the way back, if you like oysters, look for a road to the right just past Schooner Bay. This is one of four finger bays that lead from Drakes Estero, a protected body of water teeming with shellfish. **Johnson's Drakes Bay Oysters** has been around since 1957. Charlie Johnson learned from the Japanese how to farm oysters by hanging them from a platform, where they feed on the plankton-rich waters of Drakes Bay. Today they ship about half a million oysters a month. You can buy a jar right here. ☎ *(415) 669-1149.*

About three miles farther on the left is Pierce Point Road, which leads to the northernmost point of the peninsula. On the right you will skirt **Tomales Bay State Park** (11). If you take the route to **Heart's Desire Beach**, you will find a usually warm and sunny place (compared with the chilly fog of the peninsula) since it opens on Tomales Bay.

Pierce Point Road leads through some of the peninsula's richest pasture land, where cattle and sheep were raised for generations. Look for the **Historic Pierce Point Ranch** (12). Established in 1858, this is one of the oldest dairy ranches on the peninsula. Now under National Park Service management, the ranch is dedicated to the preservation of the park's cultural heritage. A self-guided trail provides information about the ranch's historic structures. *Free.*

Near the ranch is a trail leading to **McClures Beach**, a nifty pocket beach. No swimming. Pierce Point Road also leads to the **Tule Elk Reserve** and the **Tomales Point Trail**, which leads to the very north end of the peninsula.

If horseback riding is your thing, head back to Olema and follow Highway 1 south about five miles to **Five Brooks Ranch**. The "Stewart Trail Ride" is a relaxing, slow-paced ride through pastures and along the crest of a small ridge to a shady, wooded trail. There are five departures a day for this one-hour ride, which costs $30. They have myriad other rides. ☎ *(415) 663-1570.*

A great way to enjoy calm Tomales Bay is to take a trip with **Blue Waters Kayaking.** Their best-known offering is the "Morning Paddles" from 10-1. This is a naturalist-led tour that includes introductory kayak lessons for a fun adventure of paddling and nature watching. Adults cost $49 and kids under 13, $24.50. They also offer day-long trips, twilight and full-moon tours as well as overnighters. Generally, these tours run on specific weekends from April through October. ☎ *(415) 669-2600.*

Trip 22
Marin and Sonoma Counties

Central Marin

Roughly strung east and west along Sir Francis Drake Boulevard are five little towns that taken together make an interesting daytrip simply because they get you away from the usual. Today, most are mainly bedroom communities, although they each got started due primarily to the railroad that used to run through Marin.

Marin County is heavily wooded and if you were to rip through these communities at a fast pace you might miss several interesting places to visit. Tucked among the hills and valleys are some stupendous homes of today's tycoons who make their way to the city each workday for banking, oil, high tech, the law and myriad other ways to make a living.

One community has set itself up as the antique capital of Northern California. They boast 130 antique dealers along with good restaurants and specialty shops, and all the other support needed for such an endeavor.

At the last stop, we will explore the origins of mountain biking and tell you how to enjoy the numerous trails in the area.

If none of this sparks your interest, consider this an eating daytrip since some of the most enjoyable restaurants in Northern California can be found along this route.

GETTING THERE:

By car from Union Square, go up either Geary or Sutter to Van Ness. Turn right and go about one mile to Lombard, then turn left. Approximately 11 blocks later, bear right onto Richardson, which will lead you directly to the Golden Gate Bridge. On the other side of the bridge, go ten miles and take the Paradise Drive/Tamalpais off-ramp.

PRACTICALITIES:

If you plan to go "antiquing," bring money and a charge card. Otherwise, just plan to be entertained by several small towns in Northern California. It's always a good idea to bring along only what you can take out of the car with you when you stop to explore or for food.

FOOD AND DRINK:

The Lark Creek Inn (234 Magnolia in Larkspur) Located in an old Victorian home, the chef serves up award-winning American fare in a true country atmosphere. Lunch Mon.–Fri., dinner daily. ☎ (415) 924-7766. $$

Left Bank (567 Magnolia in Larkspur) French, French and more French. Les Croques (sandwiches) include grilled eggplant with roasted peppers. Terrific appetizers (Pour Commencer) and dinner entrees. Lunch and dinner daily. ☎ (415) 258-3807. $$

Il Fornaio (223 Town Center, Corte Madera) Very tempting array of Italian dishes served up in a terrific atmosphere. Pasta and pizza are only the beginning. Breakfast, lunch and dinner daily. ☎ (415) 927-4400. $–$$

Woodlands Garden (30 Sir Francis Drake Blvd. in Ross) Lovely setting in the Marin Garden Center. Seared Ahi Nicoise Salad is a treat or try the Grilled Vegetable Stack. Breakfast & lunch daily. Afternoon tea. ☎ (415) 456-9527. $–$$

Isalata's (120 Sir Francis Drake Blvd. in San Anselmo) Large restaurant that can feel intimate. Fennel Crusted Pan Seared Halibut on a Green Lentil and Spinach Saute. Delicious. Lunch & dinner daily. ☎ (415) 457-7700. $–$$

Fradelizio's (35 Broadway in Fairfax) Wide selection of pasta dishes that are reasonably priced. Famous for lasagne and ravioli. Lunch and dinner daily. ☎ (415) 459-1618. $

SUGGESTED TOUR:

Numbers in parentheses correspond to numbers on the map.

When you turn off the freeway, go right on Paradise Drive. Because **Corte Madera** (1) touches the bay and reaches into the nearby hills, there are several interesting wildlife preserves well worth exploring. Go along Paradise Drive for a mile and a quarter. On the right will be **Ring Mountain Preserve** (2), established by the Nature Conservancy in 1984 to create open space in what has become a heavily developed area. Miles of paths for walking and hiking lace the many acres area of wildflowers, pastures and hills.

Heading back on Paradise, turn left and look for signs for the **Corte Madera Marsh State Ecological Preserve** (3). This preserve stretches 210 acres along the bayfront and is home to dozens of birds like sandpipers, grebes and egrets. Unlike Ring Mountain, the paths that wind through the preserve are all level.

When you cross over the freeway you are headed for Corte Madera itself. As you approach the village, the road will dogleg left, which means you are crossing the old railroad tracks that ran all the way to Tiburon. But remember the hill for the preserve at the beginning of this daytrip? It is too high for trains to go over, so tucked at the back of the east side of

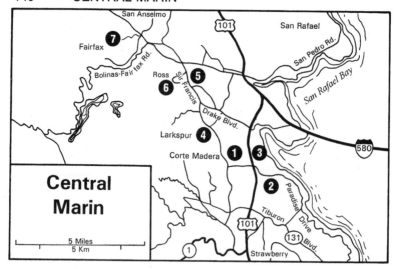

Corte Madera is an abandoned railroad tunnel, the only one in all of Marin County.

Continue on the same road, which soon leads you to **Larkspur** (4). If you turn left on Madrone, Dolliver Park is right on the corner. It is a small park of redwoods. What makes this area so unusual is that the big redwood trees are growing right out in the street.

If you grew up in a small town, Larkspur will take you back to your childhood. The main street is called Magnolia Avenue and is listed on the National Register of Historic Places. It has been called "typical of a small California town at the turn of the century."

Continue on Magnolia, which becomes College. College runs into Sir Francis Drake Boulevard. Turn left and after about one mile on the right is the nifty **Marin Art and Garden Center** (5). Originally it was part of the 10,000 acres assembled by James Ross, a shrewd Scotsman who was a director of the Northwestern Pacific Railroad. He wanted his railroad to stop at this spot and that's how the town of Ross came about. Ross was also a horticulturist and had planted many trees and flowers on the property. When his daughter married, he gave her the ten acres on which the Center now sits. Through changes of ownership, the property was nearly lost to developers.

It was saved through the Herculean efforts of Mrs. Norman B. Livermore. Today it is a unique community cooperative organization operated as a not-for-profit for the benefit of Marin County residents. Two of the original buildings are still used for Center activities. The **Octagon House** holds a terrific collection of books on art and gardens and is open to the public Tuesdays through Fridays, 11:30–3. **The Barn** is now used by the Ross Valley Players, a highly successful amateur theater group. They are the oldest continuously operating Community Theater in the nation. ☎ *(415) 456-9555 to find out about performances.* Also on the property is **Laurel House**, offering prime pre-owned goods. *Open Mon.–Sat. 11–3.* ☎ *(415) 454-8472.*

We can't forget the gardens. Towering oaks and a profusion of flowering plants mark the efforts of the garden aficionados. Among birch, laurel, holly and rhododendron are secluded dells with benches for rest. At the center of the property is the magnolia grandiflora that was originally planted by Ross' son-in-law. It started small, but grew so huge that it is an all-time favorite of photographers and painters. *Free. Open daily 10–5.*

As you leave the Garden Center, turn right and in a short distance you will approach San Anselmo. Look for Bolinas Avenue and turn left. This is church territory. In the next block on the left is one of the most distinctive churches anywhere in California. **St. Anselm Catholic Church** is the prime example of the Woodland/English style of architecture. It has dark brown wood cross pieces against cream colored plaster walls with red brick towers and walls. All that looks a bit English. But the redwood doors and walls are clearly California, to say nothing of the setting in a stand of redwoods. Beautiful stained-glass windows top off the pleasing look of this church.

Two blocks later on the right is the **Montgomery Chapel and Montague Hall**, part of the seminary on the hill above that we will visit. This church is all grey cut stone, but what makes it unusual is that several sections of it are all round. It is very foreboding and is used as a Co-preaching and Worship Center for the seminary.

Look for signs to the **San Francisco Theological Seminary** (6) and keep turning right. This will lead you up a small, steep hill to the imposing main buildings of the seminary. Built in 1892, the Victorian Geneva Hall is the main "castle" of this Presbyterian graduate school. Two heavy stone castles just below house the library and study area. The campus sits on 21 prime forested acres, and tours can be arranged by calling (415) 258-6500.

Turn left when you come back to Sir Francis Drake Boulevard. Straight ahead is antique and collectible nirvana. San Anselmo bills itself as Northern California's Antique Capital with over 130 dealers. That doesn't necessarily mean that many storefronts. For example **Creekside Antiques** is a large building with multiple spaces for 16 individual dealers. Nevertheless, you will find early American and Continental furniture, quilts, folk art, pottery, American Indian artifacts, antique toys, dolls, silver, china and rare books— just to name a few of the treasures that await you. *Creekside is at 241 Sir Francis Drake and is open Mon.–Sat. 10–5 and Sun. 12–5.* ☎ *(415) 457-1266.*

The greatest concentration of storefronts is along Sir Francis Drake, but don't overlook those on San Anselmo Avenue either. As they say of antiques and collectibles, the beauty is that, like fingerprints, no two are the same.

Another trait of San Anselmo is the many bookstores. Be sure to visit **Pa-**

per Ships Books & Crystals. This tiny spot at 630 San Anselmo Avenue is essentially a New Age store with books, gemstones and crystals. Native American goods too. The owners say a space ship hovers above the store. Hold on then, for the Millennium.

Get back on Sir Francis Drake and turn left to go to **Fairfax** (7). This is a different town than the others we have visited today. It is more down to earth. We bring you here because this is where the "soul" of mountain biking resides. There's no monument, museum or even a plaque, but believe us when we say that the two-wheeled machine with the wide tires, sturdy frame, flat handlebars and lots of gears was born in Fairfax.

It happens that a bunch of bike racers used to hang out in Fairfax. Names like Gary Fisher, Tom Ritchey, Joe Breeze and Otis Guy—all icons in the mountain biking firmament. According to legend, in the late 1970s, Fisher and Ritchey rode an old one-speed cruiser down some of the trails on Mt. Tamalpais. Not satisfied with this clunky old machine, they added gears and knobby tires. This worked much better. Then came lighter frames and bent handle bars. And soon they were racing down—and up—the tortuous trails of Tamalpais. And thus an industry was born. Last year, about three million mountain bikes were sold in the United States, some with the names of Fisher, Ritchey and Breezer.

If you would like to tackle some of these trails yourself, stop in at **Sunshine Bicycle Center** at 735 Center Boulevard in Fairfax where you can rent the latest in mountain bikes—not far from where the boys put together the very first one. Sunshine will rent you a mountain bike with front suspension for $7 an hour or $29 for the day. The latest full-suspension bike (front and rear) goes for $10 an hour or $35 for the day. Get on those trails (the store has maps) and have fun. ☎ *(415) 459-3334.*

Mostly Inland Marin

Marin County is so rich in its geographic diversity that it becomes necessary to separate it into sections. What we intend to do on this exciting daytrip is stay mostly in the interior with a side trip out to the bay.

We will explore San Rafael, Marin's county seat, and venture up to historical Novato. Both the cities mentioned are fascinating, but we will also shoot out to the bay side of Marin for a quick look at China Camp on San Pablo Bay. The camp offers great recreational opportunities and is a interesting piece of the Bay Area's history.

It is hard not to be overawed by the physical beauty of Marin, but we will also take a look at some important buildings and activities around the county.

GETTING THERE:

By car from Union Square, go up either Geary or Sutter to Van Ness. Turn right and go about one mile to Lombard, then turn left. Approximately 11 blocks later, bear right onto Richardson, leading directly to the Golden Gate Bridge. Continue on Highway US-101 approximately 8.5 miles and look for the Central San Rafael exit.

PRACTICALITIES:

Sturdy shoes are called for in this mostly urban area. It can be sunny and warm in the interior, so sunscreen and a hat are good ideas, too.

FOOD AND DRINK:

Panama Hotel (4 Bayview St., San Rafael) Located in a wonderful old hotel with a room called the "Bordello," the food is an eclectic mix of Mexican, Italian and Asian influences with lots of fresh seafood and pasta. Lunch and dinner daily. ☎ (415) 479-1623. $$

Guido's (1613 Fourth St. San Rafael) San Francisco North Beach style restaurant, named critics choice for best gnocchi's. Fresh seafood, chicken, veal and pasta. Vegetarian available. Lunch and dinner daily. ☎ (415) 453-7877 for reservations. $$

BongKot Thai Express (857 Fourth St. San Rafael) A wide range of superior Thai meals of varying hotness. A real treat are the hand-painted murals on the walls depicting the beauty of Thailand. Lunch and dinner daily. ☎ (415) 453-3350 for reservations. $–$$

Lundy's Home Cooking (1143 4th St. in San Rafael) Small local hangout. The Irish breakfast includes bacon and sausage, potatoes, eggs, toast, grilled tomato and savory pudding. Lunch & dinner Mon.–Sat. ☎ (415) 456-7669. $

SUGGESTED TOUR:

Numbers in parentheses correspond to numbers on the map.

After you exit the freeway, look for Mission Avenue and turn left. The first example of Queen Anne style architecture is at **825 Mission.** Since this home was built in 1881 before the Queen Anne style got to California, there is speculation that it was heavily remodeled along the way. At 828 Mission is an imposing structure built in 1884 called the Slick Eastland house, the home of the city's first mayor. Note the fancy stickwork brackets in the gables. It now houses law offices.

Up the street at **1130 Mission** is the Coleman House, built between 1849 and 1852 and considered to be the oldest building in San Rafael. It represents the Gothic Revival style of architecture. At **1135 Mission** is an 1891 mansion known as the DeCourtieux House, an example of early zoning. It was built with the stipulation that "no barns, stables, grocery or bar be built on the site."

Practically staring you straight in the face as you go along Mission is the **Marin County Historical Society** (1) at 1125 B St. This comprehensive museum of the area's local history commemorates the life and travel of Louise Boyd, an Arctic explorer and the first woman to fly over the North Pole. Miwok artifacts and records and photos dating back to 1860 are on display. The building, a Victorian Gothic that once belonged to the Boyd family, is listed on the National Register of Historic Places. *Open Thurs.–Sat. 1–4. Free. ☎ (415) 454-8538.*

One of the handsomest historical mansions in the town center is **Falkirk Cultural Center** (2) at 1408 Mission. Built in 1888, this fine 17-room Queen Anne mansion is situated on an 11-acre hillside estate that was put on the National Register in 1972. Falkirk is home to visual, literal and performing arts programs. Self-guided and docent tours of the house and garden are available. *Open Thurs.–Fri. 10–5. $2 donation. ☎ (415) 485-3328 for current schedules.*

At E Street, turn left and then left on Fifth Avenue. At 1104, you will find the **Mission San Rafael Arcangel** (3), built in 1817. This modest building, of Spanish Revival architecture, is actually a replica of the second-to-last in the California mission chain. The original was torn down in 1861. Based on the research and findings of the Marin Historical Society and with funds from

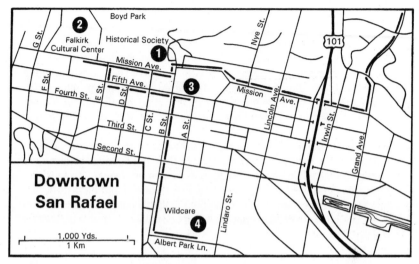

Downtown
San Rafael

1,000 Yds.
1 Km

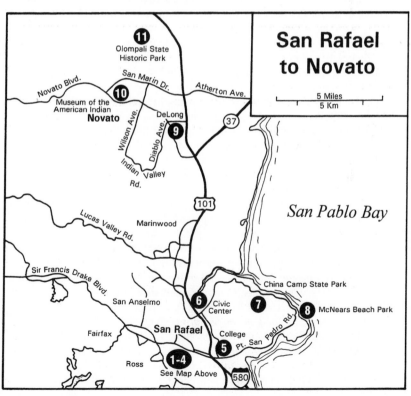

San Rafael
to Novato

5 Miles
5 Km

the Hearst Foundation, the chapel was rebuilt in 1949. *Gift shop with arti-facts. Open 10–4 daily. Free.* ☎ *(415) 454-8141.*

Follow B Street down about five blocks to 76 Albert Park Lane and turn left. It's another of the Bay Area's wondrous wild animal hospitals. This one is called **Wildcare** (4). Orphaned raccoons, injured barn owls and ailing squirrels—no matter the species—are nursed to health and returned to woodland and seashore homes. The Center has an indoor clinic and more than 20 outdoor cages for all types of animals. ☎ *(415) 453-1000 to find out about tours and walks.*

Go back to Mission Avenue and follow the signs to Grand Avenue, then turn left. More signs lead to **Dominican College** (5). Founded in 1890, the college is located on 80 wooded acres in the center of town. The four-year liberal arts institution is home to many architecturally and historically significant buildings. Campus tours can be arranged by appointment. Pick up a self-guided tour brochure from the Admissions Office in Bertrand. ☎ *(415) 457-4440.*

Get back on Grand, which becomes Villa and then on Highway US-101 North, exiting right away on North San Pedro Road East. On your left is the stunning **Marin County Civic Center** (6), designed by Frank Lloyd Wright. They say it is the last and one of the most important of his works. When he died at 92, his staff had to complete the building, so he never got to see his vision completed of a building that, ". . . makes the landscape more beautiful than it was before the building was built."

The building not only houses county administrative functions, but also includes the main branch of the county's library and the Anne T. Kent History Room. There is a separate performing arts and convention center building. Wright saw the Center's 14-acre lagoon as the focal point of the site. *Tours of the Center are held at 10:30 on Wednesdays, meeting at the Civic Center Gift Shop. To find out about performances, call (415) 472-3500.*

Next go left on North San Pedro Road, which will take you to **China Camp State Park** (7). You will wind along a country road that takes you between the round gold hills of Marin and through the marshes of the park. Once a Chinese settlement of fishermen and shrimpers, this 1,648-acre park on San Pablo Bay is now a popular spot for camping, fishing, hiking, picnicking, bird watching and a variety of water sports. A small Visitor Center, housed in the original shrimp processing plant, depicts the life of the 19th-century Chinese settlers. Several of the weather-beaten old buildings still stand along with the pier. *Camping reservations may be made by calling (800) 444-7275. Cost is $15. There is no parking along the roadway, but you do pay $2 to park at Fee Stations with facilities. Open 8 to sunset.*

As the road winds around the shoreline, look on the left for **McNears Beach Park** (8). This is one of the nicer sand beaches on the bay, although the water quality is sometimes questionable. Facilities.

Continue on the same road and turn right at Biscayne Drive for the **Pea-**

cock Gap Golf and Country Club, a splendid course that plays between the hills. *18 holes will cost you $29 Mon.–Thur., $33 on Fri. and $37 on weekends.* Well worth a round if you are a golf enthusiast.

Get back on Highway US-101 and head north for **Novato**, where you will take the DeLong/Downtown exit. Follow signs to downtown, nearly running into **Dr. Insomniac's Coffee and Tea** at 800 Grant. Besides caffeine products and other goodies, the Doctor's longish slogan is, "Drink more coffee . . . you sleep enough when you're dead." Fun place.

Go back to DeLong to the **Novato History Museum** (9) at 815 DeLong Avenue, located in the 1850 home of the Novato's first Postmaster. The displays include historical photos, records, maps, antiques, costumes and memorabilia from Hamilton Air Force base that was once the mainstay of Novato employment before it closed in 1975. *Open Wed., Thurs. and Sat., noon to 4. Donations.* ☎ *(415) 897-4320 for more information.*

If you head west on DeLong and then right on Novato Boulevard, it will take you to the **Marin Museum of the American Indian** (10) at 2200 Novato. The museum is in the 35-acre Miwok Park that offers interesting hiking trails and good picnic areas. The museum gallery primarily houses exhibits of the Coast Miwok and Pomo Indian cultures. *Hours are Tues.–Fri. 10–3, and Sat. and Sun noon to 4. Donation. Gift shop.* ☎ *(415) 897-4064.*

Turn right on Novato Boulevard and enjoy a ride through the beautiful Marin countryside. This area is typically Marin with rounded golden hills accented with deep green oaks. On level ground are one after another of Marin's famous dairy farms.

When you come to Point Reyes Road, turn left and travel one-quarter mile south of the intersection for a good example of how some of those dairy products are used. Here you will find the famed **Marin French Cheese Company.** Cheese aficionados flock here for soft ripening cheeses such as camembert, brie, breakfast and schloss. The store has all the fixings—including wines from the area—for a terrific picnic at the lake next door to the cheese plant. *Tours are daily from 10–4 on the hour. They generously provide samples at the end of the tour, which is a real treat. Their brand is called Rouge et Noir which you may have seen in your local supermarket since their cheeses are distributed all over the west.* ☎ *(800) 292-6001 for more information.*

Head north on Point Reyes Boulevard and again enjoy the stunning countryside. After about five miles, look for San Antonio Road and turn right. This will take you to Highway US-101 South. Shortly thereafter is **Olompali State Historic Park** (11), a 700-acre park created in 1990 to commemorate the fact that the area has been touched by almost every event of California history. The largest Miwok village was located here, although only the adobe of the last Headman of the Miwok people survives. There are hiking trails throughout the park, reaching to the eastern slope of Mt. Burdell. *Open 8– sunset.*

Trip 24
Marin and Sonoma Counties

Napa and Calistoga

Many have speculated about why the Napa Valley is so popular. There are lots of other fine wine-growing districts throughout California, but this 35-mile-long valley seems to have had the best public relations agent of them all.

It is estimated that more than 2 million revelers stream into the valley every year—and it keeps on growing. Weekends can see traffic jams. There is even a movement afoot to limit new wineries, but that effort probably has little chance of success.

Napa's cachet comes from many sources. It is truly a beautiful spot. The valley's rich soil supports miles of fulsome crops be they grapes, apples, wheat or other agricultural products. The valley is basically a straight line that shoots north between two wooded mountain ranges, thus giving it a clear definition. The wine is excellent. Just ask the French and other European wine growers how good Napa wines are. The answer comes from the fact that many of the valley's larger wineries have all or partial foreign owners.

Wine has been produced in the Napa Valley since the 1700s. Production grew steadily for many years and then nearly collapsed during Prohibition. It took about 30 years to make its comeback, but its real resurgence started in the early 1970s.

Say Napa Valley and most people will immediately think wine. But there's plenty to do—from the beginning in Napa Town, north to Calistoga. We'll explore these many activities during this daytrip. The good thing about the Napa Valley is that it delivers on all the wonderful things you've read about it.

GETTING THERE AND AROUND:

By car from Union Square, go up either Geary or Sutter to Van Ness. Turn right and go one mile to Lombard, then turn left. Approximately 11 blocks later, bear right onto Richardson, which will lead you directly to the Golden Gate Bridge. Continue on Highway US-101 approximately 18 miles and look for the Route 37 exit to Vallejo. Turn left on Route 29 and then right on Route 121 that will take you into Napa Town.

By car and train: You can drive to Napa and take the **Napa Valley Wine Train** with restored vintage Pullman cars that wanders through the scenic valley for 35 miles. Meals and beverages are served, and wine tastings featured. *There are three-hour excursions at lunch, dinner and Sunday brunch. Cost is $57–72.* ☎ *(707) 253-2160 or (800) 427-4124 for reservations. 1275 McKinstry St. in Napa.*

By ferry and limo. You can leave from the Ferry Building in San Francisco for a cruise to Vallejo. Twelve departures Mondays through Fridays, and five on weekends. You will be met by a limo and tour guide/driver for an eight-hour excursion through the valley by **California Wine Tours.** *$69 per person.* ☎ *(800) 294-6386. Five-hour limo tour without ferry is $39.* **Antique Tours** will take you around the valley in a convertible Packard for $60 an hour weekdays and $80 an hour on weekends. ☎ *(707) 226-9227.*

By balloon, bicycle, horse, glider, jeep and goat: see below.

PRACTICALITIES:

Taste as many wines as you want, but remember most of you will be driving. There are three ways around this: Taste the wines and then expectorate them; limit your tasting to—at the most—two or three wineries and do lots of other activities offered in Napa Valley; or take the train or ferry and limo.

Napa can be warm in during the summer months, so dress accordingly.

FOOD AND DRINK:

French Laundry (6640 Washington St., Yountville) This has the taste of France both in the food, atmosphere and service. Extensive wine list as expected. Lunch and dinner daily. Very popular, so call for reservations. ☎ (707) 944-2380. $$$+

Mustard's (7399 Hwy. 29 on Yountville Cross) They serve up what's called American/California cuisine, which means such morsels as mesquite-grilled entrees along with excellent soups and salads. Lunch and dinner daily. For reservations ☎ (707) 944-2424. $$–$$$

Wine Spectator Greystone Restaurant (2555 Main St. in St. Helena) This spectacular spot is in the Culinary Institute of America where food and wine are paramount. The massive 108-year-old Christian Brothers winery has been turned into a unique training center and restaurant that serves hot tapas and cuisines from Moroccan to Middle Eastern. ☎ (707) 967-1010. $$+

Calistoga Inn (1250 Lincoln Ave. in Calistoga) Quaint inn with its own brewery, the restaurant serves a wide variety of appetizers. Hearty sandwiches and grill plates round out the menu. Lunch and dinner daily. ☎ (707) 942-4101. $$

Dean & Deluca Market Café (607 S. Main St., St. Helena) They re-create the sights, smells and sounds of a European marketplace. Us-ing fresh, local produce and the finest meats and poultry, you can eat in or have them prepare a gourmet picnic. ☎ (707)967-9980. $–$$

SUGGESTED TOUR:

Numbers in parentheses correspond to numbers on the map.

During this daytrip, you can focus on the wines, or you can enjoy a smat-tering of tastings and enjoy the cornucopia of other attractions the valley has to offer.

A good place to start is a short walking tour of **Napa Town** (1). Take the Downtown/Second Street exit to Napa and go all the way to Main Street, then turn left. Years ago this was a busy river town with an industrial feel to it. In recent years, many of the handsome old buildings have been re-stored.

If you start on the south end of Main Street, the first thing you will come to is a grassy area called **Veterans Memorial Park.** In the block south of here is **Fagiani's Bar** at 813 Main, built in 1908. Next going north is the bank block with "The Bank That Looks Like a Bank," the **Napa Valley Bank,** at 901 Main. At 903 Main is the **First National Bank**, built in 1923. On the right is **Downtown Joe's** with a fancy ceramic front in a building that was the Oberon, built in 1934. At 948 Main is the **Winship/Smeres Building** of 1888. A favorite town gathering spot is the **Napa Valley Roasting Co.** on the right. Go there for a cup of cappucino and the town gossip. At Main and Pearl streets is the now-restored **Napa Valley Opera House.** There are no productions; it is used as a community center.

Napa has two museums of interest. The **Napa County Historical Soci-ety Museum** is located at 1219 First Street in the historic Goodman Library building. Exhibits include historical displays of pioneer tools, photos and Native American crafts. *Donations. Open Tues. and Thurs., 12–4.* ☎ *(707) 224-1739.* Another interesting museum is at 1201 Main. The **Napa Fire-fighter's Museum** collects and preserves fire-related memorabilia including four horse-drawn hose carts. *Open Wed.–Sun., 11–4. Donations.* ☎ *(707) 259-0609.*

As you head up Main Street look for the **Andrews Meat Co. and Deli** at Main and Clinton. This historic spot was once the town's leading brothel.

Before leaving the town of Napa, we must acquaint you with a popular way to see the entire valley—from the air. At 133 Wall Road in Napa is the **Bonaventura Balloon Company.** It is the premiere outfit providing balloon flights over the picturesque vineyards and wineries of the Napa valley. They have a variety of aerial and overland options, but the most popular is the three-hour adventure aloft below a huge, colorful balloon. You can custom design your flight to include a breakfast at lovely Meadowood and/or a picnic lunch in the air or on the ground. Rates range from $165–195 per person. Owner and pilot Joyce Brown is also a licensed minister, and she can perform nuptials (and handle proposals) in the air—and has on numerous occasions. Sometimes only the bride and groom go up, but other times they take up a small wedding party. Very uplifting. ☎ *(707) 944-2822 for reservations and custom rates.*

Back down on the ground, to get back to Route 29 going north, get on Second Street. Go north on 29 four miles and turn right on Oak Knoll Avenue. The **Trefethen Winery** is located at 160 Oak Knoll. The main building was built in 1886 for another winery and it is the oldest three-story gravity-flow wooden winery in Napa. Its 600 acres makes it the largest estate vineyard and winery in the valley. *Open 10–4:30 for tastings and tours.* ☎ *(707) 255-7700.*

Oak Knoll will take you to the Silverado Trail, a calmer and sometimes more scenic route than 29. Among the many boutique wineries along this route, there are three you might consider—**Clos Du Val Wine Co.**, **Chimney Rock Winery**, and **Stag's Leap Wine Cellars**—all in what's called the Stags Leap District.

Go north 4.5 miles and turn left on the Yountville Cross Road. As the road name suggests, this will take you into Yountville, a classy little town named for George Yount, who planted the first grape vines in the area. He deserves a town named after him. A shrewd operator, old George was the first U.S. citizen to receive a Spanish land grant in 1836, whereupon he built a mill. In the center of town, look for **Vintage 1870** (2), a sizable restored red brick winery building that now houses shops and restaurants. A gentleman by the name of Groezinger purchased the land from Yount for $250 and established a winery in 1870. It was in business until 1954.

Something you won't want to miss is the new **Napa Valley Museum** (3) at 55 Presidents Circle in Yountville. The museum does two things: It has fascinating exhibits on the land, the people and the art of Napa Valley; it also has an interactive exhibit called *California Wine: The Science of an Art* that takes you through a year in the wine making process. You can explore all aspects of wine making—from grape growing to bottling. *Open Wed.– Mon. 10–5, the adult admission is $3.50, students and seniors $2.50 and kids 7–17 are $1.50.* ☎ *(707) 944-0500.*

Domaine Chandon at 1 California Drive in Yountville (☎ *(707) 944-2280)* is owned by the famed Moët et Chandon in France. Be sure to see the Champagne Museum where tours of the winery start. Following the tour, sparkling wine can be purchased by the glass or bottle. There's also an excellent restaurant at the winery. *It is suggested that you call for reservations for tours and the restaurant at* ☎ *(707) 944-2892.*

Head north on Route 29 a short distance. On the left in Oakville are the rambling Spanish-style buildings of the **Robert Mondavi Winery** at 7801 St. Helena Highway. One of the first large wineries to kickstart the Napa Valley revival, this one offers excellent tours under their comprehensive Visitor Program. Several times daily there is a complimentary **Vineyard and Winery Tour and Tasting** that in about an hour covers grape growing, winemaking and the sensory appreciation of wine and food. *Reservations are recommended,* ☎ *(888) MONDAVI, ext. 2002.* Tuesday at 10 and seasonally at 2 in the afternoon there is an **Essence Tour & Tasting**, a three-hour adventure focusing on the influences of soil, climate and the artful hand of the winemaker as they unveil the mysteries of aromatic essences. *The cost is $15 and reservations are a must.*

The **Advanced Winegrowing Tour & Tasting** is for those who have taken the previous two tours. Limited to 10, it is quite an experience and is offered on Sundays and Wednesdays at 10. *Cost is $20.* **Picnic in the Vineyards** is a half-day program that focuses on all aspects of winegrowing with an emphasis on the importance of vineyards. You have lunch under a sprawling oak tree among some of their oldest vines. *Cost is $35. It is offered Mondays at 10 May–Oct.* Finally, they offer **The Art Of Wine and Food** on Fridays at 10. This is a half-day comprehensive program on wine and food that ends with a three-course luncheon created by their winery chef. *Cost is $65.* For the latter three programs, reservations are a must. ☎ *(888) MONDAVI, ext. 2022.*

As you cruise north again on Route 29, let's talk a bit about the acres of grapes on either side. If it is summertime, the leaves will be bright green and you will not see many grapes. In the fall, the leaves become multi-hued and the grapes are full grown with harvest taking place in late fall, depending on the weather during the growing season. In the winter months the vines are bare. Most vineyards plant mustard below the vines, and the sea of yellow can be breathtaking. Periodically you will see apparently useless sticks rising up throughout a vineyard. These are really perches to provide hawks a lookout for hunting pesky gophers who love to chomp on vine roots.

Next is St. Helena itself. A must is the **Silverado Museum** (4) at 1490 Library Lane if you are a Robert Louis Stevenson fan. ☎ *(707) 963-3757.* This smallish museum houses manuscripts, photos, letters and other memorabilia of Stevenson's stay in the area. In spite of its size, the museum has about 7,000 Stevenson artifacts on display including virtually all of the author's first editions. *Open Tues.–Sun., noon to 4. Admission is by donation.*

Beringer Vineyards at 2000 Main Street is a very popular stop. The family's Tudor-style mansion is open 9:30–5 for tastings. The house was built in 1848 and you can wander from room to room enjoying the architecture and furnishings. Free tours of the winery leave several times daily. ☎ *(707) 963-7115.*

After you leave Beringer, you will pass through a quarter-mile Tree Tunnel. Just at the other end, be sure to turn left into the **Culinary Institute of America at Greystone** (5), 2555 Main Street in St. Helena. It is located in a massive three-story stone building that once housed the Christian Brothers

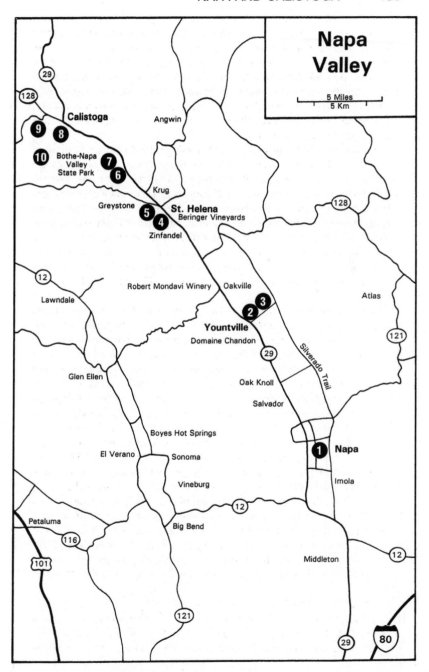

Napa Valley

5 Miles
5 Km

winery. It took 400 men one year to it build in 1889. After a $15 million renovation that took three years, it is today a bustling place where the nation's premiere chefs come to hone their skills. This is not for rookies. Students here must be Certified Chefs before they can attend classes. You can view the slick 15,000-square-foot, open-floor-plan teaching kitchens daily at 10:30, 1:30 and 3:30. The charge is $3. There are live cooking demonstrations in the state-of-the-art teaching theater on the weekends, the same hours as the kitchen viewing. Cost is $7.50. Both these activities are very impressive and probably not to be seen anywhere else in the nation. The award-winning Wine Spectator Greystone Restaurant is also in the building. See Food & Drink above.

For no cost, you can tour large sections of the first floor that include Brother Timothy's 1,800-piece corkscrew collection, and the huge cask room with an extensive collection of oak cooperage. The De Baun Museum celebrates and explores what it means to be a professional chef. Outside is the Cannard Herb Garden that consists of seven sweeping terraces of culinary herbs.

A bit farther north are two wonderful places to take a break from wine tasting. The **Bale Grist Mill State Park** (6) preserved the mill that was built in the 1800s to grind wheat when that was this region's major crop. The mill with its operating water wheel is an idyllic spot for a picnic. There's a Visitor Center where you can buy flour from the mill. On weekends, you'll see the miller grind grain with the French buhr-stones or have the chance to linger in the mill's granary while you watch and smell baking demonstrations. There is a small museum. *Open daily 10–5.* ☎ *(707) 963-2236.* An adjacent recreation area is the much larger **Bothe-Napa Valley State Park** (7). There are wonderful hiking trails through redwood and fir groves, and one that leads back to the grist mill. If you enjoy bird watching, this is the place. To cool off in the summer heat, there's a swimming pool. The native American Plant Garden is located next to the Visitor Center. Camping is available at 50 sites for a charge. *Camping reservations can be made by calling (800) 444-7275.* Full facilities. Open 8 to sunset, the park is free but you pay for swimming. ☎ *(707) 942-4575.*

Calistoga (8) is our final destination in this fully packed daytrip. It seems much less pretentious than other areas of the valley. In the center of town is the **Sharpsteen Museum** at 1311 Washington Street, founded by Ben Sharpsteen who was a fabled animator for Disney Studios. There are exhibits of that kind of work along with history about Sam Brannan, who wanted to utilize the hot springs coming from the earth to turn the area into another Saratoga, thus the name Calistoga. Brannan was quite a promoter and ladies' man. *The museum is open 10 to 4 daily in summer and noon to 4 in winter. Admission is by donation. Gift shop.* ☎ *(707) 942-5911.*

Speaking of steam, Calistoga surely is California's headquarters for multiple body indulgences. Among them are mineral baths, sauna, hot steam bath, aromatherapy, mud baths or wraps, massage, facials, mineral pools and whirlpool—you name it. There are numerous places to accomplish this sort of thing. To get ugly before getting beautiful in a mud bath, consider going to **Dr. Wilkinson's Hot Springs Mud Bath** at 1507 Lincoln. The good doctor has been at it since 1946. Costs range from $45 for a Salt Glow Scrub to $89 for mud bath with facial mask, aromatic mineral whirlpool bath, steam room, blanket wrap and one half hour massage. ☎ *(707) 942-4102.*

If you want to see, but not feel the mysteries of the Earth, go out of town about three miles to visit **Old Faithful Geyser** (9) at 1299 Tubbs Lane. The water in the geyser is 350 degrees hot and shoots 50 feet in the air about every 30 minutes. The timing depends on barometric pressure, the moon, tides and the Earth's tectonic pressures. *The park is open daily 9 to 5 in winter and an hour later in summer. Adult admission is $4, seniors $3.50 and kids 6–12 $2.* ☎ *(707) 942-6463.*

Just down the road at 4100 Petrified Forest Road is the **Petrified Forest** (10), created about six million years ago when a nearby volcano sent hot ash into the forest. The fierce heat sucked the water out of the trees and turned them to rock. Pathways lead a quarter-mile among many examples— some 100 feet tall—of trees-turned-to-rock. There's a gift shop and picnic area. *Open daily 9–5. Adult admission is $3, seniors $2 and $1 for kids 4–11.* ☎ *(707) 942-6667.*

To top off your wine tasting, consider a visit to **Schramsberg Vineyards** at 1400 Schramsberg Lane. Robert Louis Stevenson is reported to have tasted every variety grown on the premises and described it in detail in his book *The Silverado Squatters.* ☎ *(707) 942-4558 for an appointment.* This is reputed to be the oldest winery in the Napa Valley.

At the beginning of this daytrip, we said there are numerous ways to get around the valley besides car and train. Here are several options:

There are wonderful bike tours available in Calistoga that go all over the valley. **Getaway Adventures** offers daily departures to the area's secret spots along country lanes. Their Luxury Bike Wine Tour includes a top-line Cannondale, comfortable saddle and helmet. Their secret is the seasoned guide who goes along with you. Gourmet picnic lunches with Getaway are quite an event. Linen tablecloths, china, silverware plus superb food. Four wineries are visited. The all-inclusive cost is $89. They also offer a Pedal 'n Paddle that includes biking and kayaking. All day costs $99. *1117 Lincoln Ave.* ☎ *(707) 942-0332 for reservations.*

Open-air **Wine Country Jeep Tours** can take you above the valley floor and into the magnificent hills that make up the rim of the Napa Valley. The knowledgeable tour guides provide info and stories about the history of the valley. There are many offerings, but one of the most popular is Swirlin', Sippin' Ridin' in the Vineyards. *Tours range from $40 to $90.* ☎ *(800) 539-5337 for more information and reservations.*

Sonoma Cattle Company will take you deep into Robert Louis Stevenson State Park where you can ride to the top of Mount Saint Helena. The view from the summit includes the nearby geyser country and distant mountains. The park retains the wilderness aspect that inspired some scenes in *Treasure Island* and became the setting for *Silverado Squatters.* They also offer Sunset and Full Moon Rides for $45, Box Lunch and BBQ Dinner Rides from $65–90 and numerous others. ☎ *(707) 996-8566.*

If you go over to the Calistoga Gliderport, **Calistoga Gliders** will let you surf the invisible waves of air breaking over the mountains. Your glider swoops and soars on silent wings as the FAA Certified Pilot skillfully maneuvers for maximum views of vineyards, mountains and villages. A 20-minute ride is $79 for one and $110 for two. Extended rides are also available. They also offer biplane rides over the valley. Cost is $95 for one and $120 for two for 20 minutes. ☎ *(707) 942-5000.*

Calistoga Pack Goats hikes along Napa valley trails with sweeping scenic views. The goats carry water and lunch—and not you. They trek at a moderate pace accommodating beginners and family members. Goats are not anxious to jog up the trail, so the pace is easy and fun. The pack trips are weekdays 8 and 4 and weekends 8, 11 and 4. They are located at Happy Hollow Ranch on 4762 Petrified Forest Road in Calistoga. Rates start at $45. ☎ *(707) 942-5504.*

Lest you think wine is the only adult beverage available in the Napa Valley, be assured that **Napa Valley Brewing Co.** at 1250 Lincoln will happily pour you a frothy glass of their finest brews. And surprise, sake is brewed in Napa as well.

Way at the beginning of the valley, **Hakes Sake Gardens** brews Japan's national rice wine at One Executive Way in Napa. Watch the two steps of sake making—conversion of the starch into sugar; and fermentation of the sugar into alcohol. Built in 1989, their state-of-the-art facility produces about 240,000 cases annually. *Open 10–5 daily. Free.* ☎ *(707) 258-6160.*

Sonoma Valley and Santa Rosa

Sonoma and its parallel valley neighbor Napa are the best-known grape growing regions in America. Besides that relationship, they both have famous authors who lived there: Napa has Robert Louis Stevenson and Sonoma, Jack London.

But there the similarities pretty much end. Sonoma grows many different crops in its fertile soil besides grapes. Here you will find the rolling hills producing a profusion of fruits and vegetables—like delectable lettuces, vine-ripened tomatoes, corn picked that morning, bright crunchy peppers, followed by squash and pumpkins in the fall and berries, melons, apples and stone fruit in their seasons. Many of these delectables are sold by small farmers in handy roadside stands.

One wag has compared the two valleys by saying Napa is all slick Jeep Cherokees and Sonoma is working Chevy trucks. That's not to say there aren't sophisticated shops and restaurants in Sonoma, because there are.

A must-stop is the vast acreage where Jack London settled down to produce some of his more than 50 works.

We'll also go up the road to Santa Rosa, the largest city in Sonoma County. It's a bustling place with lots of fun things to do. How about ice skating with Snoopy, whose hometown is here?

It's all fun and discovery.

GETTING THERE:

By car from Union Square, go up either Geary or Sutter to Van Ness. Turn right and go one mile to Lombard, then turn left. Approximately 11 blocks later, bear right onto Richardson, which leads directly to the Golden Gate Bridge. Continue on Highway US-101 about 18 miles and look for the Route 37 to Vallejo exit. Turn left on Route 121 and follow signs to the business district of Sonoma.

PRACTICALITIES:

Lots of the Sonoma wineries and attractions open at 10 in the morning, so keep that in mind as you plan your trip. It takes about an hour to get to Sonoma. The weather is almost always warm and dry, which is why the grapes and other crops like the area so much.

FOOD AND DRINK:

A lot of what you find on tables in Sonoma (and beyond) is grown or raised right here in the valley.

Magliulo's (691 Broadway in Sonoma) This family-run Italian/American spot features fresh seafood and pastas. Gracious patio dining. Lunch and dinner daily. ☎ (707) 996-1031. $$

The General's Daughter (400 W. Spain St. in Sonoma) This is called a Sonoma Valley and Santa Rosa "Wine Country" restaurant, meaning is has an extensive wine list and gourmet dishes. Open for breakfast, lunch and dinner. ☎ (707) 938-4004. $$

il mulino (14301 Arnold Dr. in Glen Ellen) Located in an old mill with huge millwheel, this Italian restaurant's speciality is homemade ravioli. Frito Misto is made of calamari, rock shrimp, peppers and zucchini. Lunch and dinner daily. ☎ (707) 938-0588. $$

Mixx (135 Fourth St. in Santa Rosa) They work at their seasonings, which have been called "bold." Lots of fresh produce and seafood. Lunch and dinner daily. ☎ (707) 573-1344. $$

Sonoma Cheese Factory (2 Spain St. on the Plaza in Sonoma) This full deli is the perfect place to buy your picnic, or eat in the cozy outdoor dining area. The cheeses are the best. See them make the cheese right on the spot. Lunch only daily. ☎ (707) 996-1931. $

SUGGESTED TOUR:

Numbers in parentheses correspond to numbers on the map.

Head straight for the enormous town square in central Sonoma for some easygoing fun. The eight-acre Plaza is the largest of its kind in California and was laid out by General M.G. Vallejo for Mexico in 1835. Free public parking is just beyond Spain Street on First Street East.

Start your tour at the re-created **Depot Museum** (1), which tells the story of the area through an eclectic collection of artifacts, including room settings of antique furniture, costumes, books and paintings. *It is open Wed.–Sun. 1–4:30. Donations. Located at 270 First St. West.* ☎ *(707) 938-1762.*

As you walk back across the parking lot you will enter the **Sonoma State Historic Park**, made up of a number of very interesting spots. Forget about stuffy museums; these places represent Sonoma's colorful and tumultuous past. If you purchase a $2 admission to one, you can visit four (on the same

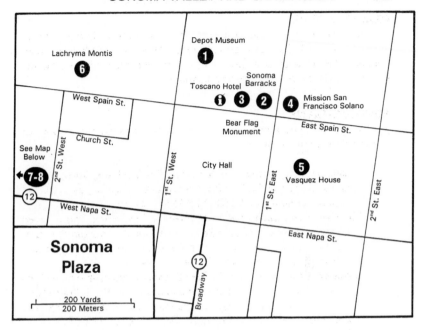

Depot Museum **1**

Lachryma Montis **6**

Toscano Hotel **i** **3**   Sonoma Barracks **2**   **4** Mission San Francisco Solano

West Spain St.

Bear Flag Monument   East Spain St.

Church St.

See Map Below ← **7-8**

2nd St. West

1st St. West

City Hall   1st St. East   **5** Vasquez House   2nd St. East

12

West Napa St.   East Napa St.

Sonoma Plaza

200 Yards
200 Meters

Broadway **12**

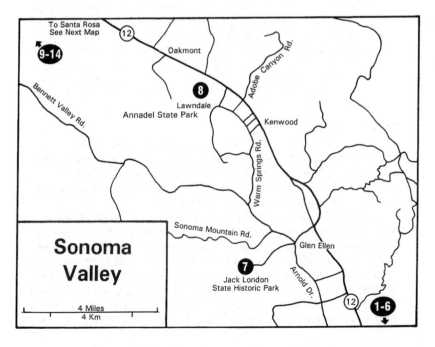

To Santa Rosa See Next Map **12**

9-14

Oakmont

Adobe Canyon Rd.

Bennett Valley Rd.

8

Lawndale
Annadel State Park   Kenwood

Warm Springs Rd.

Sonoma Mountain Rd.

Glen Ellen

Sonoma Valley

7

Jack London State Historic Park

Arnold Dr.

12

1-6 ↓

4 Miles
4 Km

day) for the same amount. They are the Barracks, the Toscano Hotel, the Mission, and the Vallejo Home.

The **Sonoma Barracks** (2) is a Monterey Colonial two-story adobe built in 1834 by General Vallejo to house his Mexican Army troops. In keeping with the geography, Vallejo remodeled the barracks as a winery in 1860. Later on, it was the U.S. military headquarters. Today it houses exhibits depicting Native American, Mexican and Early American periods of California history. *Open 10–5 daily.*

The **Toscano Hotel** (3) is a California-style woodframe building with Greek Revival details. It was built in 1852 to house Italian immigrants. As you look in on the bar and reception room, it looks like a movie set. *You can take a quick look at the lobby and bar daily 10–5. More detailed docent-led tours of most of the hotel are Sat.–Mon. 1–4.*

Established in 1823, the **Mission San Francisco Solano** (4) was the 21st and last mission built in California's "Golden Chain" that stretched from San Diego to Sonoma. Each was about a day's travel apart. This mission eventually grew into 27 rooms with over 10,000 acres of land. Today, only five rooms of the original remain. The rest is a faithful reconstruction. The mission consists of the Bell Room that was built in 1824–25; the Dining Room is filled with paintings of many of the missions in the chain; the Chapel was built in 1840–41 with the painted Eye of Heaven above the altar and the Courtyard. *Open 10–5 daily.* ☎ *(707) 938-1519.*

Practically across West Spain Street from all this good stuff in the Plaza is the **Bear Flag Monument**, a stone commemoration of the 25 tumultuous days in 1846 when Sonoma was the capital of the independent Republic of California. The story is that a ragtag band of Americans from the hills calling themselves Osos, or bears, set out to wrest control of the land from Mexico. They rode into Sonoma on June 14, 1846 and arrested the cooperative General Vallejo, then hoisted the Bear Flag of the Republic of California. Less than a month later, Americans claimed all of California for the United States and the roughnecks threw in with the Yankees.

While you are still in the area of the Plaza, walk a few steps to the **Vasquez House** (5) at El Paseo de Sonoma. It serves as the headquarters for the League for Historic Preservation. There you can pick up a walking tour map that points out 59 historic sites around the square. *Cost is $2. The house is free. Open Wed.–Sun 1–5.* ☎ *(707) 938-0510.*

Next, make your way on Spain Street and follow signs to **Lachryma Montis** (6)—which means "Tears of the Mountain"—the 20-acre estate of General Vallejo, Mexico's original man in the region who at one time owned 175,000 acres. To show his adaptability, he had this classic Yankee-style house pre-fabricated and brought around Cape Horn after America took over from Mexico. The general lived here with his 16 children, and eventually went on to become a state senator. There is a museum beside the house. State Rangers give interesting tours with commentary on its history, furnishings and personal effects of the property. *The estate is open daily 10– 5.* ☎ *(707) 938-1519.*

The **Sonoma Spa** on the Plaza at 457 First Street West offers everything from mini-massages and facials to complete natural body treatments and deluxe spa packages. The most popular package is a three-hour body treatment with facial and massage for $156. ☎ *(707) 939-8770.*

An easy way to get around—because of many mile-long walking/bike paths—is to rent a bicycle from **Sonoma Valley Cyclery** at 20093 Broadway in Sonoma. *Rates are $6 per hour or $28 for 24 hours.* ☎ (707) 935-3377.

One mile south of the Plaza you can take a 20-minute steam or diesel train trip through 10 acres of landscaped park filled with trees, animals, bridges, tunnels, waterfalls and historic replica structures at **Train-Town.** *Open daily. Tickets are $3.50 for adults and $2.50 for kids and seniors.* ☎ *(707) 938-3912.*

Now it's time for wine and cheese. **Vella Cheese Co.** is located in an elegant, old stone building at 315 Second Street East. This small facility handmakes their fine cheeses that annually win numerous awards. Try the award-winning Dry Monterey Jack that ages for months. *Open 9:30–5:50 daily.* ☎ *(707) 938-3232.*

The **Sebastiani Cask Cellars** is a few blocks from the Plaza at 389 Fourth Street East and is well worth a visit. There are free tram car rides from the parking lot, tours, picnic areas and a gift shop. *Open 10 to 5 daily, call* ☎ *(707) 938-5532.* If you go up Old Winery Road you will find the handsome **Buena Vista Carneros Winery.** It was started in 1857 by an Hungarian aristocrat who has been called the father of the California wine industry. Old and handsome, the winery is now an historical monument. *Gift shop and gallery.* ☎ *(707) 938-1266.*

Next head north on Highway 12 for a fascinating park in the hills. Turn left on Madrone and right on Arnold. The first stop should be **Jack London Village** at 14301 Arnold Drive. Here you will find the handsome **Glen Ellen Tasting Room** with a History Center that tells the story of wine in this part of the world. No charge for tasting. *Gift shop.* ☎ *(707) 939-6277.* Check out the **Olive Press** (next door) where you can see them pressing olive oil. *Free tastings. Gift shop with anything olive.* ☎ *(707) 939-8900.*

Across the street is the **Jack London Bookstore** at 14300 Arnold. Lots of used books including copies of the 30 Jack London books still in print. Prints, anthologies and anything Jack London can be found here since this also houses the Jack London Research Center. He was a prodigious writer producing 1,000 words every day. The result was 51 books and over 200 short stories. *Valley of the Moon,* a name given to all of Sonoma Valley, was his 36th novel written in 1913. *Open 10–5 Wed.–Mon.* ☎ *(707) 996-2888.*

Glen Ellen is a lovely little town of Victorians and stone buildings. Turn left. This will take you to Beauty Ranch where Jack London settled down at the age of 27, when he was already an acclaimed writer. It is said that as soon as London saw the property he knew he wanted to settle there. He said, "There are great redwoods on it, some of them 10,000 years old. There are hundreds of firs, tan-bark and live oaks, madrone and manzanita galore. There are deep canyons, streams of water, springs. It is 130 acres of the most beautiful, primitive land to be found in California."

Today, about 800 acres comprise the **Jack London State Historic Park** (7), where you can hike, picnic or stroll among the trees described by London. It's easy to immerse yourself in Jack London memorabilia (including first editions) at the museum, the House of Happy Walls, which was the house his wife built after his death. Inside are relics of the London's full and varied life: photos and writings from his sailing days in the South Pacific; a re-creation of London's bedroom and dining room; and extensive memorabilia from London's prolific career.

You can wander the haunting ruins of Wolf House, which burned to the ground before London and his wife ever got a chance to live in it. *The park is open 9:30 to sunset. Admission is $6 per car,* ☎ *(707) 938-5216 for more information.*

Horseback riding is provided by **Sonoma Cattle Co.** over the pastures and up into the hills by the park. The views are truly spectacular. *A one-and-a-half-hour ride is $40. There are other offerings as well. For reservations and more information* ☎ *(707) 996-8566.*

Another winery worth a visit is the **Benziger Family Winery** at 1883 London Ranch Road, just below the park. They pull you through the vineyard in a special jitney, stopping along the way to visit exhibits, touch vines and then sip a little. *Open 10–5 daily.* ☎ *(707) 935-4046.*

Go north on Highway 12, where you will pass the entrance to the huge **Annadel State Park** (8). Here you can hike, fish for black bass and picnic. *Open sunrise to sunset, admission is $5 per car.* ☎ *(707) 539-3911.*

Soon you will drive into **Santa Rosa** (9), Sonoma County's largest city. Follow signs to the Visitor Center at 9 Fourth Street. It is located in the **Historic Railroad Square**—a compact shopping area with a wonderful variety of specialty and antique shops and restaurants. Pick up walking tour brochures. *The Center is open Mon.–Fri. 8:30–5 and weekends 10-3.* ☎ *(707) 577-8674.*

Get ready for a good number of museums in town.

Santa Rosa has a distinguished agricultural background. Luther Burbank, certainly the country's foremost horticulturist, found the fertile soil here much to his liking and went ahead to develop 800 varieties of new flowers, fruits and vegetables. Visit the **Luther Burbank Memorial Gardens** (10) at Santa Rosa and Sonoma avenues. You can wander beautiful paths that show off his genius all year at no charge. *Docent-led tours of the Victorian home where he lived are conducted Wed.–Sun., Apr.–Oct., from 10–4. Cost is $3 for adults.* ☎ *(707) 524-5445.*

The **Sonoma County Museum** (11) at 425 7th Street is a good place to

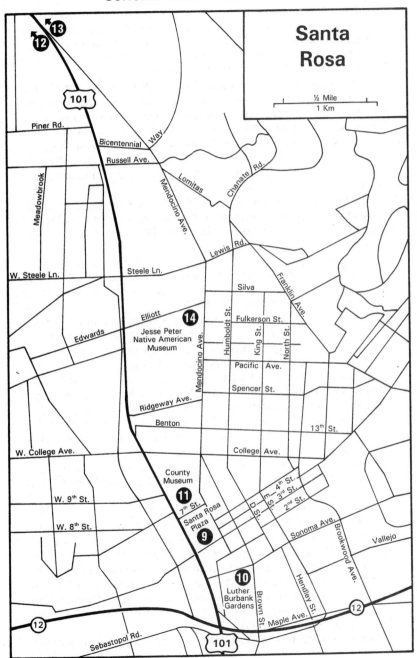

become familiar with this part of Sonoma County. It is located in the beautifully restored 1909 Post Office and Federal Building. Besides the historical exhibits, there are changing displays. *Open Wed.–Sun. 11–4. Admission is $1.* ☎ *(707) 579-1500.*

More than 50 years of aviation is represented by aircraft and artifacts including flying aircraft, static aircraft and restoration projects at the **Pacific Coast Air Museum** (12), located at 2330 Airport Boulevard. *Open Tues.–Thurs. 10–2 and weekends 10–4. $3 donation.* ☎ *(707) 575-7900.*

The **California Museum of Art** (13) at the Luther Burbank Center (on Highway 101 take the River Road exit and follow signs) exhibits paintings, sculpture and photographs from contemporary California artists. Exhibits rotate every six weeks. *Open Wed.–Sun. 11–4. $2 admission.* ☎ *(707) 527-0297.*

Honoring the cultural and artistic contributions of Native American artists, the permanent collection of the **Jesse Peter Native American Museum** (14) includes photographs, basketry, beadwork, pottery, sculpture and replicas of building sites. *Located at the Santa Rosa Jr. College, it is open Mon–Fri. 12–4. Free.* ☎ *(707) 527-4479.*

There is a one-of-a-kind facility made possible by a one-of-a-kind owner, the creator of Snoopy, Charles Schulz. It's the **Redwood Empire Ice Arena** at 1665 West Steele Lane. This is the largest ice arena in Northern California. There's a gallery where you can inspect original drawings, awards, photos and memorabilia by Schulz. *It is free and open 10–6 daily. Don't miss Snoopy's Gift Shop. The ice arena is generally open 12:30–2:30 and 3–5 daily. Cost is $ 7.50 for 12 and up.* ☎ *(707) 546-3385.*

Air Flamboyant in Santa Rosa will fly you over the vineyards, mountains, valleys, lakes and rivers of Sonoma County for an hour. It is breathtaking. The rate of $180 per person includes a hot breakfast and a bottle of champagne. ☎ *(707) 838-8500.*

Mendocino

The town of Mendocino is regarded as the jewel of this 80-mile-long coastal drive. The entire town is on the National Register of Historic Places. Innovative restaurants and a who's who of galleries and stylish shops mingle with museums, historic buildings and a first-rate art center. One of the great things about Mendocino is that it is compact, and a full range of accommodations are within walking distance of the town's attractions.

Redwoods are big in this part of Northern California, but the rugged coast is really the star. These scenic wonders taken together—giant 200-foot trees and churning ocean—were made for painting and sculpting. Thus artists flocked to the Mendocino coast like so many seagulls following the founding of the Mendocino Art Center in 1959 by visionary Bill Zacha. Today the town boasts more artists per capita than anywhere else in the United States, and remains a haven for both students and professionals.

The name Mendocino is derived from Antonio de Mendosa, Viceroy of New Spain. The captain of a Spanish ship named the cape after the viceroy. Numerous adventurers passed this way, some even landing at Cape Mendocino en route to destinations north and south.

GETTING THERE:

Head north over the Golden Gate Bridge and take Highway US-101. You will go north through Marin and Sonoma counties. After Cloverdale, look for an exit to Route 128. Take that all the way to historic Route 1, which runs along the coast. This will take you right into the town of Mendocino, approximately 156 miles from San Francisco.

PRACTICALITIES:

In the summer, the inland areas of Northern California can be rather warm, but along the coast it may be downright comfortable and sometimes chilly. Listen to this: The average daily high temperature on the Mendocino Coast in winter is 64 degrees; in summer it is 65 degrees. The cooler temperatures are created by ocean breezes and cool morning fog.

We'll do some walking today, so wear comfortable shoes.

While street addresses are included where they are known, Mendocino pays little attention to this detail. Just wander and enjoy yourself.

FOOD AND DRINK:

MacCallum House Restaurant & Gray Whale Café (45020 Albion St.) Located in an elaborate Victorian house built in 1882, this is a cozy spot. Dinners feature fine North Coast cuisine, and lunches are casual. Local wines. ☎ (707) 937-5763. $$

Bay View Café (45040 Main St.) The name says it all. You go up in one of the town's famed water towers for what is considered one of Mendocino's best view restaurants. Try for seating on the deck so you can see the ocean and headlands. Breakfast, lunch & dinner daily. ☎ (707) 937-4197. $–$$

Café Beaujolais (961 Ukiah) They're proud of their organic ingredients, some of which are locally grown. Another treat is their brick-oven bread baked fresh daily. Dinner daily. ☎ (707) 937-5614. $–$$

Gardens Grill (at the Mendocino Botanical Gardens) Applewood-grilled seafood steaks and vegetarian fare. Nice weather means dining in the beautiful Gardens. Lunch Mon.–Sat. and dinner Thurs.–Sat. ☎ (707) 964-7474. $–$$

Mendocino Hotel (45080) Main St.) Great setting for great food. Try the Grilled grape leaves for an appetizer. The TBA sandwich is turkey, bacon and avocado. For dessert, the Olallieberry Deep Dish Pie with ice cream is other-worldly. Lunch and dinner daily. ☎ (707) 937-0511. $–$$

SUGGESTED TOUR:

Numbers in parentheses correspond to numbers on the map.

A good way to become familiar with this wonderful small town is to take a walking tour. But before starting the history tour of the lovely buildings and shops, go to the end of Main Street and turn left for a marvelous walk in the **Mendocino Headlands** (1). Narrow paths take you to the very point overlooking the town bluffs. The sweeping views across the inlet, up the Big River and to town are worth this small diversion. Along the way you will see a sinkhole with a sea cave that allows water into the deep hole. Look for the stairway that will take you down the bluff to the lovely beach fronting the town.

Keep in mind, as you walk around town inspecting some of the more historic buildings, that redwood harvesting fueled the economy from the mid-1800s to the 1930s. Most of the town of Mendocino's Victorian buildings were constructed of local redwood following a fire in 1870.

The prosperity of the late 19th century and early 20th century is evident in these now-landmark buildings with their grand scale, elegant facades and beautifully-crafted interiors. Floundering during the Depression, Mendocino's last mill closed permanently in 1938. The coast slipped into a period of economic decline, which had a silver lining. When California's postwar boom brought tremendous growth to most of the rest of the state, the town of Mendocino was largely passed by. Thus it was spared wide-scale "improvements" such as the demolition of old buildings.

Today, the town of Mendocino is a State Historical District with very strict codes for signage and zoning. Any physical change to a structure must go before the Historical Review Board, and they are tough; therefore no fast food, no garish signs, and hardly any new buildings.

We suggest you start your tour on Main Street at 45270 where you will find the **Artists Co-op of Mendocino**. Upstairs are all manner of fine work by 14 local artists featuring Mendocino scenes. There are artists in residence in the studio gallery. *Open 10:30–4:30 daily.* ☎ *(707) 937-2217.*

Next on Main at 45110 is the **Panache Gallery**, with a good mix of traditional and contemporary works from a gallery that specializes in local arts and crafts. You will find a wide variety of works from all disciplines. *Open 10–5 daily.* ☎ *(707) 937-0947.*

At the corner of Main and Kasten is what's called the "Old Bank Building." With its curving lintel above the front door, it was used in the opening scene for the 1950's movie *East of Eden.* Built in 1908 for the Mendocino Bank of Commerce, it eventually became a Bank of America branch. The elaborate old vault is still there. When B of A moved out in 1983, in moved a wonderful store called **Out of This World**. They sell binoculars, telescopes, robots, science kits, games and books. ☎ *(707) 937-3335.*

On the east corner of Main and Kasten is the **Gallery Bookshop.** Beside a healthy selection of books, they have sections for local writers and musicians. While the choices aren't huge, it's fun nonetheless to see local production other than paintings. There's an excellent children's section, too. ☎ *(707) 937-2665.*

Next is the handsome old **Mendocino Hotel** with its Victorian lobby. Against one wall is a burnished metal fireplace mantel that wraps all around the fire pit—called a "surround." Beautiful antique furniture and redwood trim make this a fun visit.

Do stop in at the **Fetzer Wine Tasting Room** at 45070 Main Street next door to the hotel. They offer four tastes of the wines grown at their extensive vineyards in Hopland, north of San Francisco. With the tastings you get a commemorative wine glass. The cost is $4. Besides wine, they have a good selection of gifts. *Open 10–6 daily.* ☎ *(707) 937-6190.*

A gallery at 45052 Main will show you some of the most fantastic wood furniture, bowls and accessories anywhere. **Highlight Gallery** displays mostly works of local artisans, including those from the famed College of the Redwoods Fine Woodworking program just up the road in Fort Bragg

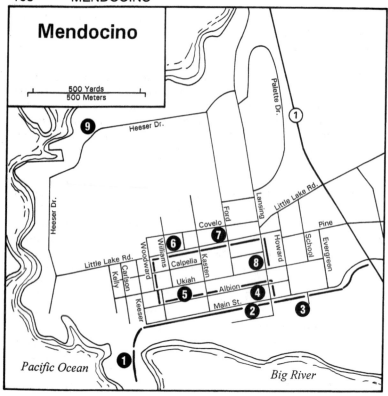

Mendocino

500 Yards
500 Meters

Pacific Ocean

Big River

(see Daytrip 27). Excellent paintings are for sale as well. *Open 10–5 daily.* ☎ *(707) 937-3132.*

Built in 1854 for town founder J.B. Ford, the **Ford House** (2) is at 735 Main on the water side of the street. This sterling facility focuses its displays and exhibits on the Mendocino Headlands State Park and the human and natural history of the Mendocino Coast. That is appropriate since the building sits on the bluff above the coast below. Ford House serves as the Visitor Center for the park and has interpretive displays of interest to all ages. *Open daily 1–4. Admission is a $1 donation.* ☎ *(707) 937-5397.*

A bit farther on Main is the handsome **Mendocino Presbyterian Church** (3). Built in 1868, it is the oldest Presbyterian Church in continuous operation in California. Unlike probably every church you have ever entered, the steeple is on the opposite end of the building from the front door. The reason is simple: Pacific Avenue used to be the main street in town and it ran along the steeple side. That street is no more, and so now you enter the church from Main Street. Sunday services are at 8:30 and 10.

If you walk to the end of Main Street you will come to the well-known **Gallery One**. This is said to be one of the coast's premier galleries, with works from over 50 painters, potters, sculptors and glassblowers. *Open 10–5 daily.* ☎ *(707) 937-5154.*

Walk back on Main Street to Lansing and turn right, and then left. At 45007 Albion Street stands the **Kelley House Museum** (4), built in 1861 for one of the local tycoons. Today you will find exhibits and displays of the area's principal activities from bygone days such as lumbering and ranching. The museum also has photos and short histories of many of the significant buildings in town. *In winter, the museum is open Fri.–Mon. 1–4. During the summer it is open the same hours daily. Admission is $2.* ☎ *(707) 937-5791.*

A couple of blocks farther on Albion is the tiny red **Temple of Kwan Tai** (5). It was built in 1852 and is the oldest Chinese temple on the North Coast. It is not open, but you can peek through the windows and see the small altar with josh sticks and other offerings. ☎ *(707) 937-5123.* Next on Albion is a fascinating shop called **Wind and Weather.** The store, which sells all manner of weather instruments including weather vanes and sundials, is located in one of the dozen or so water towers. This one was built in the mid-1800s. *Open 10–5 daily.* ☎ *(707) 937-0323.*

Continue on Albion and turn right on Woodward, then right on Little Lake. At the corner with Williams is the **Mendocino Art Center** (6). There is a terrific gallery in front, but it's more than a gallery . Also at this facility is an artist-in-residence program that serves as an educational retreat and resource center. Dozens of classes in several disciplines—fine art, textiles, jewelry and metal arts, and ceramics—are offered spring, summer and fall. Want to try your hand at silk painting? How about learning basic faux finish or capturing a likeness in charcoal? There are truly dozens of wonderful classes including Chocolate as an Art Form. *The gallery is open 10–5 daily.* ☎ *(707) 937-5818 for more information.*

Between Kasten and Ford on Little Lake are four beautifully restored and maintained Victorians that make up what is called "Bankers Row." In Mendocino's past, as the name suggests, the town's moneymen lived along here. At the corner with Ford is **Blair House** (7)—now a B & B—made famous as Jessica Fletcher's Cabot Cove house in *Murder She Wrote.*

If you turn right on Lansing, at the corner with Ukiah, you will find the lovely old **Masonic Lodge Building** (8). What makes this structure so interesting is the carved redwood statuary atop the ornate building that was built in 1866 (it took seven years to build). A Mason by the name of Erick Jensen Albertson spent his spare time in a Big River beach shack carving the figures as well as the fluted columns, arches and ceiling decorations. See if you can see the mythical figures that depict the Angel of Death, the Hourglass of Transience, the Weeping Maiden, the Anointment of Her Hair, the Acacia Branch and the Sacred Urn, the Sundered Column and the Book of Light—all are symbolic within the Masonic Order. Today, it houses a savings and loan, but the Masons still meet upstairs.

One feature of the town you won't want to miss are the dozen or so water towers spotted around the place. In the early 1800s, Mendocino sported more than 80 of these elevated towers—some as high as 60 feet with huge redwood tanks. Some are cylindrical, some angular and many were topped by windmills and cupolas. Today the dozen treasures that survived fires and winter storms are used in a variety of ways. One has been turned into a wine cellar—and six can be slept in since they have been converted to B&Bs. The town's oldest tower, built in 1857, is at Main and Hesser Streets. Standing with a decided starboard list is Captain David Lansing's tower at Howard and Main that dates to 1865.

Now it's time to play near the water—and in the mountains. Let's head for the **Mendocino Headlands State Park** (9) to cover the parts we missed at the beginning of this daytrip. The park wraps around three sides of the town, creating a needed greenbelt that contributes to the town's charm. The park consists of grassy headlands separated from the crashing surf below by dramatic, crinkled bluffs, sandy beaches and churning inlets. It offers such wonderful activities as hiking, whale watching (in winter) and picnicking. To get to the western portion, go to the end of Main and turn right, and then left which will take you to Heeser Drive. This road runs all along the headlands and eventually connects with Lansing. There is a good-sized beach along the Big River. To get there go south of town and turn left at the signs, which will take you to the mouth of the Big River.

If you want to explore one of California's last undeveloped estuaries in a canoe or kayak, check out **Catch a Canoe & Bicycles Too!** at Highway 1 and Comptche-Ukiah Road. As the name suggests, they'll also rent you a bicycle for exploring around town and up and down the coast using their handy bike map. Trek bike rentals are $10 per hour or $30 a day. Since the Big River is a tidal estuary, these fine folks will set you up with three kinds of boats such that you go up with the tide and come down with the tide. It's beautiful. Kayak rentals are $12 an hour or $36 a day. Canoes are $18 and $54 for the same time periods. A specially designed stable and fast outrigger canoe can be rented for $54 an hour. There's no day rate. ☎ *(707) 937-0273.*

Fort Bragg and the Skunk Train

The settlement that became Fort Bragg got started because of the Moho Indians, who were the original settlers of this part of the world. The federal government established the Mendocino Indian Reservation in the mid-1800s so that conflicts with the increasing number of lumbermen could be controlled. The reservation was actually moved inland and the seacoast fort abandoned a short while later.

But lumber was becoming king and thus the town of Fort Bragg started life as a lumber town in 1857—and can still lay claim to the title. Today it has a population of around 6,000. While that may be considered pretty small by many standards, Fort Bragg nonetheless is much larger than its neighbors for many miles. There is plenty of 19th-century flavor to the place, but an equal dose of the modern in retail, the arts, restaurants and lodging. Fort Bragg offers plenty of activities for the whole family.

On the south end of town is Noyo Harbor, still a traditional fishing village where you can dine on the day's fresh catch in harbor-view restaurants, or you can go out and catch your own.

Certainly the highlight of a visit to Fort Bragg is a ride on California Western Railroad's "Skunk Train." You can choose between several offerings of short trips on vintage trains through the redwood forests from Fort Bragg. We'll take you on such a trip.

GETTING THERE:

From Mendocino, go north about nine miles, which will take you right into the town of Fort Bragg.

PRACTICALITIES:

In summer and winter the inland areas of Northern California are always warmer than along the coast. The average daily high temperature on the

Mendocino Coast all year long is about 65 degrees. The cooler temperatures are created by ocean breezes and cool morning fog.

Be aware that hours for various facilities may vary between summer and winter.

FOOD AND DRINK:

The Wharf (780 North Harbor Dr.) Located right in the middle of Noyo Fishing Village, they take pride in their fresh fish. Clams, scallops, prawns, calamari. You name it and they have it right from the boat. Lunch and dinner daily. ☎ (707) 964-4283. $–$$

The Fort Bragg Grille (356 Main St.) A touch of the south with Garlic and Cheese Grits and Biscuits and Red Eye Gravy. Try the Grilled Lingcod sandwich with fresh local fish. Breakfast & lunch daily. ☎ (707) 964-1987. $

North Coast Brewing Co. (444 Main St.) Great food that includes seafood, pasta and burgers. A variety of handmade ales brewed on the spot. Dinner Tues.–Sun. Lunch on weekends. ☎ (707) 964-3400. $

Egghead's Restaurant (326 Main St.) Fresh home-made goodies that include a selection of crepes, omelets and benedicts. Try the Sloppy Dot or Wicked Witch Burger. Many salads to choose from. Breakfast and lunch daily. ☎ (707) 964-5005. $

SUGGESTED TOUR:

Numbers in parentheses correspond to numbers on the map.

Just a short way out of Mendocino going north is the **Russia Gulch State Park** (1), a good spot for hiking and mountain biking. On the ocean side is what's called "Punch Bowl," one of the many sunken sea caves along this stretch of coastline. The water enters through a tunnel that causes all sorts of churning, which creates deep-throated sounds. One of the scenic trails in the park leads to a gushing waterfall and continues on with a moderate climb into the hills. Mountain bikes are only permitted on the Fern Canyon trail. There is a rocky headland with small sandy beach. Small camping area. The day use fee is $5. ☎ *(707) 937-5804.*

A short hop later on the left look for Point Cabrillo Road. This will take you to the 300-acre **Point Cabrillo Preserve** (2) that features open meadows and windswept bluffs leading to the venerable **Point Cabrillo Lighthouse.** This was built in 1908; the impetus for its construction was the tremendous need for the region's lumber to rebuild San Francisco after the 1906 earthquake. From 1908 until 1957, the 116 marine disasters off this coast would have been much greater without the lighthouse. On Sundays from June through September at 11 a.m., docents lead walks of the area where you can learn a little coastal ecology and some Mendocino history. They tell the story of the *Frolic,* the 1850 shipwreck that changed the Mendocino coast forever

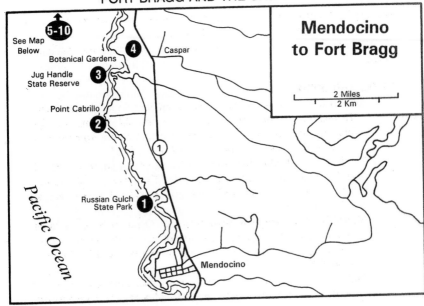

Mendocino to Fort Bragg

2 Miles
2 Km

See Map Below
Botanical Gardens
Jug Handle State Reserve
Point Cabrillo
Russian Gulch State Park
Caspar
Mendocino
Pacific Ocean

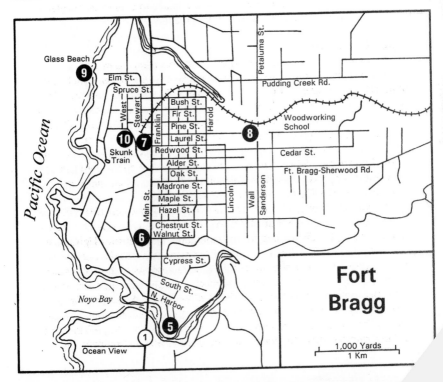

Fort Bragg

1,000 Yards
1 Km

Glass Beach
Pacific Ocean
Elm St.
Spruce St.
Bush St.
Fir St.
Pine St.
Laurel St.
Redwood St.
Alder St.
Oak St.
Madrone St.
Maple St.
Hazel St.
Chestnut St.
Walnut St.
Cypress St.
South St.
N. Harbor
Ocean View
Noyo Bay
Skunk Train
Woodworking School
Cedar St.
Ft. Bragg-Sherwood Rd.
Pudding Creek Rd.
Petaluma St.
West
Stewart
Franklin
Harold
Main St.
Lincoln
Wall
Sanderson

(see Daytrip 28). It's also a chance to visit the 1908 lighthouse that is under restoration. *Donations.* ☎ *(707) 937-0816.*

Next is the **Jug Handle State Reserve** (3). Because the 769-acre park straddles Highway 1, the beach is popular for picnicking and sunset watching, and the hills hold a fascinating hike. What makes this 2.5-mile hike so interesting is that it is really an ecological staircase. You climb five low terraces that take you both forward and backwards in time. That's because each terrace represents a piece of land uplifted from the ocean at approximately 100,000-year intervals. Pick up a self-guided brochure at the trailhead. *Always open.* ☎ *(707) 937-5804.*

A popular place is the **Mendocino Coast Botanical Gardens** (4) at 18220 North Highway 1. This marvelous spot started out as a private business founded in 1961. At 47 acres, the gardens preserve some of the most beautiful plants and trees in the area, and so the owners turned it over to the Mendocino Coast Recreation and Park District in 1992. Native coastal pines and planted groves of fragrant eucalyptus and Monterey cypress shelter the area. Two creeks flow through the gardens, and more than three miles of trail provide easy access to the coastal bluffs. *Open 9–5 in summer and 9–4 in winter. Closed major holidays. Adult admission is $6, seniors are $3, kids 13–17 $3 and 6–12 $1. 18220 N. Hwy. 1.* ☎ *(707) 964-4352.*

Next turn right on North Harbor, which will lead you down to **Noyo Harbor** (5), way below the highway bridge. If ocean fishing is your thing, consider going out with the **Telstar Charters.** In summer they offer two fishing trips a day, and in winter just one. They're experts at landing salmon, rockcod and lingcod. A five-hour salmon trip is $55, and the same time for Rockcod and Lingcod is $45. From about December through March you may want to consider a whale watching cruise, where you can catch sight of the huge gray whales. They say an average of 3,500 gray whales pass the coast during the annual migration, which is November to March. Two-hour whale watching cruises are $20. ☎ *(707) 964-8770.*

As you travel along Highway 1 look on the left for the tree nursery owned by **The Timber Company** (6), with an official address of 50 West Redwood Avenue. From the road, the green expanse of the plantings looks like grass, but under the 70,000-square-foot covers are about two million tree seedlings. A visit here helps to make sense of the tremendous scale of the timber industry in this part of the world. Georgia Pacific (of which The Timber Co. is a sister company) owns 195,000 acres of timber in Mendocino and Humboldt counties. For every tree that is harvested, GP plants five to seven seedlings, thus the huge number of redwood, blue spruce, cedar, maple, pine and Douglas fir sprouts at this location. The seedlings are raised until they're a year old, and then are planted. At an average age of 50 years, these trees will be for your great-grandchildren's homes. *The Visitor Center is open 8–4 Mon–Fri. Free admission and you can purchase seedlings for ...edwoods are usually available Oct.–Feb.* ☎ *(707) 961-3209.*

In the town of **Fort Bragg** there are definitly things to see and do. **The Guest House Museum** (7) dominates downtown from its location at 343 Main Street. This three-story Victorian, built entirely of redwood using 67,000 board feet, (what else would it be built of right here?), was constructed in 1892 for $10,000. It was the home of C.R. Johnson, founder of the Union Lumber Co. that eventually became Georgia Pacific. The exhibits tell the history of lumber in the area, but the house itself is well worth the $1 donation. Ornate woodwork can be seen in the decorative moldings, trim over the windows and doors, spindle banisters on the stairs and the block-paneled ceilings. *Open 10:30–2:30, Tues.–Sun.* ☎ *(707) 961-2823.*

For a look at the funky world of body decoration, stop up at **Triangle Tattoo** at 356B Main Street. A warren of small rooms show thousands of tattoos from Japan, India and Burma, and the Maoris in New Zealand. You've probably never seen anything like it. No charge for looking. *Open 12–7 daily.* ☎ *(707) 964-8814.*

Also in the heart of town between Redwood and Laurel streets is an area known as **North Franklin Street**, where you can shop for such goodies as antiques, collectibles, glassware and vintage clothing.

If you turn right on Laurel and go to the end (turn left on Alger just before the school buses), you will find the **College of the Redwoods Fine Woodworking School** (8). Program Director and founder James Krenov enjoys a worldwide reputation as a master craftsman who conducts a nine-month program and summer sessions. In the studio you will see artisans learning every conceivable woodworking skill. You can tour the studio and observe these talented student woodworkers in action while school is in session, but you must call first. ☎ *(707) 964-7056.*

At the end of Elm Street in Fort Bragg is a curious coastal area called **Glass Beach** (9). Hard as it is to imagine on this beautiful coast, local residents used to toss all manner of junk over the concrete bulkhead into the ocean. Glass, broken dinnerware, costume jewelry, wine bottles and other assorted junk were unceremoniously heaved onto the rocks.

The dump was closed about 30 years ago. Since then the rugged shoreline has become a beachcomber's paradise. Over the years the items that were thrown to the rocks below the headlands were thrashed and battered into what today is considered sparkling treasure that now covers the beach.

Fort Bragg has a true cultural side as well. The **Warehouse Repertory Theatre** bills itself as the "industrial strength" theater on the Mendocino Coast. Both new and classical plays are presented from February to December, and there's a summer festival as well in the company's converted warehouse. ☎ *(707) 961-2940 for current schedule and tickets.*

The **Gloriana Opera Company** presents a range of lively musical productions in its new 150-seat theater. The season is from February to December. ☎ *(707) 964-7469 to find out what's playing and for tickets.* The **Fort Bragg Center for the Arts** presents a music series in the Opera House that includes five concerts in fall, winter and spring. ☎ *(707) 964-0807 for current offerings and tickets.*

The **Symphony of the Redwoods**, a 50-member symphony orchestra established in 1983, presents four main concerts annually. There is also a chamber music series with concerts throughout the year. ☎ *(707) 964-0898 to identify concerts you may want to attend.*

Next it's time to catch the train. The famous **Redwood Route of the Skunk Train** (10) of the California Western Railroad and Navigation Company dates back to 1885 on this beautiful coastline. Regardless of how many times you've made the 40-mile trip to Willits, still the scenery leaves you in awe.

Traveling eastward from the Pacific Ocean along the scenic Noyo River toward the giant redwood trees inland, the train moves at an average of 18 miles an hour. It twists through 381 curves and crosses 30 bridges and trestles to reach the midpoint of Northspur and the final destination of Willits.

These vintage trains have carried logs, loggers, freight and passengers along the same track for over 100 years. The unusual name, **"Skunk Train,"** derived from gas engines introduced in 1925. Apparently the smell of the gas and smoke—blown upland by the coastal winds—was so strong that residents said, "you could smell them coming," thus the different name.

You have several choices with the Skunk Train. First, there are three different types of cars. Old No. 45 Steam Engine is the favorite that huffs and puffs on a half-day trip to Northspur from March through October. The Super Skunk diesel-powered locomotives deliver their cargo of passengers and freight all the way to Willits 40 miles away pretty much on a daily basis. But the true "Skunks of the Route" are the classic, vintage 1925 and 1935 Motorcars. Beautifully preserved, these cars were originally gas powered.

The train travels about 90 percent of the time through heavily wooded areas. The trees are alder, oak, white and Douglas fir, maple, pine, hemlock, bay laurel—and best of all the towering Coast Redwoods. You will learn that redwoods are the only trees that regenerate themselves since the stumps don't die. The train passes what is reputed to be a 1,000-year-old redwood next to the tracks. There are three types of redwoods: *Dawn* that grow in China; *Coast Redwoods* that grow in a narrow band along the California coast; and *Giant Sequoias* that grow inland in the Sierra Nevada (see Daytrips 37 and 38 about Yosemite).

Periodically, the train stops at various clearings since it is still used by regular passengers—either residents who can't get out during the winter months or campers getting to remote locations during the summer months. One stop is called Company Ranch, which is where the lumber companies grew cattle for meat for their workers. It may interest you to know that the Skunk Train drops off and picks up mail at 18 stops along the way six days a week.

Full-day trips are $35 for adults and $18 for kids 3–11. Half-day trips to Northspur are $25 for adults and $13 for kids 3–11. The schedule changes *between winter and summer.* ☎ *either (800) 77 SKUNK or (707) 964-6371. Reservations are recommended, especially in summer.*

For true railfans, there's a new twist. Now you can ride in the cab of the locomotive with the engineer instead of in a passenger cab. Cab riders can choose between the majestic 1924 Baldwin steam engine or a vintage diesel engine. The cost is $100 per person, based on space availability. All participants must sign a liability release. Call the same phone numbers as above for more information.

Mendocino North

Native Americans lived here as early as 9500 BC. Over the centuries tribal groups evolved, living peacefully together. The local Pomo lived in the valleys and harvested from the sea. They were well established by the time European explorers began scouting the area in their galleons in the mid-1500s.

While numerous prowling sea captains passed this way looking for safe harbors, the ever-present fog and tempestuous sea discouraged close inspection of the coastline, thus keeping the area virtually unknown to many save its native inhabitants—even at the time of the Revolutionary War.

Gold was discovered in California in 1848, and the rush was on. In 1850 the two-masted cargo ship *Frolic,* bound for a rapidly growing San Francisco with goods from Canton, ran aground about three miles north of the present town of Mendocino. While surviving crew members made their way ashore on lifeboats, the Pomo salvaged Chinese porcelain, silk and other treasures from the wreck.

The ways of the new arrivals conflicted with those of the native Pomo. By the late 1850s, the Mendocino Indian Reservation had been established near the Noyo River in what is now Fort Bragg. The reservation operated until 1866, when the native people were forced to relocate east to the Round Valley area where many Pomo live to this day.

Information about Fort Bragg is included in Daytrip 27. In this excursion, we'll go farther north to explore the coast and then the spectacular redwoods.

GETTING THERE:

From Mendocino, go north. Fort Bragg is about nine miles north. Keep going north on Highway 1.

PRACTICALITIES:

As we said above, the frequent fog keeps the coastline cool—about 65 degrees all year round. Inland areas of Northern California are always warmer than along the coast. The road north of Westport climbs high into the mountains with many curves and much up and down. Be prepared for mountain driving. The views are worth it.

There's not a large selection of places to eat on this daytrip, so you might consider picking up a picnic at **Tote Fete** at 10450 Lansing in Mendocino. They specialize in gourmet food to go. ☎ (707) 937-3383.

FOOD AND DRINK:

Pelican Lodge & Inn (38921 Hwy. 1 in Westport.) Located right in the heart of this little burg, their speciality is a huge sirloin steak. They take pride in their fresh fish and salads. Rustic old bar that's worth a visit. Breakfast, lunch and dinner daily. ☎ (707) 964-5558. $–$$

Westport Inn & Deli (on Hwy.1 in Westport.) Fresh fish and other goodies await you in this small spot on the highway. Good salads in a wide variety. Lunch and dinner daily. ☎ (707) 964-5135. $

Redwood Diner (Drive-Thru Tree Rd. in Leggett) Traditional coffee-house with full light menu. Burgers, salads and pastas for lunch and dinner daily. ☎ (707) 925-6442. $

SUGGESTED TOUR:

Numbers in parentheses correspond to numbers on the map.

After **Fort Bragg**, the next town you come to on the north coast is **Cleone** (1). This neat little burg began as a ranching community more than 100 years ago, but later joined its neighbors as a lumber town. Today its western roots are evident in the popularity of horseback riding here, available at Richo-chet Ridge Ranch.

Right at Cleone is the 1,600-acre **MacKerricher State Park** (2). What makes this area quite different from most of the rugged, steep coastline north and south of here is that it includes about ten miles of beach with sand dunes and sloping lowlands. Besides the ocean to the west, to the east are two freshwater lakes; one is stocked with trout. Fishermen can choose ocean fishing, including mussel-taking and abalone diving, or if that doesn't work out, try their hand at trout fishing.

Walkers, joggers, bicyclists and horseback riders will thrill to the seven miles of abandoned roadway that runs right between the ocean and the lakes for spectacular views. One of the outstanding features of MacKerricher is Laguna Point, where a trail leads out to great seal watching. A fairly large population of these fascinating sea creatures has taken up residence on some jagged rocks off the coast, and most times you can see these charac-ters performing all their tricks. The point is also an excellent whale watch-ing spot during the winter months. The Laguna Point trail is wheelchair accessible.

There are 153 developed campsites as well as 11 walk-in sites. In sum-mer, rangers lead hikes (including night hikes), bike rides and campfire pro-grams. *MacKerricher is open daily 8 to sunset. It is free.* ☎ *(707) 937-5804.*

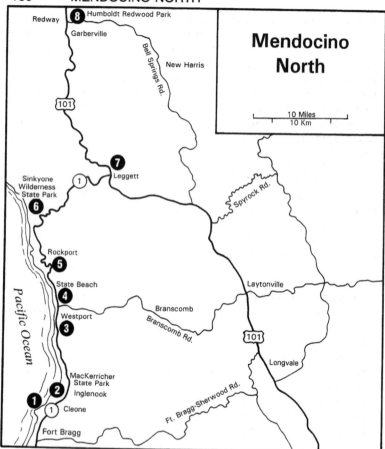

When you come out of the park you will find **Richochet Ridge Ranch** at 24201 North Highway 1. They offer group rides on the beach and in the forested areas as well. In season they also offer whale and seal watching—on horseback. How about that. One-and-a-half hour rides are at 10, noon, 2 and 4, and the cost is $35. The ranch also has private rides for $55 for the same time period. ☎ *(707) 964-7669.*

Westport (3) is the northernmost town on the Mendocino Coast. It's isolation is one of its virtues, except for the opening of abalone season in early April when divers come from far and near and the place is jumping. At least the local residents have a sense of humor—Westport's annual Great Rubber Ducky race on Mother's Day draws crowds for the race and barbecue (beef, not duck). Lodgings include both the basic and those that pamper.

About two miles north of town is the **Westport-Union Landing State**

Beach (4). Smaller than most of the other state recreation areas along this coast, it is nonetheless popular for beachcombing. It also affords excellent tide pools to discover. A word about tide pools is appropriate here. Keeping in mind the fragile nature of these natural pockets in the rocks, it is best to just look and not disturb. As an example, you might turn over a rock and expose an immobile marine animal, leaving it exposed to the sun to die. As the matter of fact, California law prohibits taking tidal invertetrates.

The park's 41 acres, along a narrow strip next to the highway, has seven campgrounds above the churning ocean below. Surf fishing, spearing and abalone diving are popular uses for this park. *Open 8 to sunset, there is no day use fee.* ☎ *(707) 937-5804.*

North of Westport, the highway wiggles its way to **Rockport** (5), which is not much more than a school and a few houses. A bit farther north the road swings east in deference to a coastline so rugged it is best explored by seasoned wilderness hikers and four-wheel drive vehicles. If you look for signpost 90.88, there is a narrow unmaintained dirt road leading to **Sinkyone Wilderness State Park** (6).

To show how rugged the terrain is at this point, it was not possible to bring the highway along this shore and that's why it shoots off east. There are no facilities in Sinkyone, so take your own water and provisions.

When you stay on Highway 1 at this point, it will take you into **Leggett** (7). This is considered the access point leading north to the majestic and mysterious giant redwoods. Right in town is the **Chandelier Tree Park.** This is 200 acres of virgin redwoods preserved in their natural state. The highlight of the park is the Chandelier drive-thru tree. It is still thriving to this day, towering 315 feet into the sky. With a girth of 21 feet, it is so named for its unique limb structure. The branches are about 100 feet up, measuring four to eight feet in diameter (which makes them bigger than many mature trees). The way they grow resembles a handsome chandelier. *The park is open daily 8 to dusk. Admission is $3.* ☎ *(707) 925-6363.*

Pushing on north, after an hour or so you will come to the dramatic **Avenue of the Giants** (8) in **Humboldt Redwood Park.** This 51,000-acre park contains the famed Avenue, 31 magnificent miles of giant, first-growth redwoods. It is considered the most outstanding display of these giants of the forest in the 500 miles of the redwood belt in California. It is also a cool place where you can hike, picnic, fish or bike. There are campgrounds throughout the area.

Just beyond Garberville is the first entrance to the park at Phillipsville. Be sure to pick up a brochure for an auto tour that points out nine attractions along the route. Half-way up is the Humboldt Redwoods State Park Headquarters with a good Visitor Center. There are a series of vide will give you full information on the area. Also included are wildlife and a special treat for kids where they can make tracks in sand of th animals. *The Center is staffed by volunteers and so it is generally op*

9–8 daily, July through Labor Day and 9–3 the rest of the year. ☎ *(707) 946-2409.*

The park's 10,000-acre Rockefeller Forest preserves nearly ten percent of the old-growth redwood forests remaining in the world. The Founders Grove, so-named for that band of hearty souls who founded the Save-the-Redwoods League, contains a loop trail. An outstanding example of giant trees you'll see along the way is the Founders Tree. No longer standing on this route was the Dyerville Giant, which was certified by the American Forestry Association as the champion redwood until it fell back in 1991. Measured on the ground, it was 370 feet tall, making it 200 feet taller than Niagara Falls.

If you go all the way to Scotia at the top end of the park, you can tour a working lumber mill. **Pacific Lumber** runs tours weekdays 8–2. It is fascinating to see the speed at which a log is turned into lumber. *Free.* ☎ *(707) 764-2222.*

South of Mendocino

The entire 80 miles of the Mendocino Coast is fascinating, and during this daytrip we'll drop down below the town of Mendocino to seek new adventures.

Many visitors have said they never tire of the beauty of the blue Pacific Ocean crashing against steep cliffs with pocket beaches here and there. And of course when you look inland, there is the deep green of pine and redwood forests. One can't forget the golden meadows, either, that seem to appear out of nowhere. Logging was the primary economic engine in this part of California for many years. It's still pretty important, but instead of nearly every stream along the coast holding several sawmills, most of that activity is now concentrated north in Fort Bragg. One industry that hasn't changed much in over 100 years is agriculture. Cattle can still be seen grazing in lush pastures and row crops are still evident in the level areas of this coast.

Also along this coast are a series of neat little towns that each have an interesting history. We'll explore all of this during this daytrip.

GETTING THERE:
From Mendocino, go south on Highway 1.

PRACTICALITIES:
The average daily high temperature on the Mendocino Coast all year long is about 65 degrees. The cooler temperatures are created by ocean breezes and cool morning fog.

In summer, you may be tempted to go in the ocean at some of the beaches along this coast. Always beware of the sometimes dangerous rip tides and "sneaker" waves that come up suddenly.

FOOD AND DRINK:
Albion River Inn (3790 Hwy. 1 in Albion) Located right above the ocean for dramatic views. *Bon Appetit* magazine says this restau-

rant is "now one of the finest to grace the Golden State shore." Dinner daily. ☎ (707) 937-1919. $$–$$$

Ledford House (3000 N. Hwy. 1 in Albion.) Traditional North Coast dining with local specialties. Spectacular ocean view. Live music nightly. Dinner daily. ☎ (707) 937-0282. $$

Greenwood Pier Café (5928 Hwy. 1 in Elk) Well known for its clam chowder. Good focaccia sandwiches. Tofu Rancheros are one of their specialities. Lunch and dinner daily. ☎ (707) 877-9997. $–$$

Bridget Dolan's Pub & Dinner House (5910 S. Hwy. 1 in Elk) Enjoyable Irish pub that serves full dinners Fri., Sat. & Sun. "Pub grub" Mon.–Thurs. nights. Local beer and wines served. ☎ (707) 877-1820. $–$$

Pangaea (250 Main St. in Point Arena) They use as much locally grown and organically pure foods as possible. Locally caught salmon is a speciality. Breast of Duck and Seared Ahi Tuna are also prime choices. Dinner Wed.–Sun. ☎ (707) 882-3001. $–$$

SUGGESTED TOUR:

Numbers in parentheses correspond to numbers on the map.

Just south of Mendocino—about three miles—is the 2,160-acre **Van Damme State Park** (1). Besides a sheltered beach (from which it is said there is the best abalone diving in Northern California), the park extends inland about four miles and affords some excellent hiking trails that total about ten miles. For those who like short nature hikes, there are two. The **Bog Trail** is about a third of a mile long, starting near the west entrance to the park.

Another one takes you to a **Pygmy Forest** that is accessible either by hiking from the entrance near the Visitor Center or from Little River Airport Road. The latter trail takes you to nature's bonsai of Mendocino cypress, Bolander pine, rhododendron and Bishop pine. Poor soil and drainage create trees about two to three feet high that might normally soar 100 feet This trail is wheelchair accessible.

There is a Visitor Center just inside the park, whose theme of "Living With the Sea" features dioramas and displays of man's relationship to the sea. *Operated by volunteer docents, the center is generally open 10–4 daily.* ☎ *(707) 937-5397. The day use fee for the park is $5. Camping is $16 per night.* ☎ *(707) 937-5804. Opposite the park on the beach side, you can rent kayaks for $15 an hour.*

Local third-generation resident Francis Jackson has researched the history of logging in the Little River area, putting together a map showing where mills and shipyards were located. Periodically he leads walking tours over what is called the "Jackson History Trail." In a gulch on the north of Little River was Peterson's Shipyard where Thomas H. Peterson built 14 lovely schooners between 1869 and 1879. Check at the entry station for dates and times for the walking tour.

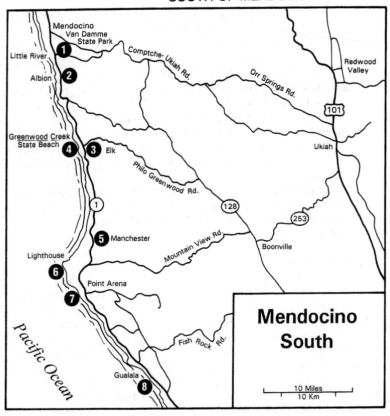

Mendocino
South

10 Miles
10 Km

Hollywood loves Little River. When James Dean stayed here during the filming of *East of Eden,* he was ordered out of the dining room of a local inn for putting his feet on the table. The rooms where Alan Alda and Ellen Burstyn cuddled in 1978's *Same Time Next Year* remains popular with couples who reserve them repeatedly at the elegant **Heritage House** at 5200 North Highway 1 in Little River.

This famed hostelry was built in 1877 as a farmhouse. Over the years the property developed quite a colorful history. During Prohibition, it was used as a base by rum runners as well as smugglers of Chinese laborers, who had been brought to the coast to work in the logging camps. If it has a distinctly New England look, it's because it was built by a couple from Maine.

Farther south is **Albion** (2), tucked alongside the Albion River. The high trestle bridge built in 1944 over the river is the last wooden bridge remaining on Highway 1. The harbor at Albion is one of the locations thought very likely to be 16th-century explorer Sir Francis Drake's 1579 fort site when he navigated the Pacific Coast. Drake still causes arguments among historians, but visitors come to Albion for respite at its fine restaurants and charming inns. During the holidays, many of the B&Bs and inns participate in an annual Candlelight Bed & Breakfast Tour. Lots of fun.

English sea captain W.A. Richardson named the town using the ancient name for Britain. He was a clever soul who built a house and sawmill on the estuary of the river. The latter was a unique design that used a large waterwheel powered by the tides to run the mill.

Next is a stretch of land known as the **Elk Coast**. Perched high on the bluffs above the Pacific Ocean, along a sparsely populated and incredibly scenic 20-mile section of Highway 1, it is truly off the beaten track. It's a secret well kept by those who know—and don't want to spoil—the real Northern California. The area begins at the Navarro River on the north, extends south through the sleepy villages of Greenwood/Elk and Irish Beach, and ends at the town of Manchester.

The tiny town of **Elk** (3) itself is nestled on a cliff-top setting as beautiful as it is secluded. A prosperous mill town at the turn of the century, Elk today is a peaceful cluster of elegant country inns, unique restaurants and shops featuring the work of local artisans. *The old mill office at 5980 Highway 1 now houses a small Visitor Center and Museum, open Saturdays and Sundays from 11–1. Lumbering and timber is the main subject of the displays. Donations.*

The terrific part of the Elk Coast are the many things to do—as well as see. **Force Ten Ocean Whitewater Tours** at 6143 Highway 1 will take you out for a unique kayak tour. You launch through the surf at Greenwood Beach and glide through sea caves and kelp forests. The professional guide will help you find star fish, sea lions, birds and hidden beaches. They have all the equipment including wet suits, and they provide instruction for novices as well as experts. *Cost is $80 for a two hour tour.* ☎ *(707) 877-3505.*

Ross Ranch Horseback Riding provides private, guided horseback rides with a lifelong resident of the Elk Coast who takes you through beautiful mountain redwoods forests just east of Elk. Or you can experience the thrill of riding on spectacular Manchester Beach. Most are two-hour rides with longer ones available too. *Cost is $19 per hour in the mountains and $24 per hour on the beach.* ☎ *(707) 877-1834.*

Make time to visit the **Greenwood Creek State Beach** (4) in Elk, directly across from the Elk Store. Most interesting are the sea stacks and coastal bluffs that are part of the 47-acre park fronted by a quarter-mile sandy beach. This was once the site of a redwood lumber mill. Great spot for picnicking and fishing. Not recommended for swimming, but you can launch a kayak here or surf cast. ☎ *(707) 937-5804.*

Head farther south for **Manchester** (5). What makes this small community especially interesting is that it is the site of another in the string of marvelous wilderness parks dotted along this coast. Turn left on Kinney Road for **Manchester State Park.** This open area along the seacoast is really for kicking back and taking it easy, or taking up some more active pursuits like steelhead and salmon fishing in winter in the two creeks that run through the park—or surf fishing along the five miles of lovely beach any time of year. Right at the point where the 1,400-acre park touches the ocean is where the San Andreas Fault—that awful creator of earthquakes in the region—makes its way into the ocean headed west.

Bird watchers have a field day observing such exotics as whistling swans among the wetlands. There are 48 rather primitive campsites spread among the grassy dunes for those hardy souls who don't want much privacy; there are ten environmental campsites as well. Camping reservations are strongly advised during the summer months. ☎ *(800) 444-7275.*

The park also includes the **Area Rock Natural Preserve** that protects many unusual underwater plants and animals native to this part of California. *The park is always open. There is no day use fee. A campsite will cost you $12 and an environmental site costs $10.* ☎ *(707) 937-5804.*

The **Point Arena Lighthouse and Museum** (6) is an historical sentinel just north of town. Follow signs and take a rather bumpy road two miles out to the lighthouse. Many a ship met its doom before the lighthouse was built in 1870. The original structure was destroyed in the 1906 earthquake; the "new" lighthouse was built in 1907. In 1976 the fog signals were silenced permanently, and a bell-buoy placed nearby. In 1977 an automated aircraft-type beacon was installed on the balcony of the 115-foot-tall tower. *The lighthouse and museum are open 11–3:30 daily. The cost is $3 for adults and $1 for kids.* ☎ *(707) 882-2777.*

Next in the southern odyssey is **Point Arena** (7). This is one of California's smallest cities, and one distinguished as a state historical district. Proof is along Main Street, where many Point Arena businesses are housed in historic buildings, some dating back to the 1800s. Among them is the Arena Theater that once was the site of vaudeville shows that definitely livened up the downtown scene. The theater is newly renovated and presents live theater and concerts as well as Hollywood and foreign films.

The very last community on this jaunt happens to be the southernmost town in Mendocino County. **Gualala** (8) is situated right at the county line in what many locals boast is the "banana belt." Born a lumber town like its neighbors, it stayed a mill town for almost a century. Just 45 years ago, Gualala could boast of four sawmills. All that has changed dramatically. After the last mill closed in the 1960s, the town actually began to grow. Those who love the land and wanted a more rural lifestyle, along with many artists, were attracted to the area.

Gualala today is a happy mix of new and old with art galleries, restaurants, boutiques and accommodations ranging from the refurbished 19th-century properties to more contemporary options.

If you want to explore the towering redwoods and lush fern canyons in the area more carefully, consider renting a bike from **Adventure Rents** located at 39175 Highway 1, just north of the Chevron Station. *Rates are $15 for two hours or $30 for a full day (rentals include helmets and water bottles).* This same outfit has kayaks and canoes so you can explore the Gualala River. What makes it special is that motorized craft are not permitted on the river, so you can adventure at a leisurely pace, upstream or down, past redwood forests, salt marshes and sandy beaches. *Canoes are $40 for two hours, $50 for a half day and $60 for a full day. Single kayaks are $20, $25 and $30 for the same time periods. They are open seven days a week.* ☎ *(707) 884-4386.*

If scuba diving is your thing, **Jay Baker Hardware** at 38820 South Highway 1 will rent you just about anything you need. *For same-day rentals of a wet suit, booties, fin, belt, gloves, hood, mask, snorkel, AB iron and AB gauge the rate is $50. The airtank, back pack and tube are an additional $22. The 24-hour rate for the same equipment is $75 and $27 respectively.* ☎ *(707) 884-3534.*

Section IV

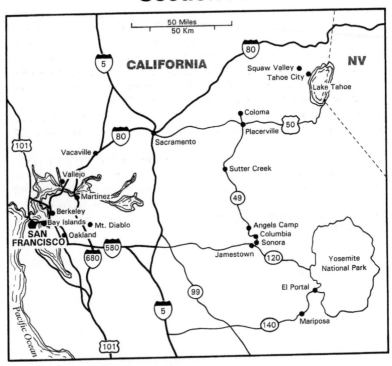

DAYTRIPS AND OVERNIGHTING
EAST OF
SAN FRANCISCO

There's always lots going on in the East Bay—from cultural events galore in Berkeley to sailboats races in Oakland to bike riding over a couple of islands that hug the east shore.

The area east of San Francisco has an intriguing past with many historical monuments and buildings of special note. Sacramento, in spite of what you might have heard of the city, deserves a good deal of your attention because of its rich history. The capital city's museums are among the finest in the East Bay—or anywhere in California for that matter.

As we progress farther east into the mountains, there's more history to be explored in Gold Country. Not only are the mountains and valleys wonders to behold, but the tales of the Gold Rush played out in big and small historical artifacts and collections are fascinating.

A couple of biggies east of San Francisco are Yosemite National Park and the Lake Tahoe area. These are two of California's most stunning natural formations. You can expect them to be popular year round.

GETTING AROUND—EAST

Daytrips to Berkeley, Oakland and Alameda can be accessed in a number of ways:

BY CAR:

Clearly this is the preferred means of getting around the East Bay. You have more flexibility to get into the hills of Berkeley and Oakland in a car.

BY BART:

This commuter train will take you right into the heart of Oakland or Berkeley. Details are in Daytrips 30 and 31.

BY FERRIES:

There is a regular ferry to Alameda. The Blue and Gold has 13 departures from the Ferry Building on weekdays and six departures on weekends. The round trip fare is $8. ☎ *(415) 705-5555*.

For the overnight Trips 37-41:

BY CAR:

For the Gold Country, Yosemite and Lake Tahoe (Daytrips 37–41), we recommend a circuit where you spend as many nights as you want in each, but you keep moving. By doing this you can take them all in. A preferred route is to take I-80 east from San Francisco and then US-50 into the mountains to Placerville. From there head either north or south to follow Highway 49, appropriately named for the Gold Rush of 1849.

When you follow Highway 49 south from Placerville, after about 40 miles and many Gold Rush towns, take Highway 120 straight into Yosemite National Park. Once you have had your fun in the park, there are two very scenic routes to get to Lake Tahoe.

If you continue on 120 through the park and out the east side, the views are fantastic. Get on US-395 going north and then US-50 to Lake Tahoe. The mountain pass on this route is oftentimes closed by snow during deep winter months. An attractive alternative (some actually prefer it) is to retrace your route on Highway 49 going north. Past Jackson turn right on Highway 88, which will take you over the mountains to connect with US-50 into Lake Tahoe. The latter route will take your breath away periodically with the mountain and lakes views that are outstanding.

BY TOUR BUS:

On Tuesdays, Thursdays and Sundays, Tower Tours will lead you to Yosemite in one day. The motorcoach leaves at 7 in the morning and returns about the same time in the evening. The fare is $99 for adults and $59 for kids 5–11. ☎ *(415) 434-8687.*

BY BUS/TRAIN:

It's possible to take a combination bus and train from San Francisco to Yosemite. Essentially you depart San Francisco by bus at 6:45 and go a short distance; then you board an Amtrak train and go most of the way; and then you take another bus to arrive in the park at 12:40 in the afternoon. For the return, you leave the park at 9 in the morning and by reverse bus/train/bus you arrive back in San Francisco at 4:20 in the afternoon. The fare is $33 each way. ☎ *(800) USA RAIL for details.*

ACCOMMODATIONS—EAST

Almost any kind of accommodation you can think of is available in this part of California. The gamut runs from rustic luxury to motels to full service campgrounds. Take your pick.

For the Gold Country, Yosemite and Lake Tahoe, it's a good idea to call the respective Chambers of Commerce or Visitors Bureaus, listed below. Most will assist you with lodging reservations.

VISITOR INFORMATION

El Dorado Chamber of Commerce
542 Main St.
Placerville, CA 95667
☎ (800) 457-6279 or (530) 621-5885

Tuolumne County Visitors Bureau
55 Stockton
Sonora, CA 95370
☎ (800) 446-1333 or (209) 533-4420

Yosemite Valley Visitors Bureau (2 locations)
P.O. Box 425
Mariposa, CA 95388
☎ (800) 208-2434 or (209) 966-2456

41729 Hwy. 41
Oakhurst, CA 93644
☎ (209) 683-4636
www.yosemite.com

North Lake Tahoe Resort Association
245 North Lake Blvd.
P.O. Box 884
Tahoe City, CA 96145
☎ (530) 581-6900
www.tahoefun.org

Berkeley

There are many storied college campuses and their surrounding towns, but this one has got to be among the best-known in the world. Sometimes called "Bezerkely," it has led the way in many civic, intellectual and business spheres.

From the beginning, this has been a college town. When the trustees of California College gathered in 1866 on a hillside overlooking the bay, they were so impressed with a poem recited for the occasion by one of their fellow trustees, Bishop George Berkeley, that they named the town after him. It was that simple.

Nestled against the rolling hills with San Francisco Bay at its feet, Berkeley enjoys a mild climate year-round. Acres of open space, neighborhood parks and city bike lanes offer a hundred opportunities to explore the outdoors. And with its wealth of cultural life, a visit to Berkeley is never dull.

The university campus could consume the better part of this daytrip, depending on what your interests are. But we will also explore some of the architecture and museums off campus. Shopping anywhere in Berkeley is great, especially along Telegraph Avenue. Consider: There are 50 plus bookstores in town.

GETTING THERE:

By car, from Union Square go down Bush and follow signs to the Bay Bridge. You will pay the $2 toll coming back. Follow Route I-80 and get off at the University exit.

By BART, walk down to the Powell Street Station. The fare is $2.65 to downtown Berkeley. Buy a ticket from the machine (some give change and others don't). Insert your ticket in the fare gate. It will be returned to you since you will need the same ticket to exit at Berkeley.

PRACTICALITIES:

Berkeley is a walking town, so wear comfortable shoes. If you go when school is in session, generally there will be more activities and buildings open to the public. That's not to say that things close down when Cal is on vacation. Berkeley is always lively.

FOOD AND DRINK:

Skate's on the Bay (100 Seawall Dr.) A fabulous European brasserie serving seafood and pasta specialities. A wonderful bar with a bay view to die for. Lunch and dinner daily. ☎ (510) 549-1900. $$

Encore Hot Pot (2067 University Ave.) Very unusual restaurant where you sit at a table with a hot pot in the middle. You go to a buffet line and choose veggies and meats to cook back at your table. Good fun and food of your own making. Lunch and dinner daily. ☎ (510) 540-8888. $–$$

Raleigh's (2438 Telegraph Ave.) Good old American dishes with Seven Signature Salads lead by Caesar Tapenade. Outdoor seating in a pleasant garden. Lots of lagers, ales and ciders on draught. Lunch and dinner daily. ☎ (510) 848-8652. $–$$

Hana Sushi Buffet (1722 University Ave. on the waterfront) Casual atmosphere serving 13 kinds of sushi and 14 different hot dishes. Salad bar. Open Mon.–Sat. ☎ (510) 841-9500. $–$$

SUGGESTED TOUR:

Numbers in parentheses correspond to numbers on the map.

Let's begin this day with an architectural walking tour of **Downtown Berkeley** (1). The starting point is the corner of University and Shattuck avenues. **Shattuck Square**, built in 1926, is a cluster of buildings that originally served as a turnaround for steam trains and later electric trolleys. The square is composed of three striking Mediterranean buildings designed by the firm that did the Oakland Paramount, Pacific Coast Stock Exchange and 450 Sutter in San Francisco. Next door is the painstakingly restored **Roos Brothers Building** at 64 Shattuck Square.

Across the street stand two significant buildings, the **Hotel Central** at 2008 Shattuck and the **Heywood Building** at 2014, both designed by the same architect, James Plachek. Next is the 1925 **Wells Fargo Building** at 2081 Center that underwent an extensive historic renovation in the early 1990s. Note the exceptional lobby space and handsome clock above the entrance. The **BART Station** built in 1970 in Constitution Square is today's counterpart to the earlier Southern Pacific Depot.

Constitution Square Building is a 1980s renovation of the early-20th-century structure known as the **Haven's Block** at 2168 Shattuck, built in 1906. Continuing to walk south down Shattuck, notice the impressive, block-long **Shattuck Hotel** at 2060 Allston. It is on the National Register and is built on the site of the original Francis Kittredge Shattuck estate.

In mid-block on Kittredge is the Art-Deco **California Theater**, a 1929 remodel of the original 1913 theater. At the corner of Shattuck and Kittredge

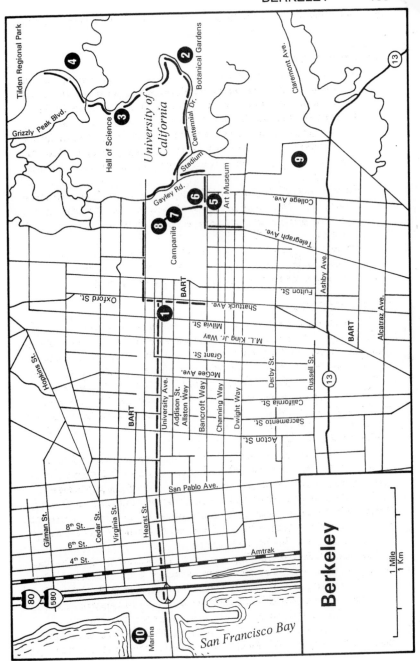

Berkeley

San Francisco Bay

1 Mile
1 Km

BERKELEY

he **Main Library**, displaying beautiful panels on two sides. In the same block is the **United Artists Theater** with its restored Art Deco facade and a lobby that rivals any other in the nation. To the left is the **Morse Block**, built in 1906 and designed by Charles W. Dickey. Note the elaborate metal cornice.

Across the street at 2271 Shattuck stands the **Tupper & Reed Building** with its Pied Piper on top. It looks like it came out of Disneyland. Next door, the **Spiro Building** boasts colorful tilework and the original arcade of display windows. Rounding out this tour is the **Whitecotton Building** at 2300, also designed by James Placheck. Currently owned by descendants of the Shattuck family, the building has undergone extensive seismic work and renovation. As you go back up Shattuck north, note the **Studio Building** at 2037 with its studio space under the tiled mansard roof. It was the first home of the California College of Arts and Crafts.

If you're in a driving mood, why not follow Shattuck north to Hearst and turn right. This will take you along the north boundary of the university. Turn right on Gayley Road and then left at the stop sign at Stadium Rimway, then left again at the next stop sign at Centennial. Now you are seriously climbing into the Berkeley hills via Strawberry Canyon.

Your first stop should be at the **Botanical Gardens** (2) at 200 Centennial Drive. This large area contains 13,000 plant species and is considered to have one of the largest plant collections in the U.S. As you wander among the thematic gardens, the views of San Francisco are outstanding. Of special note are the redwoods, the old rose section and the Chinese medicinal herb garden. There are picnic facilities and a wonderful garden shop. *Open daily 9–4:45 except Christmas. Adult admission is $3, seniors $2 and kids 3–18 $1.* ☎ *(510) 643-2755.*

Turn right on Centennial Drive and climb another mile to the superb **Lawrence Hall of Science** (3). While it is owned by the University of California, it is a public science center where people of all ages can participate in astronomy, computers and biology activities. There are interactive displays of such diverse subjects as the brain and lasers. Try your hand at calculating the odds by rolling dice. Planetarium programs, films and lectures weekly. *Open 10–5 daily except major holidays. Adult admission is $6, seniors and kids 7–18 $4 and kids 3–6 $2.* ☎ *(510) 642-5132 for more information.*

If you keep going up Centennial, it will take you to **Tilden Regional Park** (4). This 2,000-acre gem has open meadows, forests and spectacular views across the bay. There are great activities for kids such as a neat merry-go-round, the Little Farm petting zoo, steam train rides and pony rides. There's an Environmental Center, botanical gardens, picnicking sites and miles of hiking and biking trails. Lake Anza has a beach and swimmable water in summer. It is so big—with so much to do—that it is a good idea to pick up a map along the way.

The **Tilden Park Golf Course** can be played through undulating hills and valleys with row upon row of stately redwoods and Norfolk pine lining the fairways. *Greens fees are $25 Mon.–Thurs., $30 on Fri. and $38 weekends and holidays.* ☎ *(510) 848-7373 for tee times well in advance.*

The park is open 5 a.m. to 10 p.m. daily. Although the various attractions have their own hours and charges, admission to the park itself is free. ☎ *(510) 562-PARK for more information.*

As you descend Centennial, turn right on Stadium and then left on Gayley Road. Follow this to Bancroft Avenue and turn right. In a few more blocks you will come to **Telegraph Avenue**. The funky and the fun exist all along this famed street. Look over the 20–30 colorful street vendors and lots of neat stores. The street also has its share of Berkeley characters and street performers.

When you go north, Telegraph will take you right into one of the main entrances to the university. There's a **Visitor Information Center** with maps at Sproul Hall 101 to your right. The University of California at Berkeley, usually simply called Cal, is the oldest and second-largest of the nine campuses that make up the University of California system. It has close to 30,000 students in undergraduate and graduate programs. Many of the latter, like the law school called Boalt Hall, are among the top five in the nation.

U.C. Berkeley's eclectic architecture is comprised of 465 buildings with 12 million square feet. Its 1,365 acres—laid out by the redoubtable Frederick Law Olmsted—contain six libraries with some 5 million volumes. If the challenge to cover all of that is too much for you, here are some suggested highlights:

At 2626 Bancroft is the **U.C. Berkeley Art Museum/Pacific Film Archive** (5). This major campus art center includes 11 exhibition galleries, a sculpture garden and more than 800 film programs annually. The museum houses a permanent collection of Hans Hoffman paintings donated by the artist. *Open 11–5 Wed.–Sun. and 11–9 on Thurs. Closed on major holidays. Book store. Admission is $6.* ☎ *(510) 642-0808.*

Nearby in 103 Kroeber Hall at Bancroft and College is the **Phoebe Hearst Museum of Anthropology** (6). There are fascinating exhibitions and public programs usually based on the museum's exceptional archeological and anthropological collections. Enjoy the book and gift store. *Open 10–4:30, Wed.–Sun. and 10–9 on Thurs. Closed on major holidays. Adult admission is $2, seniors $1 and kids 50¢.* ☎ *(510) 643-7648.*

Most visitors to the campus are drawn to what is officially called **Sather Tower** (7), but is commonly called the Campanile. Built in 1914, it is probably the best-known landmark in the East Bay and was modeled after St. Mark's Campanile in Venice, Italy. You can take an elevator to the observation platform for stunning views all around. *Open weekdays 10–4 and weekends 10–5. Admission is $1.*

You will find one of the oldest and largest collections of fossils in America in the **Museum of Paleontology** (8), located in the Earth Sciences Building where there are lots of dinosaurs and their bony skeletons. A very topical exhibit for the Bay Area is the earthquake recorder on the first floor. *Hours are 8–9 Mon.–Fri. Free.*

For culture consider the **Berkeley Repertory Theater**, offering a mix of classics and modern theater. Tickets range from $30-$45. ☎ *(510) 204-8901 for performances and ticket information.* The **Berkeley Symphony Orchestra** offers a season that showcases Bay Area composers and the classical composers as well. Single ticket prices range from $25–$45. ☎ *(510) 841-2800.* Offering 50 diverse events—from music to theater to dance, and in every combination of the three—**Cal Performances** is a stimulating experience. Tickets go between $14 to $38 depending on the performance. ☎ *(510) 642-9988.* **Berkeley Opera** can be reached at (510) 524-5256. **Berkeley City Ballet** performance and ticket info is available at (510) 841-8913.

For current information on the arts, special events and activities in Berkeley ☎ (510) 549-8710 any time, any day.

Also of interest, but not on campus, is the **Judah L. Magnes Museum** (9) at 2911 Russell Street. Housed in this handsome old mansion are many Jewish art pieces from around the world. There are paintings by Liebermann and Chagall. This is considered to be California's premier collection of Jewish artifacts. *Open Sun.–Thurs. 10–4. Closed major holidays. Free.* ☎ *(510) 849-2710.*

It's worth a trip to the **Berkeley Marina** (10) to visit the Shorebird Nature Center at 160 University Avenue. The Center is "used to teach estuary science education to school classes," but it is open to the public as well. Inside the Center is a 100-gallon saltwater aquarium that displays creatures found in San Francisco Bay. There's also a "Touch Table" and an exhibit depicting cormorants. Some of the education programs offered are High Tides and Low Tides, where participants learn of the creatures and shoreline formations at various tides. Free. ☎ *(510) 644-8623.*

*Oakland

It's really not fair to have Oakland sit across the bay from its spectacular cousin, the City of San Francisco. In any other locale, Oakland would be a nice, comfortable place, but when it's compared to SF, the ribbing begins. Wasn't it the late columnist Herb Caen who asked if anyone else noticed that when you drive over the bridge from San Francisco you enter Oakland for free, but to go back the other way and enter SF, you have to pay $2. He could be so snide.

Two very worldly and famous authors grew up in Oakland—Gertrude Stein and Jack London. The latter was one of the most successful sellers of books in American literature. Both left after their early childhood, but there is a whole area named after London, which we will explore.

Oakland, a city of under half a million people, sports an excellent museum, a tidal saltwater lake, great parks in the hills behind the city and even its own Chinatown. The latter is much less frenetic than the one across the bay in San Francisco.

Cheek-by-jowl with the stunning new twin-tower Federal Building is a grouping of restored Victorians. That's the story of Oakland: urban renewal on a grand scale and renewal with grandeur.

GETTING THERE:

By car, from Union Square go down Bush and follow signs to the Bay Bridge. You will pay the $2 toll coming back. Follow Route 980. Take the 18th/14th St. exit.

By BART, walk down to the Powell Street Station. The fare is $2.20 to the 12th St. station in downtown Oakland. Buy a ticket from the machine (some give change and others don't). Insert your ticket in the fare gate. It will be returned to you since you will need the same ticket to exit at Oakland.

PRACTICALITIES:

Be sure to take $2 with you if you take the Bay Bridge. It's so embarrassing and inconvenient to be out of money in trying to get back to San

Francisco. Oakland can be visited any day. The weather is almost always mild and pleasant. Getting around Oakland can be confusing because there are a number of one-way streets.

FOOD AND DRINK:

Ratto's (821 Washington) In the heart of Old Oakland, their specialty is homemade pasta served in a wide variety of delicious combinations. Great live operatic and jazz on Fri. Landmark store next door. Lunch and dinner daily. ☎ (510) 832-6503. $–$$

Oakland Grill (301 Franklin) A real workingman's restaurant, they serve a Forklift Steak special that includes a sirloin, veggies, salad and fruit. Excellent three-egg omelettes. Breakfast, lunch and dinner daily. ☎ (510) 825-1176. $

Rio California Café (1233 Preservation Parkway) Their claim to fame is "A Taste of Brazil" in Oakland. The food is from south of the border and the location is a gem. Lunch and dinner daily. ☎ (510) 834-2565. $

Overland House Grill (101 Broadway) Terrific appetizers include Jalapeno Poppers, peppers stuffed with cream cheese and deep fried with ranch dressing. Soups, salads, sandwiches and pizza. ☎ (510) 268-9222. $

SUGGESTED TOUR:

Numbers in parentheses correspond to numbers on the map.

After you get off the freeway at the 18th/14th Street exit, turn left at 17th and go all the way to **Lake Merritt** (1). This is a large saltwater lake that rises with the tide in the bay. There's usually a steady stream of humanity walking, strolling and running around the 3.5-mile perimeter of the lake. Join them for a bit of exercise and enjoy the views both back toward the city and east to the hills. If you're there at dusk, you can enjoy the Necklace of Lights that encircles the lake.

Also on the north shore of the lake is the 122-acre **Lakeside Park**, originally a wildlife refuge. Today it has flower gardens and a special aviary, but the best part is **Children's Fairyland**, a three-dimensional storybook theme park. There are dozens of rides for kids, special shows and lots of attractions depicting nursery rhymes to keep young ones amused. ☎ *(510) 238-6876.*

Note that the lake is big enough for all manner of watercraft, although there is no swimming. If you are moved to leave the land and venture onto the calm water, you can rent a diverse selection of boats. The **Lake Merritt Boating Center** at 568 Bellevue Avenue will rent to you hourly: a sailboat for $6; a kayak or paddle boat for $8; or a canoe or rowboat for $6. The Center prides itself on its safety programs and lessons. They will teach you to windsurf if you have that urge. ☎ *(510) 444-3807.*

Continue your drive around the lake. After 14th Street look on the right

Oakland

500 Yards
500 Meters

Lakeside Park

Bellevue

Lake Merritt

Newton

Park St.

E. 19th St.
E. 18th St.
E. 17th St.
Foothill
E. 15th St.
International
E. 12th St.
E. 11th St.
E. 10th St.
E. 7th St.

9th Ave.
8th Ave.
7th Ave.
6th Ave.
5th Ave.
4th Ave.
3rd Ave.
2nd Ave.
10th Ave.

Lakeshore

Lakeside

Oakland Museum

Madison St.
Jackson St.
Alice St.
Harrison St.
Webster St.

Oak St.
Fallon St.

BART

20th St.
19th St.
17th St.
14th St.

Telegraph Ave.

San Pablo Ave.

BART

Franklin St.
12th St.
11th St.
10th St.

8th St.
7th St.
6th St.
5th St.
3rd St.

Chinatown

Broadway

Washington St.
Clay St.
Jefferson St.

Preservation Park

Pardee Home

M.L. King Jr. Way

Embarcadero

Jack London Square

Brush St.
Castro St.
Market St.
Filbert St.

Oakland Estuary

Alameda

(Tunnel)

880

980

880

for the large, stately Victorian home known as the **Camron-Stanford House** (2). It is the last of many Victorians that ringed the lake many years ago. Built in 1875, it was saved because it housed the Oakland Public Museum for 57 years. *You can tour it with a trained docent on Wednesdays 11–4 and Sundays 1–5. Adult admission is $4, seniors $2 and kids 12–18 $1. ☎ (510) 836-1976.*

If grand old homes interest you, there's another Oakland gem off our suggested tour. The **Dunsmuir House and Gardens** is at 2960 Perlata Oaks Court. This is an example of the Classical Revival style of architecture built in 1899. It is big at 16,000 square feet, with a Tiffany-style dome and 10 fireplaces. Set on a 40-acre estate, the grounds also include stunning gardens, a carriage house and milk barn. *The grounds can be toured Feb.–Nov., Tues.–Fri. from 10–4. Mansion tours are Apr.–Sept., Wed. 11 and 12. ☎ (510) 615-5555.*

To continue our tour after Camron-Stanford, go up to 15th Street and turn left and then left again on Madison. At 9th, turn left—this will take you to Oakland's top attraction, the:

*OAKLAND MUSEUM OF CALIFORNIA (3), 1000 Oak St., Oakland, CA 94607-4892, ☎ (510) 238-2200. *Open 10–5 Wed.–Sat., noon–5 on Sun. Closed Mon. and Tues. and major holidays. Gift shop and restaurant. Admission is $8 for adults, senior and students $6. Fri. 3–9 adults $5 and seniors and students $3. First Sun. of the month adults, seniors and students $3. ⅙.*

This tiered gem is devoted to all things California. It has three main areas of interest: The Gallery of California Art celebrates the Golden State's tremendously creative spirit; The Cowell Hall of California History unlocks the wonders of the past; and the Hall of California Ecology explores nine different natural habitats found in the state. The gardens, forests and ponds intertwined with low-level buildings are well worth a visit. At the lower level is the Great Court with outdoor exhibits. This is also a terrific spot for a picnic.

The Great Hall has changing exhibits. A fascinating recent exhibit had to do with the 150th anniversary of the discovery of gold in the hills to the east of town. Giant gold nuggets, early mining characters and other displays are outstanding. The Food Chain Diorama uses a mountain lion to show how we all compete for survival. But one of the outstanding permanent exhibits is called Dream on Wheels. What else from a museum devoted to California and its lifestyle?

After the museum, go up Oak Street to 14th and turn left. Oakland, like many other American cities, is restoring sections of its downtown. **Preservation Park** (4) is one of the most unusual urban renewal projects in which the city and a private developer have renovated 16 stunning turn-of-the-century buildings. The city added 11 buildings to the five already in place to create a true park with tree-lined streets and a central fountain. These august structures were once home to industrialists, shopkeepers, lumber merchants, saloon keepers and others.

Today, they house 45 businesses and non-profit organizations. Certain spaces are open for use by the public for meetings, receptions and classes. ☎ *(510) 874-7580 for more information.*

Also included in the park is **The Pardee Home** (5). Of all the examples of Italianate architecture in Northern California, this one is considered the finest. It is outstanding for its spacious yard and white picket fence. Also on the property is the original water tower and carriage house. Both Enoch Pardee and his son George were eye doctors who did very well. More than that, they took on political careers: they both served as mayors of Oakland. George, however, went further and served as Governor of California from 1903–07. Of special note are the thousands of artifacts collected from all over the world by George's wife Helen. *Tours of the house and grounds are Fri. and Sat. at noon. Adult admission is $5 and kids under 12 are free.* ☎ *(510) 444-2187.*

Go down 11th to Webster and turn right. This will put you into Oakland's **Chinatown** (6). Not as big or tourist oriented as San Francisco's, there's lots of good shopping and bargains nevertheless.

When you go down Broadway you will come to one of the highlights of a visit to Oakland, **Jack London Square** (7). This is the rough waterfront area where London roamed around frequently in his youth, although today it has been gentrified with its string of shops and restaurants. His cabin, where he lived during the Klondike Gold Rush, can be visited, as can the **Jack London Museum** in what is called Jack London Village. The small museum has excellent exhibits, including books and other important memorabilia. *It is open 11–6 daily. Donation.* ☎ *(510) 451-8218.*

Close by is President Franklin D. Roosevelt's yacht, the *Potomac*. All spit-and-polish, it is often called the "Floating White House." Over 12 years and $5 million has been spent to restore the 165-foot vessel. *Dockside tours are Wed. & Fri. from 10–2 and Sun. 11–3. Adult admission is $3, $2 for seniors and $1 for kids 6–17.* Of special interest to many visitors are the two-hour history cruises long the San Francisco waterfront and around Treasure Island in the bay. They are offered mid-March through November 1, with 10 and 1:30 departures on the first and third Thursdays and second and fourth Saturdays. *Cost is $30 for adults, $27 for seniors and $15 for kids 6–17. Reservations can be made by calling (510) 839-7533 ext. 1.*

Above the MacArthur Freeway in the hills above Oakland is **Dimond Canyon** (8), a good area for a hike. From Route I-580, take the Fruitvale exit, turn left on Fruitvale and go past MacArthur Boulevard to Dimond Park. The park itself has many amenities including playgrounds and basketball courts, but be sure to look for the Dimond Oak, reputed to be 200 years old and thus by far the oldest in Oakland.

Sausal Creek runs down through the canyon and the hike basically follows the creek, which is usually dry in the summer. The trail is about 3.5 miles and can get rugged in spots. Go as far as you want.

Oakland has plenty of professional sports for all tastes. The **Oakland Raiders** have moved around a bit, but they seem settled in town for the long haul. ☎ *(510) 615-4864 for ticket information.* For baseball fans, the **Oakland A's** provide plenty of excitement while chasing more homerun records. *Ticket information is available at (510) 762-BALL.* For roundball games, the **Golden State Warriors** are now playing basketball in their Arena in the Coliseum during the season. ☎ *(510) 986-2222 for ticket information.*

For the arts, Oakland stands tall. The **Oakland East Bay Symphony** plays free noontime ensemble concerts in the lobby of Lake Merritt Plaza at 1999 Harrison St.

Martinez and Benicia

This northeast section of the Bay Area has an interesting history—and should not be overlooked. It oftentimes gets forgotten with all the glamour that goes on south of these towns and hamlets.

The towns of Benicia and Martinez are actually the pincers points of the Carquinez Straits, a narrow part of the bay that leads up to the delta.

California's capital was in this region in the mid-1880s. There's also an abandoned army base that is connected to one of the country's more illustrious presidents. His name was Grant, and he was a young soldier who got in some trouble. We'll leave it at that until you take the daytrip.

The region also was the home of the famed naturalist John Muir. It would seem that he would spend his twilight years on some wilderness mountaintop, but instead he choose a fruit ranch in the community of Martinez.

Vallejo is north of Benicia and has as its claim to fame Marine World Theme Park. It is quite a mix of aquarium, zoo, circus, rides and the like.

GETTING THERE:

By car, from Union Square go to Bush and follow signs to the Bay Bridge, which is Highway I-80. You will pay the $2 Bay Bridge toll coming back. Get on Highway I-580 and a short distance later take Highway 24. Look for Highway I-680 North. Follow 680 to Martinez. The Benicia Bridge has a $2 toll, which you pay on the way there.

PRACTICALITIES:

This is a leisurely excursion into the countryside, so take sunglasses and comfortable shoes. Any time is a good time to take this daytrip.

FOOD AND DRINK:

First Street Café (440 First St. in Benicia) California cuisine in a stylish setting near the waterfront. Fresh bread daily and homemade desserts are highlights. Breakfast, lunch and dinner daily. ☎ (707) 745-1400. $–$$

Tia Theresa at the Brewery (120 W. H St. in Benicia) Housed in an historic building, this spot features artistic murals of the area. Wonderful Mexican-American food and great drinks. Live music Sat. nights. Open for lunch and dinner daily. ☎ (707) 745-2535. $–$$

Captain Bylther's Restaurant (123 First St. in Benicia) Good views of river traffic negotiating the straits. Good salads and healthy dishes for the whole family. ☎ (707) 745-4082. $–$$

Victoria's Café (701 Main in Martinez) This little café was formerly called DiMaggio's because Joe supposedly put up the money years ago. Who knows why it has a courthouse/prison theme now, but if you want to feel his aura, go there. Good basic breakfast and lunch daily. ☎ (925) 370-2722. $

SUGGESTED TOUR:

Numbers in parentheses correspond to numbers on the map.

At first this route will take you through some of the more congested areas in the East Bay. But once you start to climb the mountains and go through the tunnel, there are more open areas of pastures and round hills on the other side.

You will pass by the towns of Walnut Creek and Concord, both of which are basically bedroom communities, but with a sprinkling of high tech businesses. Many of the residents commute into San Francisco or Oakland.

Soon you will come to the old town of **Martinez** (1). The story is told of the San Francisco bartender who took the ferry daily to this little town in the East Bay and to stave off the chill of the trip, he invented the martini. It makes for a good story—whether it's true or not.

Take the Alhambra exit for the **John Muir National Historic Site** (2). Muir was born in 1838 in Scotland. In 1849, his father decided to try homesteading in Wisconsin. Eighteen years later Muir embarked on his legendary thousand-mile walk that took him from Indiana to the Appalachians and finally to the Gulf Coast of Florida. Ever restless, he sailed for California shortly after arriving.

The Sierra Nevada mountains in California were his siren call and he spent a good deal of his adult life there. He called these mountains his "Range of Light." Here he carefully studied the trees and plants and geology all along the mountain range. Muir was able to prove, against all scientific thought at the time, that the Yosemite Valley was formed by glaciers.

This was the man who really started the conservation movement in the United States in the early 1800s. Teddy Roosevelt insisted on naming Muir Woods (see Daytrip 19) after the man because of his work preserving forest and fields throughout California. Many point to Yosemite National Park (see Daytrips 37 & 38) as Muir's single greatest achievement. Some consider him the father of the National Park Service, which today administers this property.

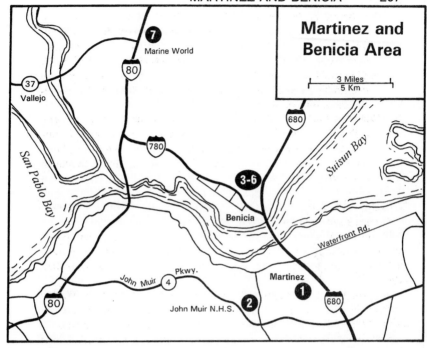

Martinez and Benicia Area

3 Miles
5 Km

Marine World

Vallejo

San Pablo Bay

Suisun Bay

Benicia

Waterfront Rd.

John Muir Pkwy.

John Muir N.H.S.

Martinez

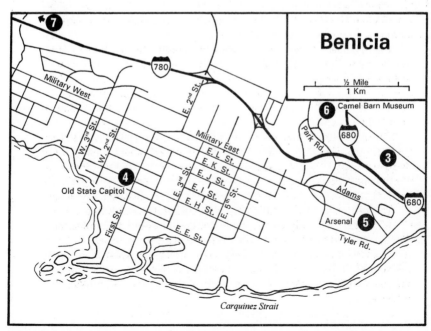

Benicia

½ Mile
1 Km

Military West

Military East

Camel Barn Museum

Park Rd.

E. L St.

E. K St.

E. J St.

E. I St.

Old State Capitol

E. H St.

Adams

E. E. St.

Arsenal

Tyler Rd.

First St.

Carquinez Strait

You can tour the eight-acre farm and his house, both of which are National Historic Sites. The 17-room house is a fascinating Italianate Victorian. You can see from the furnishings how Muir conducted his life, especially the messy study where he did much of his writing, which included 10 major books and 300 articles. It is interesting to note that on the grounds is the adobe built by Don Vincente Martinez for whom the town is named. *The home and grounds are open Wed.–Sun. 10–4:30. You can take a self-guided tour or there are guided tours at 2 in the afternoon. Adult admission is $2. There is a small gift and book store. It is located at 4202 Alhambra Avenue.* ☎ *(925) 228-8860 for more information. Partially* ♿.

Be sure to go down Alhambra into the little seacoast town of Martinez. It has a tree-lined downtown with lots of reasonably priced antiques and collectibles. This is where Joe DiMaggio was born, although there is no plaque or monument. Maybe later. Check out the tiny **Martinez Museum** at the corner of Escobar and Court Streets. It is in the Victorian Borland Home with changing displays of Martinez and Contra Costa County artifacts. *Open Tues. and Thurs. 11:30–3.*

If all this touring has made you thirsty, take a diversion to the **Conrad Viano Winery**, a real down-home affair in contrast to the toney wineries of Napa and Sonoma. It is located at 150 Morello Avenue. Open daily. ☎ *(925) 226-6465.*

When you cross over the Benicia-Martinez Bridge, you are reportedly passing the narrowest spot in the entire San Francisco Bay. To your left is San Pablo Bay, which is the northern portion of the bay, and to your right is Suisun Bay. The latter is actually the beginning of the delta region of Northern California. This is the immense waterway into which the Sacramento River and its many tributaries spill their waters coming down from the High Sierras. As you look to the right, stuck in this waterway is one of the Navy's largest mothball fleets. There are just under 100 of these vessels, including Liberty Ships left over from World War II.

Just across the bridge, take the Central Benicia exit to the seacoast town of **Benicia** (3). General Mariano Vallejo—who founded Sonoma (see Daytrip 25)—also founded this town on part of his humongous rancho when this was Mexican territory, naming it after his wife. For a while, Benicia rivaled Yerba Buena (renamed San Francisco) to the east as the trade and transportation hub of Northern California. While Benicia may have made more sense because of its location as a rail and ship junction, look at the relative size of the two cities today to tell which one won handily.

If you stop at the Chamber of Commerce, they have a handy map outlining a walking tour of some of Benicia's highlights.

At the corner of First and G streets is the handsome, historic **Old State Capitol** (4). Built in 1852, it was California's capital city for two years in 1853–54. Actually, it was the third capital after San Jose and Vallejo. The city fathers were so anxious to get the state capitol in Benicia back then that they built this building in three months, using for the six big interior post masts from sailing ships left behind in the area during the Gold Rush. You can visit the legislative chambers. *The Old Capitol is open 10 to 5 daily. Admission is $2 for adults.* ☎ *(707) 745-5435.* ♿.

We promised you a racy story about an American president in the introduction to this daytrip. Here goes: The Army found this area advantageous and so in the mid-1800s established an arsenal here. This was the time of the Mexican War, and one of the lieutenants passing through was a young man by the name of Grant. Apparently he got carried away one night with too much drink on the streets of Benicia and became so unruly that he was arrested and tossed in jail. The soldier's name was Ulysses S. Grant and he not only became Commander in Chief, but also President of the United States. Can you imagine what the media would make of a story like that today?

You can visit the remnants of the base. After visiting the Old Capitol, retrace your route and turn right and go down Military. Where Grant and Adams separate is the Spanish-style building of the **Benicia Arsenal** (5). Go down Grant and look for signs for **Johansen Square.** Within this complex is the Armory with attached **Clock Tower.** The building, with two-foot-thick walls and slots for rifles, was used as a defense post for the Carquinez Straits. Also on the property is the **Commandant's House,** an imposing 20-room mansion built in 1860 and being restored today. Stephen Vincent Benet, the well-known poet who wrote "John Brown's Body," lived here when his father was commandant of the post.

Just as you come out of the post on Adams is the **Guard House** built in 1872. What is significant about this building (the bars are still on the windows) is that here was the location of Grant's trial where he was found guilty as charged.

At the end of Adams there is a sharp right turn to Jefferson. Follow signs to visit the **Camel Barn Museum** (6) at 2024 Camel Road. In 1863 the Secretary of War had a brainstorm to use camels in the deserts of the United States for moving war materiel. A bunch of these stubborn beasts were imported and sent to the desert. Supposedly the camels did just fine in their roles, but their handlers couldn't do their jobs. Because it was such an embarrassment, the animals were shipped off to this corner of the country to be auctioned off. These four sandstone buildings were originally military warehouses and are now listed on the National Register of Historic Places. Today the museum has a variety of displays and exhibits of both the city of Benicia and the Army Arsenal. *Open 1–4 Fri., Sat. and Sun. Donations requested.* ☎ *(707) 745-5435.*

Continue north on Highway I-780 to Vallejo. Here you will find an unusual amusement park geared for families. **Marine World Theme Park** (7), besides being an amusement park, works hard at research, training and education.

Along with bumper cars and rides that include Flying Carousel, Jambo, Swan Boats and Monkey Business, there are wonderful shows. One is the Killer Whale Show, and there's also the Sea Lion, Elephant, Bird and Water Ski Shows. The Wildlife Theater presents a number of animals as an ambassador for its species. It is designed to further an appreciation for endangered species. At Dolphin Harbor, the park presents its seven bottle-nose dolphins featuring their extraordinary behavior. The show allows guests to come face-to-face with these amazing animals.

Some of the other attractions include Tiger Island where adult tigers and their cubs dive for their favorite toys. The Walrus Experience allows visitors to observe these fascinating creatures above and below the water. The Shark Experience allows you to travel underwater through the Tropical Reef inside a crystal-clear tunnel. Here you are surrounded by sharks as they swim beside you and overhead—but you are thankfully protected by strong plastic walls. There are also educational displays and material on sharks. Kids love the Elephant Encounter where the intrepid ones can ride some of the smaller versions of these giants.

The park is open 10–8 Fri.–Sun. in the spring, daily 10–10 Memorial Day through Labor Day, then 10–8 Fri.–Sun. through Nov. 1. Adult admission is $28.99, kids 4–12 are $19.99 and seniors 60+ $23.99. Admission covers almost every attraction, although there are small additional charges for riding the elephants. Parking is $6 per vehicle. ☎ (707) 644-4000.

Four Bay Islands

You won't see the hordes of visitors who go to Alcatraz or Angel islands, but that's part of the appeal of these four (of 14) other islands spotted around the bay that we'll visit in this daytrip. They're often overlooked, and they shouldn't be.

Treasure Island is attached to Yerba Buena. The former will soon be transformed into a huge housing and recreation area, and the latter is where we'll find out how the heavy ship traffic on the bay gets sorted out.

Even many San Franciscans have a hard time believing there are an estimated 3,000 Victorians in the town of Alameda. That says a couple of things. Could some San Francisco residents be a bit provincial? And further, it tells you that Alameda is an old city with an interesting past. Bay Farm Island is just a stone's throw from Alameda and, besides Yuppie residences, has a spectacular bay-side path that circles the place.

For many, the highlight of this trip will be to go aboard the fabled aircraft carrier USS *Hornet* tied up in Alameda. Through the efforts of a handful of Navy vets this treasure was saved from the cutting torch. Today, thousands stand in awe of the gaping aircraft bay under the huge flight deck.

Also in this daytrip we'll learn a bit about the two bridges that link the City of San Francisco with its many neighbors in the East Bay.

GETTING THERE:

By car, from Union Square go down Bush and follow signs to the Bay Bridge (Hwy. I-80) going to the East Bay. About half way across the Bay Bridge look for a left turn to Treasure Island. It comes up quickly, so be cautious. You will pay the $2 toll coming back.

PRACTICALITIES:

Any time is a good time to visit these other islands—with one caveat: pay attention to the opening times for the USS *Hornet* and other museums.

FOOD AND DRINK:

Luciano's (2319 Santa Clara Ave. in Alameda) They call it French Ital-

iano, which means lots of pasta, but with a French flair. Their wood-
burning oven turns out many wondrous pizza dishes. ☎ (510) 523-
3300. $–$$

The Courtyard (1349 Park in Alameda) Café, marketplace, gallery and
espresso bar rolled into one. They serve a poached salmon and
spinach salad that is tops. Or try the crab cakes that melt in your
mouth. Lunch and dinner daily. ☎ (510) 521-1521. $–$$

Linguine's Pasta & Vino (1506 Park in Alameda) So popular they kept
expanding and now it covers three storefronts. Intimate and fun, the
pasta dishes are like the Old World. Lunch and dinner daily. ☎
(510) 865-5101. $–$$

The Whole Shabang (formerly famous Crolls's at 1400 Webster in
Alameda) This is a fun place. The Oofty-Goofty is a turkey, roast
beef, salami and cheese combo. Lots of other sandwiches and salads. Jazz Fri. & Sat. nights. Breakfast, lunch and dinner daily. ☎
(510) 864-2264. $

SUGGESTED TOUR:

Numbers in parentheses correspond to numbers on the map.

Let's talk first about the bridge you are traveling on to get to these islands
in the bay. The **San Francisco-Oakland Bay Bridge** (1), completed in 1936,
carries 280,000 cars a day and is reputed to be one of the busiest bridges in
the nation. For many years it carried cars and trains, but the latter were
stopped in 1950. On the top deck is westbound traffic and the lower east-
bound. For the movie *The Graduate,* the traffic was reversed so a helicopter
could film Dustin Hoffman and Katherine Ross shooting over to Berkeley in
a convertible with her hair blowing in the sunshine.

Keep in mind that the West Bay side of the bridge was built (like the
Golden Gate Bridge) to allow huge ships to sail beneath it and so its towers
soar 500 feet above the water. The two suspension spans on the west bay
section are 2,310 feet wide and meet at a central anchorage that is bored
400 feet down due to the extraordinary depth of the water, ranging from 50
to 105 feet. This side of the bridge is by far the more attractive of the two
sections. It is 4.5 miles long. The two bridges meet at Yerba Buena Island
and for a while you travel not on a bridge but through a tunnel.

Once on the other side of the tunnel you are on the less dramatic, can-
tilever East Bay span that is about 4 miles long. The Loma Prieta earthquake
in 1989 caused considerable damage to both sides. Since then, there has
been talk of replacing the East Bay side with something more aesthetically
pleasing than the low level, pedestrian-looking bridge there now. The state
is proposing a utilitarian design, but others are pushing for a more dramatic
single pylon with multiple cables creating a spider web effect. This is so the
East Bay will have a "signature" bridge too. Meanwhile, the debate goes on.

Take the left turn lane to **Treasure Island** (2). For years this was a Navy

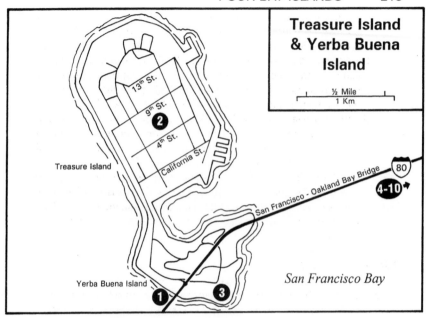

Treasure Island & Yerba Buena Island

½ Mile
1 Km

Treasure Island

13ᵗʰ St.

9ᵗʰ St.

❷

4ᵗʰ St.

California St.

San Francisco - Oakland Bay Bridge

80

❹-❿

Yerba Buena Island

❶

❸

San Francisco Bay

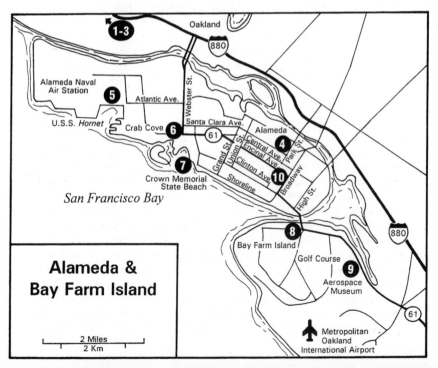

1-3

Oakland

880

Alameda Naval
Air Station

❺

Atlantic Ave.

U.S.S. *Hornet*

Crab Cove

❻

Santa Clara Ave.

61

Webster St.

Alameda

Central Ave.

❹

Park St.

Encinal Ave.

Union St.

Clinton Ave.

❿

❼

Grand St.

Shoreline

Broadway

High St.

Crown Memorial
State Beach

San Francisco Bay

❽

Bay Farm Island

Golf Course

❾

Aerospace
Museum

61

✈ Metropolitan
Oakland
International Airport

880

Alameda & Bay Farm Island

2 Miles
2 Km

Base, but it was recently given to the City of San Francisco. The island was actually built of silt from the bay and the Sacramento Delta as one of the biggest manmade islands in the world. The purpose of all this construction was to create a place for the 1939 World's Fair, which drew upwards of 10 million people. Besides all the rides and other fair accouterments, maybe many people came to see Sally Rand's Nude Dude Ranch.

Plans call for turning most of Treasure island into a giant playland for residents and visitors to the Bay Area. There used to be a museum on the base with displays of Naval operations around the bay. The museum will be reopened when the island is transformed for recreational use soon after the year 2000. In the meantime, enjoy the fantastic view of the city from this spot.

You might consider a side trip across the way to **Yerba Buena Island** (3), which was made by Mother Nature. As you leave Treasure Island, the first road on your left is Macalla. This will take you up through the heavily wooded island, where you will take an immediate right up Yerba Buena. Follow signs for the **Ship Tracking Station** run by the U.S. Coast Guard. This unique facility is like an airport control tower; however, instead of airplanes it keeps track of the 200 plus vessels that enter, leave and criss-cross the bay daily.

Coast Guard personnel will give you a briefing on how they use computers, radar and video cameras to keep everything moving safely in a body of water that extends ten miles northeast to San Pablo Bay and 40 miles southeast to Palo Alto. At its greatest width the bay measures 13 miles, with depths reaching over 200 feet just inside the Golden gate. The problem comes about because 70 percent of the bay is less than 12 feet deep. You can easily see how these ship traffic people are very important. They stress that their job is to keep vessels informed of each other and water conditions, and not to give orders like the FAA for airplanes. *You can visit any day between 9:30–5.* ☎ *(415) 556-2950 or 556-2760.*

You can follow Yerba Buena down to the water and look back up at the gracious admirals' mansions surrounded by huge lawns. Return and look for the Oakland entrance to the freeway.

Cross the rest of the Bay Bridge and follow signs to the 23rd Avenue/Alameda exit. At the next stop light, turn right and cross the small bridge, putting you on Park Street.

Alameda (4) is a wonderful old city in the East Bay that's often overlooked as place to visit. The original inhabitants were Ohlone Indians when it was all marshland and estuaries. It got westernized when two gentlemen by the name of Auginbaugh and Chipman bought over 2,000 acres in 1851 from the original Mexican land grant. They were quite the developers/entreprenuers, who to draw people to acquire lots and build houses, provided free excursions to their property in the East Bay. More than that, they supposedly gave away lots to anyone who would build a structure worth more than $50. Imagine that deal today.

The place grew slowly until the railroad lines extended to Alameda and regular ferry service began. That caused a building boom during which many of the nearly 3,000 Victorians were built. The island sported seven Navy shipyards during WWII. All that military presence gave Alameda its reputation. Today the Navy is gone, many of the Victorians have been restored and the island remains a pleasant, low-key place to live and visit.

Turn right on Santa Clara from Park. At Webster turn right then left at Atlantic. Follow signs to the giant aircraft carrier **USS *Hornet*** (5), which is tied up at a pier in Alameda Point. This ship is one of the most storied Navy warriors that significantly affected the outcome of WWII in the Pacific. It is amazing that the huge and complex ship was operational 21 months after its keel was laid.

And once it got underway, the *Hornet* wreaked devastation on the Japanese military. Consider that it destroyed 1,410 enemy aircraft and 1,250 million tons of shipping. It set Navy records by shooting down 72 planes in a day and 255 in a month. While it was under attack 59 times, it did all this without being hit by a bomb, torpedo or Kamikaze. However, in a typhoon in June 1945, the forward 24 feet of her flight deck was collapsed by heavy seas. For the next two days, *Hornet* launched aircraft off her stern as she backed into the wind.

The ship was designated a National Historic Landmark in 1991, but in spite of that it was destined for the scrap heap in 1995. A small but determined group of Navy veterans worked through 37 agencies and raised several million dollars to rescue this most worthy prize. We should be thankful for their hard work.

Today you can tour the 900-foot beauty that has been refurbished from bow to stern. There are period aircraft on display above and below deck, but the most awe-inspiring of all is to stand in the huge bay below deck and see the cavernous 900-foot-long bay where multiple aircraft were held in readiness for launch and attack. Don't miss the cramped crew's quarters and the wheel house where the Captain controls the direction and speed of *Hornet*.

Open daily 8–6. Closed on major holidays. Adult admission is $9 and kids under 6 are free. ☎ *(510) 521-8448 for more information.*

Retrace your route to Webster and turn right. When you come to Central turn right and then left on McKay. This will take you to the **Crab Cove Visitor Center** (6) at 1252 McKay. For many years, this was a giant amusement park called Neptune Beach with a whole range of amusements and activities from a skating rink to dance halls to roller coaster. That all got cleared away when Neptune went bankrupt in 1939. Today there is an attractive, but small display space with an array of three-dimensional exhibits of some of the more fascinating aspects of the marine environment in the bay. Naturalists take field trips out onto the marshes and mud flats that are part of a much larger Crab Cove Marine Reserve. *The Center is open Wed.–Sun from 10–4:30 Mar.–Nov.* ☎ *(510) 521-6887.*

After the Visitor Center, turn right on Central and right on 8th which will take you to Shoreline Drive. Make your way along this 2.5 mile-drive that parallels **Crown Memorial State Beach** (7). Beach activities are influenced by the tides. High tide is the best time to observe sea birds like loons, grebes and various ducks close to shore. Low tides are best for viewing shorebirds and intertidal organisms like clams, mussels and worms that live in the rocky bottom and mudflat areas. You can simply catch some sun along here too.

Follow this road, which becomes Broadway, and turn right on Otis, taking you over the bridge to **Bay Farm Island** (8). See—you're now on your fourth island as promised. Turn right immediately on Veteran Way to find the start of a wonderful walk along a waterfront park that hugs the shoreline. A lot of the land on the west side of the island is landfill, where many pleasant homes have been built for the young and prosperous causing it to be dubbed "Yuppieville" today. This island got its original name because of the fertile soil on the higher regions where farmers grew vegetables for neighboring cities. Today's population is around 8,000.

A lovely golf course sits in the middle of the island. You can play the **Jack Clark Golf Course** on Mondays through Fridays for $22. Twilight games cost $16. On weekends greens fees are $25 and a golf cart is $22. ☎ *(510) 864-3423 for reservations.*

A big chunk of Bay Farm Island is utilized by the Oakland Airport. If you go out Doolittle Drive and turn right on Langley Drive and then left on Boeing Street, you will find the **Western Aerospace Museum** (9). The museum's facilities are located in a vintage hangar on the airport's historic North Field. The hangar is an educational center, restoration shop and outdoor exhibition area. The hangar, now filled with historic aircraft, was built in 1940 by the Boeing School of Aeronautics and was used to train aircraft mechanics for the U.S. Army Air Corps and Navy during WWII.

The most spectacular exhibit is the four-engine flying boat built in 1946. There is a video that chronicles the history of the flying boats and shows clips of its performance in the film *Indiana Jones and Raiders of the Lost Ark. The museum and gift shop are open Wed.–Sun. and most holidays 10–4. Adult admission is $4.* ☎ *(510) 638-7100 for more information.*

As you leave Bay Farm Island, get on Central Avenue where you will come across many of the handsome Victorians for which Alameda is well known. This side of the island is known as the "Gold Coast" for its many elaborate mansions. This is specifically called the "Leonardville Heritage Area." Go to the 2000 block of San Jose to see two outstanding examples of Queen Anne style homes built by the rich who lived in Alameda. At 2103 is a modest mansion built in 1891, but a major mansion is at 2070 San Jose, erected by a wealthy builder.

Go up to Union Street. At 891 is Joseph Leonard's bayshore mansion,

Leonardville's biggest and costliest home. He built it in 1895 for $20,000. Next door at 893 is another building designed by Leonard. It was the home of Albion Morse, who was the captain of a vessel sailing between San Francisco and China for 14 years. On Clinton Avenue, go by 1832–1834. Again the elaborate mansion was designed by Joseph Leonard for Green Majors who was a mining speculator. There are many more.

For a more complete look at the background of Alameda, visit the **Alameda Historical Museum** (9) at 2324 Alameda Avenue. This small museum traces the many fascinating turn of events in Alameda's past. *Open Wed.–Fri. and Sun. 1:30–4:00 and Sat. 11–4. Admission is free.* ☎ *(510) 521-1233.*

Mount Diablo and Vicinity

The Spanish called it Monte de Diablo, or "Devil's Mountain," from an encounter with a frightening Indian at mid-slope. That's one story, but there are others about how the mountain got its name. If you climb it or ride a bike up it, as thousands do each year, you may even have your own name for this 3,849-foot peak. Many still believe spirits inhabit the mountain.

Whatever the name, Mount Diablo can be seen from just about anywhere in the East Bay and beyond. And if you can see it from a huge area below, it only stands to reason that you can see down on probably an ever bigger area from the summit. There is one guidebook that says the mountain offers "the widest view that can be seen from any point in the United States." That's quite a claim. And the park's own brochure says the view is second only to 19,000-foot Mount Kilimanjaro in Africa.

The mountain itself is part of the Mount Diablo State Park, covering a vast area that includes the Diablo Foothills Regional Park as well. There's a two-lane road winding its way to the summit, or you can hike a trail nearly seven miles (or longer) to the top. Along the way is wonderful scenery and wildlife that ranges from native birds to mountain lions.

In Danville, we'll visit the home of author Eugene O'Neill. This is where he wrote his last five plays, some of which were his best known. The upscale town of Blackhawk up the road also has a very fancy shopping mall with an interesting auto museum at one corner.

GETTING THERE:

By car, from Union Square go down Bush and follow signs to the Bay Bridge. You will pay the $2 toll coming back. Once across the bridge, take Route 24 and then I-680 south. Take the Stone Valley/Alamo exit and go along Danville Boulevard to Danville.

PRACTICALITIES:

If you decide to hike all or a portion of the trail up Mount Diablo, wear suitable footgear. There are many trails. The State Park Service gives three ratings to the mountain's trails: short, pleasant walks; moderate hikes; and demanding hikes.

FOOD AND DRINK:

Bridges Restaurant & Bar (44 Church St. in Danville) Handsome building of native woods with spectacular gardens. Imaginative menu that changes daily, featuring the finest in seasonal ingredients. Lunch Fri., dinner daily. ☎ (925) 820-7200. $$–$$$

Basil Leaf Café (501 Hartz Ave. in Danville) Terrific Italian spot with a wide selection of pastas. Two of their specialities are Linguini Herbed Marinara and Chicken Gilroy with Roasted Garlic & Pancetta. Lunch and dinner daily. ☎ (925) 838-7778. $–$$

Patrick David's (416 Sycamore Valley Rd.) Lovely café in an unusual shopping center. The Maple Cured Double Thick Pork Chop with Three Cheese Potato Cake and Green Apple Reduction is a favorite. Great salads too. Lunch and dinner daily. ☎ (925) 838-7611. $–$$

Celia's Mexican Restaurant (411 Hartz in Danville) If you love Mexican food, this place is for you. Pollo en Crema is strips of chicken with a secret sour cream sauce. Good seafood dishes too. Lunch and dinner daily. ☎ (925) 855-9300. $

SUGGESTED TOUR:

Numbers in parentheses correspond to numbers on the map.

The historic town of Danville holds lots of interesting spots. Turn right on Railroad Avenue for the **San Ramon Museum** (1), located in the old Southern Pacific Depot built in 1891. The railroad was very important to the San Ramon Valley, eventually reaching Martinez. From there the area's farmers could ship their produce and crops to the larger San Francisco market. Today, the old depot houses a museum focusing on the history and culture of the entire San Ramon Valley. *Open Wed.–Sun. 10–5. Free.* ☎ *(925) 837-3750.*

The **Iron Horse Trail** (2) passes the old depot, and will eventually cover the entire distance of the former railroad bed. Great for walking, biking and rollerblading. Take a stroll to get a sense of the valley and views to the hills on either side. Be sure to check out the **Old Danville Hotel** at 411 Hartz. It used to face the other way when it was used by passengers coming out to the valley on the train. Now it houses about 14 nifty shops. Speaking of shopping, one of the most comfortable and pleasant centers in the country is the **Danville Livery & Mercantile** at Sycamore Valley Road and San Ramon Valley Boulevard. This center was designed to complement the community's historic charm.

Before tackling the mountain, why not start out with some culture by visiting the **Eugene O'Neill National Historic Site** (3). Like a lot of people who
decide to settle in the Bay Area, O'Neill and his wife Carlotta looked north
in Marin, south on the peninsula and finally decided on the East Bay as their
"final home and harbor." When they saw the area above the wilderness, it
was apparently an easy decision.

On the 158 acres they purchased outside Danville, they built quite a
spread. O'Neill was flush with his Nobel Prize and so the house became
one of the finest around. They called it Tao House from the Chinese for "the
good, simple life." They also put in a swimming pool and extensive gardens.
This was where America's most famous playwright wrote such classics as
The Ice Man Cometh, A Moon for the Misbegotten and *Long Day's Journey
Into Night.* O'Neill won the Pulitzer for the latter, and is the only American
playwright to be honored with the prestigious Nobel Prize—so far.

After the home was restored, the National Park Service decided to open
it for the public. Furnishing of the rooms continues. Since the house is in a
gated neighborhood, it is only accessible at certain times. *Tours are at 10
and 12:30 Wed.–Sun. except major holidays, but by reservations only at
(925) 838-0249. Admission is free.*

Take Diablo Road and follow signs to the South Entrance to **Mount Diablo State Park** (4). Part way up the mountain you will find an entrance station. *The park is open 8 to sunset every day. Admission is $5 per car and $4
for seniors.* You can begin your hike here or choose from about a dozen
other hiking trails and fire roads. If you go by car, the summit is about 10
miles away.

They say of Mount Diablo: "One mountain, many names." As we mentioned at the beginning of this daytrip, one legend has it that Diablo or
Devil's Mountain came about as a name when the Spanish in 1804 stormed
into the area looking for runaway mission Indians. They surrounded an Indian village in a thicket, but when night came the stealthy natives snuck
away, infuriating the Spanish. Thus they called it *Monte de Diablo*, which
really means "Thicket of the Devil." Mistaking Monte to mean mountain,
others meanwhile started to call it Mount Diablo.

There's an 1850 version told by General Vallejo, who claimed the Spanish were sent packing when an unknown personage or evil spirit appeared
out of the mist. The name Devil's Mountain was reinforced with this tale.
Then Bret Harte published a short story in 1863 that further confused the
whole picture. Harte's version has an 18th-century priest meeting up with
the devil atop the mountain. The devil shows the good father what California will be like in the future, with hordes of Americans chasing out the Spanish. The rotten devil promised to hold back the Yankees in return for
renouncing the padre's priestly duties. They fight. Then the priest wakes up.
Sounds like opera.

However the name came about, the mountain is well worth a trip up.

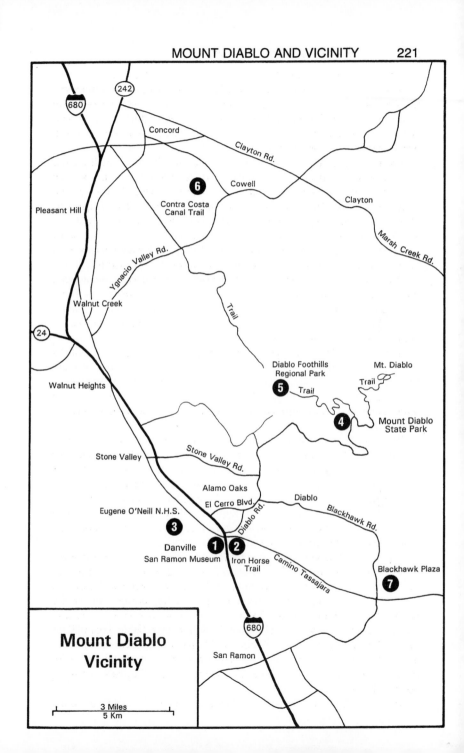

The park suggests any one of ten "short, pleasant walks"—such as Juniper Trail, Donner Creek and Sentinel Rock—that are relatively level and where the footing is firm. There are also ten "moderate hikes" that are half-day adventures. In summer you will need a hat and water, and look out for poison oak (it is a three-leaf devil that can cause unpleasant itching). In winter bring along a jacket. In the more strenuous category are the ten "demanding" hikes that are not meant to test your endurance, but to open up some of the more remote beauty spots of the mountain. These are usually day-long adventures for the experienced hiker and outdoors person. There's the Burma Road Loop, the Pine Pond-Frog Pond Loop and Mt. Olympia from Three Springs as examples. Brochures with trail maps are available at the Visitor Center.

Guided hikes and interpretive events are conducted by the park staff. You must check the bulletin board at the Visitor Center or call (925) 837-2525 to find out what's going on. If picnicking is your thing, there are over 50 sites along the park's paved roads. You can call for reservations. This is campers' paradise with 58 sites located in three campgrounds. Most campsites have piped water and restrooms with flush toilets. In summer, the campsites are first-come-first-served, but from October through May they can be reserved by calling (800) 444-7275.

Something must be said about the view from the top. Mount Diablo is so high compared to the surrounding countryside that it was selected in 1851 as the starting point for a survey of the public domain. Today, the Mount Diablo base and meridian lines are used as legal references of real estate throughout two thirds of California and parts of Nevada and Oregon.

If it is clear, you can see west beyond the Golden Gate to the Farallon Islands, approximately 40 miles away; southeast to the James Lick Observatory (see Daytrip 47) in the mountains above San Jose; south to Mount Loma Prieta in the Santa Cruz mountains; north to Mount Saint Helena in the Coast Range. North and east of Mount Diablo is the San Joaquin Valley and Sacramento Rivers that meet to form the splayed-out and watery delta. It is said that with binoculars you can even see Half Dome in Yosemite, and according to the park's brochure, ". . . the panorama visible from the top of Mount Diablo is unsurpassed in extent by any other in America or Europe, and is second only to that visible from 19,000-foot Mount Kilimanjaro in Africa." Yes, it snows lightly atop this mountain fairly often in winter.

The Visitor Center, with neat displays of the geology, plants and animals of Mount Diablo is open Wed.–Sun. 11–5.

Spread out just below Mount Diablo Park is the **Diablo Foothills Regional Park** (5). This 978 acres is bounded by the Castle Rocks of Mount Diablo and the undulating camelback ridges that form Shell Ridge. The facilities include lots of open land for trail use and nature study. There are reservable picnic sites, a swimming pool and archery range. *Open 10:30–5 daily. The all-day fees for these facilities are adults $4, kids 13–17 $3 and*

6–12 $2. The rest is open free to the public from Memorial Day to Labor Day. ☎ *(925) 462-1400.*

Just a few steps from the urbanized areas of the county is the **Contra Costa Canal Regional Trail** (6). It is a network of beautiful trails—much of which runs along a canal begun in the 1930s to supply irrigation water for local crops. Delayed by WWII, construction was complete some 20 years later. Water is pumped into the canal from the Sacramento/San Joaquin delta near Rock Slough. The water flows to Martinez (see Daytrip 32) where it is treated to become that city's and several other cities' water supply. No swimming or fishing.

Head up Sycamore Valley Road to the swanky **Blackhawk Plaza** shopping center. Besides Saks Fifth Ave. and numerous other top-scale shops, the center holds an amazing collection called the **Blackhawk Automotive Museum** (7). The building alone is an architectural masterpiece, featuring multi-levels of glass and granite. The dazzling display of antique autos is perhaps one of the best in the world. Within the 100,000-square-foot museum are some 120 classics that stagger the imagination. A tiny curved-dash Oldsmobile contrasts with hefty Duesenbergs, Lincolns and Packards. The lighting is such that the sparkle of chrome and brass and silver is almost overwhelming.

Besides the cars, there is an accompanying museum that celebrates the automobile as art. It holds nearly 1,000 artifacts in an amazing variety of media from the automobile's first 110 years. There is a gift shop and bookstore with everything automotive. *Open Wed.–Sun. 10–5. Admission is $8 for adults. Students and seniors are $6.* ☎ *(925) 736-2277.* ♿.

To Vacaville: For the Whole Family

Be prepared for variety on this daytrip. On the way to one of the largest outlet malls in the nation at Vacaville, we'll stop for some different kinds of touring. It just could be the kind of factory tour you've always wanted to do, but have never taken the time. And there's something for everyone.

Dad might like the huge Budweiser brewery, while Mom and the kids will go bananas over the equally impressive Jelly Belly factory whose product was made famous by one of our illustrious presidents. Then Dad's and Mom's spirits might pick up as we take a tour to a couple of wineries in the area. Finally, it's Dad's turn again with a tour of a large airplane facility, but Mom can come storming back when we get to what is considered the nation's largest outlet mall at the end of this daytrip.

Regardless of which member of the family is in favor of a particular tour or place to visit, it should be fun for everyone.

GETTING THERE:

By car, from Union Square go down Bush and follow signs to the Bay Bridge. You will pay the $2 toll coming back. The bridge is Route I-80. Stay on that the entire way to Vacaville. There is a $2 toll for the Carquinez Bridge.

PRACTICALITIES:

This daytrip will include some walking, so wear comfortable shoes. Be sure to pay attention to the hours and days for tours of the two factories as they vary seasonally.

FOOD AND DRINK:

Merchant & Main Grill and Bar (349 Merchant in Vacaville) Small-town California cuisine, which means it isn't snooty. Terrific fresh seafood and prime steaks. Open for lunch and dinner daily. ☎ (707) 446-0368. $–$$

Manka's Corner Deli (Manka's Corner on Abernathy) Country atmosphere to the max. This is a real down-home place in Suisun Valley. Sandwich menu a yard long plus deli items. Lunch Tues.–Sun., breakfast weekends. ☎ (707) 425-3207. $

Jelly Belly Café (2400 N. Watney Way in Fairfield) Besides burgers shaped like Jelly Bellies, there are Jelly Belly milkshakes, and ice cream and candy made on the spot. Lots of good eats in a fun place. ☎ (707) 428-2838. $

Heritage House (303 Merchant in Vacaville) Great omelettes and other hearty breakfasts. Family-style lunch. Local people hang out here. Don't expect much in decor, but abundant food. Open for breakfast and lunch. ☎ (707) 448-3900. $

SUGGESTED TOUR:

Numbers in parentheses correspond to numbers on the map.

As you tool along the lower portions of Highway I-80, it should be pointed out that this was mostly farmland at one time. Row crops and fruit trees covered some of the hills and valleys. Note that today the suburbs have sprawled out all along this freeway, although as you go farther north it becomes farmland in places once again.

About 25 miles from San Francisco, turn off the freeway at Abernathy and then right on Chadbourne, following signs to the **Jelly Belly Factory Tour** (1). It's actually the fancy-sounding Herman Goelitz Candy Factory. This is fun, fun, fun. Ronald Reagan became enamored of this fine product when he was governor up the road in Sacramento. The story goes that he took to these little goodies when he gave up smoking a pipe.

As we all know, Reagan gifted heads of state and other potentates with jars of the now-famous Jelly Belly beans. Do you remember the photos at various times in the White House of presidents and chancellors and prime ministers sitting around a low coffee table with a jar of Jelly Bellys with the presidential seal front and center? Only in America.

Jelly Bellys were first introduced in 1976, but the Reagan publicity brought tremendous changes to this 100-year-old company. At one time it was in a back alley in Oakland, but with prosperity came this new plant built in 1986. It covers 350,000 square feet, which is the size of several football fields. Today the plant can turn out 1,250,000 beans per hour or 100,000 pounds per day.

Attached to the plant is the exciting new 35,000-square-foot Visitor Center complete with restaurant, ice cream parlor and store. *Fascinating tours, where you'll learn which of the 40 official flavors is the most popular, begin here and are offered 9–3 daily.* Free. ☎ (707) 428-2838. &.

On the right as you came in on Chadbourne, you probably saw the gi-

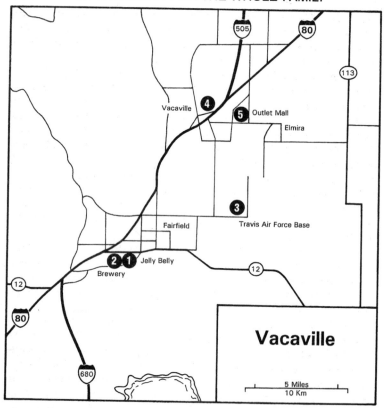

Vacaville

5 Miles
10 Km

ant **Budweiser Brewery** (2). This monster supplies beer to most of the cities and towns in the Bay Area, thus its size. The land area the plant sits on is over 500 acres, and there's speculation that perhaps someday there will be a theme park built here—like Busch Gardens in other parts of the country.

To kick off the tour, there's a brief video that takes visitors through the brewing process; however, the tour is conducted by people who really know the beer business. You are urged to ask any questions that pop into your head at the end.

With a volume that can top 21 million bottles and cans a day, this is a busy place. To keep the suds moving, the plant operates every day of the year on three shifts a day to turn out seven of the 38 Budweiser brands. During the tour, you'll see it all from bottle washing to fermentation of the hops. Naturally it is a giant assembly line that moves at a rapid pace with lots of noise.

The tour ends in a pub-like room where you can—what else—sample the product. There's something very nice about free, fresh beer after such a strenuous tour. There's a gift shop that specializes in Budweiser logo products. *Tours are 9–4 Mon.–Sat. June–Sept. and the same hours Tues.–Sat. in winter. Free.* ☎ *(707) 429-7595.* &.

When you leave the beer plant, turn left on Chadbourne, which becomes Abernathy as it crosses over the freeway. Not to push adult beverages, but now we'll head into a real rural area to sample some wine. Practically on the other side on the left is **Cadenasso Winery** at 4144 Abernathy. This is a tiny country winery where you will find excellent Chardonnays. *Open Tues.–Sun 9–5:30.* ☎ *(707) 427-3345.* As you travel along this lovely country road, look for signs to **Wooden Valley Winery.** In business since 1932, this family-owned winery turns out several medal winners from the California State Fair. Their Merlot is their most popular wine, but all the reds are excellent. All their wines are grown in the valley, and they don't distribute except through their own store. Pleasant picnic area and gift shop. *Located at 4756 Suisun Valley Road.* ☎ *(707) 864-0730.*

Again go north on Route I-80. After two miles, look for the Waterman Boulevard and Air Base Parkway exit. Going another five miles brings you to the **Travis Air Force Base** (3) and a neat aerospace museum on the grounds. Stop at the Visitor Center and be prepared to show your license, registration and insurance card.

With California's history in aerospace, this is an appropriate museum to show off all manner of flying machines. In the Air Park outdoors there are 32 different aircraft, from the tiny Gonzales biplane to the mighty Flying Fortresses. Many of these were built right here in the Golden State. Example after example from some of the better-known aerospace builders are on display. The Air Park is open every day of the year. Inside are a number of trainers and lots of memorabilia from the early days of the Air Force, including interesting photos from the Berlin Airlift. *The indoor museum is open Mon.–Fri. 9–4. Closed all federal holidays. Free.* ☎ *(707) 424-5605.*

Head north again for the wonderful little town of **Vacaville** (4). Take the exit for the Central Business District and stop in the middle of town for a snack or cup of coffee. This is small-town California at its best, with a central park and quaint shops and restaurants. A worthwhile visit is the **Vacaville Museum** at 213 Buck, almost in downtown. It sits next to the impressive Buck Mansion, a classic Victorian. The museum has substantial exhibits of old Vacaville including photos, memorabilia and models. *Open Wed.–Sun. 1–4:30. Admission is $2. During the summer months, volunteers conduct walking tours of historic Buck Avenue.*

Farther up the road is the monster **Vacaville Outlet Mall** (5), where over 130 stores hope to part you from your money. It is said that home builders in Vacaville build extra-large size closets since this mall is so close to town and offers such a cornucopia of bargains. Another wag has said Vacaville is the best-dressed small town in California because of the outlet mall. Nonetheless, it is big; there's a shuttle to take you between the three sections of the mall simply because of its size. There's great diversity in the offering—from London Fog to Florsheim to Levi's. From Highway I-80 turn off at I 505/Orange Drive. *The mall is open Mon.–Sat. 10–8 and Sun. 10–6.* ☎ *(707) 447-5755.*

*Sacramento

Many people are surprised to know that Sacramento got its start because of a big name in the Gold Rush—John Sutter. Sutter founded his settlement in 1839 as a fort ten years before the start of the Gold Rush.

Somehow Sutter finagled a 48,000-acre land grant from Mexico and set about building an adobe fort to protect his lands. He had grandiose ideas of building an empire that stretched from the rich farmland of the valley into the Sierra Nevada Mountains. He gave what is now Sacramento the high-sounding name of New Helvetia (it means New Switzerland since that's where Sutter came from).

The first gold was discovered at Sutter's Mill up in the mountains by James Marshall in early 1848. This didn't cause much commotion at first, but when merchant Sam Brannan shouted about it in the streets of San Francisco all hell broke loose. The word got around and the number of miners and camp followers swelled to around 50,000 a year later. That number doubled three years later.

What should be a happy story actually turned out quite badly for settler John. The gold fever stripped his land of workers and equipment, and things went downhill from there to bankruptcy in 1852. John Marshall also died penniless.

But Sutter's town prospered, supplying all manner of goods and services to the hungry mob scratching away in the mountains for demon gold. Because of its economic importance, Sacramento became California's capital in 1854. The railroads and Pony Express each used the town as a hub, further building its importance and population.

It is an historic city of nearly 400,000 souls, whose main occupation now is government. The city is filled with historical sites and numerous world-class museums. This will be a very interesting daytrip.

GETTING THERE:

By car, from Union Square go down Bush and follow signs to the Bay Bridge. You will pay the $2 toll coming back. The bridge is Route I-80. Stay on that the entire way to Sacramento. When you cross the Carquinez Bridge there is a $2 toll.

PRACTICALITIES:

The Sacramento area can be steamy in the summer time, so dress accordingly. Sunglasses are a good idea. Most museums and historical sites open at 10 in the morning, but several have different closing hours from winter to summer.

FOOD AND DRINK:

Frank Fat's (806 L St.) Lots of politicos hang out here. Classic Chinese dishes, choice cuts of aged steak and Frank's famous banana creme pie. Lunch Mon.–Fri. Dinner daily. Reservations ☎ (916) 442-7092. $$

Delta King—Pilothouse Restaurant (1000 Front St., Old Sacramento) Located aboard the famous *Delta King*, this spot was voted Sacramento's most romantic dinner house. Great views of the river. Reservations ☎ (916) 441-4440. $$

Il Fornaio (400 Capitol Mall) Award-winning authentic Italian cuisine. Wonderful fresh pastas and wood-fired pizzas. Fresh baked goods. Breakfast Mon.–Fri., dinner daily. ☎ (916) 446-4100. $–$$

Fat City Bar & Café (1000 Front St., Old Sacramento) Famous 120-year-old-bar accents the turn-of-the-century feel of this place. Hearty American cuisine ranging from appetizers to full dinner entrees. Reservations ☎ (916) 446-6768. $–$$

The Firehouse (1112 2nd St. in Old Sacramento) For lunch they have a smoked turkey croissant, but you must try the grilled asparagus. A good selection of seafood and pastas. Sunny courtyard in good weather. Lunch Mon.–Fri. and dinner Tues.–Sat. ☎ (916) 442-4772. $–$$

SUGGESTED TOUR:

Numbers in parentheses correspond to numbers on the map.

About 30 miles beyond Vacaville, turn off at the Downtown Sacramento exit. You will cross a high drawbridge over the Sacramento River and are now on the Capitol Mall. Go to 5th, turn left and then left again on I Street. This will take you directly into the Historic Registered Landmark called **Old Sacramento** (1). A good place to start is the **Visitor Center** at 1101 2nd Street, where you will find information about the wonderfully restored area. It wasn't always as attractive as it is now, but today it has 53 restored historic buildings that will transport you back in time to the Gold Rush days. This is where the early deals for gold and railroading and real estate were made. It was a boom town on the Sacramento River. *The Center is open 8–5 daily.* ☎ *(916) 442-7644.*

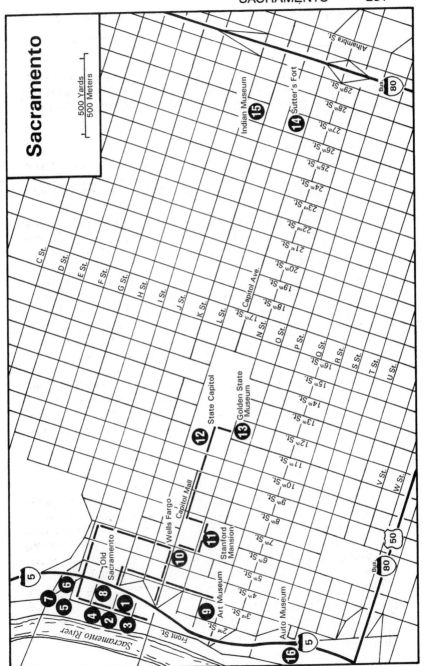

Sacramento

500 Yards
500 Meters

Walk along 2nd Street and turn left at K Street. This will take you to the **Delta King** (2) that carried passengers and cargo between San Francisco and Sacramento from 1926–41. In 1984, it was restored and is now a hotel and restaurant. While this one doesn't move, you can take an excursion on the **Spirit of Sacramento** on the river. There are all manner of trips, but a couple of examples are the one-hour Sightseeing Tour that's well narrated. *Cost is $10 for adults and $5 for kids under 12; the two-hour Luncheon Cruise with meal is $27.50 for all or $15 without lunch. These and other dinner cruises generally run Wed.–Sun. For reservations* ☎ *(916) 552-2933.*

For a quickie river tour, you might consider **River Otter Taxi Co.** that runs half-hour watertaxi trips six times daily on weekdays and 12 times on weekends. *The cost is $5; kids under 42" are $2.* ☎ *(916) 446-7704.*

You will see many horse-and-carriage outfits on the streets of Old Sacramento. It's a fun way to get around. Usually you can rent the whole carriage (and pile in as many as it will hold) for $10 for an Old Town Tour; a river tour for $25; a capitol tour is $50.

Along Front Street is the **Old Sacramento Public Market** (3), where busy commerce took place in the town's past. Here you will find a good selection of fresh California produce, meats, fish, flowers, fruit, ethnic foods, desserts and much more. Generally most stalls are open 10–6. Also along this street is the **Eagle Theater** (4) at 925 Front Street, built in 1849 (it has been reconstructed) as the first theater in California. Today the wooden-canvas structure houses a critically acclaimed theater offering professional production and an historical Old Sacramento slide show. *Operated by volunteers, the usual hours are 10–5. Donations. For information,* ☎ *(916) 323-6343; for the latest shows* ☎ *(916) 445-6645.*

If you continue down Front, you will run right into the **Discovery Museum** (5) at 101 I Street. It is located in the reconstructed red-brick building that originally housed the city water works, mayor's office and city prison. The museum provides a look at the rich cultural heritage of the area through exhibits featuring archaeology, Victorian- and Depression-era life, ethnic communities, music and popular culture. Probably the most popular exhibit is the renovated Gold Gallery featuring over 100 gold specimens from Bank of America's collection. This exhibit leads visitors through the woods to the back porch of a miner's cabin, then into a mine shaft excavated right on the museum's second floor. Changing exhibits too. *Adult admission is $4, kids 6–12 $2. Open daily 10–5.* ☎ *(916) 264-7057.*

Next door is the **Big Four Building** (6) at 113 I Street, where Collis Huntington, Mark Hopkins, Leland Stanford and Charles Crocker (see Daytrip 11) hatched their plans for the Central Pacific Railroad. Inside is the **Huntington Hawkins Hardware Store** that not only has historical displays of a typical hardware store of the 1800s, but it also sells 5¢ glass marbles and other antique wood toys. Old-fashioned lamps, baskets and other paraphernalia makes for interesting shopping. *Operated by volunteers, it is usually open 10–4.* ☎ *(916) 323-7234.*

Nearby is the:

*CALIFORNIA STATE RAILROAD MUSEUM (7), 125 I St. Sacramento, CA 95814, ☎ (916) 445-7387. *Open 10–5 daily. Adult admission is $6, kids 6–12 $3. Gift shop.* &.

Since Sacramento is where the transcontinental railroad got started, be sure to visit this spectacular facility in Old Sacramento at 2nd and I Streets. It is big and it is world-class. Considered to be the largest interpretive railroad museum in America, the 100,000-square-foot facility displays 21 meticulously restored locomotives and cars. This is all spit-and-polish brass, steel and wood. Over 40 one-of-a-kind exhibits tell the fascinating story of railroad history from 1850 to the present. Historic equipment and exhibits on the transcon railroad and 19th-century rail travel are housed in the reconstructed 1876 Central Pacific Station. One favorite is the dining car with china and tableware exhibits from all the classic railroad lines.

The same ticket will admit you to the **Central California Passenger and Depot Station** on Front Street. A reconstruction of the 1876 depot depicts the bustling activities of train travel in the mid-1800s.

You can take an excursion on a steam train of the **Sacramento and Southern Railroad** that operates over a six-mile route on weekends along the Sacramento River. This is the real thing and it's tons of fun. *There are hourly departures 11–5 Sat. and Sun. Cost is $6 for adults; kids 6–12 $3.* ☎ *(916) 552-5252 ext. 7245 for reservations.*

Next we suggest you go up to 2nd Street, and at the corner with I Street observe how the streets were raised 12 feet in 1873 to keep the area from flooding. This was a major undertaking with dirt dredged from the American River. Next walk along 2nd Street to observe the many fine old buildings restored to their earlier luster. At 2nd and J Streets is the **Pony Express Monument** (8). In April 1860, 80 young riders were able to complete the 1,966-mile mail run on horseback to St. Joseph, Missouri in fewer than ten days. What a feat.

If you would like to spread your wings and go beyond Old Sacramento, look for the Downtown Underpass at 2nd and K Sts. This will take you under two freeways and into the landscaped entrance to the **Downtown Plaza.** Here you will find numerous shops—from the majors like **Macy's** to the tiny like the **Beanery** that sells gourmet coffee. Have fun.

Close by Old Sacramento at 216 O Street is the **Crocker Art Museum** (9). The museum today is made up of two historic buildings and a modern wing all joined to make one of the finest art galleries in California. An enthralling restored Victorian built in 1873 houses the oldest public art museum in the west. Originally it incorporated a bowling alley, skating rink, billiard room, elaborate ballroom and library as well as the gallery space for showcasing several hundred paintings. The original European paintings and master drawings collections have been augmented with 19th-century California paintings, sculpture, Asian art and more recently contemporary art and photography. The original Crocker Mansion on the property houses the contemporary collection. *Open Tues.–Sun. 10–5 and Thurs. until 9 Adult admission is $4.50 and kids 7–17 $2.* ☎ *(916) 264-5423.*

By all means take the time to walk down the Capitol Mall. At 400 Capitol Mall is the **Wells Fargo History Museum** (10), which includes a fully restored Concord stagecoach. There are interpretive displays explaining the Wells Fargo Express, banking and staging operations as well as its commercial role in early Sacramento history. Original artifacts include gold, functioning telegraph, gold scales, treasure boxes and many documents of the era. *Free. Open 9–5 Mon. Fri. Closed major holidays.* ☎ *(916) 440-4161.*

Turn right on 5th and left on N Street to see the 140-year-old **Stanford Mansion** (11). This one started out a bit smaller, but Leland Stanford never did things in a small way, so he added to it over the years and built it into a 44-room home. It is an impressive and richly ornamented residence. A small adjacent building was used by Stanford when he was California's governor. *It is under restoration, so public tours are Tues. and Thurs. at 12:15 and Sat. 12:15 and 1:30. Free. Be sure to call (916) 324-0575 to confirm tour times and hours.*

Continue on to the:

*CALIFORNIA STATE CAPITOL MUSEUM (12), 10th and L St., Sacramento, CA 95814, ☎ (916) 324-0333. *You can pick up a self-guided tour brochure in any of the exhibit rooms or the Tour Desk in the basement in room B 27. Free. Good restaurant and gift shop.* ♿.

As you walk down the Capitol Mall, you can't miss this delightful building sitting at the west end of the 34-acre Capitol Park. The classic revival structure was built of brick and granite between 1861 and 1874. Its formal composition is crowned with a tiered dome above a large columned portico. The ball at the very top is covered with—what else—California gold leaf that glimmers in the sunlight. The building went through a massive restoration completed in 1982. Inside, the magnificent dome, marble mosaic floors, crystal chandeliers and monumental staircases are highlights.

What is amazing is that the building is a combination working government house and museum. On the top floors you can enter the public galleries of both the Assembly and the Senate. The Governor's office and various hearing rooms are set amidst the many hallways. There are free guided tours on the hour 9-4 daily except major holidays. It is a very impressive monument and should not be missed.

On the east side of the Capitol Building is a wonderful place to relax and enjoy the many acres of the **Capitol Park**. Among the hundreds of trees and bushes are discreet memorials and plaques to various groups. A self-guided map is available from the Tour Desk.

One of the newest museums in a city replete with them is the **Golden State Museum** (13), close by the Capitol. Located at 1020 O St., the 35,000-square-foot museum is an exploration of the phenomena we know as "California." On display is its past, present and promise for the future. The GSM features some of the vast collections of the State Archives, currently comprised of some 120 million items. Displays of authentic documents, three-dimensional artifacts, newsreels, films, holograms and a range of technology combine to explore many accounts of the state's history. *Open 10–5 Wed.– Sun. Adult admission is $6.50, kids 6–13 $3.50, seniors $5.* ☎ *(916) 653-7524.* ♿.

You might consider visiting three very worthwhile attractions slightly outside this area:

Sutter's Fort (14) at 27th and L streets is where it all started in 1839. Self-guided tours explain the exhibit rooms, which include copper and blacksmith's shops, a bakery, prison, dining room and living quarters as well as space for livestock. *Open daily 10–5. Adult admission is $3, kids 12 and under $1.50.* ☎ *(916) 445-4422.*

The **California State Indian Museum** (15) takes you back even further into the history of the area. It is the first state-run museum devoted to Indian culture and arts and crafts illustrating the lifestyle of California's earliest inhabitants. The museum is located at 26th and K Streets. *Open daily 10–5. Adult admission is $3, kids 6–12 $1.50* ☎ *(916) 324-0971.*

If you like old cars, and especially old Ford cars, plan to stop at the **Towe Auto Museum** (16) at 2200 Front Street. They invite visitors on a sentimental journey to see the development of the history of the auto in America. You can relive the early days of automobiles with a volunteer docent or go on a self-guided tour. It's all pretty neat. There are a few antique motorcycles and bicycles too. Gift shop. *Adult admission is $6, seniors $5 and kids 14–18 $2.50. Open daily 10–6.* ☎ *(916) 442-6802.*

The streets of Sacramento comprise many blocks of elaborate Victorians. Nestled along tree-lined streets, the majority may be found from 7th to 16th Streets, from E and I Streets.

Gold Country

The Mother Lode is generally considered to be the mountainous area from Downieville south to Mariposa, a swath that's about 200 miles long. During the time the gold held out, hundreds of millions of dollars were taken out of the hills and valleys of this beautiful area.

The cry of gold in late 1848 changed California forever, as well as it changed a good deal of the nation. Before gold was discovered, San Francisco was a small town of about 25,000 souls. When the gold rush got going full steam, the city by the bay was up to about ten times that size. With gold in California, the westward tilt of the nation became even more pronounced.

Obviously fortunes were made, but there were just as many—probably more—failures, including John Sutter and James Marshall who together started it all. Not everyone made money directly from mining the yellow stuff either. Many became rich by supplying the miners. They needed lodging and food and supplies, and those shrewd operators who seized on those opportunities in many cases did better than the people who grubbed for gold.

When gold fever struck, farms, homes, businesses and ships were often abandoned in favor of get-rich-quick mining. References to the legacy of the Gold Rush are frequent throughout this book. As an example, the large building columns used in the third State Capitol Building in Benicia were masts from sailing ships abandoned in the bay when the sailors jumped ship and made for the hills. See Daytrip 32.

This daytrip—loaded with things to see and do—will essentially cover the area from Coloma in the north to Sonora in the south, a distance of about 85 miles. We will highlight the more prominent spots along the route. There are more, including several side trips you may want to experience.

GETTING THERE:

From Placerville on Highway US-50, go north about nine miles to Coloma on Route 49. After Coloma, head south back through Placerville and on down the route of the 49ers.

PRACTICALITIES:

In summer the inland areas of Northern California are usually warm, but in the winter there may be snow. That's why the skiing can be so excellent in the Sierra Nevada mountains.

State Route 49 is generally a two-lane road that winds through the hilly part of Northern California. It is not a highway where you make time; rather it should be enjoyed for all the history that exists along the way. Portions are level and the speed limit is 55 mph, but certain areas can be congested—as when Route 49 is a town's main street.

There are a number of museums along this route. It's a good idea to be aware that hours for various facilities may vary between summer and winter. Most facilities—and many restaurants—are closed on Mondays.

FOOD AND DRINK:

Smith Flat House (2021 Smith Flat Rd. east of Placerville) This interesting spot is located in an 1852 Gold Rush building that exudes charm. Good food including pasta dishes with seafood. Lunch weekdays and dinner daily. ☎ (530) 626-9003. $–$$

Upstairs Restaurant & Streetside Bistro (164 Main St. in Jackson) Innovative cuisine, because the owner graduated from the California Culinary Academy. Smoked vegetables are a favorite. Good selection of salad entrees. Lunch and dinner Tues.–Sun. ☎ (209) 223-3342. $–$$

Sonora Inn (160 S. Washington St. in Sonora) California cuisine with an accent on good pasta dishes. Try their soups including the clam chowder. Breakfast, lunch and dinner daily. ☎ (209) 532-7468. $–$$

Kamm's (18208 Main St. in Jamestown) Housed in one of the historic buildings in town, they serve a good selection of Cantonese dishes. Their specialties are chow meins. Lunch Mon.–Fri. Dinner daily. ☎ (209) 984-3025. $–$$

LOCAL ATTRACTIONS:

Numbers in parentheses correspond to numbers on the map.

To get started, we suggest you head north from Placerville for a few miles to find the fountainhead of the Gold Rush in **Coloma** (1). The whole business got started when John Sutter, an early land baron, needed lumber for his settlement in Sacramento. He joined up with James W. Marshall to start a sawmill in the hills near the source of a good stand of timber.

On that fateful day in January 1848, it was Marshall who was looking in the tailrace of the sawmill and saw flecks of yellow glistening in the sun. While he and Sutter agreed to keep the whole business quiet, word nonetheless leaked out on the streets of San Francisco. The result was that Coloma sprang to life in such a fashion that the population grew to 5,000 souls by the end of 1849. It was boomtown with 13 hotels, a couple of banks and numerous other enterprises to service the horde of miners.

Today it's a tiny burg with a B&B and a handful of stores and restaurants. There's no gas station. The highlight of Coloma, however, is the **Marshall Gold Discovery State Historic Park**, with its reproduction of Sutter's Mill across the street from the museum. This 275-acre park is a must for those interested in the history of the Gold Rush. As you wander around, there are waystations to tell you of the history of the area. *The park is open daily 8– sunset.* At the Visitor Center is the **Gold Discovery Museum**, of interest to those who want to know more of the details. *The museum is open 10–5 in summer and 10–4 in winter. Closed major holidays. You pay a $5 day use fee that includes the museum, or $2 to walk in.* ☎ *(530) 622-3470.*

Also in Coloma is the **American River Nature Center**. Their programs include Kid's Discovery Days each Sunday from 12:30–2:30. During these programs kids go out into the surrounding area to learn and have fun. Cost is $5. There are free Nature Hikes on the first Saturday of each month. *The Center is open 10–4 Wed.–Sun.* ☎ *(530) 621-1224.*

Placerville (2), at 8,500 people, by comparison with Coloma is a big city. The reason it became prominent in the Gold Rush—besides the richness of its mines—was that it was a transit point for miners heading into the mountains, a wild place. It's original name was Dry Diggings, but later became Hangtown because of the lawlessness of the place. As it grew in prominence, the city fathers wanted something more sedate and thus they changed the name to Placerville.

Four famous names came out of this town: Philip Armour of the meat packing fame had a butcher shop here in the early days; John Studebaker, who would become a famed automaker, got his start here making wheelbarrows; and future railroad tycoons Mark Hopkins and Colis Huntington got started here, the former selling veggies to the miners and the latter operating as a merchant. (see Daytrip 11).

Be sure to check out the **El Dorado County Historical Museum** located west of town at 100 Placerville Drive. It offers a closer look at actual mining equipment, a blacksmith shop and a steam locomotive outside. Inside, the museum features a range of displays such as a stagecoach that carried miners, rooms and furniture of that era, and a replica of a country store. The museum has a satellite called the **El Dorado County Railroad and Logging Museum**, located three miles east of town. *Both facilities are open Wed.– Sat. 10–4 and Sun. noon to 4. The museums are free, but donations are a good idea.* ☎ *(530) 621-5865 for more information.*

In Placerville, **Gold Rush Tours** provides guided historical gold-panning and wine country tours of the neighboring countryside. *Cost is $20 per hour. They are located at 5580 Tosca Court.* ☎ *(530) 677-5122.*

You are now in for about 20-plus miles of scenic meadows, hills and mountains. A good place to stretch your legs after that journey is in **Amador**

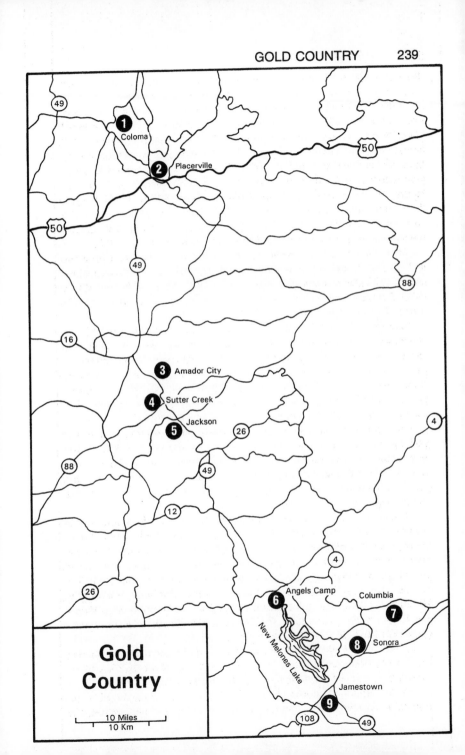

Gold Country

10 Miles
10 Km

City (3). This little town on the bend in the road was the site of the Keystone Mine that operated from 1853–1942. It was among the most prolific gold producers, turning out $24 million in gold ore. Now the town is a quaint place with a number of antique shops and the **Amador/Whitney Museum,** open weekends noon–4. What makes this tiny museum interesting is that it presents exhibits of the Mother Lode from a woman's perspective.

Just over the hill is **Sutter Creek** (4), which while it has a gold mining background, nonetheless seems like a small New England town with clapboard houses, white picket fences and a lushly planted B&B in the center of town. In its heyday, the mines in this area produced $40 million in gold. After that ended, the town prospered with a large lumbering business that continues to this day. Well worth a stop.

Next on this journey south to rediscover the excitement of the Gold Rush is the town of **Jackson** (5). It started out as a waystation providing water for cattle and the troops trudging off to find their fortunes in the minefields. That lead to a number of merchants setting up businesses here as well. In 1850, however, quartz deposits rich in gold were found and off the town went in search of demon gold. Two famous mines were developed here. The Kennedy and Argonaut Mines produced upwards of $80 million in gold before they were shut down in 1942. At a park one mile north of town you can see the huge Kennedy Tailings Wheels.

However, at the **Amador County Museum**, located at 255 Church Street, you can inspect a working model of the Kennedy Mine. In a restored brick home, named the Brown House after a famous judge, you can inspect all manner of furnishings, equipment, utensils and other accouterments of this period. *The museum is open Wed.–Sun. 10–4. The mine model costs $1 for adults and 50¢ for kids 6–12, but the home museum is free. Donations are encouraged.* ☎ *(209) 223-6386.*

The **Kennedy Gold Mine** can be toured on weekends from March through October. Guided surface tours are conducted where you can view many historic foundations, including the huge stamp mill that is in arrested decay. You need to be prepared to walk a bit on uneven ground, up and down hills and several stairs. *Cost is $5 for adults and $3 for kids 6–12.* ☎ *(209) 223-9542.*

Angels Camp (6) is about 28 miles south of Jackson. It is named for George Angel who founded a trading post here in 1848. The town boomed and George became rich. Like most of its counterparts, this town was pretty rowdy, with lots of fascinating characters. That made fodder for a couple of master storytellers—Messrs. Mark Twain and Bret Harte—both of whom spent time in this very spot actually working for short periods in the mines.

The town has a literary background. It was the setting for Mark Twain's first short story, *The Celebrated Jumping Frog of Calaveras County.* It is also said to be the locale for Bret Harte's *Luck of Roaring Camp.*

There are many historic buildings in town, and prominent among them is the **Angel Hotel** where it is reported that Mark Twain heard many of the stories that later turned into some of his more famous tales. The hotel is now offices and isn't open to the public. Another good place to actually see and feel Gold Rush paraphernalia is the **Angels Camp Museum** at 753 Main Street. *It is open daily 10–3 from Mar.–Oct. From Nov.–Feb. the hours are 10–3 Wed.–Sun. Admission is $2 for adults and 50¢ for kids 6–12.* ☎ *(209) 736-2963.*

Twelve miles south of Angels Camp is **Columbia** (7) where in 1850, so the story goes, a handful of miners grubbed 30 pounds of gold from the stream in two days. Stories like this hyped others to flock to the area, and before it was over, Columbia yielded $87 million in gold at 19th-century prices. Unlike hundreds of other towns in the Mother Lode, this little town never really went away. In a master stroke, the State of California decided way back in 1945 to preserve a typical Gold Rush town, and thus was born the **Columbia State Historic Park**.

Today there are over 40 buildings in a town that looks much as it did in the mid-1800s. What makes visiting the park so popular is that it is alive— with shops, a bank, the newspaper and plenty of things to do and see. You can shop for "antique" wood toys made right in the building that originally housed a hardware store, drink beer in an original saloon and buy oil lamps like the miners used in a period mercantile store. The **Columbia Stage Line** is an authentic stagecoach that operates 10:30–4:30 on weekends year round and daily May 15–Labor Day. The stagecoach winds through pic-turesque terrain on a unique coach road. *Adults can ride in the coach for $5, kids 12 and under $4.50. To ride shotgun is $1 more.*

The **Columbia Stables** on the park grounds assists you on horseback in discovering old gold diggings and a scenic canyon with fascinating lime-stone formations exposed by miners over a century ago. *Beginning rides cost from $9–$45.* Other examples are the 45-minute Gold Seekers View at $20; the one-hour Back Country Explorer at $25 and the three-hour Back to the Past at $65. ☎ *(209) 532-0663 for information and reservations.*

At the **Matelot Gulch Mine Supply Store** in the park you can pan for gold right on the spot. For $5 they will include some gold in your sluice gate and for $3 you get to look for your own. Better still, tours of the only active work-ing gold mine in the state are offered daily. Take a careful look for the quartz vein that gold formed in millions of years ago. Expert guides take you through 800 feet of tunnel where you'll discover what "stopes," "side drifts," and "glory holes" are all about. *Tours are at 10:30 daily.* ☎ *(209) 532-9693. The park is open every day except Christmas 9–5. Amazingly, it's free.*

At a major bend in the road is **Sonora** (8), reportedly one of the wildest and woolliest towns in the Mother Lode. It got started with miners from Mex-ico, and conflicts soon started with the American miners. Gold was very im-portant to its early existence, but it also became a transport and trade hub for cattle ranching and timber products from the surrounding area. Today,

Sonora is still prosperous because of agriculture and forestry. A walking tour of downtown will take you past memorable 19th-century architecture. Pick up a map at the museum.

The **Tuolumne County Museum and History Center** at 158 West Bradford Avenue is a fascinating way to learn more about the gold country. You will see gold as it came out of the ground in various forms as well as the history of gold mining in this area. There are terrific displays of historical events that took place here. *Open Sun. & Mon. 9–4, Tues.–Fri. 10–4 and Sat. 10–3:30. Donations.* ☎ *(209) 532-1317.*

Jamestown (9), founded in 1848, is our next—and final—stop. What makes "Jimtown," as the locals call it, interesting is that unlike most of the other towns in the Mother Lode, gold is still mined here in the streams and deep quartz veins south of town. Apparently there was lots of gold to begin with (they say the rich Woods Creek once yielded a 75-pound nugget), and they're still finding it. You might want to try your hand at some gold panning, so contact **Gold Prospecting Expeditions**. After practicing in their old livery stable location, they will take you to the real thing where you can try your luck for $20 for an hour. They also have half, full and multiple day expeditions. ☎ *(209) 984-GOLD.*

Be sure to make time for a visit to the **Railtown State Historic Park**, found downtown on Fifth Avenue. Included is the actual roundhouse of the Sierra Railway. The building and restored rail cars and engines are such beauties that Hollywood often uses them for films. *The park, open daily 10–5, is free, but tours of the roundhouse cost $2.50 for adults and $1.50 for kids.* Well worth it. On weekends, there are excursions on one of the steam trains. Be sure to call for reservations at (209) 984-3953.

Yosemite I

This park is so huge and has so much going on that we have broken it into two daytrips. If you're a hiker and backpacker and want to camp, that certainly is available to you. Most people come to Yosemite for several days simply because there's so much to see and do.

This daytrip visits the southern part of the park, including Yosemite Valley, the most popular area.

If you don't want to do anything but wander around and stare at the scenery, that will take a considerable amount of your time. After all, John Muir spent several years doing that along with his research in the late 1800s. But there are lots of activities too. Just the free classes—included are various nature walks, talks and hikes—alone could keep you busy for several days.

Over the years, many have extolled the virtues of Yosemite and thus the park plays host to upwards of four million people annually. And therein is a point. July and August are usually the most crowded, so if you can arrange your time for a spring or fall visit, you will find the park less congested. Winter is another matter. Some of the roads are closed when the snow begins to fall, but there is downhill and cross-country skiing, snowshoeing, ice skating and winter nature hikes.

GETTING THERE:

Most people come by car. From the west, Highways 120 and 140 take you into the park. Highway 41 comes straight up and through the South Entrance to the park. From the east, take Highway 120 over Tioga Pass. However, this route is usually closed from late fall until late spring, depending on the weather conditions. 24-hour road and weather reports are available at (209) 372-0200. The cost to enter the park by car is $20, valid for seven days.

It's possible to take a one- or two-day tour of the park by motorcoach. **Via Adventures** has departures from Merced ($38) and Mariposa ($20). ☎ *(888) 727-5287. The entry fee is included.*

Those who come on foot, by bicycle, motorcycle or horse pay $10 each, valid for seven days.

PRACTICALITIES:

It would be nice, but you cannot make a reservation to visit Yosemite, except of course for the hotels and campgrounds inside the park. The camping reservation number is (800) 436-7275.

Auto access can be a problem on some spring and summer weekends and very busy holidays, and so on these occasions cars may be temporarily restricted. Regardless, you're usually better off parking your car and taking the free tram anyway.

Keep in mind that complimentary shuttle bus service will take you through a good portion of the valley on a regular schedule. The shuttle bus services most of the major trailheads, the Valley Visitor Center, Yosemite Museum and the Indian Cultural Exhibit—and more. Take advantage of it to cut down on traffic and air pollution. The schedule runs from June 15–September 7 from 7–10. Except for early morning and later at night, the shuttle bus operates every ten minutes.

FOOD AND DRINK:

Yosemite Lodge Cafeteria (at Yosemite Lodge) Great food that includes salads, pastas and burgers, plus many other selections for the whole family. Breakfast, lunch and dinner daily. $–$$

Four Seasons Restaurant (near Yosemite Lodge) Located right in the middle of the valley, this family restaurant serves a varied menu of American dishes. Open for breakfast and dinner. $

Meadows Ranch Café (5024 Hwy. 140 in Mariposa) Fresh gourmet food and sandwiches. Their specialty is BBQ meats served country style. Breakfast, lunch and dinner Tues.–Sat. ☎ (209) 966-4242. $

Jackalopes Bar & Grill (1122 Hwy. 41 in Fish Camp) Fun place for sandwiches and burgers. If you're there on the weekends, they have live music. Lunch and dinner daily. ☎ (559) 683-6555. $

LOCAL ATTRACTIONS:

Numbers in parentheses correspond to numbers on the map.

If you come up from the south on Highway 41 through Fish Camp, just inside the park entrance is the breathtaking **Mariposa Grove** (1) of giant sequoias. These are among some of the oldest and largest living things on Earth. Grizzly Giant is said to be 2,700 years old and many believe it is the oldest living sequoia on Earth. There is a free tram from Wawona to the grove—and it is advised because of narrow roads. Three times daily there are ranger-lead tours of the grove beginning the end of June and usually through September. A guided tram tour winds through these awesome giants offering views of the Fallen Monarch, Clothespin Tree, fallen Wawona

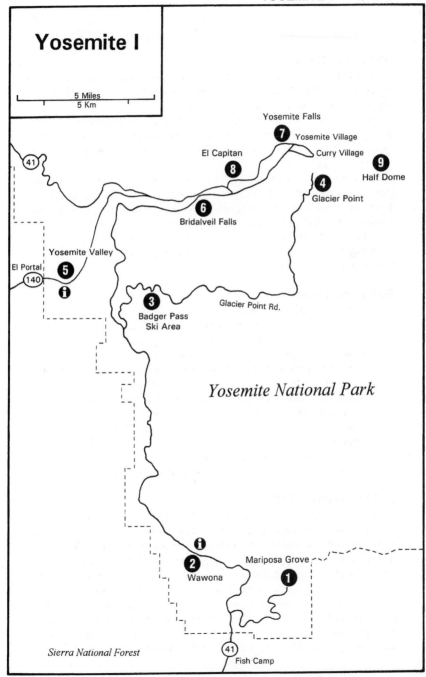

Tunnel Tree and more. *The tram costs $8 for adults, $7.25 for seniors, $4 for kids 4–12.* You can walk through as well. The **Mariposa Grove Museum** offers giant sequoia displays, books, maps and information. *Open 9–4:30.*

A bit farther is what was once an Indian village called **Wawona** (2), with its Victorian-style hotel and classic **Wawona Golf Course.** This challenging nine-hole course can be played during the warmer months. *Rates are $13 for nine holes and $19.50 for 18 holes.* ☎ *(209) 375-6572 for tee times.* Also of interest is the **Pioneer History Center.** See horse-drawn wagons, a covered bridge and historic buildings from Yosemite's past. You can take a stage ride to experience the adventure of horse-drawn travel in the early days of the park. The center is always open. The **Wawona Information Station** has information about the park's activities, wilderness permits, trails, books and maps. *Open 8:30–4:30 (closed for lunch).*

If you come to Yosemite in the winter and enjoy snow, next is the **Badger Pass Ski Area**, offering downhill and cross-country skiing. Snowboarding has become very popular recently and is offered as well. There is plenty of lift up the mountain with a triple and two double chair lifts. Badger offers complete ski schools for all abilities. *The rates for lift tickets are: weekend all-day adults $28 and kids under 12 $13; midweek all-day adults $22 and kids under 12 $13. There are two-day cross-country overnight guided tours that include all meals, lodging, guide and instruction for $110. Other packages are also offered. Turn at Chinquapin Junction on Hwy. 41 for Badger Pass.* ☎ *(209) 372-8444 for more information. You can get a snow report by calling (209) 372-1000.*

Following the same directions, you can go beyond Badger Pass to one of Yosemite's awesome viewing sites called **Glacier Point** (4), from which you can see the whole sweep of Yosemite Valley spread out 3,200 feet below. Half Dome and the High Sierra are also clearly visible from here. One of the favorite viewing times is sunset, and many visitors time their trip to Glacier Point for viewing under a full moon. It is truly one of the most dramatic sights in Yosemite. There are numerous ranger-led walks to explore scenic points in the Glacier Point area. Check with the information station for specific walks.

Another approach to the park is from the west on Highway 140 out of Mariposa. This route follows the Merced River to the **Arch Rock** entrance to the park. Routes 41 and 140 meet at what is considered the beginning of **Yosemite Valley** (5). This is the main gathering point for visitors to the park. The Yosemite Valley Visitor Center in the Village offers information, maps, books, exhibits and a multilingual One Day in Yosemite program. Be sure to see the video that provides a good introduction to the park. *Open 8–7.*

Yosemite Village has several other spots to see, too. The **Yosemite Museum** displays the cultural history of Yosemite's Miwok and Paiute people from 1850 to the present. There is also a good gift shop. *Open 8:30–5:30 daily.* The **Ansel Adams Gallery** exhibits the handsome photography of

Adams and other contemporary photographers. *Open daily 8:30–6:30.* 📷 *(209) 372-4413.* The **Nature Center at Happy Isles** is a family-oriented nature experience that includes wildlife dioramas, wildlife tracking tips and interactive displays. *Open 9–5 daily.* All of the above are wheelchair accessible.

The valley itself is essentially a flat area with sheer walls on either side. On the valley floor are stands of trees and open meadows filled with wildflowers. The **Merced River** flows through the valley, providing recreation of all sorts. The sheerness of the valley walls mean waterfalls that are most plentiful in late spring and early summer.

Among the more prominent waterfalls are **Bridalveil Falls** (6), which the native Indians called "Pohono" or spirit of the wind. The bridalveil moniker comes from the fact that the wind usually swirls around the cliff face and in so doing lifts the falling water and blows it back and forth creating a delicate mist. An astonishing fact about this waterfall is that it may look small, but in reality it is the equivalent of a 60-story building. **Yosemite Falls** (7) is near the Yosemite Lodge. This spectacular wall of water is one of the tallest in America, cascading down 2,425 feet.

Two of the better-known geologic features of the valley are **El Capitan** (8) and **Half Dome** (9). The former is an enormous granite monolith that soars almost 3,600 feet skyward from the valley floor. Some are intrepid enough to climb its sheer face on their own; or if you feel like you would like some assistance with your rock climbing, call **Yosemite Mountaineering School** in summer at (209) 372-8453 and winter (209) 372-8344.

The big one, however, is Half Dome. This 87-million-year-old giant stands guard over the entire valley from its location at the east end. The other half is thought to have fallen away when the glaciers that formed these mountains receded. This mountain is 8,842 feet, and in the summer you can climb to the top by taking the Mist or John Muir Trail. It can be a one- or two-day climb that should be done with a companion. Maps and information are available from the Visitor Center.

And speaking of getting into these mountains on foot, this is hiking nirvana. There are over 800 miles of hiking trails parkwide. The **Mist Trail**, mentioned above, is one of the most popular in Yosemite Valley. It starts at Happy Isles, and along the way you come to 317-foot **Vernal Falls** and 600-foot **Nevada Falls**. While considered strenuous in places, most people in decent shape will find this a real treat. **Four-mile Trail** is a more direct route to Glacier Point and is considered quite strenuous. To make your life easier, however, there is the hiker's bus, which will take you to Glacier Point so you can hike down.

The park officially lists ten day hikes from the short half-mile to Bridalveil Falls to the strenuous 17-mile roundtrip to the top of Half Dome. For guided naturalist-led hikes and backpacking adventures call (209) 379-2321.

If you'd like to experience the valley in a more casual way, consider taking the **Valley Floor Tour**, which is a two-hour, 26-mile tram tour through the heart of Yosemite. A knowledgeable guide describes the geology and history of the park. It runs all year and costs $17. The **Mariposa Grove of Big Trees** is a six-hour trip from the valley to the giant sequoias in the grove. There's a stop at the Wawona Hotel, where a buffet lunch is available for an additional charge. This tour costs $34. A half-day tour from the valley to Glacier Point is available for $20 round trip. Some folks take it one way to hike Glacier Point either up or down. One-way cost $10. These tours depart from the Yosemite Lodge. ☎ *(209) 372-1240 for more information.*

Touring and hiking aren't the only activities in Yosemite by a long shot. There is horseback riding in the valley and at Wawona and Tuolumne Meadows. Some of the **Guided Saddle Trips** offered are a Two-Hour Scenic Ride that departs several times a day and costs $35. The Half-Day Scenic Ride leaves at 8 and 1 and costs $46. On Sundays only, an All-Day Scenic Ride is offered to Yosemite's backcountry. The cost is $70. *Reservations are recommended, so* ☎ *(209) 372-8348.*

With 12 miles of paved paths, bicycles are a popular way to get around the entire valley. They can be rented from **Yosemite Concession Services** at either Yosemite Lodge or Curry Village. ☎ *(209) 372-8319. Offered Apr.– Nov., the rates are $5.25 per hour or $20 for the day. Bike and trailer cost $10.50 per hour or $33 for the day. They also have strollers, wheelchairs and helmets.*

When the Merced River is running at the right depth, you can partake of it in a raft during the summer months. *Rentals are available by calling (209) 372-8341. Daily rates from 10–4 (which include life jacket, paddle and shuttle) are $12.75 per person and $10.75 for kids.*

The classes and programs offered in the park are endless. There are free art classes each day, spring through fall and during the Christmas holidays at the **Art Activity Center**. At the **Yosemite Museum**, Native American cultural programs are offered frequently.

In winter, there is ice skating at Curry Village on an outdoor rink. *Skates can be rented for $2. Rates for skating are $5 for adults and kids $4.50.*

Some words about using the park: Bears are a real problem, because when people leave food out or in their cars, bears will go after it. If you are camping, by all means use the metal containers provided by the Park Service. Each year campfires, cigarettes and human carelessness cause unwanted fires in Yosemite. Never smoke while walking or in an area with flammable materials. Crush butts completely before throwing into garbage containers. Never throw butts out the car window. If you're bicycling, California law requires those under 18 must wear helmets. Bikes are prohibited on pedestrian and hiking trails.

Yosemite II

The history of Yosemite includes Indians, explorers, gold seekers, naturalists and now visitors. The big draw has always been the incredible natural beauty of the place. It is said that the Miwok Indians first inhabited this area about 10,000 years ago. Their name for Yosemite was *Ahwahnee*, which means "place of gaping mouth." That loose translation holds true for most visitors even today. It's little wonder the park draws over four million visitors a year.

Around the 1830s, explorers started making their way into the area. Many had no concern for natural beauty, but people like Galen Clark worked with President Abraham Lincoln to sign the Yosemite Grant in 1864. This is considered the foundation on which most state and national parks are patterned.

We can also thank one of the best-known naturalist/explorers of all, Scotsman John Muir, for a big push in the creation of Yosemite. Not only did he explore and research the area thoroughly over many years, he also persuaded influential Americans, including President Teddy Roosevelt, to come to Yosemite for visits. Muir was so enthusiastic about saving the area for future generations that Roosevelt began the process of starting a governmental agency that eventually became the National Park Service.

Muir's message was simple and straightforward. "Wildness is a necessity. Mountain parks and reservations are useful not only as fountains of timber and irrigating rivers, but as fountains of life."

During this daytrip, we'll explore the area to the north of Yosemite Valley. Be sure to review the previous daytrip for information about the valley and south.

GETTING THERE:

If you come in on Highway 120 from the west, turn left on Tioga Pass Road, the continuation of 120. Coming from the east, you will be on Highway 120. However, this route is usually closed from late fall until late spring, depending on the weather conditions. 24-hour road and weather reports are available at (209) 372-0200.

On Highway 140, turn left on Big Oak Flat Road and then right on Tioga Pass Road. From the south, you will go into Yosemite Valley for a short distance and cross over the Merced River to Big Oak Flat Road. Then turn right on Tioga Pass Road.

Most people come by car, although there are motorcoach tours available as well. In winter, you can take a two-hour sightseeing tour of the valley in a warm motorcoach. These tours leave frequently from hotels. ☎ *(209) 372-1240.*

PRACTICALITIES:

Just on a day visit, it's not possible to make a reservation for Yosemite, except of course for the hotels and campgrounds inside the park. The camping reservation number is (800) 436-7275.

The National Park Service can restrict auto access on some spring and summer weekends and very busy holidays. Regardless, you're usually better off parking your car and taking the free tram anyway.

Keep in mind that complimentary shuttle bus service will take you throughout the valley on a regular schedule. The shuttle bus services most of the major trailheads, the Valley Visitor Center, Yosemite Museum and the Indian Cultural Exhibit—and more. Take advantage of it to cut down on traffic and air pollution.

The cost to enter the park by car is $20, valid for seven days. Individuals in a bus, on a bicycle or horse, or walking pay $10 for seven days. If you think you'll be back many times, a Yosemite Pass, good for a year, is $40.

FOOD AND DRINK:

The Ahwahnee Dining Room (In the Ahwahnee Lodge) Certainly Yosemite's grandest dining. The room itself is like an English manor house with high ceilings and appropriate furniture. Men will wear coat and tie at dinner. Truly a lovely dining experience. ☎ (209) 252-4848. $$–$$$

Evergreen Lodge (33160 Evergreen Rd. near Camp Mather) Try the Honey Stung Chicken or their specialty, Baby Back Ribs. Fresh Salmon. Vegetarian Brochette. All served in a very rustic atmosphere. Breakfast and dinner daily Apr.–Oct. ☎ (209) 379-2606. $–$$

PJ's Café (18986 Main St. in Groveland) Sit down or take out, this busy place serves up a variety of good foods including pizzas, sourdough sandwiches, salads and burgers. Beer and wine too. Breakfast, lunch and dinner daily. ☎ (209) 962-7501. $

Tuolumne Meadows Grill (in the park at the Lodge) Hearty breakfast

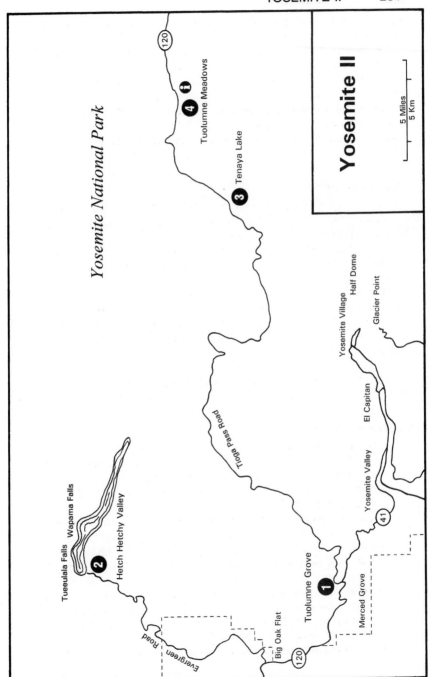

to get you set for an active day, or a wide selection of sandwiches to sustain you during the day. ☎ (209) 252-4848. $

LOCAL ATTRACTIONS:

Numbers in parentheses correspond to numbers on the map.

At the junction of Big Oak Flat Road and Tioga Road is the spectacular **Tuolumne Grove of Giant Sequoias** (1), a huge grove of huge trees. It contains one of the last two trees you can walk through in Yosemite. The **Dead Giant** was tunneled through in 1878 after it was destroyed by fire. A self-guided walk through the woods with factual waystations tells the story of the grove and its inhabitants.

An historic road runs through the grove to the Big Oak Flat Entrance Station. This also serves as a wonderful hiking trail—or for cross-country skiing in winter. From the parking lot to the grove is a little over one mile, quite steep in places.

Before the entrance station you can take Evergreen Road for a forty-five minute drive to **Hetch Hetchy Valley** (2). Geologists say that at one time this was the same as Yosemite Valley, with dramatic waterfalls, soaring domes and a peaceful river running through it. Some of those features are still visible today. On the north side of the valley, there are two waterfalls—**Wapama** and **Tueeulala**—that can be seen during the months when water is plentiful. Look for Hetch Hetchy Dome just beyond the waterfalls.

The name Hetch Hetchy comes from the Miwok, who used it to describe an edible plant that grew in this part of the countryside. The importance of Hetch Hetchy as a water source for the millions who live in the Bay Area can best be described as we did in Daytrip 42, Woodside and Portola Valley. There we suggested that you stop at the Water Temple (officially called the Pulgas Temple) on Skyline Boulevard south of San Francisco. At that very spot is the outlet for water coming down a many-miles-long aqueduct from Hetch Hetchy Reservoir into the huge Crystal Springs Reservoir that wanders along the coastal mountains. Life in the Bay Area would be considerably different without the Hetch Hetchy Reservoir that reaches up into this valley for several miles.

If you walk to the center of O'Shaughnessy Dam, there are plaques to tell you about the construction. Continuing on, there are good trails that will take you along the north side of the reservoir.

Tioga Road itself is about 40 pleasant miles of forests, meadows and lakes. It was originally built as a mining road, and in 1961 many of the twists and turns were straightened out. Keep in mind that it is closed in winter, generally from late October to late May.

This is considered the high country, and the views are spectacular. Be sure to stop at **Tenaya Lake** (3), said to be one of the largest and most scenic lakes in the Sierra Nevada mountains.

Next is **Tuolumne Meadows** (4), the largest subalpine meadow in the

California mountains. In broad expanses of open meadows, you can some-times see bighorn sheep grazing. The **Tuolumne Meadows Visitor Center** will help you with park orientation, trail information, books, maps and interesting displays. *Open 9–7 daily.* ☎ *(209) 372-0263.* ♿.

If you have the urge to get out and explore the area, consider taking a guided **saddle trip** starting at the meadows. Only available in the summer, there are two-hour, half-day and full-day trips for all abilities. The longer trips usually take you to spectacular waterfalls and numerous lakes dotting the countryside. *Rates range from $35–70.* ☎ *(209) 372-8427.*

Trip 40
Overnighting—East

Tahoe North

Tahoe has got it all: A gorgeous big lake surrounded by miles of jagged peaks, tons of summer and winter activities for the whole family, and wonderfully clear water and air. On the latter point, Mark Twain said, "To obtain the air the angels breathe, you must go to Tahoe."

Contrary to popular belief, the Tahoe Basin wasn't created by the collapse of a volcanic crater. Instead, about 25 million years ago the basin sank between two parallel faults as the mountains on either side rose.

The lava flowing from Mt. Pluto on the north shore spilled a dam across the basin's main outlet. Water from snowfall and streams flowing into the basin gradually created a lake several hundred feet higher than the present lake. Eventually a new outlet was eroded, creating the present path of the Truckee River.

Glaciers formed during the Ice Age, scouring away loose rock and reshaping the canyons into broad U-shaped valleys. As the glaciers melted, they left behind brilliant bays, jagged peaks and polished ridges.

All that geologic activity millions of years ago left us with a treasure to enjoy today. Be sure to take care of it. And yes, be sure to read the next daytrip to fully appreciate the Tahoe area.

GETTING THERE:

Coming from Sacramento in the west or from Reno in the east by car, the most direct route is Route I-80. To go practically to the northernmost tip of the lake, you can take Highway 267 down to King's Beach. Highway 89 from Truckee leads south to Tahoe City, about a third of the way down on the west shore.

PRACTICALITIES:

The Tahoe area is blessed with two very distinct seasons. Summer is playtime on the lake and river, as well as in the mountains. Winter is mostly mountain play. Regardless, there's plenty to do any time of year.

Another fact to keep in mind is that three-quarters of the lake on the west

254

side is in California and the remainder of the lake on the east side is in Nevada. If a game of chance interests you, there's some of that on the east side of the lake.

Be aware that hours for various facilities may vary between summer and winter; and some places just close down in winter.

To avoid summertime traffic day or night, the Tahoe Trolleys are fun and easy, and they go most everywhere. *Cost is $2 all day, 10–10.* ☎ *(530) 541-7548.*

FOOD AND DRINK:

Black Bear Tavern (2255 W. Lake Blvd. in Tahoe City) Traditional New England atmosphere with a mix of "Old Tahoe." You will enjoy the sizzling sirloin steaks, wild boar and venison—and the seafood. Dinner daily. Reservations ☎ (530) 583-8626. $$–$$$

PlumpJack Café (at the Squaw Valley Inn) Sister restaurant to the critically-acclaimed PlumpJack in San Francisco. Gracious dining in an Alpine setting. Casual bar for joining friends. Lunch and dinner daily. Reservations ☎ (530) 583-1576. $$–$$$

Hacienda de la Sierra (931 Tahoe Blvd. in Incline Village) If you love Mexican food, this is your place. Real classy. Their specialties are fajitas and margaritas, but choose from a wide menu selection. Lunch and dinner daily. ☎ (775) 831-8300. $–$$

Grazie! (700 N. Lake Blvd. in Tahoe City) Great Italian food they call "Progressive." That means innovative dishes with Old-World style. Combine that with a lakeside setting and you have a real winner. Lunch and dinner daily. ☎ (530) 583-0233. $–$$

Jason's Beachside Grille (8338 N. Lake Blvd. in King's Beach) Fresh home-style food that includes seafood, steaks and salad bar. Lunch and dinner daily. ☎ (530) 546-3315. $

LOCAL ATTRACTIONS:

Numbers in parentheses correspond to numbers on the map.

We suggest you come down Highway 89 from Route I-80. If you can resist getting to the lake for a bit, there's some good fun in store at **Squaw Valley** (1). You may remember this beautiful place as the site of the 1960 Winter Olympics. Whether you're there in the summer or winter, there's plenty to see and do.

Let's start with the summer season. The key to all sorts of activity on the mountain is to take the **Cable Car** up to High Camp at the 8,200' elevation. In a place of a million dramatic views, the ones from this gondola are among the best. *The cable car runs daily from 9:40 a.m. to 9 in the evening. The adult rate is $14; seniors are $12 as are kids under 12. After 5 in the afternoon the rate is $5.*

Located in the Cable Car barn is the **Headwall Climbing Wall**, where people of all ages can try their hand at rock climbing on a 30' and a 45' simulated rock surface. *$10 per person for unlimited climbing time.*

Once at High Camp, take your pick among activities from tame to extreme. **Hiking** here is marvelous. There are easy-to-follow trails from short and easy to those of Olympic proportions. Full-moon hikes are very popular. A large **Swimming Lagoon**—open 11–9—can be great fun at this altitude. *A cable car/swim package is $19 for adults and $10 for kids 12 and under.*

The **Mountain Bike Park** also offers a wide range of trails from beginner to world-class challenging. *The park is open 9:40–5 daily and the package includes the cable car ride and unlimited use of the park for $19.*

Now comes the fun part. How about standing on an 80' platform looking over a 500' cliff for some good old **Bungee Jumping?** Think of the views of mountain ridges and the lake in the background. *The cost is $45 per person for the first jump; subsequent ones the same day are $15.* ☎ *(530) 583-JUMP for reservations.*

Squaw Valley Stables at 1525 Squaw Valley Road offers nine guided one-hour rides daily from May through October. *The cost is $19. There are three two-hour rides daily that cost $38 and a half-day ride costs $60. Pony rides for kids 10–4 cost $6 for a half-hour when you lead.* ☎ *(530) 583-RIDE.*

The green valley that spreads out as you approach the Squaw base facilities holds a stunning golf course at the **Resort at Squaw Creek**. The par-71 course was designed by Robert Trent Jones. *Greens fees (including cart) are $85 in spring from May 24–June 20 and fall from Sept. 23–Oct.20. During the summer months the greens fees are $110 for 18 holes.* ☎ *(530) 583-6300 ext. 6936.*

Now it's wintertime. Squaw Valley is certainly best known for its skiing. In fact, the ski area spans six high Sierra peaks covering about 4,000 acres. They say the open bowls are similar to European skiing. *To get up the slopes (on a wide variety of lifts) to schuss down, the daily rate is $30 for adults; $15 for juniors 13–15 and seniors 65–75; and $12 for kids 12 and under. Those over 75 ski free. All these lift tickets include the cable car.*

But winter activities don't end with skiing. One of the area's newer activities is **Tubing.** Hop on a snowtube, choose a lane and enjoy the ride. *The package for cable car and two hours of tubing is $19 for adults and $10 for kids 12 and under.* **Ice Skating** on a rink similar to one used during the Olympics is also available in winter. *The Skating Pavilion is open 11–9, summer and winter. Rates are the same as for tubing.*

If all that has tired you out, head south to **Tahoe City** (2) for a calmer experience at two wonderful museums. **Gatekeepers Museum/Marian Steinbeck Basket Museum** is located at 120 West Lake Boulevard in William B. Layton Park. The reconstructed museum is on the original site of the gatekeeper's cottage; for years he was the person responsible for measuring the depth of the lake and letting water out through the gate down the Truckee

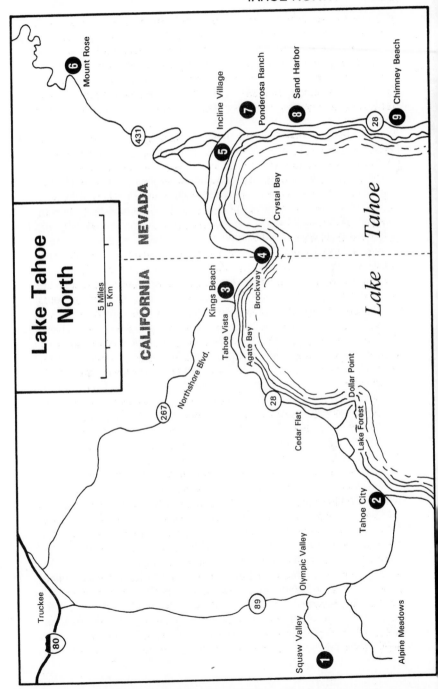

Lake Tahoe
North

5 Miles
5 Km

CALIFORNIA NEVADA

Lake Tahoe

Truckee

80

Squaw Valley

Olympic Valley

89

Alpine Meadows

Tahoe City

2

Lake Forest

Dollar Point

28

Cedar Flat

Northshore Blvd.

267

Kings Beach

Tahoe Vista

3

Agate Bay — Brockway

4

Crystal Bay

5

431

6 Mount Rose

Incline Village

7 Ponderosa Ranch

8 Sand Harbor

28

9 Chimney Beach

1

River. With its rich history, the museum tells fascinating stories of Lake Tahoe's early days right up to the present. A new wing holds 800 Native American baskets, ranging from those measuring 3 feet wide to detailed miniatures one-quarter inch in size. *Open May 1–June 15 and Labor Day– Oct. 1, Wed.–Sun. 11–5. The same hours, but daily during the summer. Admission is a $2 (or more) donation.* ☎ *(530) 583-1762.*

On the way to the museum be sure to stop at "Fanny Bridge," which spans the Truckee River just as it comes out of the gates from the lake. The trout grow to humongous size because they have no predators here and people throw them food. Those looking over the railing expose their fannies in a line.

The **Watson Cabin Museum** is listed on the National Register of Historic Places as the oldest building in Tahoe City. It illustrates Tahoe life at the turn-of-the-century. *Open Mid-June to Labor Day, 12–4 daily. Admission is by donation.* ☎ *(530) 583-8717.*

Many people enjoy floating down the Truckee River in a raft starting in Tahoe City. **Mountain Air Sports** will rent you a raft, paddles and safety vests for $20 per person (kids under 12 are $15). ☎ *(530) 583-7238.*

There are numerous guided whitewater rafting trips in this part of the world. One that may intrigue you is offered by **Tributary Whitewater Tours** on the Little Truckee River. It is a seven-mile run with several Class 2–3 rapids. During the three-and-a-half-hour trip the river passes through the high Sierra desert, along tree-lined banks and through a small mountain town. Life jackets and paddles are provided along with safety instructions. *Cost on weekdays for adults is $60 and kids $54; weekends are $75 for adults and $67.50 for kids. They offer numerous other trips.* ☎ *(530) 346-6812 for reservations and information.*

Tahoe Trips and Trails in Tahoe City offers hiking and mountain biking tours by day or multi-day. A day-long guided hiking or walking tour that includes snacks, entrance fees and transportation is $39 per person. A similar tour, but on mountain bikes, costs $40 per person. Front suspension bikes can be rented for $30 a day. In winter, they offer a Snowshoe Tour for $49 per person. Their "Tahoe Sampler" is an ideal way to have several experiences like hiking, biking, lake kayaking and more. ☎ *(530) 583-4506.*

You can enjoy hands-on sailing or just sit and relax with **Tahoe Sailing Charters** in the Tahoe City Marina. They take you out on the 33-foot sloop *Avalanche* for a two-hour cruise along the north shore at either 10, 1 or 4 p.m. *Cost is $35 per person. A two-hour Sunset Cruise with refreshments and appetizers is $45 per person. Inquire about their sailing lessons, which start at $50 for a two-hour session.* ☎ *(530) 583-6200.*

We must not overlook the popular winter activity of cross-country skiing available on the north shore from **Lakeview Cross-Country Ski Area**, located two miles east of Tahoe City. Various trails cater to all abilities—from the meandering Meadow Lark trail for beginners to the more challenging

Bear Trail or the Red Tail Trail for seasoned skiers. There are 65 kilometers (about 35 miles) of machine-groomed backcountry trails with set tracks and skating lanes. *Open 8–5 daily Thanksgiving to Easter, weather permitting. Cost for adults all day is $15, afternoon $12 and twilight $5. Kids 13–17 and seniors pay $12, $9 and $4 for the same time periods. Kids 7–12 are $6, $6 and $4 for the same time periods. Snowshoe rentals are $15 all day and $10 half day.* ☎ *(530) 583-9353.*

Also in Tahoe City is the fun **Tahoe Gal**, a replica of an old sidewheel paddle boat. A one-and-a-half-hour cruise along the scenic west shore gives you views of historical sites and some of the most lavish real estate in the west. Foremost is the Kaiser Estate, well-known as the location for *Godfather II*. Daily scenic shoreline cruises offered by **North Tahoe Cruises** cost $15 for adults and $5 for kids. They also offer a three-hour-plus cruise of Emerald Bay and surrounding area. ☎ *(530) 583-0141.*

Next on the itinerary is **Kings Beach** (3). The story is that a wealthy southern Californian by the name of Rob Sherman owned this land along the beach. He was an inveterate gambler and lost the property to Mr. King in the early 1930s. *Today this is a terrific sand beach open to the public daily from 6 a.m.–10 p.m. The day use parking fee is $5 or you can walk in for free.* All manner of water activities are available here from **Kings Beach Aqua Sports.** If zooming up in the air on a parachute while being pulled by a speeding boat tickles your fancy, then you can take a 15-minute ride for $45. Experienced waterskiers can trail a boat here for $25, or they offer half hour lessons for $50. You can rent a pedal boat or kayak for $15 per hour, or if speed is your thing, a Jetski will cost you $45 for a half-hour or $80 for an hour. ☎ *(530) 546-2782.*

There is a wonderful paved bike path that runs from Dollar Point on the north shore to Meeks Bay halfway down the west shore, mostly along the waterfront. It is a MUP (multi-use path with walkers, joggers and in-line skaters), but a great experience on a bike. You can rent a mountain bike from **Tahoe Bike and Ski** at 8499 North Lake Boulevard at King's Beach. A standard bike is $5 an hour, half-day $15 and all day $23. A suspension mountain bike is $7.50, $15 and $33 for the same time periods. They also have a Basic Downhill Ski Package for $11 a day, a performance package for $16, snowboards $17 and cross-country $9. ☎ *(530) 546-7437.*

At Tahoe Vista you can rev up your engines on the lake with a powerboat from **North Tahoe Marina.** A 21-foot Invader with a 230-hp engine that seats up to nine people can be rented for $85 per hour, $320 for four hours and $600 for eight hours. They have several other powerboats available as well. Water-skis, tube or wetsuit can be rented for $15 per day. ☎ *(530) 546-8248.*

At **Crystal Bay** (4) or **Stateline**, be sure to stop in at the beautifully restored **Cal-Neva Lodge**. This venerable resort straddles the California/Nevada line, so you can gamble in half the hotel. The Indian Room houses an historical display of Washoe Indian artifacts. At one time Frank Sinatra was an owner until the State of Nevada stepped in and made him divest his interest because of his sometimes shady friends. ☎ *(702) 832-4000.*

Because you have now crossed into Nevada, there are more opportunities to try your hand at some gaming. The **Tahoe Biltmore Lodge/Casino** is at Crystal Bay, #5 Highway 28. It offers a neat casino and good, reasonable food.

Turn right and head into **Incline Village** (5), a classy little village of upscale condos and homes with three-car garages. It got its name from the Incline Railway that labored up into the hills to bring down logs in the 1800s. The **Hyatt Regency Lake Tahoe** is a four-star/four-diamond resort with a good sized casino. The hotel is across the road from a sandy beach, at Lakeshore and Country Club Drive in Incline Village.

There are two world-class golf courses in Incline, both designed by Robert Trent Jones: the **Championship Course** at 955 Fairway Boulevard and the **Mountain Course** at 690 Wilson Way. On the par-72 6,900-yard Championship Course you will find tightly cut fairways bordered by towering pines and stunning views of the lake. *Off-season greens fees are $90 regular and $45 twilight; high season fees are $115 regular and $60 twilight.* ☎ *(888) 236-8725 for tee times.* The Mountain Course is carved out of the pines and it demands more accuracy than distance. *Greens fees on this course for the off-season are $40 regular and $25 twilight; high season is $50 and $30.* ☎ *(702) 832-1150 for tee times.*

The **Incline Village Tennis Complex** has seven courts in a beautiful setting. Rates are $9 per hour for adults and $5 for 12 and under. Lessons are available. ☎ *(702) 832-1235 for court reservations.*

Before continuing around the lake, you might consider a side trip up **Mount Rose** (6) for a sweeping view of the lake and surrounding countryside. Turn up Country Club Road, and then up on Highway 431. Go up about four miles to a viewing area where markers will point out highlights of the lake and mountains. If you were to continue on this route over 9,000-foot Mount Rose, you will come to Reno about 30 miles away with its lively, neon-lit downtown. If you make this trip, be sure to see the new **Legacy Casino** right downtown with its huge dome with old mining equipment, melodrama and inside weather changes. It's quite a show.

Past Incline Village, watch for signs to **Ponderosa Ranch** (7) location of the *Bonanza* TV series. Here you'll find all your old favorites. Take a tour of the Cartwright Ranch House. There's an entire Old West Town with an authentic saloon. Breakfast hayrides are a whole lot of fun. You start with a haywagon ride through tall timber. Then sit down to scenic views of the lake with Ben's scrambled eggs, Hop Sing's sausage, flapjacks, juice, coffee and fun. *Open 9:30–5 daily, Apr.–Oct. Adult admission is $9.50, kids 5–11 $5.50. Food is extra.* ☎ *(702) 831-0691.*

Those continuing down the east side of the lake will soon find the **Lake**

Tahoe Nevada State Park, a 12,000-acre shore-to-backcountry area with stunning aerial views of the lake. There are 65 miles of trails and dirt roads for hiking, mountain biking and horseback riding. Foremost among the trails is the spectacular **Flume Trail**, carved out of the edge of the mountain 2,000 feet above the lake shore. This trail follows a precarious route dug out of the granite cliffs more than a century ago. The usual starting point for this is **Spooner Lake**, located at the junction of Highways 28 and 50. There are many other trails as well. ☎ *(702) 831-0494.*

Also in this wondrous park are four hidden beaches—and a fifth that isn't really hidden. Less than a mile from Incline Village is the appropriately named **Hidden Beach**, a sandy beach protected by great piles of granite boulders. **Sand Harbor** (8) is a developed beach with picnic area, boat ramp and full facilities. *The day use parking fee is $6, or you can walk in for free.* About two and a half miles south of Sand Harbor is **Chimney Beach** (9) with a small parking lot on the left side of the road. A mile farther south is another small parking lot with facilities at the top of a fire protection road, which descends to **Secret Harbor** at the lake's shore. A final point to reach on the east shore is just another few miles down the road. A locked Forest Service gate marks the entrance to a dirt road leading to a half-mile hike down to **Skunk Harbor.** Have fun.

Trip 41
Overnighting—East

Lake Tahoe South

There are some facts about Tahoe that are worth knowing. For instance, Lake Tahoe is the largest Alpine lake in North America. Its water is 99.7 percent pure, which is about the same as bottled water. They say it's so clear that a dinner plate can be visible 75 feet below the surface. The lake's surface elevation is 6,225 feet above sea level.

The region has a dry and comfortable climate with an 80 percent chance of sunshine throughout the year. It averages about a foot of snow in the lower elevations, but of course in the mountains that number jumps up considerably. Squaw Valley reports that they usually get 450 inches annually.

Lake Tahoe is 12 miles wide, 22 miles long, and has 72 miles of shoreline—including many bays and inlets. A drive around the lake is possible, but as a daytrip it might frustrate you since there is so much to do; you might be caught between trying to keep a schedule and being constantly tempted to stop and enjoy. Regardless, circling the lake is called "The Most Beautiful Drive in America."

That's why we've divided the area into a north and a south section. Even that will tax your energies with so much to see and do. Be sure to read the preceding daytrip to get the full flavor of the area.

GETTING THERE:

Coming from Sacramento in the west, if you choose Highway US-50 it will take you straight to South Lake Tahoe. From Reno in the east, take US-395 to US-50 south.

PRACTICALITIES:

Many areas have two seasons, but not many can offer plenty to do in either summer or winter. Summer is a mix of playtime on the lake as well as in the mountains and along the river, but winter is mostly mountain play. Any time of year, there's plenty to do.

Keep in mind that three quarters of the lake on the west side is in California and the remainder of the lake on the east side is in Nevada. Those interested in a game of chance will find there's enough of that on the east side of the lake.

Be aware that hours for various facilities may be different between the summer and winter seasons. Some actually close in winter.

To avoid summertime traffic day or night, the Tahoe Trolleys are fun, easy and they go most everywhere. *Cost is $2 all day, 10 a.m.–10 p.m.* ☎ *(530) 541-7548.*

FOOD AND DRINK:

Grumpies (787 Emerald Bay Rd. in South Lake Tahoe) Fun place for the whole family, with a long list of pastas and sandwiches. A good appetizer is the Veggie Egg Rolls with Plum Sauce. Breakfast, lunch and dinner daily. ☎ (530) 542-1717. $

Lyon's (3310 Lake Tahoe Blvd. in South Lake Tahoe) They have soups that are meals in themselves. The Prime Rib Chili Bowl is a favorite. Lots of burgers and fresh fish too. Breakfast, lunch and dinner daily. ☎ (530)541-7751. $

Cowboy's (2244 Hwy. 50 in South Lake Tahoe) Hearty food that includes big burgers. Best known for the Wagon Master, a charbroiled top sirloin served on a sourdough roll. Breakfast, lunch and dinner daily. ☎ (530) 541-4488. $

The Beacon Bar & Grill (on the beach at Camp Richardson) What a location! The food is very good too. Sandwiches and salads for lunch. For dinner try the Filet of Pacific Salmon. Entertainment most afternoons outside on the West Deck. Breakfast, lunch and dinner daily. ☎ (530) 541-0630. $

LOCAL ATTRACTIONS:

Numbers in parentheses correspond to numbers on the map.

If you come from the west on US-50, it will take you right to **South Lake Tahoe** (1). Here you will find all manner of things to do. Go left on Highway 89. In summer there are numerous wonderful activities on the lake.

If fishing is your thing, you might consider contacting **Kingfish Guide Service.** These people have been pulling big and small fish out of the lake for many years, and they can make it an enjoyable experience by steering you in the right direction. Aboard the 43' vessel *Kingfish* they provide tackle, rods, reels and refreshments, and they can help with a one-day license, which is $9.70. Rates are $65 for six hours, during which everyone on the boat catches their limit of two Mackinaw trout. Reservations ☎ *(530) 525-5360.*

What seems like a logical use of land is the **Tahoe Paradise Sports Complex**, located on Highway 89 just after you turn off US-50. In summer, the verdant land is used for a 4,100-yard executive golf course and in winter it turns into groomed trails for snowmobiling. *If you walk the golf course the*

greens fees are $32; with a cart they are $45. Snowmobiling costs $35 per half-hour. ☎ (530) 577-2121.

Look for historic **Camp Richardson** (2) at Highway 89 and Jameson Beach Road, just 2.5 miles from the "Y" where 89 breaks away from US-50 The area has gone from an Indian gathering place to a lumber camp to a resort, and has had several owners. Today it is operated under a permit from the United States Forest Service that owns the land. These folks have a laundry list of interesting activities—summer and winter—to keep the whole family happy. For example, there's kayak water polo for the ambitious in your group.

But let's start with summer. The 120-acre site includes such wonderful activities as "**Coffee with a Naturalist**," starting in the Camp Richardson Hotel (on the National Register of Historic Places) at 9:30 every other Wednesday. After coffee, you take a personalized historic walk with a Forest Service ranger. Sticking with morning activities, they offer a **Breakfast Horseback Ride**, where you take a brisk morning ride to bacon and eggs, hotcakes and cowboy coffee. Cost is $28. The stables include many other rides such as two-hour **Trail Rides** for $35 and a **Steak Ride** through wooded trails to a western steak barbecue. Cost is $35.

On land, you can rent a **mountain bike** for $30 and ride all day through cool forest trails. Tandem, cruiser and kid bike rentals are also available. The Forest Service **Pope-Baldwin Bike Trail** runs all along here, connecting several beaches, the Tallac Historic Site, Camp Richardson and the Taylor Creek Visitor Center.

There's even a **Climbing Rock** where for $4 you can try your legs and hands at scaling rock formations from entry level to more advanced. Or, rent in-line skates for $20 all day.

On the lake, check out the Marina where if you want to power yourself, how about a **kayak** rental for $15 an hour for a single and $20 for a double? Fun **paddle boats** are $15 an hour. For the thrill of power, they offer **Jet Skis** for $75 per hour. A **power boat** to take you anywhere on the lake is $85 per hour.

In winter, they offer **Sleigh Rides** that take you through snow-laden trees and along trails to beautiful views. The cost is $12 per person. **Cross-Country Skiing** can be enjoyed by the whole family. Use of equipment and the trails cost $16 for a half-day and $25 for a full day for adults. Kids are $11 and $19 for the same time periods. For another good wintertime exercise, **Snow Shoeing** can be exhilarating. Rentals are $11 for a half-day and $15 for all day.

There's more, but you'll have to discover for yourself. ☎ *(530) 542-6584 for full information.*

Right next to Camp Richardson is the **Tallac Historic Site**, a real taste of the old Tahoe that includes three lovely waterfront estates on Pope Beach. At the **Valhalla Mansion** there is the Indian Museum, open 10–5 during the summer months. Admission is by donation. The Valhalla Boathouse Theater has productions all summer long. The large **Pope Estate** can be toured on Wednesdays, Fridays, Saturdays and Sundays at 1 and 2:30 from Memorial Day to Labor Day. *Cost is $2.50. Reservations are a must at (530) 541-4975.* When visiting this historic site, also look for the old-growth pines that are reputed to be 400 years old, and enjoy the non-native plants of the Pope Arboretum and the gardens of all three estates.

Just up the highway on the left is the road to **Fallen Leaf Lake** (3). It is tiny compared to Lake Tahoe, but the area reminds many of the Old Tahoe with a slower pace and neat older buildings. The trailhead to the **Desolation Wilderness** is at this point. This area is the most heavily used wilderness per capita in the U.S. It contains 63,475 acres of sub-alpine forests, glacial lakes and valleys, and granite peaks. Parts of the **Pacific Crest Trail** and the **Tahoe Rim Trail** pass through the area. The latter is a scenic 150-mile hiking and horseback trail due to be completed in the next five years. The trail is generally moderate, with altitude changes from 6,300 to 9,400 feet. Dayhikers pay a $3 parking fee. Campers must have a wilderness permit and pay $5 per person per night. ☎ *(530) 644-6048.*

Again, up Highway 89 on the right is the **United States Forest Service Taylor Creek Visitor Center** (4). *Open daily from 8–5:30 June–Sept. and weekends only in Oct. 8–4.* The center offers a wide range of maps, brochures and wilderness permits. The interpretive programs called "Patio Talks" are very informative. Several self-guided trails leave from this spot. ☎ *(530) 573-2694.*

A highlight of the area is the **Stream Profile Chamber**, just a half-mile walk down the Rainbow Trail. This innovative exhibit lets you see what it would be like to go below the surface of Taylor Creek. At floor-to-ceiling glass bay windows, you can see live trout, crayfish, insects and frogs in action without getting wet. It's a wonderful way to see an entire ecosystem up close. *Open late June–Sept. 8–5 daily and Oct. weekends 10–4.*

Next, we're off to the famous **Emerald Bay** (5). Evidence that Tahoe was once the summer playground of the very rich can be seen at **Vikingsholm**. You take a one-mile hike down to an authentic Scandinavian castle built in 1929. The castle, both from the outside and interior, seems totally appropriate in this Alpine setting with its hand-hewn timbers, decorative trim and native stone. Mrs. Lora J. Knight patterned the castle after several she visited in Scandinavia, using a Swedish architect for authenticity. When she purchased the 237 acres in 1928, she also acquired the only island in Tahoe, Fannette Island, where she had a teahouse.

It is almost exactly as she left it in 1945. *Open 10–4 June to mid-Sept.* There are docent-led tours every half-hour, and you can walk the grounds. Try to get Helen Smith as your docent since she spent 14 summers in her youth as a guest in this very house. Helen knows all about the place first hand. *Admission is $3.* ☎ *(530) 525-7277.*

The castle is within the much larger **D.L. Bliss/Emerald Bay State Park** (6). The 1,830-acre park offers camping, picnicking, swimming and fishing, and has full facilities. Rubicon Point, within the park, is one of the most spectacular vistas of the lake and surrounding area. If you went eight feet off the shore at Rubicon, you could stack the Empire State Building and the Washington Monument on top of each other and still have 20 feet of water left on top. *There is a $5 per day parking fee or you can walk in free.* ☎ *(530) 525-7277.*

Farther up the highway is **Sugar Pine Point State Park** (7), open 6 to sunset. There are numerous good nature trails including one for the handicapped. Within the park is a Nature Center with good exhibits of the wildlife of the area. Along the shore stands the sumptuous **Ehrman Mansion**, open 11–4 daily during the summer months. This stately summer home includes three stories of ornate furnishings and decor. *There are six tours daily starting at 11. The house is open July-Labor Day.* ☎ *(530) 525-7277. Adult admission is $2 and kids 5–12 are $1. The park's phone number is (530) 525-7982.*

It wouldn't be Emerald Bay without a cruise out onto the lake. The **Tahoe Queen,** an authentic sternwheeler, is one of the most enjoyable, offering scenic daytime and dinner-dance cruises. The clarity of the water in the lake is evident from the boat's special glass-bottom viewing area. In the winter, they will shuttle you to Squaw Valley with an uproarious après-ski party on the way back. *Rates for the two-hour-and-15-minute Emerald Bay Cruise are $16 for adults and $8 for kids 4–12.* ☎ *(530) 541-3364.*

A breathtaking way to see the lake and surrounding countryside is to float silently from a hot-air balloon. **Lake Tahoe Balloons** offers flights year round. What is especially different about these flights is that they take off and land from the deck of the Tahoe Flyer, the world's only balloon launch and recovery vessel authorized by the Coast Guard. Take your camera and warm clothing. A half-hour flight is $99. After the one-hour flight they take you to a champagne brunch at Café Roma at Caesar's Resort. Cost for the latter is $165 per person. Free shuttle service from your hotel. *Reservations* ☎ *(530) 544-1221.*

Next we suggest you retrace your route to the junction of US-50 and follow signs to the spectacular resort of **Heavenly Valley** (8). The resort's 4,800 acres are a playland in summer and winter. Take the **Aerial Tram** daily between 10 a.m.–9 p.m. In winter, the tram is open 9–4 on weekdays and 8:30–4 on weekends. Just steps from the tram is the **Tahoe Vista Trail**. This two-mile-long pathway is the ticket to a natural wonderland. You'll see massive sugar pines, giant granite boulders and fields of wildflowers. You can pick up a map for a self-guided tour of the Tahoe Vista Trail, or you can take guided tours scheduled at 11 and 1 daily during the summer months.

Winter is when Heavenly shines. There are 82 runs served by 26 lifts. Besides superb skiing, the views are divine. The deep blue lake contrasts with the green mountains. Adult lift tickets are $47 for the weekends and $45 for weekdays. Half-day is $33. Kids 6–12 are $22, teens 13–15 $34 and seniors over 65 $22. ☎ *(702) 586-7050.*

A wonderful way to see the east shore of the lake is to take a cruise on the 50-foot **Woodwind II** from Zephyr Cove. They really sail this multi-hull beauty, providing exceptional stability and lots of thrills. They depart four times daily during the summer months and spend one hour and 45 minutes exploring the beautiful shoreline on the east side. Adults cost $18, seniors $16 and kids 3–12 $9. There's also a Sunset Champagne Cruise where you can enjoy the evening light with a complimentary beverages. Cost is $26. *Reservations (702) 588-3000.*

Section V

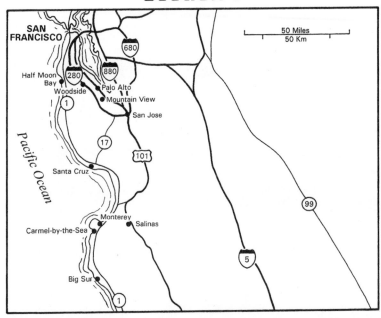

DAYTRIPS AND OVERNIGHTING
SOUTH OF
SAN FRANCISCO

If you think of the peninsula area of San Francisco as more of an bustling business-like region, you would be partially right. After all, Silicon Valley sits south of the city and it's very industrious. There are other pretenders outside of Boston and in Boulder, Colorado, but there's nothing like the concentration of high tech firms around San Jose. Some call it the mothership of high tech worldwide—and it is. As visitors, there are numerous ways to enjoy this aspect of the area south of San Francisco.

There are mountains on the peninsula and south as well. These lovely, wooded hills were practically stripped bare to provide timber for the city during the Gold Rush. The results of this activity—and in some cases the wealth it created—can be explored for lots of fun.

Ah, the seacoast. Once again, it is a tremendous draw for visitors. Monterey Bay is a huge semi-circle encompassing a trench deeper than the

Grand Canyon. The resulting sea life is an amazement to behold. Pushing farther south, a visit to fabled Big Sur can be a soothing experience.

GETTING AROUND—SOUTH

BY CAR:

The preferred means of getting around the area south of San Francisco is on four wheels you control. The key word is flexibility to get into the hills or to the seashore or around various towns.

BY BART:

This commuter train will take you part way down the peninsula, but it doesn't put you in the right places for daytripping.

BY TRAIN:

Commuter trains run regularly and speedily to areas on the Peninsula. We provide information on taking CalTrain to Palo Alto in Daytrip 43 and San Jose in Daytrip 46.

ACCOMMODATIONS—SOUTH

There are wonderful luxury hotels, working ranches and historic B&Bs where you can settle yourself to explore the Monterey/Carmel area for several daytrips.

Three bed and breakfast spots operated by the Four Sisters Inns are worth your time to consider. The Victorian **Gosby House** in Pacific Grove has been welcoming guests to the Monterey Peninsula for over 100 years. You're fed almost constantly, and the 22 rooms are individually decorated with fine English antiques. Some have fireplaces. Also in Pacific Grove is the 1888 Victorian mansion known as **Green Gables Inn.** This one only has 11 rooms divided between the main house and the carriage house. But boy, do they have views. The Monterey Bay Aquarium is only a five minute walk away.

Tucked away in a quiet corner of Carmel is the **Cobblestone Inn**. The 24 rooms—all with fireplaces—wrap around a slate courtyard and English garden. There's a giant fireplace in the lobby. Very Carmel.

To throw a broader net to find accommodations on the Monterey Peninsula, you can call the nice people at (800) 555-WAVE. They can book you into your choice of about 40 different hostelries. More specific to Carmel and Carmel Valley is the Roomfinder Service. Call them for assistance with accommodations all over the peninsula at (800) 847-8066.

VISITOR INFORMATION

Palo Alto Chamber of Commerce
325 Forest Ave.
Palo Alto, CA 94301
☎ (650) 324-3121

San Jose Convention and Visitors Bureau
333 W. San Carlos St., Suite 100
San Jose, CA 95110-2720
☎ (408) 295-9600 or 977-0900
www.sanjose.org

Half Moon Bay Chamber of Commerce
520 Kelly Ave.
Half Moon Bay, CA 94019
☎ (650) 726-5202

Santa Cruz County Visitor Council
701 Front St.
Santa Cruz, CA 95060
☎ (800) 833-3494 or (831) 425-1234

Monterey Peninsula Chamber of Commerce
(Also covers Carmel)
380 Alvarado St.
Monterey, CA 93940
☎ (800) 555-WAVE or (831) 649-1770
www.infopoint.com/sc/cvc/

*Woodside and Portola Valley

As you cruise along the highway or wind you way on just about any road in this area, you are bound to see snatches of gargantuan homes in the wooded hills. These country estates belie what Woodside once was. In the early 1800s, it was thinly populated with rascals who jumped ship up north in San Francisco and down south in Monterey. Today there are still just a few folks who live in the area, but now they are a refined lot with a decidedly genteel lifestyle.

Woodside got its start when a man by the name of John Copinger was awarded another of those huge land grants by the Mexican officials. Copinger got his hands on 12,000 acres that included stately redwoods and many other prime stands of tall trees. Because the cities and towns north of here were beginning to come alive, the demand for lumber was strong, and so sawmills popped up here and there in the hills and valleys. Many of the sailor-miscreants went to work in the lumber operations.

As in lots of places in the Bay Area where there were large stands of accessible trees, these hills were practically stripped bare as demand for lumber zoomed because of the Gold Rush in the mid-1800s. Can you imagine what would happen in these environmentally sensitive communities if that happened today? Fortunately, many areas around Woodside and Portola Valley are heavily wooded again as a result of the second-growth stands of redwoods and other indigenous trees. But there are only a handful of the really big old giants left.

We will spend some time in one of the big mansions in Woodside, and then travel through the wooded hills and valleys of the area.

GETTING THERE:

By car from Union Square, go down Stockton, which becomes 4th after Market Street. At highways US-101 and I-80 go south, and after a few miles get on I-280 south. Follow that past Hillsborough. Take the Black Mountain/Haynes Road exit and go right, then left on Skyline Boulevard.

PRACTICALITIES:

It's a good idea to leave around 9 in the morning to avoid commuter traffic. That leaves time for a leisurely breakfast in the city before heading to this country area. There are excellent hikes and walks, so wear comfortable shoes.

FOOD AND DRINK:

Buck's Restaurant (3062 Woodside Rd.) This is an original, with memorabilia collected by owner Jamis MacNiven, The Big Cheese. How about a steam-powered bicycle? The food is really good too. Hot dungeness crab with melted cheese. Breakfast, lunch & dinner daily. ☎ (650) 851-8010. $ –$$

Quail's Nest Café (at Filoli) Good soups and foccacia bread sandwiches. There's a special Quail Sack Lunch with a sandwich, pasta salad, fruit and cookies. Open Tues.–Sat. 9:30-2:30. ☎ (650) 364-8300. $

Robert's Market (corner of Canada Rd. & Whiskey Hill Rd.) They stand in line at the deli on weekends for picnic fixings. Terrific sandwiches and salads. Try the smoked turkey. Open everyday 8–8. $

Alpine Inn (3915 Alpine Rd.) Been in continuous operation for 146 years, the last 40 under the ownership of the Alexanders. Basically a beer and burger place, very popular with Stanford students. Herbert Hoover's initials are on one of the carved-up tables. Great outdoor seating by the creek. Lunch and dinner daily. ☎ (650) 854-4004. $

SUGGESTED TOUR:

Numbers in parentheses correspond to numbers on the map.

Although it may not always look like it, when you get on **Skyline Boulevard** (1) in Hillsborough, you are driving through some of the most expensive real estate in the nation. Hidden here and there among the hills and valleys are the sumptuous mansions of such names as Levi Strauss, Hearst, Davies and Crosby, just to mention a few. The wooded area on your right—on the other side of the Crystal Springs Reservoir—is the 23,000-acre Peninsula Watershed Natural Area.

When you come to the stop light, turn left and then right for the continuation of Skyline Drive. After a couple of miles look for the entrance of the **Old Sawyer Camp Trail** (2) on the right side of the road. This is a level, paved trail that runs for about 16 miles, basically along the shore of the reservoir. On weekends, it can be popular with joggers, bike riders and walkers. This is a very pleasant way to get some exercise.

Four miles down the road on the right you will come to what the residents call the Water Temple, officially named the **Pulgas Temple** (3). This is a pleasant interlude with grassy areas and plantings leading up to an eight-column temple that marks the spot where the Hetch Hetchy aqueduct—which brings precious water down from the Sierra Nevada Mountains—spills into the Crystal Springs Reservoir. The Greek columns and plantings signal the significance of water to California's well-being.

Continue on Canada. On your right will be a blue sign for Filoli:

*FILOLI (4), Canada Road in Woodside, CA 94062, ☎ (650) 364-2880. *Open mid-Feb. to early Nov., Tues.–Thurs. for guided tours at 9:30, 11:30 and 1:30; reservations needed; Fri. and Sat. for self-guided tours from 10–2; Adult admission is $10, kids 2–12 $1. Gift and garden shop.* ♿.

As you approach **Filoli** you may recognize it as the mansion used for the opening shots of the TV show *Dynasty*. They only used the exterior for shooting. Filoli is the Georgian Revival mansion of William Bourn, who was one of the original gold barons. Filoli means: *Fight* for a just cause; *love* your fellow man; and *live* a good life. These are fitting words for a man who became a millionaire getting lots of gold out of the hills. As the matter of fact, they say his home has about 200 pounds of gold in various forms throughout.

Bourn became even richer by bringing another substance out of the hills and mountains. This time it was water. As a shrewd businessman, Bourn realized early on that the growing population in this area would need good drinking water, and so he developed a way to bring it out of the mountains and store it for the nearby citizens. That's the reason for the Crystal Springs Reservoirs you passed on the way down.

He built his spectacular and tasteful mansion in 1916 at a cost of $500,000. It includes 17 fireplaces and 43 rooms that tell a story about the man who built it. There's a vault for the family silverware just off the kitchen. Look especially for the lightness of the Drawing Room where the ladies gathered after dinner, in contrast to the richness of the Library to which the gentlemen retired. Let your mind place Bourn in the black-walnut-paneled, book-lined library thinking great business thoughts. It goes on and on with gorgeous Oriental rugs and other priceless furnishings to culminate in the Grand Ballroom, with crystal chandeliers and murals of the Lakes of Kilarney in Ireland and Muckross House, which Bourn purchased for his daughter.

Before making your way to the gardens, be sure to notice the beautiful floral arrangements that are everywhere in the mansion. Each Monday, the gardeners go about the grounds cutting blossoms that are made into stunning arrangements by an army of volunteers.

Those who like gardens will thrill at the 16 acres surrounding the house. The gardens are a succession of separate areas or garden rooms, each with

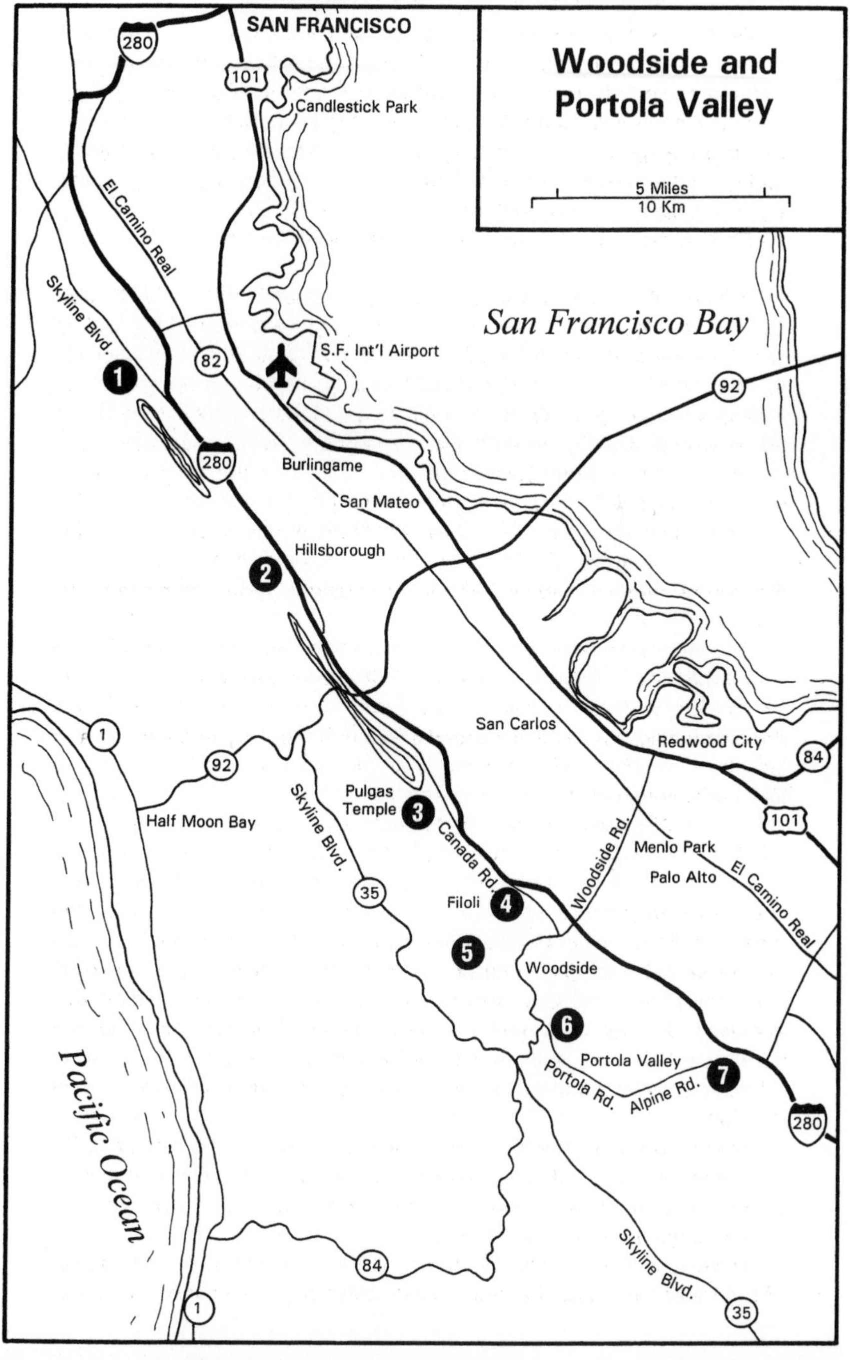

Woodside and Portola Valley
5 Miles
10 Km
SAN FRANCISCO
280
101
Candlestick Park
El Camino Real
Skyline Blvd.
San Francisco Bay
82
S.F. Int'l Airport
1
92
280
Burlingame
San Mateo
2
Hillsborough
San Carlos
Redwood City
84
1
92
Half Moon Bay
Pulgas Temple
3
Skyline Blvd.
Canada Rd.
101
Woodside Rd.
Menlo Park
Palo Alto
El Camino Real
35
Filoli
4
5
Woodside
6
Portola Valley
7
Portola Rd.
Alpine Rd.
280
Pacific Ocean
84
1
Skyline Blvd.
35

a distinctive character. While much of it is very formal, there is a blending with natural features that transitions into the surrounding countryside.

Filoli is a big property covering about 650 acres. There are escorted nature hikes on Mondays through Saturdays at 10. These marvelous adventures take you on a three-mile trek through some of the forested areas of the estate. You must have a reservation.

As you leave Filoli, turn right on Canada and then right again on Woodside Road. Heading toward the mountains, turn right on Albion Road for a look at some of the grander homes in the neighborhood. Turn right on Kings Mountain Road, and two miles up you will come to **Huddart County Park** (5). The road is quite narrow and winding, with a heavy tree canopy created by redwoods and other towering trees. Near the present borders of this 973-acre park were five sawmills in the mid-1800s. If you are in a hiking mood, this will fulfill your every wish with miles of trails. Great spot for a picnic. *The park is open 8 to sunset.* ☎ *(650) 851-0326. $4 entry fee per car.*

When you come back down turn right on Tripp Road. At the intersection on the right will be the historic **Woodside Store** (6). The building has been restored and today is a museum operated by the San Mateo County Historical Society. *Open Tues. and Thurs. 10–4 and Sat. and Sun. noon to 4.* The story of this store is the story of the area. It is on the property that once was a redwood shingle mill owned by Mathias Parkhurst. His partner was a dentist by the name of Robert Tripp. In 1851 they decided to open this store to provide the necessities—and whiskey—to the growing number of lumberjacks working the sawmills. Tripp had his office here, and you can see his original chair and dental instruments. In 1859, Tripp served as the small community's dentist, bartender, postmaster and grocer. It thrived and has survived to this day. *The museum is free.* ☎ *(650) 851-7615.*

Continue on Tripp, which rejoins Woodside Road. After three-quarters of a mile, look on the right for **Wunderlich Park** at 4040 Woodside Road. This is the former home and land of the coffee tycoon James Folger. The home is not visible, but the large, handsome stables are still used by private horse owners. Since this is horse country, it may interest you to know you can't rent a horse in Woodside or Portola Valley simply because many of the old trails go right through private property. The park includes the **Alambique Trail** with three hiking sections: a flat two-mile course; a 2.5-mile trail called The Meadows; and a 4.8-trail called Skyline Boulevard.

Turn right coming out of the park, and a short distance later is Highway 84 that goes over the mountains to the San Gregorio. This becomes a pretty tortuous climb, but is worth going about two miles up for the views.

When you come back down, take a sharp right on Portola. This road winds its way through wooded areas and along the creek. At one time on the left, this was the 2,000-acre Mountain Home Ranch where pioneer Charles Brown started the first sawmill on the peninsula in 1847. You can just see the red-tiled roof of his adobe, believed to be the oldest structure in San Mateo County.

Turn left at Alpine Road. After just about a mile you will come to the **Alpine Inn** (7), a famous watering hole built in 1852. Remember in the earlier part of this daytrip where we talked about the scoundrels who jumped ship and settled in the area to cut and mill timber? This is where they hung out, gambling and fighting and drinking. Needles to say, it has been through Prohibition, several owners and name changes. It became Rosotti's in the late 1940s, a name that many still call it.

The Inn is actually now a State Historical Landmark as the oldest California roadhouse in continuous use. Do stop here for refreshments.

Palo Alto

This is the third time that the name Leland Stanford turns up. The first was in Daytrip 11 when we talked about Nob Hill in San Francisco and the fact that the Stanford Court Hotel is built on the site of the original Stanford mansion. He was one of the Big Four railroad barons. The second time was in Daytrip 36 when we explored the Stanford Mansion in Sacramento, built by Leland and his wife when he was governor of California in 1861.

Today, the centerpiece of this daytrip is the lovely Stanford University campus in Palo Alto. Stanford and his wife Jane came to California in 1852. He immediately set about building his fortune, mostly through construction of the transcontinental railroad. Part of his holdings was a large farm and ranch called the Palo Alto Stock Farm in this very area. Here he bred and raised horses on what was the largest trotting horse farm of its kind in the country.

Tragedy struck his son Leland Junior when they were on a trip in Italy in 1884. At 16, he contacted typhoid fever and died. The heartbroken parents returned to the peninsula and decided to found a university in memory of their son. Thus was launched one of the nation's most distinguished universities, originally called the Leland Stanford Junior University.

We'll also visit the next town of Menlo Park with some very interesting things to do.

GETTING THERE:

By Train, take a taxi to the CalTrain Railroad Depot at Fourth and King Street. ☎ (800) 660-4287 for times and fare.

By car from Union Square, go down Stockton, which becomes 4th after Market Street. Get on Route US-101 going south and get off after about 25 miles at the University exit.

PRACTICALITIES:

One of the most practical ways to make this trip is on public transportation. When you get to Palo Alto, we suggest either walking or riding a bike. You will see plenty of both in this town. Either way, wear loose clothing and comfortable shoes.

FOOD AND DRINK:

Crescent Park Grill (546 University Ave.) Neat California-style restaurant serving nouvelle cuisine. Smoked Trout, Grilled Merquez Sausages are highlights. Lunch Mon.–Fri. and dinner daily. ☎ (650) 326-0111. $–$$

Stickneys (1 Town & Country Village) Coffee shop supreme. Forty-plus-year history of serving the community terrific seafood, beef and Mexican dishes. Leave room for a wide range of fabulous desserts. Breakfast, lunch and dinner daily. ☎ (650) 324-0317. $–$$

Prolific Oven Bakery and Coffeehouse (550 Waverly St.) These are baked goods to die for. There are 14 types of pastries and muffins, and 15 flavors of cookies. French-style cream cakes are highlighted by orange custard. Open daily for breakfast and dessert. ☎ (650) 326-8668. $

The Rose & Crown (547 Emerson) Tucked away is this little pub with terrific pub food. How about Rose & Crown Rarebit? Ploughman's Lunch is wedges of Cheshire & Stilson, roll and house-pickled onions. Lunch and dinner daily. ☎ (650) 327-ROSE. $

SUGGESTED TOUR:

Numbers in parentheses correspond to numbers on the map.

If you choose to cover this daytrip on a bike, rentals are available from **The Bike Connection** at 2086 El Camino Real. ☎ *(650) 424-8034 for reservations. Daily rates are $15 for a three-speed and $20 for a mountain bike. Open 10–6 daily.*

Get on University and head west straight into the campus. Today, there are over 14,000 students in undergraduate and graduate programs at **Stanford University** (1). Currently the university has more than 70 departments in seven schools: Business, Earth Sciences, Education, Engineering, Humanities and Sciences, Law and Medicine. The Stanford faculty is one of the most distinguished in the nation. Among the 1,300 faculty members are eight Nobel Laureates, four Pulitzer Prize winners, 178 members of the American Academy of Arts & Sciences and 104 members of the National Academy of Sciences.

There are dozens and dozens of interesting buildings, and we will give you information about a few of them. Jane and Leland Stanford originally laid out the master plan for the campus in collaboration with the distinguished designer, Frederick Law Olmsted. They wanted a monumental plan in memory of their son, who died at age 16. The campus' architecture is basically a mix of Mission Revival and Romanesque. Arches and long arcades connect the sandstone buildings accented with red tile roofs. The original central campus buildings have grown to occupy about 1,200 acres.

A good place to start is **Visitor Information Center** (2) in Memorial Hall opposite the Hoover Tower. *It is open 10–4 daily. Closed major holidays. You can catch campus walking tours here at 11 and 3:15 daily. For those who don't want to walk, there's a cart tour daily at 1 in the afternoon. Reservations ☎ (650) 723-2560. There are no tours during the first week of classes, final exams and academic holidays. Campus maps are available here.*

In the middle of the campus, as expected, is the **Inner Quadrangle**, the handsome courtyard focal point. The 12 original classroom buildings are joined by arcades with **Memorial Church** and the surrounding **Outer Quadrangle.** *The church is open 8–5 weekdays. Sunday services are at 10.*

Hoover Tower (3) honors one of the school's more notorious graduates, Herbert Hoover, who was the nation's president from 1929–33. If you want to look over the whole campus, this 285-foot tower is the way to do it. *Open daily 10–4. Adult admission is $2 and $1 for seniors and kids under 13. Closed during finals, breaks between academic sessions and the first week of classes each quarter. ☎ (650) 723-2053 for more information.*

At the present, the tower houses the **Hoover Institution on War, Revolution and Peace**. On the ground floors are exhibits and memorabilia of the school's famous alum. There are changing exhibits from the posters, photos, letters and other documents of the of the Hoover Institution Archives collection. *Open Tues.–Sun. 11–4 Free. ☎ (650) 723-3563.*

Be sure to check out the recently remodeled **Museum of Art** (4) at Museum Way and Lomita Drive. During the 1989 earthquake this prize facility took a major hit, but is back with even better offerings. It features a contemporary collection of paintings, sculpture, prints and drawings. The Stanford Collection is mostly memorabilia from Europe collected by Leland Stanford, Jr. Before his untimely death at 16, this young man was quite the amateur collector. Many are classical antiquities. *Open Wed.–Sun. 11–5 and Thurs. until 8. Free. ☎ (650) 723-3469.*

A remnant of Leland Stanford's Palo Alto Stock Farm is what's called the **Red Barn**. After Stanford's death, the Stock Farm went downhill until all the horses were gone. On Campus Drive West, this handsome Victorian barn is worth the visit. It is still used for boarding horses.

After you leave the campus, go to 315 Homer Avenue where you'll find the **Museum of American Heritage** (5) located in the lovely old Williams house and gardens. It is devoted to the display of electrical and mechanical devices commonly found in homes and businesses from 1800–1950. This is a wonderful way to trace the development of such critical tools as calculators, cash registers, cameras and many more. *Open Fri.–Sun. 11–4. Admission is by donation. ☎ (650) 321-1004.*

Find your way to Cowper Street where you will pass through what's col-

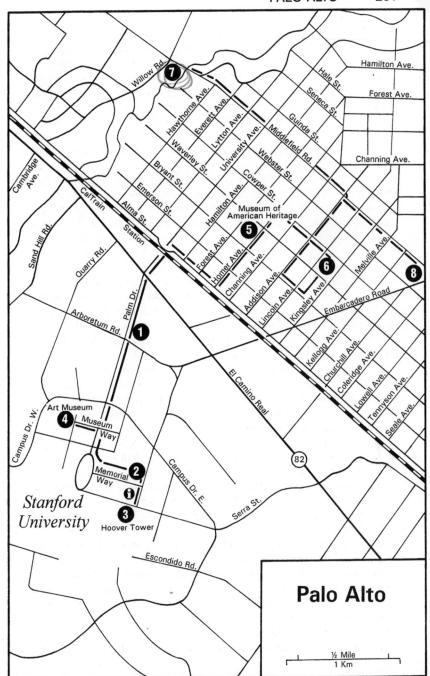

Palo Alto

called **Professorville** (6). This area is listed on the National Register as a Historic District. It is the older part of Palo Alto, where the teachers built homes as the campus began to develop in the early days. If you go by 1061 Bryant, you will come to the **Sunbonnet House**, designed in 1899 by the inestimable Bay Area architect Bernard Maybeck for a professor by the name of Emma Kellogg. There are many other beauties in this area. Walking tours of the Professorville Historical District are on the 1st, 3rd and 5th Saturdays at 10 in the morning. ☎ *(650) 299-8878.*

While on Bryant, check out 1044, which was the childhood home of brothers Russell and Sigurd Varian. You may remember they founded **Varian Corp.** after they invented the klystron tube in 1937. This tube is the real backbone of modern microwave electronics. There's hope for all of us when you consider one brother was a college dropout and the other was dyslexic. Varian was the first tenant in the fabled Stanford Tech Park. Today the company has 4,000 employees in 15 buildings.

At 367 Addison, there's a plaque that commemorates the spot where Stanfordites **Bill Hewlett and David Packard** founded their empire. For heavens sake, it was in the garage where the Packards were renting a house. Nonetheless, this very spot is called the "Birthplace of Silicon Valley."

If shopping is your thing, check out the **Stanford Shopping Center.** They call it Northern California's most cultivated collection of stores, in a breathtaking garden setting. The biggies include Neiman Marcus, Nordstrom, Macy's and Bloomingdale's. Many other colorful shops as well, with good restaurants throughout. *180 El Camino Real. Call the concierge at (800) 772-9332.*

Close by at Willow Road and Middlefield are the offices and testing areas for **Sunset Magazine** (7). Be sure to take the walking tour of the spectacular garden that includes four experimental plots gardens. As you pass through the massive carved oak doors, the first thing that hits you are the 1.2 acres of brilliant green grass. The surrounding gardens were designed by Thomas Church, the dean of western landscape architects. Church created a garden with distinct areas representing the major climate zones of the west. The flowers are stunning. You will frequently hear from other guests what you are probably thinking, "Why won't my (whatever flower) bloom like theirs?" *Garden tours are open for walking weekdays 9–4:30. There is no charge.* ☎ *(650) 321-3600.*

Just down the road is the wonderfully creative **Junior Museum and Zoo** (8) at 1451 Middlefield Road. In a lovely garden setting you can visit over 100 animals including raccoons, bobcats, hedgehogs, ferrets, exotic pheasants and geese, and many species of reptiles. You meet the animals through their Animal Encounters program. They also have changing interactive exhibits. *Open Tues.–Sat. 10–5, Wed. 1–8 and Sun. 1–4. Admission is by donation.* ☎ *(650) 329-2111.*

Also well worth a visit is the **Allied Arts Guild** at 95 Arbor Road. Here you will find a plethora of artists' works for sale, including pottery, painting, sculpture, weaving and more. There's plenty of talent here to choose from, with some very good bargains. There are neat gardens too. ☎ *(650) 325-3250.*

One of the best known bicycle stores in the nation is called **Wheelsmith** at 2180 El Camino Real. The owner, Ric Hjertberg, has a wonderful collection of racing bikes. ☎ *(650) 493-9022.* Worth a visit.

Trip 44
Peninsula

Half Moon Bay and Coastside

A good deal of the interest in Half Moon Bay is that it's close to San Francisco (only about 25 miles south), yet it seems a world away. Part of the isolation is due to the precarious coastal route to get there from the big city, but more so is the winding, mountainous route from the east. Both of these roads (the only two ways to get the Half Moon Bay besides boat) were originally trails of the Costanoan Indians.

The town of Half Moon Bay and its neighboring villages along the coast—Montara, Moss Beach, San Gregorio and Pescadero—are usually referred to as "Coastside." Coastside was first discovered by foreign explorers in 1776 when Captain Gaspar de Portola founded Mission Dolores in San Francisco and sent the mission's cattle, horses and oxen down the coast to graze. That began a long history of agriculture that is still very evident today.

In the 1840s, land grants were deeded to early Spanish settlers. Later, Mexican and Chilean laborers settled along Coastside and the town of Half Moon Bay became known as Spanishtown. A rich mixture of immigrants came in another wave in the late 1800s and the various ethnic groups—Canadians, Chinese, Germans, Irish, Italians, Scots, Portuguese and Pacific Islanders—each left their marks on the region.

GETTING THERE:

By car from Union Square, go down Stockton to Market, which becomes Fourth. Follow signs for US-101 South. This will take you directly to I-280. Take this freeway south about 20 miles. Look for Skyline Boulevard and Highway 92 to Half Moon Bay, which is about eight miles over mountains.

PRACTICALITIES:

There may be coastal fog during the summer months, usually in the mornings. There are some excellent and easy hikes to redwood forests and along the coast, so wear comfortable shoes. Sunglasses are a good idea.

FOOD AND DRINK:

Chart House (8150 N. Cabrillo Hwy., Montara) Famous for its daring, wrap-around picture windows, the dramatic setting is best at sunset when the salt mist rises from beach below. Hand-cut steaks, fresh seafood and lavish salad bar. ☎ (650) 728-7366. $$

The Shore Bird (390 Capistrano Rd. in Princeton-by-the-Sea) Your table will overlook the harbor and fishing boats. Pepper-crusted Yellow Tuna is one of many fresh fish delicacies. Another favorite is the Pan Fried Calamari Steak. Lunch and dinner daily. ☎ (650) 728-5542. $–$$

Miramar Beach Restaurant (turn on Magellan to 131 Mirada Rd.) So close to the water that the waves sometimes splash up on the building. Originally a Prohibition roadhouse, this great spot has a colorful history. Seafood is their specialty. Lunch & dinner daily. ☎ (650) 726-9053. $–$$

La Di Da (500 C Purissima in central Half Moon Bay) Fun, funky interior with lots of color and things going on. Live music on weekends. Calzones, salads and other good eats. Breakfast, lunch and dinner daily. ☎ (650) 726-1663. $

LOCAL ATTRACTIONS:

Numbers in parentheses correspond to numbers on the map.

As you dip down on Highway 92 on your way to Half Moon Bay, you will see Crystal Springs Reservoir on both sides of the road. This signals the start of the rather tortuous, but very picturesque climb and then descent to the coast. Consider that during the 1800s, you could take the same route in a stage coach that took about eight hours travel time.

Once at the summit, the downward slope reveals deep valleys and more and more farms tucked back into the flat areas. In the fall, you have never seen so many pumpkins, for this is one of the nation's premiere pumpkin patches. Almost any time of year, however, you will see flower farms in profusion. Lots of Christmas tree farms too, since agriculture of all types is still a mainstay of the Coastside area. Stop at **T&E Pastorino Floral** at 12511 San Mateo Road or Highway 92 for a full range of flowers and produce. *Open 9–6 daily.* ☎ *(650) 726-2445.*

And since things grow well here, so do grapes. Stop by the **Obester Winery** at 12341 San Mateo Road. They are best known for their Pinot Noir. Good champagne and organically grown Chardonnay too. *Open daily 10–5.* ☎ *(650) 726-9463.*

As you approach the end of the road, look for Main Street at the first stoplight and turn left. This is the start of the **Historic District of Half Moon Bay**

(1). On the left is the original redwood home of **Pablo Vasquez**, who was the son of a Mexican ranchero. Built in 1869, this home at 270 Main was the center of Vasquez' rather raucous lifestyle that included many festive parties, bull fights and horse racing. A bit farther on is the **Pilarcitos Creek Bridge**. This concrete reinforced span was the first of its kind in San Mateo County when it was built at the turn of the century. The man who mapped out the town of Half Moon Bay, Estanislo Zaballa, built the **Oldest Building** in 1859 at 326 Main. **The Bells of Half Moon Bay** are next at corner of Main and Kelly Ave. Originally, there were bells above and bells below on a special stand. Those on top called the firemen and those below, school children. In the next block is historic **City Hall** "that looks like a bank" at 501 Main. It looks like a bank because is was preceded by three banks as original tenants. Turn left on Kelly and right on Johnson, and that will take you to the **Half Moon Bay Jail and Historical Museum** at 505 Johnson. Built in 1911, the two tiny cells were soon inadequate for the spirited, lively community. *It is open to the public Fri. 1–3 and Sat.–Sun. 11–3. Donations.* ☎ *(650) 726-7084 for more information.* A bit farther on Johnson is the **Community Methodist Church**, built in 1872. This quaint little church with about a dozen pews has beautiful stained-glass windows.

If you retrace your route to Kelly and turn left, this will take you to **Half Moon Bay State Beach** (2) at Francis Beach, one of the largest all along this coastline. Great for walking and sunning at certain times of the year, however the swimming is always questionable and best avoided because of cold, rough water and uncertain undertows. *The beach park is open 8 in the morning until sunset. Day use fees are $5. Campsites can be rented for $16 overnight.* The Coastside Trail starts at this beach and runs all the way to Vallejo Beach just south of Pillar Point Harbor, a distance of about three miles. ☎ *(650) 726-8819 for information. Full facilities.*

At Highway 1 (Cabrillo), go south about a half a mile and turn left at Higgins Purissima Road. Another half-mile up on the right is the **Johnston House** (3), built in 1853 and listed on the National Register for Historic Places. In an area where the early Spanish influence is still quite evident, it is pretty amazing to come across a classic Eastern-style salt box so typical of New England and the East. Sitting all alone on a knoll, the style of this white clapboard house is Yankee; yet the hand-hewn timbers and pegs inside are of redwood, which is decidedly California. *The San Mateo County Historical Association leads docent tours the third Saturday of the month from 11–3. Donations.* ☎ *(650)726-0329.*

If you follow the same road up another four miles you will come to the **Purissima Creek Redwoods** (4), an Open Space Preserve. Look for the small, unmarked parking lot at the sharp bend in the road. There is a 1.25-mile gentle, broad trail where you will find lush forests of giant redwoods, fields of wild flowers and fern-lined creek beds. Well worth a visit. *Open 8 to sunset.* ☎ *(650) 691-1200.*

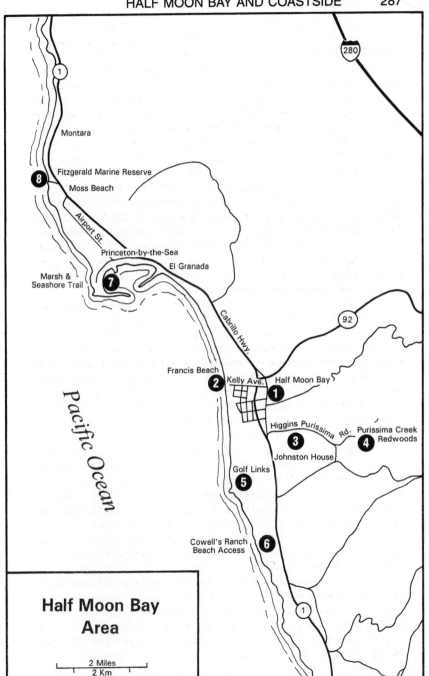

280

1

Montara

Fitzgerald Marine Reserve

Moss Beach

8

Airport St.

Princeton-by-the-Sea

El Granada

Marsh & Seashore Trail

7

Cabrillo Hwy.

92

Pacific Ocean

Francis Beach

2

Kelly Ave.

Half Moon Bay

1

Higgins Purissima Rd.

Purissima Creek Redwoods

3

Johnston House

4

Golf Links

5

Cowell's Ranch Beach Access

6

1

Half Moon Bay Area

2 Miles
2 Km

When you come back to Highway 1, turn left and travel about half a mile. On the right is the **Half Moon Bay Golf Links** (5), which just happens to be one of the most scenic courses in the world. The older Links Course was designed by Arnold Palmer and Francis Duane and plays inland. The newer Ocean Course's claim to fame is that you can see the beautiful Pacific Ocean from all but two of its 18 holes. It took 20 years to build, principally because California so carefully guards its coastline and hearings and permits took that long. *The Ocean Course greens fees are $95 Mon.–Thu., $115 Fri.–Sun. The Links Course greens fees are $85 Mon.–Thu. and $105 Fri.–Sun. All fees include a cart.* ☎ *(650) 726-4438 for tee times.*

Back on the highway, turn right and go south again about a mile. On the right is the **Cowell's Ranch Beach Access** (6). When the county purchased sections of the old Cowell Ranch it ran from the mountains to the sea, and so recently they opened a path down to the ocean. According to park aides Kevin Jacobs and Tom Estrada, the half-mile path is quite a treasure since access to the ocean here is limited because of the steep cliffs. A stairway actually leads down to a pocket beach with very rough water. *Sunset Magazine* recently rated Cowell's as one of the Ten Best Beaches in Northern California, calling it "Best New Beach Access." *Don't swim because of strong undercurrents. Partial facilities.* The dark green crop on the left as you walk down the path is artichoke.

To complete the loop from San Francisco over the mountains to Coastside, it now suggested that you make your way back along the coast to the city. When you head north on Highway 1, about a mile north of Half Moon Bay is **Sea Horse Ranch** and its accompanying **Friendly Acres Ranch**. Between them, they have 200 horses and ponies offering a wide variety of rides. You can ride on your own on trails and beaches, or go with a guide. An example is a two-hour beach ride for $35. *No reservations needed, but* ☎ *(650) 726-2362 or 726-8550 for more information.*

At Capistrano Road, turn off Highway 1 to Pillar Point and Princeton-by-the-Sea. Go past the harbor entrance to Prospect Way and turn left. Turn right on Broadway, then immediately left on Harvard to the end. Turn right on West Point Avenue; this will take you to the Pillar Point parking lot and the start of the half-mile **Marsh and Seashore Trail** (7). This fresh and salt water-fed marsh is pretty small, however you will likely see great blue herons, snowy egrets and killdeers. The real treat is to follow the trail around the point to the breakwater on the far side. This offers terrific views of the harbor and mountains all along Coastside. You may see sea lions sunning on the craggy rocks offshore. Don't even think about approaching any sealife since this area is part of the huge Monterey National Marine Sanctuary.

Back at the harbor, you may want to consider some ocean fishing. **Huck Finn Sportfishing** can book you onto one of the many professionally crewed boats in Pillar Harbor. They offer rock fishing year round for $38 from 7 in the morning until 2 in the afternoon, and salmon fishing seasonally for $48.

January through March, whale watching cruises go out on weekends for three hours at 10 and 1:30 for $20. ☎ *(650) 726-7133 for reservations and more information.*

As you make you way north toward San Francisco, a final suggested stop is at **Fitzgerald Marine Reserve** (8) in Moss Beach to inspect the fascinating tidepools. Take California Avenue off Highway 1 in Moss Beach and stop at the Interpretive Center. Docent-led tours cover about half a mile of exposed tidepools, where you can see hermit crabs, purple shore crabs and starfish. As you make your way from the sheltered sandy cove at the south end of the Reserve, you pass through the tangled garden of an old estate. *Full facilities.* ☎ *(650) 728-3584.*

Trip 45
Peninsula

A Good Way to Mountain View

Those many souls who commute on Highway 101 south of San Francisco will tell you that it can be pretty drab and boring along the bay. We wouldn't think of putting you through something like that when there are three splendid parks along 101 to Mountain View—to make the trip very interesting.

The three parks are distinctively different, and many residents aren't even aware of them as they sleepily head for San Francisco in the morning and wearily stagger home in the evening. But you're on vacation; and with our help we'll have you go up on a mountain for a spectacular view, go down by the bay to learn about the environment, and go out on to the marshy baylands to learn about birds and plants.

Our destination is Mountain View, which is the northern boundary of Silicon Valley. It's not an especially big town, but it's been through a rebirth and is a very pleasant place to view a small California town.

This daytrip is mostly all about nature—nature in an area that isn't often thought of as being attractive. Let's go.

GETTING THERE:

By car from Union Square, go down Stockton, which becomes 4th after Market Street. Look carefully for signs after four blocks and get on Route US-101 going south. After about 5.5 miles, take the Sierra Point exit. Turn right at the stop sign and then left on Tunnel. At the stoplight, turn right on Bayshore Boulevard. Follow that to Guadalupe Canyon Parkway and go left. Follow signs to the San Bruno Mountain Park.

PRACTICALITIES:

These are not necessarily hikes, but pleasant walks, so wear comfortable shoes. It can be cool on top of the mountain in the winter time. Down along the bay, it can also be cool in winter, but warm in summer, so dress accordingly.

FOOD AND DRINK:

Scott's Seafood Grill & Bar (2300 E. Bayshore, Palo Alto). Popular omelette and espresso bar in the morning. Blackened mahi mahi and peppered yellowfin tuna are specialities. Mocha cheese cake for desert. Breakfast, lunch and dinner daily. ☎ (650) 856-1046. $$

Taj Mahal Indian Cuisine (185 Castro in Mtn. View) Lunch buffet with all-you-can-eat for under $7. Choose from 23 items. Lots of chicken curries to choose from along with seafood Indian style. ☎ (650) 968-8008. $–$$

Man Bo Duck (360 Castro in Mtn. View) Combination Family Dinners are winners. The chef recommends Peking Duck. Rainbow Chicken has three types (lemon, Tai Chin and with snow peas). Lunch and dinner daily. ☎ (650) 961-6638. $–$$

Colonel Lee's Mongolian BBQ (304 Castro in Mtn. View) Lunch is all-you-can-eat for under $6 and dinner is the same for a little more than $10. Full menu of delicious Chinese dishes served in a fun atmosphere. Lunch and dinner daily. ☎ (650) 961-1491. $–$$

SUGGESTED TOUR:

Numbers in parentheses correspond to numbers on the map.

When you say Brisbane or San Bruno to most San Franciscans, they will usually turn up their noses. That's because this is mostly an industrial area, although San Bruno has a good deal of middle-class housing. And on the mountain we'll drive up, there are big mansions going up.

Don't let all that distract you from visiting **San Bruno Mountain Park** (1). If you've been to San Francisco before and come in from the airport or up from the south by car, you can't miss the roundish San Bruno Mountains on your left just after the airport. They don't look like much from the freeway, but the one we'll tackle is well worth a visit.

The fact that the park holds 14 rare or endangered plant species might make some snobby San Franciscans chortle, but it does. Further, it's not known by many that this open space is 2,360 acres smack in the middle of the peninsula's highly urbanized area. There's a good deal of wildlife, and if you feel vigorous, there are about eight miles of hiking trails. Be sure to go to the summit of the 1,314-foot mountain for a spectacular view all around the area. As the matter of fact, while not a terribly high mountain, San Bruno nevertheless affords the best view of the area south of San Francisco.

The park has full facilities including good picnic spots. It is open 8–8. No dogs or pets. There is a self-regulated entry fee of $4 per car. No fee for seniors or the disabled. ☎ *(650) 355-8289 for more information.*

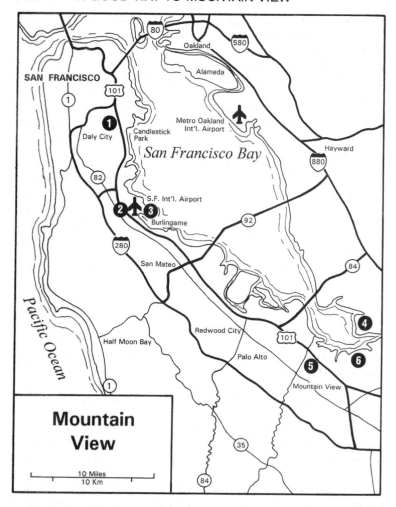

Get back on US-101 and head south again. The airport will start to loom on your left, and unlikely as it may seem, we are headed for a park that's in the shadow of this transportation beehive.

Go south about 8.5 miles and look for the Poplar Avenue exit. Look for signs to Coyote Point Drive and the entrance to the park.

Amazing as it may seem, the 670-acre **Coyote Point Park** (2) is laid out with several miles of biking and walking trails. There's a handy map you can pick up at the park entrance that shows all the trails. By all means, get you feet under you and explore some of this wonderful area.

But it's just not all trails through the eucalyptus and other indigenous trees. There's even a sizable beach at the bay shore, where during the summer you can pick up a tan. It's pebbly, so don't look for white sand. *The firing range is located near the golf course. Adults can fire three hours for $5; kids under 19 $3. Open weekdays nights Mon., Wed., and Fri. 7-10.*

If golf is your thing, the pubic **San Mateo Golf Course** adjoins the park. It can be played weekdays for $21 and weekends for $26. Twilight games after 3:30 are $15. The course is particularly challenging because just as you're about to putt, a 747 may be making its final approach overhead, but that just prepares you for when you make the pro tour and play with the crowds and TV cameras in your face. Good practice. It's a good idea to call ahead for reservations at (650) 347-1461.

Many consider the highlight of this park the **Coyote Point Museum for Environmental Education** (3). As the name suggests, this facility is situated in the ideal place to educate us all about how fragile our environment really is—especially in the Bay Area. It is done in such a way that you actually learn a lot while having fun. All exhibits revolve around the bay and the bay region. There are three descending exhibits that tell about the major components of the area—the bay itself, the mountains and the ocean—and how they interact.

Designed for self-guided tours, the museum can be very absorbing. *Open 10–5 Tues.–Sat, and 12–5 on Sun. Admission is $1 for adults and kids are 50¢.* ☎ *(650) 342-7755 for more information.*

The park has full facilities including good areas for picnics. The park entrance fee is $4 per car. The museum is in addition to the park entrance fee. Open 8–8. ☎ *(650) 573-2592.*

Go south once again on US-101. After 14 miles, look for the Embarcadero exit in Palo Alto. Turn left or east on Embarcadero and go to the end of the road.

The **Baylands Nature Preserves** (4) is also called the Palo Alto Baylands. If you want to see native birds, it is said that over 100 species inhabit the area including owls, ducks, hawks, herons and more. Be sure to find your way to the Interpretive Center, which has lots of information on the flora and fauna. Guides will take you on a tour of the preserve on a system that includes a raised boardwalk and levees. You can do it yourself, but the information from the trained guides makes it well worth going with them. There's a cute story about the rangers building a sizable natural swimming pool filed with bay water in the Preserve. Just as it was finished, the ducks moved in and chased the people away. Roll reversal in nature chasing out humans. There's a six-mile loop trail the runs throughout the Preserve.

The Interpretive Center is open Wed.–Fri. and weekends from 1–5. The Preserve is open 8 to sunset daily. There is no admission. ☎ *(650) 329-2506.*

Normally, guidebooks about the Bay Area don't take you to **Mountain View** (5). Its better-known neighbors such as Palo Alto and Menlo Park overshadow this pleasant small town on the peninsula. But it's worth a visit to see the transformation of a formerly rather plain farm community into a spiffed-up boomer town influenced by the dozens of high tech companies in the area—including Netscape.

The newly refurbished and leafy downtown (it's only six blocks long) tells an interesting story of the area. There are seven Chinese restaurants along with Chinese furniture and food stores. In the long ago, Mountain View was all about fruit orchards, and this ethnic group came to work in the many farms that covered the area. The orchards are all gone now.

Besides ethnic restaurants—that also includes Indian, Thai, Japanese and Italian—Mountain View loves books. There are three bookshops in downtown. The best-known is called **Printer's Ink** at 301 Castro. It includes a popular café.

Mountain View has further set itself apart by building a stunning new City Hall, Center for the Performing Arts and Library complex that adds to the allure of this small town. ☎ *(650) 903-6000 to find out what's playing in the Center.*

Take Castro east (it becomes Moffett) to get to the National Aeronautics and Space Administration facility, better known as the **Ames Center** (6) at Moffett Field. The very size of the buildings alone are pretty staggering. This is a fascinating facility, the largest outside of NASA headquarters in Houston. It concentrates on aircraft safety and design. You start in an auditorium with a video explaining the work that is done at this facility. White-coated scientists can be seen working on new aircraft design in several wind tunnels, one of which is the world's largest at 80 feet high and 120 feet wide. The big one is one of 20 at this facility. *Tours are free. Reservations must be made in advance.* ☎ *(650) 604-6497.*

*Urban San Jose

The people in San Jose are determined to get out the word that their city is the largest in Northern California. With a population of 874,000, they claim the city itself is bigger than San Francisco (surprise!), Boston, Washington D.C., Seattle, Miami, Denver and New Orleans.

Size matters in this case because of the myriad things to see and do in the area. It is impossible to do it all, so make your choices carefully.

For your tummy, there are many great restaurants and 50 wineries in the area, with a couple right in town. A wine tour is a good way to get your arms around this activity. Many people come for their heads. What else would you expect in San Jose than a spectacular high tech museum? San Jose's fascinating history is portrayed in parks and buildings and exhibits starting with an adobe structure built in 1797. That's only the beginning.

There is so much to see and do in this exciting region that we've made the daytrip into two: Urban San Jose (this trip) and Outside San Jose (the next daytrip). You may want to scan both to pick and choose between them, or do them separately. In any case, you'll have lots of fun.

GETTING THERE:

By car from Union Square, go down Stockton, which becomes 4th after Market Street. At routes US-101 and I-80 go south and after a few miles get on I-280 south. Follow that for 40 miles, then take the Bird Street exit. Left on Bird, then right on San Carlos Street.

By train, take a taxi to the CalTrain Railroad Depot at Fourth and King streets. The round-trip train fare is $9. ☎ (800) 660-4287 for departures.

PRACTICALITIES:

With nearly 300 sunny days per year, San Jose registers a 70-degree annual average temperature. At midday, it can be quite warm, but pleasant year round.

Many of the museums are closed on Mondays. Take sunglasses and comfortable shoes.

FOOD AND DRINK:

71 Saint Peter (71 N. San Pedro St.) Fun spot serving Nouvelle California Cuisine. Crispy Roasted Duck with raspberry pepper demi glace and Seafood Linguine are favorites. Lunch and dinner daily. ☎ (408) 971-8523. $–$$

Shark & Rose (69 N. San Pedro St.) A true pub feeling that serves a killer Shark Sandwich and Shark Tacos. Best Fish Soup in the bay area. Pastas and many other shark specialities. Lunch Mon.–Fri. Dinner daily. ☎ (408) 287-6969. $–$$

Gombei Restaurant (193 E. Jackson St.) Crowded and popular Japanese spot in the heart of Japantown. Chicken Teriyaki, Deep-fried Shrimp and Pork Cutlet don are favorites. Terrific noodle dishes too. Lunch and dinner Mon.-Sat. ☎ (408) 229-4311. $–$$

Peggy Sue's (29 N. San Pedro St.) Hollywood, Porky Pig, Great Balls 'o Fire, and T-bird are the names of some of regular sandwiches. Our Gang or Sid Caesar and more are for Big Appetites. Lunch and dinner daily. ☎ (408) 298-6750. $

SUGGESTED TOUR:

Numbers in parentheses correspond to numbers on the map.

After exiting I-280 make your way to Woz Way to visit the **Children's Discovery Museum** (1). This place is great for the whole family, with 150 interactive exhibits where you can crank, test, listen, prod, taste and tinker. Learn how electricity is generated, experiment with water and create artwork from recycled goods. *Open Tues.–Sat. 10–5, Sun. noon–5. Adult admission is $6, seniors $5, kids 2–18 $4. ☎ (408) 298-5437.*

Nearby is:

*THE TECH MUSEUM OF INNOVATION (2), 145 South Market, San Jose, CA 95113, ☎ (408) 279-7150. *Open Memorial Day to Labor Day daily 10–6 (until 8 on Thurs.); rest of year Tues.–Sun. 10–5. Closed Jan. 1, Easter, Thanksgiving, Christmas. Adults $8, seniors $7, kids 6–18 $6 IMAX theater extra; joint ticket available.*

The Tech, as it's known for short, provides insight into San Jose's famous industry—high technology. Housed in 132,000 square feet of space are four themed exhibit galleries: Innovation, Exploration, Communication and Life Tech. You will be able to see how computer chips are made, design your own roller coaster or make your own movie in The Tech's Digital Studio. If you want to really get crazy, you can ride a virtual bobsled or "fly" with a jet pack simulator. For more stimulation, there's also an IMAX Dome Theater. All of it is a wonderful experience.

At the corner of San Fernando and Market is the **San Jose Museum of Art** (3). What is remarkable about this fine facility is an agreement with the

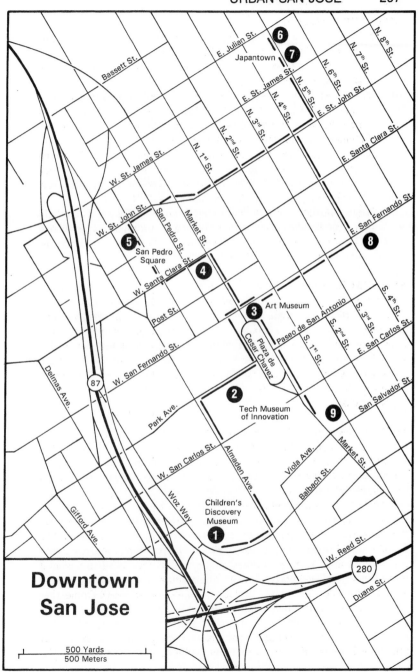

Downtown
San Jose

500 Yards
500 Meters

famed Whitney Museum in New York to share exhibits back and forth from each other's permanent collections. From the Whitney you'll see art by renowned talents such as Georgia O'Keefe, Edward Hopper and Andy Warhol. One of the museum's recent exhibits was (what else?) *Alternating Currents: American Art in the Age of Technology. Open daily 10–5, Thurs. 10–8. Adults $6, seniors and kids 6–17 $3. Café and gift shop.* ☎*(408) 294-2787.*

For those interested in the fabric of life, consider a stop at the **American Museum of Quilts & Textiles** (4) at 60 South Market Street. There are regularly changing exhibits of quilts and textiles from around the world as well as the museum's own collection. *Open Tues.–Sun. 10–5 and Thur. until 8. Admission is $6, seniors and students $4 and kids under 13 free.* ☎ *(408) 971-0323.*

Continue up Market to **San Pedro Square** (5), where there is plenty to see and do. The **Peralta Adobe** at 184 West John Street is the city's oldest structure, built in 1797. It is named after pueblo official Comisionada Luis Peralta, one of the state's first millionaires. He occupied the adobe until his death in 1851. Display cases in this humble home tell the story of California's first civil settlement. *Open Tues.–Sun. 11–4 for guided tours and 11–3 for self-guided tours. Tours of the adobe and house start with an excellent video. Adult admission is $6, seniors $5 and kids $3. Museum store.* ☎ *(408) 993-8182. Partially* ♿.

Directly across the street is the **Fallon House** at 175 West St. John. This is an opulent 1850s home of one of San Jose's early mayors. Well worth a visit. Admission and tours are combined with the Peralta Adobe. ☎ *(408) 993-5437.*

A few blocks from the city center is **Japantown** (6), which dates back to the late 1880s when Japan-born bachelors migrated to the Santa Clara Valley. Today it is a flourishing area of homes and shops. Be sure to check out the exterior of the massive 1910-built Issei Memorial Building. Next door at 535 North Fifth Street is the home of the **Japanese American Resource Center/Museum** (7). It features heritage photos of Japanese-Americans who first came to the area in 1890. *Open Sun., Thur. and Fri. 11–3. Admission is by donation.* ☎ *(408) 298-4303.*

Classical music lovers might want to visit the **Center for Beethoven Studies and Museum** (8), located at the corner of 4th and San Fernando on the San Jose State University campus. This nifty museum will slake your thirst for all things Beethoven, including some original manuscripts—and even a lock of his hair. *Open Mon.–Thur. 1–5 and Fri. 1–4. Free.* ☎ *(408) 924-4590.*

Next are a number of attractions outside the city center. If you go south on Market, you will come to what's called **SoFA** (9), an acronym for South First Area. It is a smart section of cafés, restaurants, nightclubs, classic theaters and art galleries. Look for the **Wine Galleria** at 377 South First Street, where you can taste and purchase a variety of Santa Clara wines. *Open Mon.–Sat. 5–midnight and Sun. 2–10.* Not exactly next door, but fairly close, the **J. Lohr Winery** at 1000 Lenzen Avenue produces a line of outstanding varietals including non-alcoholic wines. Wine tasting and limited tours are available. Open all year. ☎ *(408) 288-5057.*

San Jose has numerous outstanding performing arts programs available to visitors:

The **American Musical Theater of San Jose** presents exciting full-scale musical productions from the largest professional musical theater company in the bay area. ☎ *(408) 453-7100 to find out what's playing. Their season runs from Oct.–June.* The **Northside Theatre Company** at 848 William Street by contrast is a small and quaint theater with live performances for audiences of 75. Their presentations are suitable for families. ☎ *(408) 288-7820 for the current shows.*

The **San Jose Repertory Theatre** recently opened in a spectacular new theater building. It is considered the South Bay's only fully professional residential theater company, offering a wide variety of contemporary and classic plays. ☎ *(408) 291-2266 to find out how to enjoy their efforts.*

Opera San Jose is a professional, regional opera company performing many of the classics in the Montgomery Theater at 2149 Paragon Drive. The season runs from November until May. *The phone number for current operas is (408) 437-4450.*

Nationally acclaimed, the **San Jose Cleveland Ballet** presents a full schedule of dance. This professional ballet company is ranked among the top 10 in the nation. ☎ *(408) 288-2820 to find out about programs for the season, which runs Oct.–May.*

Perhaps best known among the many cultural activities in San Jose is the **San Jose Symphony.** The season is September until June, during which the orchestra presents a full schedule of classics along with the Kickback Series and Super Pops! *Their number is (408) 287-7383.*

Outside San Jose

Many people have heard the term "Silicon Valley." Most know that it refers to a business region densely populated with high tech companies. But ask the average person who doesn't work in the technology industry or doesn't live in Northern California where Silicon Valley is and what there is to do, and you're sure to stump the majority. Here are some answers:

What is Silicon Valley? The actual term owes its popularization to the late Don Hoefler, a City of Santa Clara engineer and editor of a major engineering journal. He began using the insider's term in trade journals in 1971. The tag succinctly described the region that almost overnight spawned myriad companies based on computers.

Where is Silicon Valley? The high tech boom and silicon-based semiconductor industry were born in Santa Clara County around metropolitan San Jose during the 1960s. While you won't find many maps defining Silicon Valley's boundaries, people generally consider it to run from San Mateo on the north, the Santa Clara mountains to the west, San Francisco/Diablo mountains to the east and Morgan Hill to the south. That's a big territory.

San Jose, described as the capital of Silicon Valley, serves as the world headquarters for such high tech companies as Adobe, Cisco Systems and Netcom. Close by are such stalwarts as Hewlett-Packard, Apple, Intel, National Semiconductor, Advanced Micro Devices and dozens of others.

San Jose has an eccentric side as well. Mix that with great wealth from making weapons and you have the 160-room mansion of the Winchester heiress, with hidden tunnels and doors that open into walls. The observatory built on a hill outside of town was founded by one of the more whimsical Gold Rush millionaires. And would you believe that Alexander Eiffel (yes, the guy who designed the tower in Paris) came to town in the 1880s to study a huge tower in the middle of San Jose to get ideas?

For total excitement, you can fly an actual combat aircraft and engage in six aerial dogfights even though you don't know how to fly. These people have taken up about 14,000 people and claim safety first—and then fun.

San Jose and the surrounding area have so many exciting things to see and do that we've made the area into two daytrips. It might be a good idea to check out the previous one (Urban San Jose) to see whether you want to do both, or combine those items that interest you into one.

GETTING THERE:

By car from Union Square, go down Stockton, which becomes 4th after Market Street. At routes US-101 and I-80 go south, and after a few miles get on I-280 south. Follow that for 40 miles, then take the Bird Street exit. Left on Bird, then right on San Carlos St.

By train, take a taxi to the CalTrain Railroad Depot at Fourth and King Street. The round-trip train fare is $9. ☎ (800) 660-4287 for departures.

PRACTICALITIES:

With nearly 300 sunny days per year, San Jose registers a 70-degree annual average temperature. At midday, it can be quite warm, but pleasant year round.

Many of the museums are closed on Mondays. Take sunglasses and comfortable shoes.

FOOD AND DRINK:

Agenda Restaurant, Lounge & Speakeasy Room (399 S. First St.) As the name suggests, this is a fun place for food and libations. The Speakeasy Room is a secret, but they'll let you in anyway. Dinner daily. ☎ (408) 287-3991. $$

Palermo Ristorante Italiano (394 S. Second St.) The aroma and atmosphere make you feel like you're in Roma. Wide variety of pasta dishes that are lip-smacking terrific. Lunch and dinner daily. ☎ (408) 297-0607). $$

Casa Castillo (200 S. First St.) The heritage of this fine spot goes back to when the Mexicans came to work in the surrounding fields. Authentic Mexican food with just the right touch. ☎ (408) 971-8132. $$

California Sushi & Grill (1 E. San Fernando St. in the Double Tree San Jose) Slick place with a huge variety of scrumptious sushi. The chefs were trained in Japan and really have the touch. Lunch and dinner daily. ☎ (408) 436-1754. $–$$

SUGGESTED TOUR:

Numbers in parentheses correspond to numbers on the map.

After you get off the freeway and turn on San Carlos, go to Market and turn right.

Head farther south on Market, turn left at Keyes and then right on Senter. This will take you to **Kelley Park** (1), which is 156 acres of parks, museums and gardens with something for the whole family. It was once part of a 600-acre estate covered with prune, apricot, cherry and walnut orchards. *Admission to the park is free, but there is a $3 parking fee charged every day.*

If you're looking for calm, visit the **Japanese Friendship Garden** patterned after the famous Chorale Park in Japan. Feed the brilliantly colored Koi fish, or just enjoy the serenity. *Open 10–sunset. Admission is free.*

If you have kids along, another attraction of Kelly Park is the **Happy Hollow Park & Zoo** (2) at 1300 Senter Road. It offers a creative children's play area and an amusement featuring outstanding puppet theater. Kids usually thrill to the small animal zoo with petting area. *Open daily 10–5. Admission is $4.50 for those 2–64, $3.50 for seniors and under 2 free.* ☎ *(408) 295-8383.*

Many say the prime feature of Kelley Park is the **San Jose Historical Museum** (3) at 635 Phelan Avenue. This 25-acre outdoor museum includes a collection of faithfully reproduced homes, businesses and other historical landmarks as they existed at the close of the 19th century. A.P. Giannini's tiny and original Banca d'Italia—that became San Francisco's behemoth Bank of America—is here. But one of the most curious exhibits is a tower in the middle of Main Street. Shortly after electricity came to San Jose in the 1800s, one city official had the zany idea to illuminate the whole city with one giant tower to save on individual street lights.

It lit up the town all right, but the livestock and people found it a little too much. It finally fell over in a storm and that was the end of that. But before it did, Alexander Eiffel came over from France to study the tower's construction. Maybe this is when San Jose got its high tech start—way back then. The tower in the museum is a re-creation. *Open Tues.–Fri. 9 to 5; weekends noon-4:30. Adults $6, kids $4.* ☎ *(408) 287-2290.*

If you go east on Santa Clara, it becomes Alum Rock Avenue, which will lead you up to the **Lick Observatory** (4). This is one of the world's most powerful telescopes, and it got there as a result of a whimsical and wealthy Gold Rush tycoon by the name of James Lick. In the 1870s he became obsessed with astronomy and was convinced there was life on the moon. To prove all this, he wanted to build a giant telescope smack in the middle of San Francisco. He got turned down, so he searched around and came up with Hamilton Mountain to the east of San Jose as a location. *You can drive up the 4,200-foot mountain to the observatory that is open daily 10–5 except major holidays. Terrific views. Free.* ☎ *(408) 274-5061.*

Going north on I-680 takes you to Fremont and an unusual park. Situated on 250 acres, the **Ardenwood Historic Farm** (5) is a certified organic farm. It brings to life the workings of a 19th-century operation using turn-of-the-century farm tools and machinery. Animals actually pull wagons, railcars and plows. *Open Tues.–Fri. 10–4. You can tour just the grounds Tues. and Wed. for a fee of $1 for adults and 50¢ for kids. On Thurs., Fri. and Sat.*

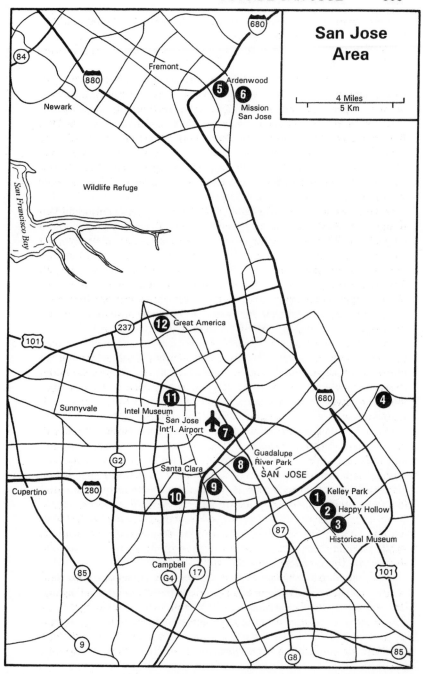

San Jose
Area

4 Miles
5 Km

guides explain and demonstrate the way of farm life in a bygone era via a tour of the old house, a horse-drawn tram and the blacksmith shop. Admission on these days is $5 for adults, $4 for seniors and kids 4–17 are $3.50. ☎ *(510) 796-0663.*

Close by is the **Mission San Jose de Guadalupe** (6), located directly off I-680 in Fremont. Begun in 1797, the mission is the 13th in the chain of missions founded in California. Mission San Jose stands at the foot of Mission Pass and at one time welcomed travelers on their way to the San Joaquin Valley and the Mother Lode gold mines. A nifty restoration project was completed in 1996. *Open daily 10–5. Admission is by donation.* ☎ *(510) 657-1797.*

Come back down I-680 to Berryessa Road, taking that west to US-101, then go north. Follow signs to the **San Jose International Airport** (7). Here a company by the name of **Air Combat USA** will provide you with a thrilling experience where you actually fly air-to-air combat—whether you've ever flown before or not. This is not a simulator. You actually take the stick of a state-of-the-art military trainer aircraft and engage in aerial dogfighting. In business since 1989, they have flown 14,000 of these "missions" with their clients. For the price of $795 for the Basic Air Combat Maneuvers, you get flight gear, a briefing, formation flying, aerial dogfights and a video of your flight. They fly out of San Jose April through December, usually on the middle of the month weekend. ☎ *(800) 522-7590 for actual dates and more information.*

Come back down Highway 87 to Taylor and head west, where you will come to the **Guadalupe River Park and Gardens** (8). This is a delightful three-mile park that runs along the river. You can walk from the Discovery Meadow in front of the Children's Museum to Arena Green.

If you get on Taylor it soon turns into Naglee Avenue. At the corner with Park, look for the **Rosicrucian Egyptian Museum and Planetarium** (9). This is the largest collection of ancient Egyptian artifacts on the West Coast. There are also planetarium shows on astronomy and ancient cultures. *Open daily 10–5. Gift shop. Adult admission is $7, seniors and students $5 and kids 6–15 $3.50. There is an additional charge for the planetarium of $4 for adults, $3.50 for seniors and students and $3 for kids.* ☎ *(408) 947-3636.*

Naglee turns into Forest. Turn left on Winchester. Just ahead is the **Winchester Mystery House** (10) at 525 South Winchester. Guaranteed you've never seen anything like this one. It is a gorgeous, sprawling 160-room manse that shows the screwy side and the innovative side of Sarah Winchester, heiress to the Winchester rifle fortune. There are unexplainable oddities such as doors opening into blank walls and staircases going nowhere. But she was sharp, too, designing such innovations as carbide gas lights, clever window catches patterned after the Winchester trigger and inside window cranks—all in use at the turn of the century. *Open daily in summer 9–8; and on weekends in winter, generally 9–4. They offer several ways to* see this treasure: the guided house and grounds tour is $13.95 for adults, $10.95 for seniors and $7.95 for kids 6–12; a second Behind-the-Scenes guided hard-hat tour of never-before-seen places (such as the basement and stables) is $10.95. You can take a combined tour for $21.95; $18.95 for seniors. ☎ (408) 247-2101.

If you go north on I-880 to US-101 a few miles from San Jose, look for the Santa Clara turnoff, which will take you to the **Intel Museum** (11) at 2200 Mission College Boulevard. This high tech attraction is located at the headquarters of one of the most famous names in Silicon Valley. Designed as a self-guided tour, you can use hands-on exhibits to learn about computer chips and how they are manufactured. Open Mon.–Fri., 8–5. Free. ☎ (510) 765-0503.

A bit farther north is another fun experience for adults and kids. **Paramount's Great America** (12) is one of those dressed-up, cleaned-up amusement parks of the 1990s. Discover Hometown Square, Yankee Harbor and County Fair. Take a train through Northern California's largest provider of entertainment, Paramount's Great America. Open 10–8 weekends, Nov.–May and daily June–Oct. Adult admission is $31.99 for those 7–59, $20.00 for those 60+ and kids 3–6 are $18.50. ☎ (408) 988-1776.

Santa Cruz

This is one of those great beach towns that dot the California Coast. It is unusual for Northern California because you can actually swim here most of the time without chilling out or getting dumped by the breakers. That's because the coast curls to the east at this spot, creating a south-facing exposure for the beach.

Sunset Magazine has rated Santa Cruz as one of the 10 best in Northern California, calling it the "Best Beach Town." Long ago, the town was a resort for blue-collar San Franciscans who would travel here by horse or train. These were the original daytrippers from up north. Someone explained that that's why there is no grand old hotel in the middle of town. Santa Cruz is only about 90 minutes from San Francisco.

There's the golden sand beach and gorgeous coastline, yes, but in the hills above town is a lovely university campus, which we'll visit. In the mountains to the east are two wondrous parks that honor the coast redwoods and other giants of the forest. We'll go there too.

Getting to Santa Cruz can be lots of fun. Let's go.

GETTING THERE:

By car from Union Square, go down Stockton, which becomes 4th after Market Street. At routes US-101 and I-80 go south and after a few miles get on I-280 south. Follow that to the Santa Cruz Route 17 exit. After you go over the hill and start down the other side take the Mt. Hermon Road exit. Wind you way through the mountains to Felton. Turn west on Graham Hill Road.

PRACTICALITIES:

Santa Cruz, while on the ocean, is usually pleasantly warm all year. Do plan to go in the water at this lovely beach, at least during the summer months, so take appropriate beachwear. Sunglasses and comfortable shoes are good ideas. If you go hiking, watch out for poison oak. Remember the saying, "Leaves of three, let them be."

FOOD AND DRINK:

Casablanca (101 Main St.) Right on the beach. Dine with a view that is unsurpassed. Entrees feature fresh fish from local waters, like Pan Seared Snapper. Dinner daily and brunch on Sunday. ☎ (831) 426-9063. $$

Hobee's (740 Front St.) The soup and salad bar is one of the best around. Very fresh. Also a wide range of burgers and sandwiches. One of the best selections is their Asian Wrap. Lunch and dinner daily. ☎ (831) 458-1212. $–$$

Stagnaro's (also called Gilda's on Municipal Wharf #37) This immigrant family started in the fishing business here in 1879. Stagnaro family members still run the place. Lots of great seafood with a great view of the beach. Breakfast, lunch and dinner daily. ☎ (831) 423-2010. $–$$

Empire Grille (6250 Hwy. 9 in Felton) Nifty small spot in this rustic mountain town. Owner is from Hawaii, so try the Mahi Mahi sandwich. Terrific pastas and salad entrees. Lunch and dinner daily. ☎ (831) 335-2127. $

SUGGESTED TOUR:

Numbers in parentheses correspond to numbers on the map.

As you tool up the hills through giant trees, the temperature drops and the aroma of redwoods and other tall trees invades your senses. What a way to get to the beach.

Follow the directions above to the small, attractive town of **Felton** (1). In the center of town is the well-known **Covered Bridge**, supposedly the only one on the West Coast. It is a State Historical landmark.

Go out Graham Hill Road a short distance, where you will find the **Roaring Camp & Big Trees Railroad**. What a terrific trip in an old-fashioned steam passenger train! The run is six miles round trip from Roaring Camp to Bear Mountain, the pinnacle of the Santa Cruz mountains. The route passes the Big Trees Grove of coastal redwoods, which incidentally was the first redwood grove to be purchased (in 1867) for the preservation of these giants. California was into ecology even then. On your way you pass through such Christopher Robin-like spots as McSkunk Junction, Grizzly Flats, Shotgun Pass and Westside Junction. *This particular one-hour-and-fifteen-minute trip runs once daily on weekdays and three times on weekends, and costs $13.50 for adults and $9.50 for kids. From July to November, they run a roundtrip through the mountains to the beach in Santa Cruz twice daily. Rates are $15 for adults and $11 for kids. No reservations taken, but* ☎ *(831) 335-4484 to confirm trip times.*

On the way down Graham Hill Road you will come to the **Henry Cowell Redwoods State Park** (2). It is nearly 1,800 acres with huge redwoods, rushing streams, canyons and open meadows. The Ohlone Indians were the

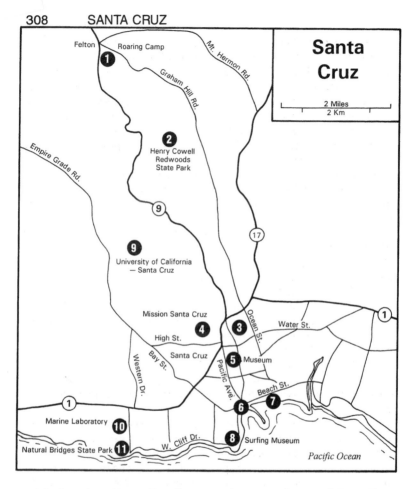

original settlers. Henry Cowell at one time owned most of Santa Cruz County, and it is his descendants who helped create this marvelous natural preserve. The park is laced with numerous trails that range from easy walks to more challenging climbing. Mountain biking is allowed on certain trails. Camping is encouraged at over 100 sites. Overnight camping fees are generally $15 depending on the season. There is a $6 fee for day use. *The park is open 8–sunset.* ☎ *(831) 438-2396 for camping information.*

Redwood Adventures offers a range of guided hikes. Their expert naturalist guides offer 1.5- to 3-hour and full-day hikes through some of the oldest and most spectacular redwoods in Central California. Rates vary depending on the size of the group. ☎ *(831) 338-1191 for more information.*

As you come over the mountain by car, there is the ocean and the town of **Santa Cruz** (3) laid out before you. You come out on Ocean Street. Turn right at Water Street and follow signs to **Mission Santa Cruz** (4) at High and Emmett streets. This small but handsome church is a living testament to the interplay between California's rich Spanish and Native American heritages in Santa Cruz. *It is open 10–4 Thurs.–Sat. and 10–2 on Sun. Admission is by donation.* Next door is the Mission Galleria with a range of interesting gifts. Across the square stands one of the town's beautiful old Victorians. The **Willey House** was built in 1887 for one of Santa Cruz's prominent bankers. It is a private residence.

Go back down Water and turn right on Pacific. Straight ahead is the newly refurbished downtown section called **Pacific Garden Mall** that runs between Water and Cathcart streets. This comfortable promenade is lined with unique shops and restaurants.

Turn left on Cooper Street and right on Front for the **Museum of Art and History** (5) at 605 Front Street. The Center is a blending of the Art Museum of Santa Cruz with the Santa Cruz County Historical Trust. The result is a presentation of visual and cultural experiences focused on regional history and modern art. Don't miss the docent-led tours. There are lectures and a film series as well. Around the corner is the **Museum Store in the Octagon.** This historic building was built in 1882 and was once the county's Hall of Records. *The museum is open noon–5 Tues.–Sun. and noon–7 on Fri. Admission is $3.* ☎ *(831) 429-1964 for more information.*

While downtown, you might want to check out **Santa Cruz Harley-Davidson** at 1148 Soquel Avenue, if such is your passion. It's a combined store and museum with some delicious vintage Harleys. *Open daily 10–5.* ☎ *(831) 421-9600.*

Next you might consider going straight to the **Municipal Wharf** (6), so follow signs down Front Street. This can be great people watching, especially the patient local fishermen and crabbers. There are shops and restaurants all along this half-mile breakwater. Stop in at **Made in Santa Cruz** on the Wharf for goods and crafts from local artisans. It's a good idea to check the weather and surf conditions at the Lifeguard Headquarters right on the Wharf. There is a charge for parking on the Wharf.

If you are interested in some ocean fishing, **Stagnaro Fishing and Cruises** on the Wharf has charters available. Rates are $42 for adults and $35 for kids under 16 for eight hours of salmon fishing March through September. Year-round deep sea fishing for snapper and cod costs $32 on weekdays and $36 on weekends for about seven hours of chasing after fresh Pacific seafood. Be sure to call in advance to find out if the weather permits going out, and for reservations. They also offer one-hour Bay Cruises at 3 in the afternoon for $5. ☎ *(831) 427-2334.*

There are really three main beaches in town. **Cowell's Beach** is on the north side of the Wharf and is the area where most of the surfers hang out waiting for the perfect wave. It is backed by moderate cliffs with a cave midway along this stretch of shore. You can take surfing lessons from **Cow-ell's Beach 'n Bikini** right across from the Wharf. The $50 cost includes a board and wetsuit and an hour and a half of personalized instruction. If you want to do it on your own, you can rent a surfboard for the day for $15 and a wetsuit for the same. A body board or skim board will cost $10 for the day. ☎ *(831) 427-2355.*

Appropriately, **Santa Cruz Beach** is the main strand on the south side of the Wharf. It is very popular on warm summer days. Going south, to complete the circle is **Twin Lakes Beach**, formed by the harbor and a pond behind it. It tends to be warmer since it's more protected by adjacent cliffs. Lifeguards are on duty only during the summer.

Santa Cruz was originally built by the railroad tycoons as a place for daytrips from the city up north. To attract crowds, the famous **Boardwalk** (7) was built in the early 1900s. It has all manner of amusements, including the famous Giant Dipper roller coaster that hurls you to and fro with flashes of beach and then mountain and up and down. Still in operation is the venerable Cocoanut Grove that continues to play big bands on occasion. The restored Boardwalk area, a seeming throwback to another era with penny arcades and salt water taffy, opens daily at 11 a.m. during the summer months; it opens at noon on winter weekends. You pay for each attraction separately. ☎ *(831) 426-7433.*

As one of the more popular wave riding spots on the West Coast, you would expect a **Surfing Museum** (8) in Santa Cruz. It is located just north of town at West Cliff Drive and Lighthouse Point in the lighthouse. It is small, but there are lots of boards of all sizes and shapes that trace the history of surfing from its start in Hawaii. *Open noon–4 daily except Monday. Admission is by donation.* ☎ *(831) 429-3429.* On the way to the museum, be sure to look at the sweep of Monterey Bay with seals cavorting offshore, and the town of Pacific Grove way in the distance.

To visit what is considered one of the most beautiful college campuses in the country, retrace your route, turn left and head up Bay Street for the **University of California—Santa Cruz** (9). Turn left at Empire Grade to reach one of the gems on this campus. It is the Arboretum, nestled on 150 acres on the west side of campus. Its main mission is to develop new plants for the Northern California region. In defined sections, this facility grows native plants from Australia, New Zealand, South Africa and the Mediterranean. A wonderful place to wander. *It is open daily 9–5. There is no charge.* ☎ *(831) 427-2998.*

When you go back down Empire Grade, turn left on Glenn Coolidge Drive. The entire campus was originally part of the Cowell Ranch, and remnants of some of the vintage buildings can be seen as you enter the campus. The first impression is one of vast open spaces. There are no structures on the open, golden hills, but the real campus is set in redwoods, looking like a place you really want to be if you're in college. Make a loop by coming down Hagar Drive.

At the traffic light, turn right on Empire Grade and then left on Western Drive. As you might expect, the university is also very much involved in the ocean. Unlike its more showy neighbor to the south, the Monterey Aquarium, the **Joseph M. Long Marine Laboratory** (10) on the north side of the bay is much more research oriented. Among many other activities, scientists and students work with sea lions and dolphins to learn such behavior as their communications capabilities. What is neat is to observe the students, both undergraduate and graduate, work with these wondrous sea animals. *The lab, located at 100 Shaffer Road, is open Tues.–Sat. 1–4. Adults $2, seniors and students $1.* ☎ *(831) 459-4308.*

Next door is **Natural Bridges State Park** (11). This is not a large beach, but the park is about 65 acres. That makes it a good one to get together for a picnic. Enjoy the lovely Pacific Ocean rolling in all the way from Japan. At one time, there were several stone bridges created from the wave action, from which the park got its name. There is only one arch left. As a submergent coast, portions of California along the water have been falling into the sea for centuries—unlike the East Coast, which is an emergent coast and therefore is rising. There are good tidepools along the water. In the winter, hordes of Monarch butterflies make this their home. *Open 8–sunset.*

*Monterey and Pacific Grove

This town is a magnet for visitors for many reasons. One of the prime ones is its location at the south end of the scythe-shaped Monterey Bay, a beautiful and serene body of water that has shaped the town in so many ways. Another reason for visiting Monterey is the history of the place.

The Spanish arrived and settled—and left a deep imprint. Succeeding groups like the Portuguese and Asians came as seamen for whales, and then for sardines and other salable fish. We know only too well their impact from the stirring writing of John Steinbeck, who is now celebrated further in a wonderful new museum of his life.

In 1777, Monterey became the official capital of both *Alta* (upper) and *Baja* (lower) California. The town remained the capital of Alta California under both Spanish and Mexican rule, until Mexico revolted from Spain in 1822.

After years of dispute between Mexico and the U.S., Commodore John Sloat arrived in Monterey and raised the American flag over the Custom House, ending Mexican rule in July, 1846. The state convention met at Colton Hall in September 1849 to frame a state government, rather than a territorial one.

The first legislature, however, met in San Jose, not Monterey. In 1850, California was admitted to the Union and the following year, Monterey became incorporated as a city.

We will visit these historical spots and many others during this fascinating daytrip. Another reason for visiting that can't be overlooked is the incredible variety of activities available in Monterey: whale watching, kayaking, hang gliding, golfing, biking, scuba diving, auto racing, sport fishing, sailing—and wine tasting.

Pacific Grove has its story too. We'll explore Monterey's neighbor to discover its treasures.

GETTING THERE:

By car, from Union Square, go down Stockton, which becomes 4th after Market Street. Get on Route US-101 and go south. Follow signs to Salinas and take the Main Street exit. This route will take you about two-plus hours. Follow signs to the National Steinbeck Center.

If you want to wander down incredibly scenic Highway 1, from Union Square go west on Geary Street. Cross Van Ness and go several blocks, turning left on Webster Street. Approximately nine blocks later, turn right on Fell Street. Follow this, which changes to Lincoln, until you come to 20th Avenue and turn left. Turn left again and then right on 19th Avenue. This becomes Highway 1 and depending on how long you dally along the way, this route will take you about four-plus hours to reach Monterey.

PRACTICALITIES:

It can be chilly along the coast in Monterey, so take a sweater or jacket. Nonetheless, sunglasses and sunscreen will be beneficial. Take swimwear if you plan to kayak or scuba dive. Good, comfy shoes too.

Note that some facilities have different summer and winter hours.

FOOD AND DRINK:

Sandbar & Grill (#9 Wharf #2 in Monterey) This is on the quiet wharf. They say you can see cute sea otters "romping tableside." Great view of the harbor. Oysters, crab, shrimp, snapper, you name the fish—meat dishes too. Breakfast, lunch and dinner daily. ☎ (831) 373-2818. $$

Paradiso (654 Cannery Row) They call themselves a California-Mediterranean dining experience, which means sunny dishes from sunny lands. Terrific fresh seafood in a great setting. Wood-burning pizza oven. Lunch and dinner daily. ☎ (831) 375-4155. $$

Wharfside (60 Fisherman's Wharf) This one is on the more crowded wharf. Excellent pastas including a full range of raviolis—try the crab. Plenty of fresh fish. Sit outdoors on nice days for views of the bay. Lunch and dinner daily. ☎ (831) 375-3956. $-$$

Fishwife at Asilomar Beach (1996½ Sunset Dr., Pacific Grove) Situated at the end of the stunning ocean drive from Pacific Grove. They serve a full range of great seafood dishes. Lunch and dinner daily. ☎ (831) 375-7107. $-$$

SUGGESTED TOUR:

Numbers in parentheses correspond to numbers on the map.

Salinas has been called the "Salad Bowl of the Nation" because of the huge lettuce and other vegetable fields in the area. The many growers and their famous native son, John Steinbeck, had a very uneasy relationship for many years. All that has changed with the opening of a new museum honoring this most talented writer:

NATIONAL STEINBECK CENTER (1), One Main St., Salinas, CA 93901, ☎ (831) 796-3833. *Open 10–5 daily except major holidays. Gift shop and bookstore. Adult admission is $7, seniors and students $6 and kids 11–17.* ♿.

Just because the man had so much to do with popularizing this part of the world, we suggest you start this tour in Salinas where the famous author was born. The new Center honors and preserves the legacy of John Steinbeck and his writings. This facility is a wonder at bringing alive Steinbeck's most memorable books, mostly through seven unique galleries that take you on an interactive journey using multi-sensory exhibits. It's like no other museum you've seen before.

The exhibits are far from stuffy or dull. In the gallery depicting his book *Travels With Charley* sits the actual camper truck Steinbeck used on his countrywide odyssey. TV and movie clips along with excellent sound and lighting bring the author's writing alive. In the art gallery are changing exhibits relevant to Steinbeck's work and the diverse culture of the Salinas Valley.

Next take Route 68 17 miles west to downtown **Monterey**.

A good way to orient yourself to the history of the area is to take the two-mile **Path of History Walk** (2). Go to the Visitors Bureau at 380 Alvarado Street for a map. The self-guided tour can begin at any point along the route. Look for gold tiles set in the sidewalk. Large tiles and street signs mark points of special interest.

The maps show 46 sites along the route, but don't panic with that overload. Most are adobes and old homes of figures from the past. One you will not want to miss is **Colton Hall** (3), the site where California's first constitutional convention was held in 1849. *The museum, at Madison and Pacific Streets, is open daily 10–noon and 1–5.* ☎ *(831) 646-5640. Free.*

A good way to get an assisted historical overview is to take the walk with a guide. This kind of tour covers fifteen key sites, including such well-known places as the **Custom House**, the **First Theater of California**, and the **Cooper Molera Adobe**. *Walking tours are daily at 10:30, 12:30 and 2:30. Cost is $5.* ☎ *(831) 649-7118.*

There are lots of other neat attractions, including two art museums. The **Monterey Museum of Art at La Mirada** (4) is located at 720 Via Mirada. The museum is in one of the handsome old Monterey homes surrounded by magnificent gardens and picturesque stone walls. With the addition of the Dart Wing in 1993, the museum added four contemporary galleries and changing exhibitions. *Open Thurs.–Sat. 11–5 and Sun 1–4. Admission is by donation of $3.* ☎ *(831) 372-3689.* A sister institution is the **Monterey**

Salinas

200 Yards
200 Meters

183
68
W. Market St.
Stone St.
E. Market St.
National Steinbeck Center ❶
Central St.
Church St.
Cayuga St.
Lincoln St.
Salinas St.
Main St.
Monterey St.
Pajaro St.
E. Gabilan St.
68
Soledad St.
W. Gabilan St.

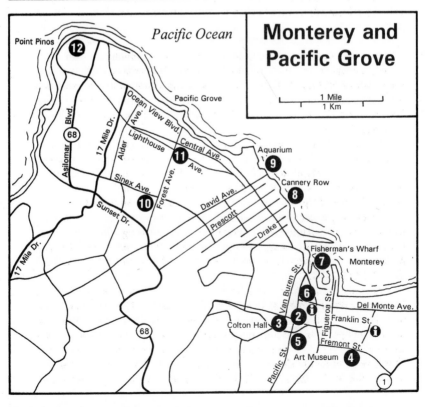

Monterey and Pacific Grove

Pacific Ocean

1 Mile
1 Km

Point Pinos ⓬
Pacific Grove
Asilomar Blvd.
68
17 Mile Dr.
Ocean View Blvd.
Alder Ave.
Lighthouse Ave.
Central Ave.
⓫
Sinex Ave.
Forest Ave.
⓾
Sunset Dr.
David Ave.
Prescott
Drake
17 Mile Dr.
Aquarium ❾
Cannery Row ❽
Fisherman's Wharf ❼
Monterey
❻
❷ ℹ
Van Buren St.
Del Monte Ave.
Figueroa St.
Franklin St.
Colton Hall ❸
❺
ℹ
Pacific St.
Fremont St.
Art Museum ❹
68
1

Museum of Art (5) at 559 Pacific Street, which has been called "the best small town museum in the United States." Its seven galleries feature California art, early Christian, Asian, American folk, ethnic and tribal art. *Open 11–5 Wed.–Sat. and 1–4 on Sun. Admission is a $3 donation.* ☎ *(831) 372-5477.*

To get a good taste of Monterey's seafaring heritage, be sure to take in the **Maritime Museum of Monterey** (6). Exhibits celebrate and showcase the sometimes tumultuous, but always fascinating fishing, whaling and trading history of this town. *Located at 5 Custom House Plaza in Old Monterey, it is open 10–5 daily. Adults are $5, seniors $4 and kids $3.* ☎ *(831) 373-2469.*

Monterey's **Fisherman's Wharf** (7) served many purposes before it became the promenade of fish markets, shops and restaurants that it is today. Originally a pier where trading schooners unloaded cargo, it was built in 1846. At that time California was not a state and Monterey was the major port on the Pacific. There are actually two wharfs; one is very busy and the other calm.

In the past, sardines, salmon, albacore, tuna, mackerel, rock cod and squid were just some of the crops from the sea to cross the well-worn planks of the wharf. Today, you can go sportfishing with **Sam's** at #84 Old Fisherman's Wharf. If you go out for deep sea cod on the 65′ *Star of Monterey,* the rates are $30 on weekdays and $34 on weekends. They will issue you a one-day California fishing license for $6.50. You can rent rods and tackle as well. ☎ *(831) 372-0577.* From May to November consider going out with **Whale Watch** to scout for humpback and blue whales and dolphins, as well as sea lions and sea otters. The six-hour trip (from 9–3) is lead by marine biologists. Cost is $39 for adults and $33 for kids. It leaves from Sam's. ☎ *(831) 375-4658.*

There are all manner of water activities available on Monterey's bay, including sailing, scuba diving and kayaking. If you want to paddle around the bay singly or in a double kayak, try **Monterey Bay Kayaks**. Their rates are $25 for a single kayak including wetsuit. A three-and-a-half-hour tour of the bay with a guide is $45. ☎ *(831) 373-5357.* Two-hour excursions of the bay in a wonderful 30′ sailboat are offered by **Carrera Sailing** on Fisherman's Wharf. The cost is $25. ☎ *(831) 375-0648.* A simple 25-minute harbor cruise in a glass-bottom boat is $5.95 for adults and $3.95 for kids 12 and under. It is offered by **Seal Life Tours** at 90 Fisherman's Wharf. ☎ *(831) 372-7151.*

Immortalized by John Steinbeck as "a poem, a stink, a grating noise, a quality of light, a tone, a habit, a nostalgia, a dream," in a book by the same name, **Cannery Row** (8) today is all of that but the stink and noise. In its heyday, there were 18 canneries. For many sardine canners, the waterfront was their whole life, encompassing both work and play. The sardines disappeared in the late 1940s from over fishing as well as currents and environmental factors. That was it. Today you can find a multitude of shops, galleries and restaurants occupying most of the space.

Cheek-by-jowl with the Row is the world-acclaimed **Monterey Bay Aquarium** (9). What makes it lots of fun is that is focuses on the mysteries and wonders of Monterey Bay and surrounding sea. Not many people know it, but the channel leading out of the bay reaches 10,000 feet down, making it deeper than the Grand Canyon. A new feature is an exhibit called The Outer Bay Wing, which is a million gallon depiction of the open ocean. Of interest to all is the three-story kelp forest. If you've ever wondered how waves happen, there's a terrific exhibit of this phenomena, as well as lots of hands-on touch pools. The sea otters can be hilarious in a special exhibit. All-in-all, a wonderful experience given in most part by the family of David Packard of Hewlett Packard fame. *Open 10–6 daily but extended hours from 9:30–6 during summer and holidays. Adults $15.95, seniors and youth $11.95 and kids under 13 $6.95. For information* ☎ *(831) 648-4888. Advance tickets* ☎ *(800) 756-3737.*

Next, get on Ocean View Boulevard and head for **Pacific Grove** (10). This attractive little burg on the peninsula got started as a Methodist retreat in 1875. The combination of fragrant pines and fresh salt air soon brought many more people than the early worshipers. The town is filled with handsome Victorians, many of which have plaques telling the names of original owners and construction dates. If you like antiquing, this is the place. Go to the Chamber of Commerce on Central between 16th and 17th streets, where you can pick up a fun Historic Walking Tour map.

The **Pacific Grove Museum of Natural History** (11) is as good an excuse as any to visit this wonderful small town on the very tip of the peninsula. The museum highlights the unique natural history of the entire Monterey County. That means exhibits about the rocky shoreline as well as back into the open countryside. Of special interest are the exhibits on the huge Monarch butterfly population that arrives in Pacific Grove starting in October. Millions of Monarchs from the Rocky Mountains west have been making their way to Pacific Grove for eons, seeking a warmer clime during the winter months. It is truly a phenomena of nature. Information at the museum will lead you to the best viewing areas. *The museum is located at Forest and Central avenues. Open 10–5 Tues.–Sun.* ☎ *(831) 648-3116. Free.*

Out on Ocean View Boulevard is **Point Pinos Lighthouse** (12), the oldest continuously-operating lighthouse on the West Coast. Built in 1855 as one of six beacons to aid navigation along the treacherous coastline, its main function was to guide ships into Monterey Bay. *Open 1–4 Thurs., Sat., and Sun. and most holidays. Take a guided tour for the best experience. Free.* ☎ *(831) 648-3116.*

Sports are a big part of life on the peninsula. Car racing at famed **Laguna Seca Raceway** is in its fourth decade of operating world-class auto and motorcycle race events. ☎ *(800) 327-SECA for a schedule of events.* To get a bird's eye view of the peninsula, consider sky diving, available from **Sky-dive Monterey** at the Marina Airport. ☎ *(888) BAY-JUMP. Rates are $179 for a tandem jump where your partner, thankfully, is an instructor.*

Golf is everywhere. The Del Monte course at 1300 Sylvan Road is a 6007-yard course popular with residents and visitors. Greens fees are $65 plus a cart. ☎ *(831) 373-2700.*

Fabled events are a big part of the scene in Monterey. Among some of the better-known are the **Whale Fest,** usually the middle of January. It offers special events and programs during peak migration season. ☎ (831) 644-7588. One of the best-known of all events in the country is the **Monterey Jazz Festival**, held in September. The festival continues to redefine jazz, drawing top-name artists for three days of observance of this American art form. The **Monterey Wine festival** is also a very popular event, usually held in March. It is the oldest continually-held wine festival in the country, and features three signature tasting events, a large bottle auction and entertaining and informative seminars.

*Carmel-by-the-Sea and Big Sur

For many people who have not been there before, the name Carmel-by-the-Sea evokes the image of a mysterious and remote seacoast town like no other in the world. That's a pretty accurate depiction of the real thing. You'd have to add the aroma of pines and the white sand beach and Clint Eastwood and an old mission to flesh out the image.

Everything is done in good taste in Carmel. Part of that stems from the strict ordinances concerning any type of signage and the architecture of homes and commercial buildings. There are no street numbers in town. After all, Carmel began as an artists' and writers' colony. Why bother with such mundane details?

Carmel has been called "a village in a forest setting," but that leaves out one of the forces of nature that has shaped the town and surrounding area from the beginning. The gorgeous Pacific Ocean at the base of the town has created a coastline in either direction that is one of dramatic rocky points and tiny bays, of twisted cypress and open meadows. Access to the captivating coastline is via the private 17 Mile Drive, originally built in 1880 as a diversion for guests at the Hotel Del Monte.

Of California's many historic missions, by far the most significant is in Carmel. It is rich in history and splendor.

Inland from the town itself is another important destination. Carmel Valley is quite a contrast from the town. The valley, primarily an agricultural area, also has wineries, horse ranches and world-class golf. Unlike its seacoast neighbor, the valley is mostly sunny and warm. To the south is the rugged beauty that is Big Sur. It was once the unexplored and unmapped wilderness called "El Sur Grange," the Big South. We'll explore all of this in this daytrip.

GETTING THERE:
Coming from the north on Highway 1, follow signs to Monterey. As you

make your way through town, get on Ocean View Drive, which becomes Sunset Drive. This will lead you to the Pacific Grove Gate of the famed 17 Mile Drive.

PRACTICALITIES:

The weather along the seacoast can be chilly, so take a light jacket or sweater. In the valley, the temperature can climb, so be prepared for that too. Comfortable shoes for walking plus sunscreen and sunglasses will make for a pleasurable trip.

Since the **17 Mile Drive** is a private road, there is an entry fee of $7.50 per car. The views alone are well worth the admission. ☎ *(831) 625-8426.*

FOOD AND DRINK:

The Oaks Dining Room (One Old Ranch Rd. at Carmel Valley Ranch) They work hard to gather fresh, local produce and the result is an "Award of Excellence" from Wine Spectator. Breakfast, lunch and dinner daily. Reservations ☎ (831) 624-2858. $$$

Pacific's Edge Restaurant (located in the Highlands Inn about five miles south of Carmel) You sit high above the coast with sweeping views that may distract you from your fixed-price dinner, which includes Maine Lobster, Crusted Salmon and Veal Medallion. A la carte too. Lunch and dinner daily. ☎ (831) 622-5445. $$–$$$+

Hog's Breath Inn (between 5th and 6th on San Carlos in Carmel) This is Mr. Eastwood's contribution to the culinary side of town. Decent food in a fun atmosphere. Don't expect Clint to wait on you. Lunch and dinner daily. ☎ (831) 625-1044. $$–$$$

Il Fornaio (Ocean Ave. at Monte Verde) Totally Italian including the atmosphere. Try the Agnolotti Di Pesce which is hand-crafted pasta filled with braised sea bass, crab and scallops. Lovely. Breakfast, lunch and dinner daily. ☎ (831) 622-5100. $–$$

Cottage Restaurant (Lincoln between Ocean & 7th in Carmel) Claims of homemade foods are for real. For breakfast try the Pannetone French Toast. Have you had artichoke soup? It's a must among 100 entrees. Breakfast and lunch daily. ☎ (831) 625-6260. $

SUGGESTED TOUR:

Numbers in parentheses correspond to numbers on the map.

The best place to start your tour of Carmel is to get on the **17 Mile Drive** (1). This spectacular road will take you through famed **Pebble Beach**, home to seven public and private golf courses with some of the most famous names in golfdom. The first of the three public courses you will come to is the **Links at Spanish Bay** (2). It is a par 72 wonder that snakes along the seacoast with the blue Pacific crashing below. All 6,078 yards are sure to be

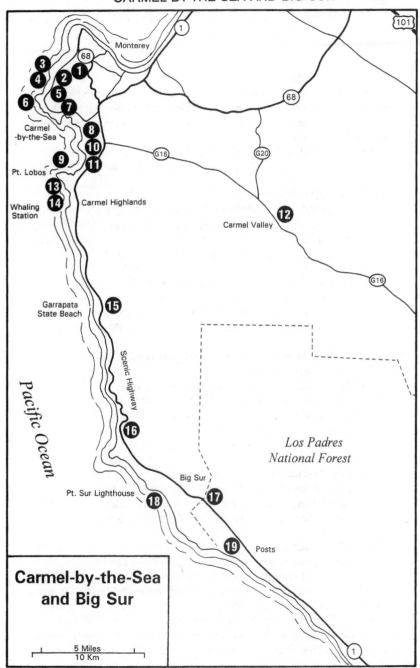

Carmel-by-the-Sea
and Big Sur

5 Miles
10 Km

difficult, if not for the course itself, for the distraction that comes from the scenery. The cost is $165 per round plus a cart.

Spanish Bay was so named because Juan Portola camped here in 1769 while searching around for Monterey Bay. There are picnic tables that are great for enjoying the views.

A short distance later is **Point Joe** (3). This famous point marks the spot where many a sea captain and crew met their fate, thinking it was the entrance to Monterey Bay. Note the ocean at this point is called "The Restless Sea" because of the turbulence of sea and spray.

Look for signs for **Bird Rock** (4), a landmark home to shoreline birds and herds of sea lions and harbor seals. There is a one-mile self-guided nature walk that begins at Bird Rock. It is in this area that the 11th Cavalry practiced riding and saber handling for use in World War II. Today you can take a beach trail ride at the **Pebble Beach Equestrian Center.** Riding times are at 10, 12, 2 and 3:30, where you explore the beauty of the peninsula. Cost is $45 for scheduled rides. ☎ *(831) 624-2756.*

The next public golfing is at **Spyglass Golf Course** (5), which comes with its own set of challenges. It is a fairly long course at 6,346 yards; again with views that are impossible to ignore. The name alone is pretty neat. Fees are $200 plus cart per round.

After several miles you will come to the renowned **Lone Cypress** (6). This remarkable old cypress is silhouetted against the Pacific Ocean as it clings seemingly to bare rock. It is the copyrighted trademark of the Pebble Beach Co. and a little sign says you can't take its picture. It seems like lots of artists have been inspired by it nonetheless.

Another choice for golf is the **Pebble Beach Golf Links** (7), which has been called indescribable in its beauty. Just think of all the famous Hollywood types who have marched along these fairways. With the sky-high greens fees of $275 plus cart come the bragging rights to having played Pebble Beach. *You may make reservations at any of the three public courses by calling (800) 654-9300.*

Eventually you will come to the Town Gate, and at that point you are in **Carmel** (8). Before you start your tour of Ocean Avenue, which is the main village thoroughfare, be sure to enjoy the white sand of the beach at the foot of town. It's not recommended for swimming, but the expanse of sugar-like sand is wonderful for walking or just sitting.

Now proceed up Ocean Avenue. If you like browsing in quaint shops, there are about a hundred of them. Reflecting its art heritage, the town claims 70 galleries, many of which feature local artists. If you stop by the **Carmel Business Association** on San Carlos between 5th and 6th they will give you a terrific walking tour map.

As mentioned earlier, Carmel got its start as an artists' and writers' colony. Many well-known authors such as Upton Sinclair and Sinclair Lewis hung out here at one time. Poet Robinson Jeffers built a hillside home outside of town called **Tor House** (9), at 26304 Ocean View Avenue between Stewart Way and Bay View Avenue. Beside the house he built a stone tower with spectacular views of the ocean. It took four years for Jeffers to build Hawk Tower, which he did by rolling stones from the beach up to the tower entirely by hand. *Docent-led tours are hourly every Fri. and Sat. from 10–4. Cost is $7 for adults.* ☎ *(831) 624-1813.*

For a change of pace, consider walking through the 35-acre **Mission trail Park** (10). You can enter from Forest off Ocean Avenue and enjoy displays of native grasses, trees, shrubs and wildflowers. Midway through the park is the impressive **Flanders Mansion**, which serves as offices of Carmel Heritage.

Nearby is the:

*CARMEL MISSION BASILICA AND MUSEUM (11), 3080 Rio Rd., Carmel, CA 93921, ☎ (831) 624-3600. *Open Mon.–Sat., Sept.–May, 9:30– 4:15; June–Aug. 9:30–7:15, Sun. 10:15–4:15. Admission is $2. Partially* &.

No matter how many other California missions you may have visited, this one is the most impressive because of its size and grandeur. It was the second of California's historical missions built in 1771 by Father Junipero Serra. Since he was the mission founder, it served as his headquarters and residence until he died in 1784. He is buried in the sanctuary.

There are several handsome buildings (and a huge open courtyard), but the present stone church is considered the gem of all the missions. It was built in 1793, after Serra's death, of stone quarried from the nearby mountains. The dome, belltowers and exterior have a Moorish flavor. Stone caternary arches form the vaulted ceiling and a unique star-shaped window culminates this early architectural masterpiece. Like most of the state's 21 missions, this one fell into disrepair and ruin. Through the painstaking restoration efforts of Harry Downie, a multi-talented artisan, the mission and church have been brought back to life.

The buildings and grounds are significant enough that Pope John-Paul II visited here in 1987. Some claim the mission is the most beautiful church in all of California, which is some distinction. See for yourself.

Next head for **Carmel Valley** (12) by getting back on Highway 1 and following signs. The valley is a bit different than the town with its pastoral setting of rolling ranch land, streams and forests. Some people prefer the valley to town because of its country pace and the variety of activities.

The buildings for the **Chateau Julien Wine Estate** trick you into believing you are in France—until you look beyond and see the golden California hills. It has a casual elegance that makes a visit well worthwhile. *Free tastings are Mon.–Fri. 8–5 and Wed. 11–5. The address if 8940 Carmel Valley Rd.* ☎ *(831) 624-2600.*

Rancho Canada Golf Club has two courses, both par 71s; East is 6,109 yards and costs $55 for greens fees; West is a bit more challenging at 6,324 yards and costs $70. They are located one mile from Highway 1 on Carmel Valley Road. ☎ *(831) 624-0111 for tee times.*

If horseback riding is your thing, **The Holman Ranch** (it's a private 400-acre estate) has a variety of terrific rides into the hills and around the valley. They offer guided trail rides such as the Hopalong Cassidy, which is a one-hour ride through oak-studded hills for $30. Another treat offered by Holman is their Lone Ranger, a VIP ride custom designed for experienced riders who have a sense for adventure. Cost is $100. Reservations for these and other activities are requested. ☎ *(831) 659-2640.*

About three miles south of Carmel is **Point Lobos State Reserve** (13). This wonderful sprawl of land jutting out from the rocky coastline has had an interesting history. The original inhabitants were Ohlone Indians, who prospered on the plentiful food supply from the mountains and the sea.

Over the years many ethnic groups brought a variety of commercial activities to Point Lobos. The Portuguese arrived around 1862 and established a whaling station. The **Whaling Station Museum** (14) documents this period with exhibit panels describing the workers and their families. The museum also includes examples of the old melting pots and a huge whale skeleton. *Open 11–3 daily.*

Throughout the Reserve are dozens of trails that wind along the coast as well as into the interior. A schedule of guided walks for the month is posted at the entrance station.

There is scuba diving in Whalers and Bluefish Coves as well. Proof of certification is required and permission to dive is provided at the entrance gate. Make reservations by calling (831) 624-8413. *The 400-acre Reserve is open in summer from 9–6:30 and in winter from 9–4:30. The cost is $7 per vehicle ($6 for seniors) although you can walk in for free.* ☎ *(831) 624-4909.*

When you leave the Reserve turn right, which will take you south. Highway 1 can be tortuous at times as it snakes its way along this gorgeous coastline. Consider that for many years the old Coast Trail, which was little more than a wagon trail, was all that linked the homesteads and commercial enterprises along this 90-mile stretch.

To get down to the ocean, look for **Garrapata State Beach** (15), about 11 miles south of Carmel. While the sand is quite nice, the water may be too cool for swimming. But that doesn't stop the nude sunbathers who sometime appear in the summer months. No facilities. ☎ *(831) 667-2315.*

Back on the highway turn right to go south. In 1937, the present highway was completed after 18 years of construction at considerable expense—even with the help of convict labor. The highway has since been declared California's first **Scenic Highway** (16) and most would agree that it provides a driving experience unsurpassed in natural beauty and scenic variety.

Today in **Big Sur** (17), you will not find the normal trappings of a travel destination. There is no town or village, no golf course or movie theater. But that's exactly the point of Big Sur. Big Sur's history dates back to the 1830s when two Mexican land grants were awarded. Neither grantee settled on the land, and it wasn't until some 40 or 50 years later that the first permanent settlers arrived. In the following decades, other hardy souls came to stake out their homesteads. Their names are immortalized on landmarks such as Mt. Manuel, Pfeiffer Ridge, Cooper Point, Dani Ridge and Partington Cove. Some of their descendants still live in Big Sur.

In the early days, besides the old Coast Trail, slow-poke steamers transported heavy goods and supplies to the area and harbored at Notley's Landing, Partington Cove and the mouth of the Little Sur River. With all the fog, navigation was treacherous, so in 1889 the **Point Sur Lighthouse Station** (18) began sending its powerful beam to protect ships from the hazards of the coastline. *Tours take approximately three hours and they are Sat. at 10 and 2; Wed. at 10 and 2 (Apr.–Oct.); Mon. at 10 (June–Aug.). The cost is $3. Volunteers also lead moonlight tours.* ☎ *(831) 625-4419.*

Besides the stunning scenery on both sides of the road, there is abundant wildlife all along this stretch.

The migratory path of the California gray whale passes by this coastline. From late November to early February, these giant mammals head south to their breeding and calving grounds off Baja California. The whales are easily spotted by their periodic spouting and they are often seen traveling together in large "pods." From late February through early April the whales return to their northern summer feeding grounds in the Bering Sea.

Most of the offshore area of the coastline has been declared a refuge for the California sea otter, that cute and playful little sea creature. They live in the abundant kelp beds. Sharp eyes and concentration are needed to detect and observe them.

Many of the homes you see clinging to the shoreline were built by a collection of artists and writers, among them Henry Miller. Actually, along the Big Sur River Valley is what's considered an artists' colony of several hundred homes. Tucked into a grove of trees on the mountain side of the highway is the tiny **Henry Miller Memorial Library** (19). There are manuscripts and other paraphernalia of the famed writer. The bookshop has just about everything the man wrote. *Open Tues.–Sun. 10–4.* ☎ *(831) 667-2574.*

Index

Special interest attractions are listed under their category headings.

HISTORY MUSEUMS:

LIGHTHOUSES:

LITERARY INTEREST:

Daytrips

•OTHER AMERICAN TITLES•

DAYTRIPS HAWAII
By David Cheever. Thoroughly explores all of the major islands—by car, by bus, on foot, and by bicycle, boat, and air. Includes many off-beat discoveries you won't find elsewhere, plus all the big attractions in detail. 288 pages, 55 maps. ISBN: 0-8038-9401-5.

DAYTRIPS FLORIDA
By Blair Howard. Fifty one-day adventures from bases in Miami, Orlando, St. Petersburg, Jacksonville, and Pensacola. From little-known discoveries to bustling theme parks, from America's oldest city to isolated getaways—this guide covers it all. 320 pages, 47 maps, 28 B&W photos. ISBN: 0-8038-9380-9.

DAYTRIPS NEW ENGLAND
By Earl Steinbicker. Discover the 50 most delightful excursions within a day's drive of Boston or Central New England, from Maine to Connecticut. Includes Boston walking tours. 336 pages, 60 maps, 48 B&W photos. ISBN: 0-8038-9379-5.

DAYTRIPS WASHINGTON, DC
By Earl Steinbicker. Fifty one-day adventures in the Nation's Capital, and to nearby Virginia, Maryland, Delaware, and Pennsylvania. Both walking and driving tours are featured. 352 pages, 60 maps, 48 B&W photos. ISBN: 0-8038-9376-6.

DAYTRIPS NEW YORK
Edited by Earl Steinbicker. 107 easy excursions by car throughout southern New York State, New Jersey, eastern Pennsylvania, Connecticut, and southern Massachusetts. 7th edition, 336 pages, 44 maps, 46 B&W photos. ISBN: 0-8038-9371-X.

• IN PRODUCTION •

DAYTRIPS PENNSYLVANIA DUTCH COUNTRY & PHILADELPHIA

By Earl Steinbicker. Completely covers the City of Brotherly Love, then goes on to probe southeastern Pennsylvania, southern New Jersey, and Delaware before moving west to Lancaster, the "Dutch" country, and Gettysburg. There are 50 daytrips in all. 304 pages, 54 maps. ISBN: 0-8038-9394-9.

Daytrips

• EUROPEAN TITLES •

DAYTRIPS GERMANY

By Earl Steinbicker. 60 of Germany's most enticing destinations can be savored on daytrips from Munich, Frankfurt, Hamburg, and Berlin. Walking tours of the big cities are included. 5th edition, 352 pages, 67 maps. ISBN: 0-8038-9428-7.

DAYTRIPS SWITZERLAND

By Norman P.T. Renouf. 45 one-day adventures in and from convenient bases including Zurich and Geneva, with forays into nearby Germany, Austria, and Italy. 320 pages, 38 maps. ISBN: 0-8038-9417-7

DAYTRIPS SPAIN AND PORTUGAL

By Norman P.T. Renouf. Fifty one-day adventures by rail, bus or car—including many walking tours, as well as side trips to Gibraltar and Morocco. All of the major tourist sites are covered, plus several excursions to little-known, off-the-beaten-path destinations. 368 pages, 18 full-color photos, 28 B&W photos, 51 two-color maps. ISBN: 0-8038-9389-2.

DAYTRIPS IRELAND

By Patricia Tunison Preston. Covers the entire Emerald Isle with 50 one-day self-guided tours both within and from the major tourist areas. 400 pages plus 16 pages of color photos; 58 photos in all, and 55 maps. ISBN: 0-8038-9385-X.

DAYTRIPS LONDON

By Earl Steinbicker. Explores the metropolis on 10 one-day walking tours, then describes 40 daytrips to destinations throughout southern England—all by either rail or car. 5th edition, 336 pages, 57 maps, 94 B&W photos. ISBN: 0-8038-9367-1.

DAYTRIPS FRANCE

By Earl Steinbicker. Describes 45 daytrips—including 5 walking tours of Paris, 23 excursions from the city, 5 in Provence, and 12 along the Riviera. 4th edition, 336 pages, 55 maps, 89 B&W photos. ISBN: 0-8038-9366-3.

DAYTRIPS HOLLAND, BELGIUM AND LUXEMBOURG

By Earl Steinbicker. Many unusual places are covered on these 40 daytrips, along with all the favorites plus the 3 major cities. 2nd edition, 288 pages, 45 maps, 69 B&W photos. ISBN: 0-8038-9368-X

DAYTRIPS ITALY

By Earl Steinbicker. Features 40 one-day adventures in and around Rome, Florence, Milan, Venice, and Naples. 3rd edition, 304 pages, 45 maps, 69 B&W photos. ISBN: 0-8038-9372-8.

DAYTRIPS ISRAEL

By Earl Steinbicker. 25 one-day adventures by bus or car to the Holy Land's most interesting sites. Includes Jerusalem walking tours. 2nd edition, 206 pages, 40 maps, 40 B&W photos. ISBN: 0-8038-9374-4.

HASTINGS HOUSE
Book Publishers
Norwalk CT
FAX (203) 838-4084
Phone orders toll free (800) 206-7822
Internet: www.hastingshousebooks.com

About the Author:

David Cheever lived in Marin County and worked in San Francisco before moving to Hawaii. His penchant for running, biking and walking caused him to venture into practically every corner of Northern California. With relatives in San Francisco, he still makes frequent trips to the Bay Area seeking new adventures to bring to his readers. Cheever is a marketing executive who lives in Honolulu with his family, and is the author of *Daytrips Hawaii,* another book in this series.